Handbook of
Information Technology
in Organizations and
Electronic Markets

Editors

Angel J Salazar
Manchester Metropolitan University Business School, UK

Steve Sawyer
Pennsylvania State University, USA

World Scientific

NEW JERSEY · LONDON · SINGAPORE · BEIJING · SHANGHAI · HONG KONG · TAIPEI · CHENNAI

Published by

World Scientific Publishing Co. Pte. Ltd.

5 Toh Tuck Link, Singapore 596224

USA office: 27 Warren Street, Suite 401-402, Hackensack, NJ 07601

UK office: 57 Shelton Street, Covent Garden, London WC2H 9HE

Library of Congress Cataloging-in-Publication Data
Handbook of information technology in organizations and electronic markets / edited by
  Angel J. Salazar and Steve Sawyer.
    p. cm.
  Includes bibliographical references and index.
    ISBN-13 978-981-256-478-8 -- ISBN-10 981-256-478-0
    1. Information technology--Handbooks, manuals, etc. 2. Management information
systems--Handbooks, manuals, etc. 3. Organizational change--Handbooks, manuals, etc.
I. Salazar, Angel. II. Sawyer, Steve, 1960–

  HD30.2.H3642 2006
  658'.05--dc22

                                                                    2006044627

British Library Cataloguing-in-Publication Data
A catalogue record for this book is available from the British Library.

Printed in Singapore.

Foreword

Organizations can take many forms. But all relate different individuals together within a framework such that they work toward some common goals, without which the organization would not long survive. The members of an organization will usually have their own distinctive interests and ambitions, and may even be unaware of the guiding objectives of the organization that they work for (or are otherwise embedded in – for instance, students in a school or college, patients in a hospital). But the organization is structured so as to channel the activities of workers and other participants in pursuit of its specific goals. Different sorts of organizations may have different goals – profit maximization and/or long-term growth, securing some aspect of quality of life of participants or clients, and so on. Whatever the organizational mission, whatever the social relations that structure its members' practices and procedures, information is integral to the functioning of organizations: so much so that one way of looking at organizations is treating them as information-processing systems.

Organizations are often contrasted with markets – organizations are considered to be hierarchically structured ways in which goods and services are produced and delivered, whereas markets are envisaged as more horizontally structured environments in which goods and services can be exchanged. Despite the idealized notions of markets in economic theorizing, markets, as much as organizations, are institutional constructs, with frameworks of rules and regulations, regulatory and policing bodies, and formal and informal practices and procedures adopted by those taking part in them. Information is of course fundamental for these participants (and the regulatory and policing bodies) to set processes for goods and services, establishing their quality and issues surrounding their production and use, and so on.

Information is integral to these institutions (and any other institutions one might care to examine, such as families, governments, scientific communities, etc.). Understanding the nature and implications of new information technology (IT) for them is thus vital, if we are to fully understand the transformations that they are going through. New IT has provided huge and rapid increases in the speed at which information can be captured, communicated, stored, and processed, in the volumes of information that can be handled in all of these ways, and in the cost-effectiveness of these processes. It enables the digitalization and digital processing of information that originates as text, visual or auditory input, and indeed any data that can be captured by sensor (thus the emergence of such terms as mechatronics, chematronics, biosensors and bioinformatics). Since the development of the microprocessor, there has been a remarkably steady and rapid trend of increasing information-processing power, as exemplified by Moore's Law and its numerous analogues for information storage and communication. One result is a steady evolution of understanding by entrepreneurs and managers, professionals and other employees, and indeed by practically the entire spectrum of social actors, of the scope for applying new IT to access and use information about a huge range of organizational and market phenomena.

None of this is entirely new. The postal system and telegraphy, the canal and railway systems, the use of cheap and accurate clocks, weighing machines, and calculating machines and printing presses: all of these were important tools that played their roles in the industrial revolution and its emergent systems of mass production and consumption, alongside the justly celebrated steam engine and factory system. (Mumford, of course, argued that the clock was fundamental for the factory system – while the application of steam power to the printing press was important for the "knowledge society" of the nineteenth century, as symbolized by the Society for the Diffusion of Useful Knowledge, for example.) New technologies for storing and communicating information enabled changes in the spatial reach of organizations and markets, and new understanding about what sorts of information could be delivered in what forms and speeds enabled changes in how organizations and markets were designed[1,2]. There are many new features of the application of new IT – not least the pace of contemporary technological change. But the reconfiguration of organizations and markets around new information technologies is far from being uniquely novel.

There are lessons to be drawn from the past then, as well as from our more recent experience. Of course, we can see the dictum that "knowledge is power" is continually reinforced. But we can also see that control over the production, distribution, and use of knowledge by no means simply remains in the hand of established oligarchs and monopolists, corporate champions and managerial elites. New ways of creating and using knowledge – including new technological instruments and systems that can be applied to this end – can be used by aspirant groups to gain footholds and even to overturn longstanding hierarchies. The PC revolution was hailed as the "triumph of the nerds" in that it reflected and reinforced the acquisition of power by new technical elites in the corporate power structure, for instance. More generally, new firms arise – Microsoft! – and particular functions within firms achieve a new strategic importance (e.g., Information Systems departments); the balance of economic power across nations can shift as capabilities are developed in booming fields. So, while we learn (again) that knowledge is power, we learn also that new IT is not always used solely to shore up existing social relationships.

Indeed, successive generations of information and communications technologies have very different characteristics, which have been associated with changing opportunities for access and action on the part of social groups with extremely varied capabilities and resources. While there seem to be some fairly stable trajectories – for example, increasing surveillance of citizens and employees in Western societies – these are a matter of social choice (especially in the post-9/11 security environment) as much as of technological capacity. Other developments seem to be much less clear-cut – for instance, if early mainframe systems tended to be centralizing, and PCs facilitated a shift to decentralized end-user power, the rise of networking has restored at least some power to central system mangers. The pace of technological change, furthermore, has often outstripped organizational learning. Managers and employees are still coming to understand how they can most effectively use equipment and software that is already well on the way to being supplanted by newer systems. The linkage between social and organizational innovation on the one hand, and technological change on the other, is extremely imperfect. This contributes to the scope for shaping organizations and markets on the part of multiple actors: no parties are so powerful and well-informed as to be able to control the implementation and use, and predict the results, of innovations.

In this complex context, the *Handbook of Information Technology in Organizations and Electronic Markets* is especially welcome. The chapters – some focusing more on empirical studies, some reviewing the burgeoning literature, some articulating new conceptual approaches or critical perspectives on received approaches – contribute significantly to the process of social reflection about the changes that are underway. They help us move beyond our local learning about organizational and market change, to engage with broader perspectives about the directions, processes, and rationales behind this change.

Sometimes a handbook is presented as the last word on a subject. There are no such pretensions here. What we have is indeed a stocktaking, but more importantly it is a vantage point from which to view a rapidly evolving terrain. Read it, enjoy the view – and hopefully you will have a better idea as to which parts of the landscape you want to explore more fully, or even to try yourself to shape.

Ian Miles
March 2006

References

1. Beniger, J. R. *The Control Revolution: Technological and Economic Origins of the Information Society*, Harvard University Press, Cambridge, MA, 1986.
2. McMahon, P. *Global Control: Information Technology and Globalization Since 1845*, Edward Elgar, Cheltenham, England and Northampton, MA, 2002.

Acknowledgements

This handbook would not have been possible without the contribution of the authors, reviewers, collaborators, the publishing team at World Scientific Publishing, and the love and support of our families. The authors, who were approached by the editors, allowed the necessary time from their busy diaries and enthusiastically embraced the ideals of this ambitious academic project from the onset. Each chapter was blind reviewed by at least two reviewers, who had explicit guidelines on how to assess the intellectual merit and quality of the commissioned manuscripts. Thanks to the authors who kindly agreed to blind review manuscripts, as well as:

Dimitris Assimakopoulos
Sebastian Bruque
Regis Cabral
Shawn Clark
Neil Clarke
Robert Davison
Alvaro Escribano
Lawrence Green
Gottfried Haber
Scott Johnson
Helmut Krcmar
Stephen Little

Harald Mahrer
Robin Mansell
Natasha Munshi
Enrique Pelaez
John van der Pijl
Michael Santoro
Detlef Schoder
Alexander Siegel
Richard Southwick
Sven Walter
David Walters

Thanks to Ian Miles for giving us time for meetings to talk about the project and for writing his up-to-date and punchy foreword. Thanks to Geoff Walsham and Rolf Wigand for their direct and constructive comments about the scope and focus of the handbook.

Thanks to Mathew Woodwark, Martin Todd and John Stageman for their support and sponsoring the website for the handbook (www.itransform.net) which was operational during the initiation and reviewing stages of the project. The website helped the editors provide useful updates and guidance for both authors and reviewers.

Thanks to Jill Kickul, Lisa Gundry, and Lori Rosenkopf, for sponsoring our workshop during the Academy of Management conference in Hawaii, which was directly related to this project. The workshop allowed the editors and authors to share valuable ideas and experiences.

Particular thanks to Jesse Hedge Hohenstein, Edward Thomas and Michael Tyworth for helping us to assemble, prepare, integrate and index the collection.

Thanks to Juliet Lee for believing in our project and for her enduring patience in seeing it through.

Special thanks to Andrea Elizabeth and Daniel, and, Sandy, Morgan and Casey, for their love, understanding and support.

Angel Salazar
Steve Sawyer
July 2006

Contents

7   Culture, Community and Identity   352
8   ICTs and Changing Social Relations in the Household   357
9   Conclusion   360
References   361

Chapter 17   Knowledge Management, Technology and
             Organization   365
1   Introduction: Thinking about Technologies and
    Organizations   365
2   A Knowledge-Based Approach   367
3   Data versus Information   370
4   From Imagination to Practice   372
5   From the Knowledge We Have to the Knowledge
    We Haven't   376
6   On Radical Constructivism   379
7   Pulling KM Together   383
8   Conclusion: The Relationship between Organizations
    and Technology   385
References   389

Chapter 18   Knowledge and Labor Theories of Value: Can they
             be Reconciled?   395
1   Introduction   395
2   Has Knowledge Replaced Labor as the Loci of Value?   396
    2.1   Evidence for the ascendance of knowledge and
          ICT processes as a source of value   397
    2.2   Evidence against the notion that knowledge/learning
          processes have become the loci of value creation   398
    2.3   Knowledge and labor in the "labor" (production)
          process   400
3   Reconciling Knowledge and Labor Theories of Value   401
    3.1   Linkages between labor and knowledge in
          value-creation processes in labor processes   403
    3.2   Value = "socially necessary" inputs to production,
          assessed by cost   405

List of Contributors

Colin G. Ash
School of Management Information Systems, Edith Cowan University,
Perth, WA 6027, Australia

Michael Barrett
Judge Business School, University of Cambridge, Trumpington Street,
Cambridge CB2 1AG, United Kingdom

Walter Brenner
University of St. Gallen, Institute of Information Management,
Mueller-Friedberg-Strasse 8, CH-9000 St. Gallen, Switzerland

Bruno Cassiman
IESE Business School, Avenida Pearson 21,
08034 Barcelona, Spain

John Cawood
Department of Information and Communications,
Manchester Metropolitan University, Rosamond Street West,
Manchester M15 6LL, United Kingdom

Katherine M. Chudoba
MIS Department, College of Business, Florida State University,
Tallahassee, FL 32306-1110, USA

Malte Dous
University of St. Gallen, Institute of Information Management,
Mueller-Friedberg-Strasse 8, CH-9000 St. Gallen, Switzerland

Geert Duysters
ECIS and Department of Organization Science and Marketing,
Faculty of Technology Management,
Eindhoven University of Technology,
P.O. Box 513, 5600 MB Eindhoven, The Netherlands

George Giaglis
ELTRUN - The eBusiness Center,
Department of Management Science & Technology,
Athens University of Economics and Business,
47A Evelpidon Str. & 33 Leukados, T.K. 113 62 Athens, Greece

Stephen Jaros
Department of Management, Marketing and E-Business,
Southern University, Baton Rouge, Louisiana 70813, USA

J. David Johnson
College of Communications and Information Studies,
105 Grehan Building, University of Kentucky,
Lexington, KY 40506-0042, USA

Peter Keen
Department of Information and Communication Technology,
Faculty of Technology, Policy, and Management,
Delft University of Technology,
P.O. Box 5015, 2600 GA Delft, The Netherlands

Alex Kofinas
Manchester Metropolitan University Business School,
Aytoun Street, Manchester M1 3GH, United Kingdom

Lutz Kolbe
University of St. Gallen, Institute of Information Management,
Mueller-Friedberg-Strasse 8, CH-9000 St. Gallen, Switzerland

Liping Liu
College of Business Administration, The University of Akron,
Akron, OH 44325-4801, USA

John Loonam
School of Business Studies, University of Dublin, Trinity College,
Dublin 2, Ireland

Joe McDonagh
School of Business Studies, University of Dublin, Trinity College,
Dublin 2, Ireland

Joseph P. McGill
College of Business - Kean University, Union, NJ 07083, USA

Adamantia Pateli
ELTRUN - The eBusiness Center,
Department of Management Science & Technology,
Athens University of Economics and Business,
47A Evelpidon Str. & 33 Leukados, T.K. 113 62 Athens, Greece

Brian T. Pentland
Department of Accounting and Information Systems,
Michigan State University, E. Lansing, Michigan 48824-1122, USA

Sajda Qureshi
Department of Information Systems and Quantitative Analysis,
College of Information Science & Technology,
University of Nebraska-Omaha,
Omaha, NE 68182-0392, USA

Kevin Real
College of Communications and Information Studies,
105 Grehan Building, University of Kentucky,
Lexington, KY 40506-0042, USA

Nadine Roijakkers
ECIS and Department of Organization Science and Marketing,
Faculty of Technology Management,
Eindhoven University of Technology,
P.O. Box 513, 5600 MB Eindhoven, The Netherlands

Gaby Sadowski-Rasters
ECIS and Department of Organization Science and Marketing,
Faculty of Technology Management,
Eindhoven University of Technology,
P.O. Box 513, 5600 MB Eindhoven, The Netherlands

Angel Salazar
Manchester Metropolitan University Business School,
Aytoun Street, Manchester M1 3GH, United Kingdom

Steve Sawyer
Pennsylvania State University, 301F IST Building,
University Park, PA 16802, USA

Ann Seror
Faculty of Administrative Sciences, Laval University, Quebec City,
QC G1K 7P4, Canada

Sandra Sieber
IESE Business School, Avenida Pearson 21,
08034 Barcelona, Spain

J.-C. Spender
Leeds University Business School, Leeds LS2 9JT, United Kingdom

Bindiganavale S. Vijayaraman
College of Business Administration, The University of Akron,
Akron, OH 44325-4801, USA

Sven C. Voelpel
International University Bremen, College Ring 2,
D-28759, Bremen, Germany

Mary Beth Watson-Manheim
Department of Information and Decision Sciences, 2426 University Hall,
601 S. Morgan Street MC 294, University of Illinois, Chicago,
Chicago, IL 60607-7124, USA

Introduction

Angel Salazar[*] and Steve Sawyer[†]

[*]Manchester Metropolitan University Business School, UK
Email: a.salazar@mmu.ac.uk

[†]Pennsylvania State University, USA
Email: sawyer@ist.psu.edu

The diversity of issues, levels and perspectives in contemporary studies of the roles, values and uses of information and communication technologies (ICT, or IT in short) raises important questions about the degree of integration between the fields of strategic management, the sociology of organizations and their underlying disciplines (i.e., economics, sociology, psychology, anthropology). For instance, to what extent is a coherent and cumulative body of theoretical knowledge on the roles and uses of IT in contemporary organizations emerging? As research continues to advance in each of the disciplinary areas concerned with the strategic impact, organizational, social and economic transformation enabled by information technology, it becomes increasingly important to consider areas of integration across disciplinary perspectives:

> The "...diversity of perspectives need not lead to fragmentation and a lack of consensus, however. Indeed, multiple views are vital to scientific advancement and do not condemn the field to an excess of unsubstantiated assertions disguised as new theories. *What is required is an epistemology capable of encompassing diverse, even seemingly contradictory, approaches*"[1] (p. 23, emphasis added).

The aim of this handbook is, therefore, to promote interdisciplinary progress by publishing original review chapters that synthesise and conceptualise prior studies in relevant research themes. To achieve the high quality levels needed, the selection of expert authors, central and emerging topics and rigorous peer reviewing have been central criteria for this proceeding. The handbook's contents embrace multiple studies and a broad range of theoretical perspectives. The handbook includes relevant work by scholars who are part of recognised international communities of researchers. Chapters have been evaluated by members of an international review and advisory board, and assessed for their substantial contribution to the development of theoretical understanding by synthesising prior research and providing a conceptual foundation for future research.

Prior published reviews have focused on the organizational implementation, integration and alignment of new information technologies at the individual, group, organization and market level of analysis[2,3]. The theoretical and empirical issues of past reviews encompassed IT-enabled organizational change, and more recently, learning and knowledge management. There is, however, a growing number of empirical studies that are looking at converging issues such as strategies for creating value and processes of transformation in organizations and electronic markets. The scope of this handbook includes the impact and transformation related to the functioning of organizations and inter-organizational networks, and the transformation and dynamics of electronic markets. More specifically, the editors identified the strategic impact and transformation processes in organizations and electronic markets as the two major areas that encapsulate the growing number of empirical studies.

IT-Enabled Transformation in Organizations

The academic literature highlights the role of collaboration, knowledge sharing and learning in competitive strategies and innovation. The intensity and pace of innovation in knowledge-intensive and hypercompetitive industries has brought the need for organizations to exploit their collaborative networks to boost their own innovation capacity. There is strong evidence in the academic literature that firms are adopting new information technology both intra-organizationally and inter-organizationally. The implementation and exploitation of information technology enables the virtualization of social relations and work processes, which may span the traditional organizational boundaries of the firm. Recent literature highlights the relationship of new technologies and new organizational forms, such as "virtual organizations" and "virtual inter-organizational networks". The Internet is enabling the creation of inter-organizational networks, such as virtual customer-supplier communities[4,5]. Large companies and specialist supply firms have grown to become virtual inter-organizational networks with their partners acting essentially as knowledge brokers in many of the value-creating relationships. A supplier can use the Internet in such a way that it can interconnect information systems across multiple sites in the value chain and let information flow across functional boundaries.

Competitive strategies can be enhanced by the implementation of virtual organizational forms based on complex, interdependent social networks and knowledge-sharing relations, which are in turn enabled by developments in information technologies such as web-based applications and electronic communication. This is a key driver for providing completely new products and services. Innovation can originate from enabling dialogue between stakeholders about their products and services[4,5].

IT-Enabled Transformation in Electronic Markets

The implementation and use of information technology is enabling electronic commerce and markets, which are characterized by multi-channel transactions and relational processes which may span different activities of the value chain. Research shows that firms are gradually moving in the direction of outsourcing most aspects of their value chain and relying heavily on strategic alliances and collaborations with specialist and intermediary companies to become more flexible and faster to market[6,7,8]. Firms are merging at a rate of trillions of dollars per year. Firms are selling, spinning off, or outsourcing their non-core activities at a high rate. These developments are united by a single threat, and that is the role of economies of scale and scope, which can be enhanced by the use of information technologies. Firms are entering into increasingly wider alliances and evolving networks of firms through electronic means. This includes the emergence of firms whose business strategies and marketing, production and innovation activities are essentially enabled by internet-based information technology infrastructures, applications and services[6,7].

Electronic markets have evolved into interconnected one-stop shops, providing specialized services with affiliate firms. Worldwide Internet Commerce, both Business-to-Business (B2B) and Business-to-Consumers (B2C), will reach $12.8 trillion in 2006 as estimated by Forrester Research. Electronic business models have evolved from basic electronic procurement and electronic commerce into more complex electronic market "ecosystems". These electronic market environments are characterised by rapid exchange of information within a virtual network of customers and suppliers working and evolving together to create and re-create value-added processes. Scholars have suggested that electronic businesses are not just members of certain industries but parts of an ecology that incorporates different industries, where the driving force is not pure competition but co-evolution[8].

Overview of Chapters

In Chapter 1, Liu and Vijayaraman adopt the premise that we are entering a fourth generation of e-business. The focus of this fourth generation of e-business is on information integration. Two emerging e-business technologies, e-services and radio frequency identification (RFID), are discussed and their roles in cross-boundary information integration reviewed. This review includes the basic concepts of these technologies, a critical assessment of their current status, and a discussion of the challenges to their adoption.

In Chapter 2, Barrett reviews the contemporary conceptual positions regarding interplay between information and communication technologies (ICTs) and organizational change and the implications for new modes of organizing. This review includes key dimensions of intra-organizational and inter-organizational forms that can be facilitated by advances in ICTs, and the potential of the ICT to enable changing organizational forms. This review includes the technological imperative, structurational approaches, and an extended discussion of the emerging perspective of "practice lens" approach.

In Chapter 3, Chudoba and Watson-Manheim focus on virtual work environments, as many of today's organizational designs require adaptive responses to overcome barriers to collaboration. Much of the research has focused on characterizations of explicit discontinuities in the virtual work environments (VWE). As understanding has increased, many have come to consider the VWE as a hybrid condition or as a continuum with varying degrees of virtuality. This suggests a more fluid conceptualization of discontinuities in the VWE, rather than a finite set of attributes. Drawing from our research in several Fortune 100 companies, all with a strong global presence, we found that the *process* of working in the VWE has a greater impact on performance than simply the presence of one or more discontinuities. By focusing on *how* work happens in the VWE, we highlight the adjustments and adaptations that those in the VWE make.

In Chapter 4, Johnson and Real address the role of human agency in brokering the integration of information technology in organizations involved in electronic markets. We review literature on organizational integration and implementation of information technologies and conclude there has not been much agreement about the types of integration that are possible or a synthetic framework that can be used to organize this literature. Organizational integration is defined in terms of its various types, and each of these types involves differing levels of alignment, organizational learning, skills, impacts on work processes, structural change, uncertainty management, resistance, transaction costs, and impacts on electronic markets. We address one key gap in current research by considering the differing brokerage roles in these types. We end this chapter by discussing implications for policy and everyday life in terms of transaction costs, human agency, and communication.

In Chapter 5, Loonam and McDonagh review the concepts and premises of enterprise systems. Enterprise systems are large software packages that promise to seamlessly integrate organizations' business processes. The chapter begins with an historical tour of the evolution of enterprise systems. This is followed by highlighting implementation trends for enterprise systems, before moving on to discuss factors deemed necessary for the successful implementation of these systems. A critique of critical success factors is provided, which clearly demonstrates that empirical investigations must go deeper in order to fully explain the implementation of enterprise systems.

Through Chapter 6, Pateli and Giaglis review the impact of advanced information and communications technologies (e.g., ERPs, Internet Commerce, etc.) on the current way of doing business, which has raised the interest of researchers on describing and analyzing the new internet-enabled business logic. Early research in the area of information technology strategy and management has made it explicit that the introduction of advanced IT technologies is a complex issue, and as such it should be examined not only from the IT infrastructure viewpoint, but also in terms of organizational strategy, structure and operations. Drawing on a critical review of selected studies on business models, a multi-theoretical framework to examine research on business models under a set of established strategic, organizational, social and information system development and management perspectives is developed.

In Chapter 7, Seror develops a framework for analyzing the future development of virtual infrastructures in service delivery systems illustrated in the health care context. Market dynamics and control mechanisms define the logic of system structures, processes and ideologies. Ideology, defined as the integrated theories and values that constitute a coherent socio-political system, is expressed in patterns of stakeholders' participation in the financing, administration, and regulation of service delivery, including the roles of government, service providers, and consumers. Four configurations describe how telecommunications technologies, the Internet, and grid computing shape virtual infrastructures in the health care context. These configurations are motivated by professional, citizenship, consumer, and managerial values. The analysis further suggests that the open source software movement may influence the ideologies of service delivery systems, particularly through grid infrastructures.

In Chapter 8, Voelpel, Dous, Brenner and Kolbe illustrate Siemens' efforts to establish a sustainable, global knowledge-sharing system. This includes both the description of the technical platform used for the transfer of knowledge, and how Siemens addressed those crucial aspects that are required to anchor a knowledge-sharing initiative within an organization. The case study culminates in six key learning aspects for Knowledge Management practitioners on how to support the global transfer of knowledge by establishing a knowledge culture within the organization.

In Chapter 9, Qureshi and Keen suggest that in order to mobilize knowledge where there is demand for it, it has to be activated. It considers the knowledge identity of the person whose knowledge is to be activated and uses these identities to analyze a case study in which highly distributed knowledge is activated. The analysis of a case study reveals "activation conditions" that delineate processes in which electronic collaboration technologies can be most effective. This has implications for the transformation of organizations and creation of collaborative work environments that enhance knowledge activation in organizations. The chapter concludes with implications and recommendations for activating knowledge in organizations.

In Chapter 10, Pentland, using organizational ecology as a starting point, outlines a framework for studying the ecology of inter-organizational routines in e-commerce. From this perspective, the adoption of e-commerce technology can be viewed as a population-level phenomenon, rather than a firm-level phenomenon. Net-based technologies are distinctive because they require integration with the systems of *other* organizations, as well as one's own internal systems. It makes sense to study technology adoption at the firm-level for technologies whose impact is limited to the boundaries of the firm. But for technologies ranging from EDI to ebXML and beyond, the main goal is to facilitate inter-organizational relationships. For these kinds of technologies it is better understood as a *population*-level phenomenon. This chapter concludes with a framework for the study of populations of inter-organizational routines.

In Chapter 11, Roijakkers, Duysters and Sadowski-Rasters identify insights from the communication literature and evaluate their relevance for improving our current understanding of inter-firm learning in international networks of knowledge-intensive companies. While the sharing of technical knowledge and effective inter-firm learning have been related to general characteristics of knowledge networks, such as centrality and tie strength, very few researchers in the networking literature have studied learning in the context of the personal communication network underlying alliance networks. Their critical examination of the networking literature has shown that a number of important research questions that relate to CMC and strategic alliances have, until now, remained largely unanswered. They try to fill that gap by providing an integrated view of the use of CMC in international alliance networks.

In Chapter 12, Ash critically reviews different extant frameworks for strategic planning and outsourcing. The review highlights the objectives, benefits and limitations of the various frameworks, and summarises their strategic principles and assumptions. The conceptual frameworks used were chosen for their coverage of the topic of strategic sourcing, their historical and strong case-based development.

In Chapter 13, Kofinas develops two alternative ontological perspectives on IT-enabled innovation: the New Economy perspective and the a-modern perspective. In the former the role of IT in enabling innovation is paramount, while in the latter view IT is not important and what matters is how IT is utilized to bring about innovation. These two perspectives are utilised to analyse the challenges that multinational companies face in the global electronic markets. The resulting dialectic will illuminate the changes that are taking place within multinational companies (MNCs) and in their interactions with the broader international context.

In Chapter 14, Cassiman and Sieber focus on the roles of the Internet and new opportunities for value creation. The new technology simultaneously affects demand and costs structures leading to a radical transformation of existing market structures. Appropriation of any value created has, therefore, become more challenging. Furthermore, as the Internet impacts industries in several ways simultaneously, they find that simply analyzing the effect of Internet on pricing behavior and price dispersion misses the point of industries being transformed, which clearly affects the pricing power and possibilities of individual firms. In this paper they provide a conceptual model for analyzing the different elements within the dynamics of industry transformation and understanding the impact of Internet on market structure. They further illustrate the different concepts with actual case examples.

In Chapter 15, McGill focuses on how IT has transformed relationships among firms in manufacturing, electronic commerce, and research intensive industry sectors, emphasizing a number of contextual factors that may either create or limit these transformations. The contribution of this chapter is to link the IT and strategic management literatures and to provide a starting point for future research that focuses on the intersection of IT and strategy. The chapter unfolds as follows. The next section examines theories of economics and management and their connection with IT-enabled transformation, followed by a selective review of industry sectors focused on manufacturing, electronic commerce, and research and development. The chapter concludes with a synthesis and discussion of IT-enabled transformation.

In Chapter 16, Cawood begins with a review of some key examples of those theories which seek to account for the role of ICTs and information in creating new forms of social structure. Here, the underlying issue of technological determinism will be addressed and a guide given to the differing perspectives and methodologies which have arisen from approaches such as post-modernism and post-industrialism. The second part of the chapter includes an examination of the theoretical models of social structures in the age of the Web and the growth of research into network culture, community and identity. In the last part of the chapter, the consumption of ICTs in households will be discussed in relation to changes in family structure and emergent patterns of home life.

In Chapter 17, Spender relates technologies to organizations, theorizing their interaction and the essential learning processes as people within organizations adopt technologies. Drawing from radical constructivism and central to this theoretical critique are three key fundamental distinctions: realist and interpretive, intellectual and practical, and rationality and creativity distinctions.

In Chapter 18, prompted by the emerging importance of information and communication technology in today's global political economy,

Jaros critically discusses the notion that "knowledge", or more specifically, "learning processes" which leverage ICT, would serve as a better root metaphor for understanding the nature of value creation in contemporary capitalism. This proposal suggests that knowledge and learning systems, often embedded in non-human assets such as communication networks, workflow configurations, robots, and computer information systems, have usurped the role of production labour as the source of value in modern corporations. More specifically, Jaros re-evaluates evidence of the "correctness" of Jacques's view that knowledge/ICT has largely replaced labor as the source of value in global capitalist production processes. He concludes that it has not, and therefore describes how they can be reconciled. Jaros then assesses the political utility of this reconciliation. In other words, what is the value of a theory of value that recognizes both knowledge and labor inputs? Speaking from a critical-political perspective: irrespective of the empirical correctness of the LTV or KTV or any theory of value, Jaros questions what is the value of using the KTV as a "metaphor" to describe global capitalism and advance the economic welfare of all employees, technical or manual?

In the concluding chapter, Salazar and Sawyer give a critical overview of selected representative studies focusing on IT-enabled transformation innovation at the level of the organization and markets. This overview provides key insights regarding the type of empirical issues scholars have traditionally focused on, including the theoretical lenses they have applied. This overview discusses existing strategic management theories applied to information technology studies, including the resource-based view and transaction cost economics, as well as more recent theoretical developments such as the relational and dynamic capabilities perspectives, organizational learning and knowledge management, neo-institutional theory, and adaptive structuring and practice perspective. This overview concludes with a discussion of the implications of remaining problematic areas for the possible extension and integration of current and emergent theories.

Table 1. Overview of Chapters

1	Liu and Vijayaraman	Review	E-commerce & information integration technologies
2	Barrett	Review	ICTs and organizational change
3	Chudoba and Watson-Manheim	Empirical	Virtual work environments
4	Johnson and Real	Review	Organizational integration and implementation of ICT
5	Loonam and McDonagh	Review	Enterprise systems' concepts and trends
6	Pateli and Giaglis	Review	IS and management perspectives
7	Seror	Framework	Virtual infrastructures in service delivery (in health care)
8	Voelpel, Dous, Brenner and Kolbe	Empirical	Knowledge management
9	Qureshi and Keen	Empirical	The mediating role of collaboration technologies in activating knowledge
10	Pentland	Framework	Ecology of inter-organizational routines in e-commerce
11	Roijakkers, Duysters and Sadowski-Rasters	Review	Inter-firm learning in knowledge-intensive networks of organizations
12	Ash	Framework	Strategic planning and outsourcing
13	Kofinas	Framework	Two models of IT-enabled innovation
14	Cassiman and Sieber	Framework	Dynamics of industry transformation and impact of Internet on market structure
15	McGill	Review	IT and transformation in various industry sectors
16	Cawood	Review	Contrasting theories of IT and use in home and family
17	Spender	Theoretical critique	Technology relationships with organizations
18	Jaros	Theoretical critique	Knowledge/ICT and labor as source of value in global capitalist production processes
19	Salazar and Sawyer	Review	IT-enabled transformation innovation at the level of the organization and markets

References

1. Baum, J.A.C. and Rowley, T.J. Companion to Organizations: An Introduction. In Joel A.C. Baum (Ed.), *Companion to Organizations*, Blackwell Publishers, Oxford, 2002.

2. Dewett, T. and Jones, G.R. The role of information technology in the organization: a review, model and assessment, *Journal of Management*, 27, 2001, pp. 313-346.

3. Kauffman, R.J. and Walden, E.A. Economics and Electronic Commerce: Survey and Research Directions, *International Journal of Electronic Commerce*, 5(4), 2001, pp. 5-116.

4. Scott-Morton, Michael. *Information Technology and the Transformation of the Corporation in the 1990s*, Oxford University Press, 1991.

5. Brews, P. and Tucci, C.L. Exploring the Structural Effects of Internetworking, *Strategic Management Journal*, 25, 2004, pp. 429-451.

6. Mata, F.J., Fuerst, W.L. and Barney, J.B. Information Technology and Sustained Competitive Advantage, A Resource-Based Analysis, *MIS Quarterly*, 19, 1995, pp. 487-505.

7. Kim, E., Nam, D. and Stimpert, J.L. The Applicability of Porter's Generic Strategies in the Digital Age: Assumptions, Conjectures and Suggestions, *Journal of Management*, 30(5), 2004, pp. 569-589.

8. Salazar, A., Hackney, R. and Green, L. (Eds.) The Strategic Impact and Diffusion of Electronic Commerce Technologies and Services, Special Edition, *International Journal of Information Technology and Management*, 4(2/3/4), 2004, pp. 123-126.

CHAPTER 1

Information Integration:
A Review of Emerging E-Business Technologies

Liping Liu and Bindiganavale S. Vijayaraman

College of Business Administration
The University of Akron
Akron, OH 44325-4801, USA
Email: liu@acm.org; vsb@uakron.edu

1 Introduction

There is no consensus on what constitutes e-business or e-commerce[1]. As the term implies, e-business is the conduct of business on the Internet. IBM, who was the first to use the term in October 1997, defines *e-business* as the transformation, through the use of Internet technologies, of business activities involving information collection, organization, and exchange. In essence, e-business aims at improving business processes by replacing traditionally paper-based processes with Internet-based applications. As a special case, *e-commerce* refers to the buying and selling products and services over the Internet[2]. In practice, e-business and e-commerce are often used interchangeably, and other related terms such as e-tailing, e-procurement, and e-marketing are also used in special occasions.

Conducting business electronically is not new; for three decades corporations have been using EDI (electronic data interchange) over private networks to exchange business documents such as Invoices, Purchase Orders, Bills of Lading, and Acknowledgments. What makes e-business a phenomenal trend today is, however, the advent of modern e-business technologies, which have been developed to take advantages of the Internet's low-cost, widespread accessibility, and its potential for integrating information across the boundaries of devices, organizations, and physical locations.

In the last ten years, e-business technologies have undergone four generations of transitions from static web pages, to interactive media, and to dynamic commerce[3,4]. Early adopters of e-business primarily used static web sites for broadcasting business information. The second generation web sites began to support information requests and customer profiles, moving beyond the one directional information flow of the initial web sites. The third generation e-business technologies transformed relatively primitive web sites into the world of e-commerce, transferring the Internet into a new sales channel[5,6]. By enabling continuous interaction, they presented businesses with a new way to exchange information and to reach customers that is independent of the physical presence of the traditional "brick and mortar" storefronts. For example, they allowed customers to browse products, fill shopping carts, and make purchases from anywhere and at any time. They also allowed distributors to check for inventory availability and automate reorder generation, and vendors to take advantage of on-line invoicing and faster electronic payment cycles.

The focus of e-business today is on information integration with the aim at transforming business processes across organizations and throughout the entire value chain, including customers, suppliers, distributors, and even competitors, and extending the Internet to the physical world. The challenge is to automate last-mile processes at the edge of the Internet, including capturing data into computer systems and moving data from one system to another. These processes are still largely manual, becoming the bottleneck of corporate workflows and the inhibitor to newer e-business initiatives.

The inefficiency of one manual process may easily offset the gain in productivity of many e-transformed processes. This is evidenced by the failure of EDI initiatives. Corporations once believed that EDI was the solution to their business problems but found their expectations largely unfulfilled; EDI implementations only automated the flow of information between trading partners while leaving manual and/or inefficient processing activities remained for both senders and receivers. For example, many companies simply sent their incoming EDI transactions to the printer while traditional manual processes remained unchanged.

The e-business era has not solved this last-mile problem and companies are still facing the same challenge as before. The majority of businesses today are still in an extremely disintegrated state. Most businesses still rely heavily on information delivered on paper, whether it is machine print, handprint, handwriting, tick boxes or bar codes[7]. Almost all but the smallest organizations have multiple systems that do not communicate with each other[8]. About 75% of companies are still in the process of integrating their front office with back-office systems[9] and 71–91% of executives could not access information from different systems in a single view[10]. As each Internet ready e-business application hits the market, companies are faced with new, costly integration projects to connect these applications to existing business applications and legacy systems. A recent survey in US found that 74% of executives believed that information integration was their top priority[11], and companies spent up to 25 percent of their technology budgets trying to integrate (and reintegrate) their business systems. A similar survey in the UK reveals that 69% of organizations saw a lack of integration impacting productivity, while 57% felt it would decrease revenues if not addressed. Furthermore, 43% of the respondents are currently working on projects driven by the need for better integration and more than 50% of companies had integration requirements in half or more of new projects[12].

Responding to the challenge, newer e-business technologies, including radio frequency identification (RFID) and e-services are emerging to take up the core of the fourth generation e-business revolution. RFID is a technology that captures product data and track inventory throughout its supply chain without human interaction, enabling the Internet to reach the physical world[13]. E-services refer to a group of technologies, including web services and grid services that create an open standard and emerging trend for application and information integration[14]. In this chapter, we review these two emerging technologies from the perspective of supporting cross-boundary information integration. We introduce the basic concepts of these technologies and show how they may be used to meet the challenge to the fourth generation e-business era. We provide critical assessments of their current status and identify the challenges to their adoption.

2 Information Integration

E-Business today is challenged to create the real-time enterprise that is responsive and proactive in the face of current business events[15], and develop new ways to respond the new types of market demand — online orders that provide immediate payment but also bring expectations that the product will be delivered just in time[4]. This entails a high-level of information sharing and functional integration across the entire supply chain. For example, it requires that suppliers are able to monitor the inventory level of their products in stores and shops worldwide, dispatch new shipments when necessary, track shipping and routing status in the distribution channel, and receive payments upon delivery.

There are two particular challenges to the fourth generation e-business era. The first challenge is the disconnection between logical and physical worlds, leading to the asynchrony of data and underlying physical objects. A database is simply a model of the real world and information maps its entities, relationships, and dynamics. Unfortunately, creating and updating such a map has never been automatic and manual processes are the state-of-art. In the logical world, information may travel at the speed of light but it jams or stops at the point of the disconnection, waiting for human interactions. In material handling and manufacturing applications, for example, these processes include shipping, receiving, bookkeeping, product sorting and counting, order fulfillments, material assembly, and monitoring the status of work-in-process, machine utilization, worker attendance, and other measures of factory operations and performance. Manual processes are also prevalent in other business settings such as retail sales and inventory control, warehousing and distribution center operations, mail and parcel handling, patient identification in hospitals, check processing in banks, and security systems.

In a typical organization, more than 90% of information is still on paper[16]. With the rise of e-business, the need for automatic processing of this information is greater than ever. Research in this area is ongoing under the umbrella of automatic identification and data capture (AIDC), which refers to data collection by means other than manual notation or keyboard input. AIDC technologies can be broken down into roughly six categories: Biometric, Electromagnetic, Magnetic, Optical, Smart Cards, and Touch. They include fingerprint identification and verification, hand geometry, iris scan, signature identification and verification, voice recognition, facial thermography, magnetic stripe, magnetic ink character recognition, bar code data capture, optical character recognition, machine vision, smart cards, touch screens, button memory, and pen-based computing. All these technologies require no keyboarding but human involvement or presence to certain extent in the data capture process. Thus, they are not suitable for collecting a large amount of data for material handling and manufacturing applications.

The second challenge is the lack of technical interoperability between systems. A typical personal example can illustrate the case. For instance, today I decide to attend a conference and so go to their web site to register. At this point, I would like my calendar to have an entry, and my Outlook to download the contact information. I would like my travel agent to access the same information to make flight and hotel reservations. I would like my GPS to download the addresses and compute the best routes to get around. I would also like my Quicken to register associated expenses. I would like to do all this with one click. Unfortunately, currently I cannot. What I in fact have to do is to manually enter the time into my calendar, laboriously cut and paste contact details into my address book, retype the same information into the travel agent's reservation system, and transfer invoices into my Quicken.

The revelation about student visa approvals for 9/11 hijackers is another example. Like many government agencies, INS has dozens of separate systems that do not communicate with each other. INS admits that the problem in this case was that the contractor that notifies schools of student visa approvals gets its information from INS on paper, which must then be manually entered. INS approved the visas well before September 11th, but it took years for the paperwork to catch up.

Years of piecemeal deployment have created a phenomenon common in all organizations where there are numerous non-compatible systems[8]. Each was developed or purchased to provide a specific function and many have been developed on different platforms using different languages, creating numerous barriers between the systems.

Interoperability is often lacking at two levels: applications and information sources, and manifested in symptoms like application inaccessibility, workflow discontinuity, and information heterogeneity. For example, it is often the case that the output of one application has to be reprocessed to be input into the other or combined with the output of the other. In the literature, data heterogeneity has long been recognized and it includes *structural heterogeneity* — different systems store data in different structures, or *semantic heterogeneity* — different systems do not understand the meaning of each other's data[17]. Manual processing is often the only viable approach to handling data heterogeneity. Companies often hire dedicated staff to do nothing more than translate information from one format to another, or enter data generated by one system into another.

Breaking down application barriers has been the central theme of research and development under the umbrella of EAI (enterprise application integration). EAI solutions typically include the following five components[18]: Message-oriented middleware, application servers, adapters, adapter development frameworks, and workflow and process management tools. Middleware serves as the glue to connect two otherwise separate applications. Increasingly it is used in the development of applications which communicate across platforms as they traverse the Internet. Different approaches have been proposed as a platform for middleware solutions, including CORBA (the Common Object Request Broker Architecture), DCOM (Distributed Component Object Model), EJB (Enterprise JavaBeans), RMI (Remote Method Invocation), and DSOM (Distributed System Object Model). Consequently, middleware is largely proprietary in nature and the languages used are generally not compatible. This makes it difficult to connect middleware islands inside a single organization. Crossing the boundaries between the islands is the key challenge to businesses as they try to incorporate e-business applications[8].

The EAI approach has had some success and may be the best solution for specific, mission critical and high-performance systems. However, EAI has some serious limitations and drawbacks when it is applied to enterprise-wide integration and inter-enterprise integration. EAI solutions depend on many point-to-point links that connect specific elements and functions of each system. Every one of these links has to be created and maintained and every integration project is beyond connecting one organization to a few partners. Instead, each organization has multiple information nodes sending and receiving transactions to an array of internal and external data sources and applications. For example, a customer may demand integration with its ERP system so that it can search for new products, view production schedule, track order status, and update sales ledger information. This would require at least four separate interfaces and probably four different platforms. Imagine 100 nodes join in a network, and each uses a unique piece of software on a unique computing platform. Using middleware technologies, each node would have to incur significant expense writing custom bridges to "hardwire" to the other 99 nodes. Once implemented, each of these links is inflexible and needs to be updated to respond to any changes to the integrated systems or the processes. If one node changes its internal system, all other nodes would have to respond. If a new node needs to join the network, all have to incur an enormous cost of entry to maintain the status of integration. In fact, complexity and bespoke nature demands, for each integration project, hundreds of hours of EAI consultant's time in addition to the cost of the middleware solution itself. Gartner estimates that 40% of a project's costs and time are spent on integration issues. It further predicts a $500,000 entry point and 12 months to see any value even from discrete internal integration projects[8].

Research on information integration has focused in three areas: schema integration, semantic mediation, and ontology merging[19]. The general problem is to define a global schema over a set of local schemas[20]. Schema integration[21] as well as its implementations, e.g. CLIO[22], focuses on resolving relation and attribute conflicts between to-be-integrated schemas. Semantic mediation introduces a mediator as transparency layer that hides the distribution of information providers from applications, and focuses on integrating new data sources into the mediator[19]. Ontology merging was initiated in artificial intelligence[23] and is now studied under the umbrella of *semantic web*, which is an extension of the current web in which information is given well-defined meaning[24], and a set of portable standards to represent ontologies, enabling Internet search engines to retrieve information in a much more intelligent way. Research in this area focuses on representing and finding term-matching relationships for resolving semantic heterogeneity[25], and developing languages to represent ontologies and processing mechanisms[26].

Research has generated a few commercial products like IBM's DataJoiner[27] and Attunity's Connect (attunity.com) and tens of research prototypes, including TSIMMIS[28], information manifolds[29], SIMS[30], MIX[31], DIKE[32], and ODB-Tools[33]. Unfortunately, all these technologies have focused on integrating a previously known fixed set of data sources and developing an integrated schema for these sources. They lack the flexibility to handle dynamically changing sets of data providers and they do not aim at semantically integrating the data of different providers[34]. Adding a new data source typically requires human processing, and often leads to loss of information that does not fit in the global schema. These technologies may be used locally to transform the data of a provider into a common domain schema compliant representation.

3 Radio Frequency Identification

Radio Frequency Identification (RFID) overcomes the limitation of traditional AIDC solutions, and is a technology that captures data or track inventory with minimum human intervention. Unlike other AIDC solutions, RFID is the non-contact, non-line-of-sight nature of the technology for data retrieval (www.AimGlobal.org). Data that is stored on RFID tags can be read through a variety of substances such as snow, fog, ice, paint, crusted grime, and other visually and environmentally challenging conditions, where barcodes or other optically read technologies would be useless. This has many significant implications to e-business. For example, using a barcode system, if a pallet arrives at a dock door, it will not be registered until an operator walks over and scans it. The number of operators available to perform the scanning limits the data rate that the barcode system can generate. In RFID, however, the acceptance of the pallet can happen automatically by using a reader to constantly monitor its space for incoming shipments. In this way, RFID systems have more of a sensor-network or monitoring-system flavor than do bar-code systems[35].

A basic RFID system consists of three main components[36]- an RFID tag, a scanner, and a computer. Antennas emit radio waves that send or receive data to and from the RFID tags. A scanner (receiver) is then used to capture the data and send the information to a computer system for interpretation, storage, and action.

There are two main types of RFID tags being used today; active and passive with passive being the more commonly used and the least expensive. Each type has its own advantages and disadvantages. *Active* tags contain built-in batteries and an internal transmitter, and are capable of transmitting up to 64 KB data. They are continuously powered and able to send and receive data at all times. Active tags are usually much larger in size and more expensive than the passive tags. Active tags generally have a much shorter lifespan than passive tags. The main reason to justify the use of an active tag is its range of communication; an active tag's read range can extend well beyond 300 feet.

Passive tags do not contain an internal power source or transmitter and must be activated through an RF signal from a reader in order to transmit information. They can be extremely small and have a long operating life. The cost of a passive tag can be as low as only a few cents per tag, making them much more affordable for companies wanting to track low-cost product. Generally, passive tags have a much shorter read range than active tags do. Most passive tags must be within a few inches to a few feet of a reader in order to transmit data.

RFID tags can store more information than any other devices currently in use for identifying inventory items. All RFID tags contain microchips that have either "read-only" or "read-write" memory. A chip with "read-write" memory allows for the original data on the tag to be read, modified, or overwritten. On the other hand, a chip with "read-only" memory comes stored with pre-existing data from the manufacturer of the tag that can be read but not modified. Many passive tags use "read only" memory in order to keep their overall cost down.

In a sense, RFID technology is not new. One of the first recorded uses of RFID technology dates back to World War II, when RFID transponders were used as a means to distinguish friendly aircrafts from enemies. The real innovation in RFID, however, is probably not in the technology itself, but in its application to real world situations[37].

Today, the primary application of RFID is to locate, identify, and track objects with the goal to reduce costs, wastes, production cycle time, and inventory[38]. RFID tags allows for much-improved tracking and inventorying of products, especially where multiple products and product-lines are involved. They can help provide operational efficiencies and improve stock level transparency in short shelf-life product distribution in supply chains[39]. They can also potentially be tied into security systems, helping to prevent theft of product.

The benefits of RFID include improved data accuracy, enhanced asset visibility, reduced information latency, reduced out-of-stocks, reduced inventory, reduced shrinkage, improved forecasting, enhanced product pedigree, reduced costs of product recalls, improved accuracy for return processing, reduced product counterfeiting, theft deterrence, etc. A study by Accenture[40] indicates that the retailers implementing RFID technology will reap "significant improvements" in both supply chain operations and inventory accuracy, including increasing revenue up to 1 percent, cutting working capital by 2 to 8 percent, and reducing fixed assets by 1 to 5 percent. The most significant is their claim that retailers can achieve up to a 65 percent reduction in in-store labor expenses when it comes to received goods and a 25 percent drop in stocking and cycle counting, and would totally eliminate the need for physical counting. RFID would also reduce product loss by nearly 1 percent in sales.

It is not surprising that, with such potential benefits, large retailers such as Wal-Mart, Target, and Tesco are making it mandatory that their suppliers use RFID tags. This is quite a big demand, but most of the suppliers are left with no other choice than to upgrade their current supply chain systems in order to integrate RFID technology. It is estimated by Yankee Group that over the next three years, manufacturers will spend $2 billion on RFID tags and another $1 to $3 billion on related infrastructure to implement RFID tags[41]. Indeed, it is this initial "start up" expense that challenges many manufacturing companies. They will be forced to make a decision if the up-front cost is worth the benefit or if they simply cannot afford to make the move. Some may choose to wait until deployment cost comes down further as tags and equipment cost becomes more affordable. A study by AT Kearney[42] concluded that, "retailers can expect extensive inventory and labor cost savings from the adoption of RFID technology, but some consumer product manufacturers will face higher costs and delayed benefits from adopting the technology." In other words, RFID technology is expected to result in "long term" cost savings by retailers and eventually manufacturers but, due to initial startup costs, it may take a while for those savings to be passed on to everyday consumers. According to Alvarez[43], by 2008-2009, enterprises will tag more than 70% of their assets and generate operating cost reductions of 1-3% through reduction of lost assets, improved tracking of asset maintenance, and protection of assets from theft, fraud, or injury.

In addition to retailers, other industries and government agencies are also looking forward to using RFID. For examples, Sullivon[44] noted an application by Georgetown University Hospital's Blood Bank and a study of RFID wristbands in comparison to the use of barcodes. MeadWestvaco Intelligent Systems is evaluating the inventory tracking solution of RF tags in order to assist the U.S. Food and Drug Administration with its multi-faceted approach, which has been launched to reduce and/or eliminate counterfeit drugs. Garskof[45] noted a few applications: 1) A Las Vegas casino is expected to begin implementing RFID-enabled gambling chips to stop counterfeiters and spot high rollers; 2) MasterCard will debut a contact-free RFID payment chip called PayPass that will be available in credit cards and Nokia cell phones; and 3) Helena Regional Airport (Montana) is installing new RFID-enabled ID readers, complete with onboard fingerprint sensors, to keep tabs on its employees.

RFID has the potential to automate supply chain processes and allow companies to determine the exact location of their products in real time. Highjump (3M) was one of the first vendors to develop RFID supply chain software. Other big name vendors including Sun, SAP, Oracle, and IBM are rewriting their existing enterprise applications to integrate RFID data[46]. In 2004, Microsoft announced its first RFID supply chain management pilot project. Microsoft plans to market its RFID software to mid-sized companies, which total 39 million worldwide.

Even though everyone in the supply chain sees some benefit from RFID, the manufacturers will end up paying for the cost of tags. It is estimated that it could cost a combined $2 billion dollars for the top 125 manufacturers to implement RFID tags[42]. Indeed, the main criticism of RFID technology is that it is too expensive and it is unlikely that the investment will pay off implementing at the item level tagging[39]. The majority of manufacturing companies do not expect a positive ROI although retailers were very optimistic[47]. Despite some early trials of RFID tags at item level by Gillette and Tesco, the ROI for item level tagging remains to be a concern for many companies because the costs of tags and associated infrastructure are still greater than anticipated benefits[48].

Although cost is a concern, lack of worldwide tag standards posts a bigger challenge to RFID adoption. The standards for RFID technology are still evolving. EPC Global is currently working with its member organizations to establish standard for tags. The acceptance of these standards depends on big retailers such as Wal-Mart, Target, Tesco, and other companies requiring suppliers and manufacturers to use tags that use a common standard.

Another challenge is the management of voluminous data the RFID system will create and the complexity of the system integration[49]. Implementation of RFID will generate a massive amount of data that needs to be stored, processed, and used in real time. RFID systems will therefore need to be integrated with existing data warehouses and other e-business systems. This will only complicate the difficult task of information integration. Existing systems may not be able to cope with the level of data or the complexity RFID technology may bring. The continuous flow of product data as an item moves through a supply chain demands that e-business systems be scalable to support the data flow, capable of distributed data gathering, and able to route and integrate information to internal applications and external business partners.

The debate that revolves around privacy and security currently dominates the press. Unfortunately, empirical data and clear analysis are scarce. The perception among consumers is that RFID will violate their privacy. RF tags can take suppliers and distributors beyond where the product was manufactured, its shipping history, and the date and time it went through the store's checkout. Electronic readers could take the information from the tag and feed it into a computer database, which can then perform any operations, for example, to determine when last time you purchased toilet paper was or which books you bought. In addressing this issue, a bill was presented to the California State Senate in 2004 concerning the use of RFID. It outlines three requirements for a business to use an RFID system that can track products or people: Tell customers it's using RFID, get consent to track or collect any information, and detach or destroy RFID tags on products before the customer leaves the store[50].

Some authors have a different take on the privacy issue. For example, Cline[51] believes that the privacy scare is simply overblown. "No company or government agency will be secretly scanning your house to find out what products you have purchased, because there is no feasible way to do so." He also admits that, if RFID chip-makers do not soon allay these fears, the escalating public emotion about this issue may effectively ban the most valuable implementations of this remarkable technology. Bacheldor[50] confirms this assessment. IBM recently conducted a study on the Cost of Privacy[51]. Based on 44 U.S.-based multinational companies, they found that setting up a privacy program office is the costliest part of privacy efforts at major corporations. They suggest that privacy is not something to be taken lightly and the privacy program will not come without expense or effort but it is an aspect of the future that must be evaluated and considered very carefully.

4 E-Service Technologies

E-service technologies are developed in response to the interoperability problem. Among them, web services and the Grid are the latest trend and the hottest sector in the information technology industry. A few years ago, *application services* were proposed to provide packaged applications over the Internet as an alternative to hosting them in house[52]. Sharing a similar vision, *web services* aim at providing modular software components to achieve collaborative computing via Internet protocols[53]. The *Grid* seeks even larger-scale sharing of computational and informational resources across platforms, devices, and institutional boundaries[54]. Although the grid was positioned to be independent of the Internet, it is now rapidly converging with web services to form a single set of standards[55] and has conveniently served as a marketplace for exchanging web services[56], as an environment to organize web services[57], or as a framework for architecting next generation information systems[58].

4.1 *Web services*

The idea of web services is not new. For many years, application services provision (ASP) has been a business model of supplying and consuming computational services over computer networks. In this model, a provider assumes responsibility of buying, hosting, and maintaining a software package on its own facilities, publish its user interfaces over computer networks, and provides its clients with a shared access to the published user interfaces. The client organizations, on the other hand, subscribe and receive the application services through the Internet or a dedicated network connection as an alternative to hosting the same application in house.

The ASP model essentially allows organizations to hand over the responsibility of systems deployment or its execution to an outside vendor while still satisfying self-information needs. It reduces the complexity associated with the traditional make-or-buy model while allowing an effective control of the deployment costs and risks[59]. It can amortize expenditures over the entire client base, enabling it to improve quality of services, security, and risk reduction measures that individual client may find cost-prohibitive.

Despite the benefits, the growth of the ASP industry has been slow. Some researchers have attributed the problem to limited user satisfaction[60]. However, some community has tended to blame users for not being ready for change[61], and has attributed the problem to limited end-user acceptance. Liu and Ma[62] empirically examined this problem based on the technology acceptance model[63].

The ASP model enables multiple organization to access a central data repository and therefore, provides a relief to the interoperability problem. For example, in the medical industry, physicians who subscribe to the same ASP may share patient data. However, the ASP model does not meet the need for information integration especially for data exchange between business partners. Instead, like ERP or EAI solutions, it simply replaces the old silos with large data islands. In the last few years, most ASPs have struggled financially and never gained widespread acceptance. No vendor is big enough to provide services to all partners in the supply chain. In the medical industry, for example, no software vendor today is able to cover every aspect of HIPAA compliance[64].

Embracing the idea of the ASP, Web services improve upon the EAI approach to systems integration. The interoperability problem with middleware has forced companies including Microsoft and IBM to seek a new open standard, i.e., web services, for distributed computing across applications, platforms, and devices. Unlike middleware solutions, web services are loosely coupled software components that exchange XML-based data[14]. Web services have the following distinct characteristics[65]. First, each web service represents a business function or business service, whose interface is exposed to the Internet and accessible by another program remotely[66]. It encapsulates a task; when an application passes a message (e.g., data or instructions) to it, the service processes the input and, if required, generates an output message back to the application. Second, all messages are written in XML-based text, which follows SOAP (the Simple Object Access Protocol) coding and formatting specifications, instead of cryptic binary strings. This enables web services to communicate with other applications that may be developed in different programming languages and reside on different platforms[67]. Third, web services are self-describing; each is accompanied by a description, written in the WSDL (Web Services Description Language), regarding what it does and how it can be used. Fourth, web services are discoverable; service consumers can search for and locate desired web services through UDDI (Universal Description, Discovery and Integration) registries.

A simple marginal costs perspective would suggest that each organization can expose some or all functionalities of its internal legacy (open or proprietary) systems as web services. These services can be as simple as scheduling appointments, validating credit cards, browsing product catalogs, or submitting invoices. They can also be as complex as the functions carried out by an entire supply chain, customer relation management system, or ERP applications. These services hide their internal complexities such as data types and business logics from their users, but expose their programming interfaces using the WSDL and their locations using UDDI protocols. Since every service complies with one set of web services standards, there is no need for writing custom bridges in order to accommodate different computing platforms. Instead, organizations can exchange data by directly invoking data exchange services.

Web services might provide businesses with an idea platform for information integration. Essentially, web services allow code to speak to code without human intervention. This will enable organizations to create an integration platform capable of crossing internal boundaries between intra-enterprise applications and connecting middleware islands with middleware-to-middleware integration. The business press calls such an integration platform SOA (service-oriented architecture)[68] or software bus[8]. Technically, SOA refers to an application architecture within which all functions are defined as independent services with well-defined invokable interfaces that can be called in defined sequences to form business processes. SOA aims at simplifying the integration of disparate systems. The traditional EAI approach quickly leads to hundreds of custom bridges for every new application or process change, whereas SOA requires just one integration point for each. New systems and platforms can be plugged in to a software bus to be immediately integrated with all the other systems on the same bus. SOA can be also used to integrate middleware islands and thus leverage existing EAI investments[8]. For example, an organization that may have selected a CORBA-based integration in one area and DCOM for another can integrate the two without discarding either.

Organizations can extend the SOA beyond the boundaries of the enterprise to link to suppliers and customers, and offer collaboration with outside systems via the same architecture. They can leverage SOA to establish a single connection to each vendor or customer organization rather than building point to point connections. If one organization were to change how a certain function is processed internally, as long as the programming interface does not change, the rest of the world can remain still. Thus, the cost of entry and exit will be greatly reduced.

To realize the benefits of SOA, of course, five infrastructure management issues must be resolved[68]: 1) security management that handles validation or authorization of the request, encryption, and decryption; 2) deployment management that allow services to be moved around the network for performance, availability, or other reasons; 3) logging management for auditing, metering, and tracking; 4) dynamic rerouting for fail over or load balancing; and 5) maintenance management.

Web services have the potential for instant connectivity with a universe of services over the Internet. However, some authors have reservation, believing it is a mirage e.g.,[8]. They caution that the security issues will make it very difficult for any organization to really trust its core processes to unknown third parties that they found on the Internet. According to a recent survey by ITToolBox.com, 54% of participants indicated that they are currently using web services for integration while 42% cited security concerns as the biggest challenge to widespread acceptance of web services. Another challenge is with complexity. At present, web services are capable of device-to-device communication but not much so of workflow processing. Although they have the potential to combine individual services into more complex, orchestrated services that will realize sophisticated business process and workflow automation, such composition and orchestration is still on the drawing board [69–71].

4.2 *Grid services*

Besides security and complexity issues, the logistics of distributing web services is also a concern[72]. Regardless how easy it is to search for and locate a web service through a UDDI registry, after all, a consumer may have to contact the provider and negotiate a service contract. If there are thousands of web services to be subscribed, it is practically impossible for anyone to contact these many providers individually and renew contracts periodically. At the same time, service providers are facing another dilemma. Since a web service is usually a small component, it may not be cost effective to spend money to market the service in a distinctive way. However, a lack of marketing effort will reduce the consumer awareness about the service, which in turn, will reduce the number of subscribers. Consequently, most providers cannot even afford the expense of maintaining their services and may have to exit, leading to a shrunk service market that diminishes the viability of web services as a business model.

Then how do we resolve this logistic issue? One approach is to have a few large providers responsible for assembling and delivering suites of web services or packaged applications to consumers. The approach might work, but it may be insufficient because these providers, like other consumers, still need to find and negotiate contracts for required services. What seems more desirable is to have a global market for efficient exchange of web services between service consumers and providers. This solution leads to the notion of a service grid, which is a distributed computing infrastructure consisting of large and diverse sets of distributed resources and services. The concept revolves around the idea of service creation and delivery through coordinated resource sharing and problem solving in dynamic, multi-institutional virtual organizations[73]. Peer-to-peer computing (P2P) was an early implementation of a service grid[74]; it aggregates the unused computing power of individual personal computers into a computer power grid to create a virtual supercomputer. With the advent of web services, now grid and web services are rapidly converging to form a single set of standards and technologies as manifested in the Open Grid Services Architecture[55], which is so promising that many people believe it is one of ten key emerging technologies that will change the world[75].

Enabling collaborative computing, grid services have the potential to serve as an effective market mechanism for distributing web services. A service grid may act as an intermediary between service providers and service consumers and break a typical many-to-many business (between providers and consumers) into simple one-to-many relationships. It buys web services from the providers and then sells the services to consumers. Then consuming web services becomes as easy as watching TV programs from a cable network or obtaining electricity from a power grid; requesting and delivering web services becomes as easy as plugging an appliance into the grid. In the meantime, those small service providers do not have to incur prohibitive expenses to advertise and run its businesses. They can focus on their core business — developing and upgrading web services, and then plug the services into the grid to sell.

Taking advantage of grids, new approaches have been proposed for information integration[34]. These include semantic mediation systems tailored to peer-to-peer architectures and data grids for the management of massive amounts of distributed data. P2P systems are highly dynamic, allowing for ad-hoc addition and removal of data sources. Instead of a fixed, global schema, P2P architectures couple the peers directly and map their local schemas via domain relations and coordination formulas[76] or peer mappings[77]. An application directly sends a query to a single peer using its local schema, which may access other peers to answer the query. Using UDDI, discovery services may be implemented to achieve location transparency and can be searched by mapping logical domains and predicates onto actual data sources. In a medical application, Liu and his colleagues proposed the notion of a data grid for managing patient records[56,72], which spreads over loosely coupled data nodes and works together with a separate service grid that utilizes the data resources. Research has mostly focused on replica management and consistency issues[34]. In the case of medical records, however, applications do not need to send complex queries over various data sources but use the grid to find one data source that has the file they need. There is no need for data integration or merging. The main issue here is probably the lack of a privacy control protocol that specifies how medical records at each node might be accessed and secured[56].

5 Conclusion

E-business technologies have undergone four generations of transitions. The Internet today offers unlimited potentials for transforming business processes, from making online orders to managing inter- and intra-organizational interactions and building customer and vendor relations. E-transformation has accelerated most of business processes and information flows. However, the bottleneck is at both ends. In typical organizations, more than 90% of information is still on paper and the majority of information systems are still in an extremely disintegrated state.

The challenge to the fourth-generation e-business era is to bring e-transformation throughout the entire value chain. It entails transforming last-mile processes, including capturing data into computer systems and moving data from one system to another. These processes are still largely paper-based and become the inhibitor to new e-business initiatives. In particular, there are two obstacles to overcome. The first is the disconnection between logical and physical worlds, leading to the asynchrony of data and underlying physical objects. The second is the lack of technical interoperability between distributed systems.

Research on information integration has produced tens of products, technologies, and prototypes to meet the challenges. AIDC technologies aim at collecting data without human interaction. A lot of progress has been made in the areas of optical recognition and machine vision. However, most technologies are still not suitable for material handling in e-business applications. RFID is one of few emerging AIDC technologies on the e-business scene, which has the potential to extend the Internet to the physical world but it may take time to realize its promise. RFID, the technology for managing supply chain, is continuously evolving. Many benefits such as supply chain visibility will materialize only when RFID technologies work with complementary technologies like Bluetooth and GPS[13]. RFID standards and products such as tags, scanners, and software are evolving rapidly. Companies that are trying to implement RFID technology will have to make short term strategic plans based on the current technology and standards but will have to develop long term strategic plans based on appropriate information resources and projections. Companies should determine how to integrate RFID technology with their existing e-business systems that connect to their partners. Real time tracking of all the items in the supply chain and making effective use of the data generated by RFID technology could be a big challenge to many companies.

System interoperability issue arises in the form of application inaccessibility, workflow discontinuity, or information heterogeneity. Human interaction is often the only viable approach to resolve the issue. Using proprietary middleware, EAI offers some success in making point-to-point connections between fewer systems. However, it becomes too expansive and complex when it is applied to enterprise-wide integration and inter-enterprise integration. Emerging web service technology offers a great promise in advancing the mission of EAI. Instead of incompatible middleware, it offers open standards and protocols that enable XML-based communication across platforms, devices, and languages. Instead of point-to-point connections, it allows service oriented architectures that reduce complex many-to-many connections in typical EAI projects; within an organization, integration is as simple as plugging a system into a software bus, and between organizations, integration is as simple as connecting two software buses. Instead of integration with a specific set of systems, emerging grid services promise an open architecture for collaborative computing over the Internet; integration becomes as simple as plugging an appliance into the power grid. Someday, a business may find itself in a position not dealing with one specific vendor for performing a certain process, say validating credit cards or shipping orders. Rather it will deal with a grid that offers a line of similar services that the business can choose, negotiate with, and use on the fly.

What follows the fourth generation e-business? We have seen where the train is going from its base station: the Internet eliminates the constraints of time and space and allows people to conduct businesses anywhere and anytime. After information integration, distance collaboration will be the next theme of e-business initiatives. Through e-transformation, jobs that are usually performed on corporate campuses can now be performed over the Internet. Thus, fifth generation e-business technology will redefine the landscape of employment and enable virtual corporations. It will open up more opportunities for job outsourcing and improve resource optimization and labor division for the mankind.

References

1. Riggins, F.J. and Rhee, H.-S.S., Toward a unified view of electronic commerce. *Communications of the ACM*, 41, 1998, pp. 88-95.
2. Kosiur, D., *Understanding Electronic Commerce*. Microsoft Press, RedMond, WA, 1997.
3. Mackey, C., The Evolution of E-Business. *Darwin*, 2003 May 1.
4. Moncla, B., *The Convergence of E-Business and Business Intelligence: The I-Business Hurricane*. 2005 [cited 2005 April 8]; URL: http://datawarehouse.ittoolbox.com/browse.asp?c=DWPeerPublishing&r=%2Fpub%2FAS070601.pdf.

5. Amor, D., *The E-business Revolution*. Prentice Hall, Upper Saddle River, NJ, 1999.

6. Kalakota, R. and Whinston, A.B., *Frontiers of Electronic Commerce*. Addison-Wesley, Reading, MA, 1996.

7. Brierton, R., *Automatic data capture - why handprint is a challenge*. 2001 [cited 2005 April 15]; URL: http://www.findarticles.com/p/articles/mi_qa3947/is_200108/ai_n8963346.

8. Baker, S., *The three steps to Web service integration*. 2002 [cited 2004 April 15]; URL: http://searchwebservices.techtarget.com/originalContent/0,289142,sid26_gci841585,00.html.

9. Maselli, J., Lack of Integration Hurts CRM Efforts: Study. *InformationWeek*, 2001 December 19.

10. Anderson, H., *2004 Systems Integration Survey*. 2004 [cited 2005 June 7]; URL: http://www.healthdatamanagement.com/html/SISurvey061004.cfm.

11. Anderson, H., Tackling the Challenge of Systems Integration. *Health Data Management*, 2005 April 8.

12. M2Communications. *Data Integration Still Important to UK It - Report*. 2005 August 17 [cited 2005 September 1]; URL: http://projectmanagement.ittoolbox.com/news/dispnews.asp?i=132666.

13. Walker, J., *et al.*, *What You Need to Know About RFID In 2004*. 2003 [cited 2005 April 15]; URL: http://www.forrester.com/ER/Research/Brief/0,1317,33298,00.html.

14. Stal, M., Web services: Beyond component-based computing. *Communications of the ACM*, 45(10), 2002, pp. 71-76.

15. Abbas, A., Productivity paradox and information technology, in *Grid Computing: A Practical Guide to Technology and Applications*, A. Abbas (Ed.), Charles River Media, Inc., Hingham, MA, 2004, pp. 19-29.

16. Hemphill, B., *File Act or Toss*. 2005 [cited 2005 June 7]; URL: http://www.appearfirst.com/business/business_37.html.

17. Kim, W. and Seo, J., Classifying schematic and data heterogeneity in multidatabase systems. *IEEE Computer*, 24(12), 1991, pp. 12-18.

18. Ruh, W.A., Maginnis, F.X., and Brown, W.J., *Enterprise Application Integration: A Wiley Tech Brief*. Wiley, New York, 2000.

19. Gupta, A., Ascher, B.L., and Martone, M.E., Registering Scientific Information Sources for Semantic Mediation. In the 21st International Conference on Conceptual Modeling. 2002. Tampa, FL.

20. Ramesh, V. and Ram, S., Integrity Constraint Integration in Heterogeneous Databases: An Enhanced Methodology for Schema Integration. *Information Systems Research*, 22(8), 1997, pp. 423-446.

21. Batini, C., Lenzerini, M., and Navathe, S.B., A Comparative Analysis of Methodologies for Database Schema Integration. *ACM Computing Surveys*, 18(4), 1986, pp. 324-364.

22. Miller, R.J., *et al.*, The Clio Project: Managing Heterogeneity. *ACM SIGMOD Record*, 30(1), 2001, pp. 78-83.

23. Uschold, M. and Gruniger, M., Ontologies: Principles, Methods, and Applications. *Knowledge Engineering Review*, 11(2), 1996, pp. 93-155.
24. Berners-Lee, T., Hendler, J., and Lassila, O., The Semantic Web. *Scientific American*, 284(5), 2001, pp. 34-43.
25. Wache, H., *et al.*, Ontology-based Integration of Information — A Survey of Existing Approaches. In IJCAI-01 Workshop: Ontologies and Information Sharing. 2001. Seattle, WA.
26. Hendler, J. and McGuinness, D., The DARPA Agent Markup Language. *IEEE Intelligent Systems*, 15(6), 2000, pp. 67-73.
27. IBM. *DataJoiner Implementation and Usage Guide*. 1995 [cited 2005 June 7]; URL: http://www.redbooks.ibm.com/redbooks/pdfs/sg242566.pdf.
28. Garcia-Molina, H., *et al.*, The TSIMMIS Approach to Mediation: Data Models and Languages. *Next Generation Information Technologies and Systems*. 1995.
29. Levy, A.Y., Rajaraman, A., and Ordille, J.J. Querying Heterogeneous Information Sources Using Source Descriptions. In 22nd Conference on Very Large Databases. 1996. Mumbai (Bombay), India.
30. Knoblock, C.A., *et al.*, Modeling Web Sources for Information Integration. In 15th National Conference on Artificial Intelligence. 1998.
31. Baru, C., *et al.*, XML-Based Information Mediation with MIX. In International Conference on Management of Data (SIGMOD). 1999.
32. Palopoli, L., Terracina, G., and Ursino, D. The System DIKE: Towards the Semi-Automatic Synthesis of Cooperative Information Systems and Data Warehouses. In ADBIS-DASFAA Symposium. 2000.
33. Beneventano, D. and Bergamaschi, S. Extensional Knowledge for semantic query optimization in a mediator based system. In International Workshop on Foundations of Models for Information Integration (FMII-2001). 2001.
34. Schwarz, T., *et al.*, Efficient Domain-Specific Information Integration in Nexus. In Workshop on Information Integration on the Web. 2004. Toronto.
35. Sarma, S., Integrating RFID. *Queue*, 2(7), 2004, pp. 50-57.
36. Finkenzeller, K., *RFID Handbook : Fundamentals and Applications in Contactless Smart Cards and Identification*. John Wiley & Sons, New York, 2003.
37. Brewer, A., Sloan, N., and Landers, L.L., Intelligent Tracking in Manufacturing. *Journal of Intelligent Manufacturing*, 10, 1999, pp. 245-250.
38. Want, R., The Magic of RFID. *Queue*, 2(7), 2004, pp. 40-48.
39. Kärkkäinen, M., Increasing efficiency in the supply chain for short shelf life goods using RFID tagging. *International Journal of Retail & Distribution Management*, 31(10), 2003, pp. 529-536.
40. Internetweek.com. *Accenture Finds Significant Benefits With RFID*. 2003 June 12 [cited 2005 September 1]; URL: http://www.internetweek.com/showArticle.jhtml?articleID=10300865.
41. Barlas, D., *$4.2 Billion RFID Opportunity*. 2004 [cited 2005 September 1]; URL: http://www.line56.com/articles/default.asp?articleID=5361&TopicID=3.

42. ATKearney., *Meeting the Retail RFID Mandate.* 2003 [cited 2005 June 15]; URL: http://www.atkearney.com/shared_res/pdf/Retail_RFID_S.pdf.

43. Alvarez, G., RFID Helps Enterprises Increase Return on Assets Through Tracking. *InformationWeek*, 2004 December 21.

44. Sullivan, L., RFID Tested Against Barcodes. *InformationWeek*, 2004 March 15, p. 16.

45. Garskof, J., The Many Faces of RFID Tech. *Popular Science*, 2004 April.

46. Schwartz, E., *RFID Ripples Through Software Industry.* 2003 September 26 [cited 2005 April 20]; URL: http://www.infoworld.com/article/03/09/26/38NNrfid_1.html.

47. Osyk, B.O. and Vijayaraman, B.S., RFID in the Warehousing Industry: Where Do WERC Members Stand? *WERC Watch*, 2005 May 19.

48. Luckett, D., The Supply Chain. *BT Technology Journal*, 22(3), 2004, pp. 50-55.

49. Helders, B. and Vethman, A.J., Beyond 2005: How RFID will change the GSC. *Chain Store Age*, 2003 December, pp. 39-48.

50. Bacheldor, B., Bill Aims at RFID Privacy. *InformationWeek*, 2004 March 1, p. 16.

51. Cline, J., The RFID Privacy Scare Is Overblown. *Computerworld*, 2004 March 15.

52. Fantasia, A., Decoding ASPs. *Harvard Business Review*, 78(10), 2000, pp. 33-42.

53. Ferris, C. and Farrell, J., What are web services? *Communications of the ACM*, 46(6), 2003, pp. 31-34.

54. Foster, I., Computational Grids, in *The Grid: Blueprint for a Future Computing Infrastructure*, I. Foster and C. Kesselman (Eds.), Morgan Kaufmann Publishers, San Francisco, CA, 2004.

55. Gannon, D., *et al.*, *A Revised Analysis of the Open Grid Services Infrastructure.* Indiana University, Bloomington, IN, 2002.

56. Liu, L. and Ramaprasad, A., An integrated e-service framework for electronic medical records. In 7th International IEEE Conference on E-Commerce Technology. 2005. München, Germany.

57. Zhuge, H. and Liu, J., Flexible retrieval of web services. *Journal of Systems and Software*, 70(1–2), 2004, pp. 107-116.

58. Hagel, J. and Brown, J.S., Your next IT strategy. *Harvard Business Review*, 79(9), 2001, pp. 105-113.

59. Dewire, D.T., Application Service Providers. *Information Systems Management*, 17(4), 2000, pp. 14-19.

60. Susarla, A., Barua, A., and Whinston, A.B., Understanding the Service Component of Application Service Provision: An Empirical Analysis of Satisfaction with ASP Services. *MIS Quarterly*, 27(1), 2003, pp. 91-123.

61. Voelker, K.G., *Primer on Electronic Medical Records.* 2002 [cited 2002 January 3]; URL: http://www.elmr-electronic-medical-records-emr.com/electronic_medical_record_Primer.htm.

62. Liu, L. and Ma, Q., The Impact of Service Level on the Acceptance of Application Service Oriented Medical Records. *Information & Management*, 42(8), 2005, pp. 1121-1135.

63. Davis, F.D., Bagozzi, R.P., and Warshaw, P.R., User Acceptance of Computer Technology: A Comparison of Two Theoretical Models. *Management Science*, 35(8), 1989, pp. 982-1003.

64. MacVittie, L., Survivor's Guide to 2003: Business Applications. *Network Computing*, 13(26), 2002, pp. 78-85.

65. Flessner, P., XML Web services: More than protocols and acronyms. *Software Development Times*, 2001 August 15, p. 31.

66. Fremantle, P., Weerawarana, S., and Khalaf, R., Enterprise services. *Communications of the ACM*, 45(10), 2002, pp. 77-82.

67. Deitel, H.M., *et al., Web Services: A Technical Introduction.* Prentice Hall, UpperSaddle River, NJ, 2002.

68. Channabasavaiah, K., Holley, K., and Edward M. Tuggle, J., *Migrating to a service-oriented architecture.* 2003 [cited 2005 April 20]; URL: http://www-106.ibm.com/developerworks/webservices/library/ws-migratesoa/.

69. Kraunelis, L., Schmelzer, R., and Bloomberg, J., *Using Web Services for Integration.* 2002 [cited 2005 April 20]; URL: http://www.xml.org/xml/wsi.pdf.

70. Srivastava, B. and Koehler, J., Web Service Composition — Current Solutions and Open Problems. In Workshop on Planning for Web Services. 2003. Trento, Italy.

71. Pistore, M., Supporting the Composition of Distributed Business Processes: Research Challenges. In WWW Service Composition with Semantic Web Services. 2005. Compiegne University of Technology, France.

72. Liu, L. and Ma, Q., Emerging e-business technologies for electronic medical records. *International Journal of Healthcare Technology and Management*, 6(1/2), 2004, pp. 1-22.

73. Foster, I., *et al., The Physiology of the Grid: An Open Grid Services Architecture for Distributed Systems Integration.* The Globus Project: www.globus.org. 2002.

74. Oram, A., *Peer-to-Peer: Harnessing the Power of Disruptive Technologies.* O'Reilly & Associates, Inc., Sebastopol, CA, 2001.

75. Foster, I. and Kesselman, C., 10 Emerging Technologies That Will Change the World: Grid Computing. *Technology Review*, February, 2003, pp. 33-49.

76. Bernstein, P.A., *et al.*, Data management for Peer-toPeer Computing: A Vision. In 5th International Workshop on the Web and Databases. 2002. Madison, Wisconsin.

77. Halevy, A.Y., *et al.*, Schema Mediation in Peer Data management Systems. In 19th International Conference on Data Engineering. 2003. Bangalore, India.

CHAPTER 2

ICTs, Organizational Change and New Modes of Organizing

Michael Barrett
Judge Business School
University of Cambridge
Trumpington Street
Cambridge CB2 1AG
United Kingdom
Email: m.barrett@jbs.cam.ac.uk

1 Introduction

In this chapter, we examine the interplay between information and communication technologies (ICTs) and organizational change and the implications for new modes of organizing. We start by briefly reviewing some key dimensions of intraorganizational and interorganizational forms, which can be facilitated by advances in ICTs. Throughout this discussion, the focus is on the promising potential of the technology to enable changing organizational forms. Subsequently, we take a closer look at the relationship between ICT and organizational change shifting the discussion from a more causal, technological imperative, whereby technology determines a particular form in the organization to focus on organizing and the role of agency. Our focus is on structurational approaches to ICTs and organizational change, which examine the interaction of human agency and structure, technology being influenced by the context and individual strategists. More recently, researchers have developed the 'practice lens' approach, which depart from earlier perspectives that purport technology as embodying structures and emphasize technologies-in-use or technology-in-practice which recognize the role of human agency in enacting the use of technology.

This practice-based perspective has been challenged as privileging human agency over social structures and technological features, with researchers calling for further recognition of the role of social influences,

institutional forces and networks. Other researchers have suggested that
the practice perspective does not go far enough in rethinking
organization change as pervasive and ongoing, instead the charge is that
it has been inappropriately focused as being dependent on specific
technologies. For example, the generic characteristics of groupware
mean lend itself by its very nature to enactment by users. Instead, the
literature on organizational becoming recognizes pervasive reflexivity at
both individual and collective levels. This focus on reflexivity,
intimately connected to identity, is important in understanding the
relationship of ICTs and organizational change, and has received
growing recognition in the literatures on ICTs and globalization and
ICTs in developing countries. We also call attention to the role of
temporality and human agency in organizational change, which though
very important is rarely developed adequately. The penultimate section
of this chapter recognizes recent calls by researchers for a renewed
emphasis on the role of networks and institutional forces. We conclude
by urging researchers to appropriately combine insights and perspectives
from organization studies and information systems in charting fresh
research directions for understanding ICTs and organizational change.

2   ICTs and Changing Organizational Forms

Advances in information and communication technologies have long
been recognized for their impact on organizational form.   Throughout
the ages, technologies as varied as the interoffice memos, file system,
and telephones have enabled coordination and control in bureaucracies[1]
and distributed forms of organization[2]. Two alternative organizational
forms have dominated the literature, namely markets and hierarchies,
though with the rise of the Internet in a knowledge based society
alternative forms have abounded such as networks[3] virtual
organizations[4], and knowledge communities[5].
    Fulk and DeSanctis[6] summarize major changes that are taking place
in electronic communication technologies and the evolution in
organizational form. They suggest that five features of ICTs have
important advancements and consequences for organizations and their
form: dramatic increase in the speed of communications, reductions in

costs of communication, rise in bandwidth, vastly expanded connectivity, and integration of communication with computing technologies enabling communal capabilities in communication. In the context of globalization of business, environmental pressures including heightened market volatility require a shift from managerial hierarchy and divisional structures to more decentralized, flexible approaches to coordinating activities[7]. It is therefore not surprising that many organizations are not just adaptively responding to the environment in developing a new form[8] but are proactively involved in designing and implementing ICTs to enable new organizational forms with varying levels of success[9]. The reality is a complex mix of possibilities such that it is not appropriate to consider a single new organizational form but to focus on dimensions of forms, both intraorganizational and interorganizational, that are linked to ICTs[10].

One dimension of intraorganizational forms is a change in vertical control with a flattening of hierarchies and a leaner organization leading to a thinner middle management layer. ICTs can allow technology-based coordination and control with a reduction in human-based coordination[11]. A second dimension of intraorganizational form is the use of ICTs to support horizontal coordination through: 1) electronic workflow, 2) concurrent engineering for product design, 3) stockless production whereby ICT reduces in-process inventory, and 4) virtual organizations which leverage ICTs to support mobile workers performing service work. A third dimension refers to the reduction of the size of the organization. Re-engineering and trends towards lean dispersed forms of organizing coordinated by ICTs have facilitated smaller organization size. The Internet has fuelled the trend towards 'demassification' and increased outsourcing of value activities such as applications development, ICT infrastructure and business processes. These activities are increasingly being performed in offshore locations[12] with the growth of global software work, and this has meant that increasingly the size of the core organization and the scope of the value activities performed in-house has shrunk[13]. There is a trade-off, however, between reduction in organization size and the ownership and control of key segments of a firm's value activities.

ICTs facilitate developments in electronic markets over hierarchical forms of organization and the development of the network organization as a mixed mode of organization combining both hierarchy and market mechanisms. ICTs can facilitate MNCs as global network organizations which are not simply a central core with tentacles but a dense set of inter-connected organizations which are themselves embedded in networks that span the globe[14], though in reality there are challenges in using ICTs to support the management of work across time, space, and culture[15]. Finally, ICTs have the potential to support new organizational forms with communication cultures to enhancing learning and innovation[16], though once again management issues of time, space, and culture challenge the effective use of knowledge communities or communities-of-knowing[17].

ICTs also support an increasing number of new interorganizational forms. With the rise of outsourcing and collaborative planning between organizations and their suppliers, the importance of ICTs in supporting interorganizational coupling has increased. Technologies such as EDI and the Internet facilitate tight coupling between buyers and suppliers, both in dyadic forms and in the form of electronic markets. Typical examples of the latter include electronic trading in financial services, the pharmaceutical industry[18], and the airline industry. Other emerging technologies such as radio frequency identification (RFID), as a ubiquitous technology promise identification and real time monitoring across the global supply chain[19] and new forms of the electronic integration effect[20].

3 Structurational Approaches to ICTs and Organizational Change

The previous sub-section has focused on the range of promising possibilities of new organizational forms that *can* be facilitated by ICTs, which reflects the causal status of technology on organizational forms. A number of researchers have challenged the populist view of ICT-enabled transformation of work and new organizational forms[21], with ICT being viewed as a 'driver' of change. We move from this more technological deterministic view to a more processual, emergent view, which focuses on the gradual unfolding of the technology-organizational relationship[22].

We focus on structuration as a dynamic process perspective to study ICTs and organizational change. This approach examines organizational change as the negotiated process between technologies and human agency within organizational environments. In this short paper, we do not review structuration theory per se but would refer the interested reader to a recent extensive review of structuration theory and IS research[23].

Early structurational approaches to studying technological change[24] shifted the focus from technologies causing organizational change and new structural forms to treating technology as an *occasion* for structuring. His study of the introduction of identical CT scanners into the radiology departments of two different hospitals showed very different organizational and structural outcomes and social processes. Barley's work advanced our understanding of the complex technology-organization relationship by tracing the relationship between action and structure over time and how the new technology was related to new ways of working at the action level, which was related to changes in structure. Similarly, Robey and Sahay's[25] study of the introduction of geographical information systems (GIS) in two county governments reported radically different experiences and consequences of use of the technology, patterns of communications between departments, and the way work was accomplished and transformed. Barley's[26] early work was followed by a number of researchers trying to explain the relationship between ICTs and change[27]. Orlikowski and Robey[28] drew on structuration theory as a model for understanding the nature of ICTs and their role in structuring of organizations. Orlikowski[29] provided a role for users to modify technologies through their ongoing interactions with them. Her structurational model of technology develops a duality of technology which recognizes both technology as having material properties built into it by its designers, so that structures are embedded in technology, and also that technology is shaped by users' interactions who attach different meanings depending on their context of use. Orlikowski[30] uses this structurational model in her case study of the development and use of CASE tools designed to improve productivity in a consulting firm. Her study shows how technical consultants were influenced by institutional knowledge and norms of software development processes. Furthermore, the actions of consultants using the new CASE tools were mediated by the assumptions and demands built into them. She also emphasizes that knowledgeable actors, who are reflexive of their actions and consequences, are able at any time to potentially undermine institutionalization of development practices.

In a parallel stream of research, Walsham[31] draws on and links models of context and process[32] via structuration theory in understanding organizational change associated with ICTs. His analytical framework synthesized multiple components namely: the *content* of any organizational change program associated with ICTs, the *social context* of a computer based IS, *social process* involving taking a cultural and political perspective on organizational change associated with IS and broader multi-level contexts, and a final component linking social context and social process via structuration theory. He conceptualizes IS as embodying interpretative schemes, providing coordination and control facilities, and encapsulating norms, and which are drawn on in the social processes which take place in organizations[33]. As Jones and Karsten[34] suggest, the use of these earlier structurational models have been drawn on in later studies to explore phenomenon related to groupware and organizational change[35], impact of the Internet on the real estate industry and the work of realtors[36] amongst others.

Another set of conceptual developments inspired by elements of structuration theory for studying ICTs and change have developed around the technological frames of reference (TFR) perspective[37]. This approach which gives primacy to the interpretive scheme modality and dimension of structuration theory, has been adopted and adapted by a number of researchers for studying ICTs and organizational change in different contexts[38]. This socio-cognitive approach to ICT and organizational change suggests that technological frames, as a subset of members' organizational frames, guide their interpretations and actions related to ICT development, adoption and use and thus influence change processes and outcomes. Incongruence of these frames by individuals in different stakeholder groups have been found to explain outcomes of change processes.

For example, Orlikowski and Gash[39] demonstrate how incongruence between managers, technologists, and users contributed to low levels of adoption and use of a Lotus Notes groupware system. The vast majority of TFR studies give little attention to socio-cognitive influences beyond the organizational boundary in understanding ICT and organization change. One exception is Barrett's[40] adaptation of TFR analysis in examining the implementation of EDI systems in an insurance market's setting, which identified the importance of market institutions as a key frame domain within an institutional field. In this way, institutional logics permeate organizational boundaries and influence users' technological frames. Significant incongruence was identified between users and technologists/market leaders who were implementing the EDI system[41]. Other recent work[42] has also shown that incongruence may vary across frame domains, groups and over time, leading to frequent frame shifts. A critique of TFR studies has been that its underlying ontology privileges stability over change[43], with organizations viewed as stable social structures in which change is exceptional and episodic. Such change is externally triggered but with organizational structures returning to status quo or to a new equilibrium after negotiations with ICTs. In sum, the majority of TFR studies have been static in orientation focusing on how frames influencing stakeholders' interpretation and actions related to a new information technology change at different points in time. In these studies, incongruence of frames and their consequences are subsequently assessed.

An alternative, more dynamic, perspective is an enacted view of ICTs and organizational change with change being conceptualized as an ongoing improvisation grounded in the ongoing practices of organizational actors and not orchestrated by top management[44]. Later work in this tradition surrounds the 'practice lens' for examining the effect of technologies on the organization[45] which shifts the earlier focus of technology embodying structures to emergent structures, technologies-in-practice, that are instantiated in the ongoing use of technological artifacts. In other words, transformations of organizational practice are not caused by technology nor realized from the embodiment of social structures within the technology. Rather, transformations or significant organizational change may result over time as users enact technologies in response to their local experiences.

4 ICT and Organizational Change in the Context of Globalization

Giddens[46] argues that it is the pervasive reflexivity in the context of globalization that differentiates this era from previous epochs: "the susceptibility of most aspects of social activity, and material relations with nature, to chronic revision in the light of new information or knowledge."[47]. Drawing from Giddens and other social theories, Tsoukas and Chia[48] suggest that the practice lens on ICT and organizational change, while emphasising human agency and enactment in practice[49], does not adequately account for this pervasive reflexivity in contemporary business. They argue for a rethinking of organizational change to more fully recognize the pervasive, radically process-oriented nature of change. Their ontology suggests that change should not be thought of as a property of organization but that organization must be thought of as a pattern that is constituted, shaped, and emerging from change. They develop the concept of organizational becoming as a way of rethinking organizational change as 'the reweaving of actors' webs of beliefs and habits of action as a result of new experiences obtained through interactions'[50]. Accounts of change, therefore, should be more directly connected to practitioners' lived experiences and actions.

Organizational becoming therefore inherently recognizes reflexive modernization in processes of globalization, whereby institutional reflexivity is linked to people increasingly exercising their inherent capacity for reflexive thinking[51]. More recently, IS researchers have been drawing on Giddens' theory of globalization in studying ICTs and organizational change, particularly in the two areas of ICTs and globalization and ICTs in developing countries.

Firstly, earlier research on ICTs and work transformation in global financial markets, Barrett and Walsham[52] developed a conceptual scheme by drawing on Giddens theory of globalization and social transformation to examine electronic trading in the London Insurance Market. Their scheme links the macro level changes associated with the introduction of new technologies and the challenges of work transformation of the professional groups. In so doing, they illustrated how Giddens general theory may be extended to explicitly include the role of information technology for understanding transformation and social change, and conclude with some key practical implications on electronic trading in the London Market. Scott[53] draws on similar themes of reflexive modernity developed by Beck[54] and Giddens to understand the role of decision support systems on the transformation of lending advisers and credit risk in the rapidly changing retail banking sector.

Another stream of research drawing on Giddens theory of globalization is the IS in developing countries literature. For example, Nicholson and Sahay[55] draw on this theory to examine time/space and globalization in examining offshoring of software development between British multi-nationals and Indian software vendors. A particular focus of their case surrounds the political and cultural issues, which developed in the globalization of software development. Bada's[56] longitudinal study in the banking sector in Nigeria examines the introduction of BPR involving computerization and networking of branches. In so doing, he draws on global theorists such as Giddens and critiques them for an inadequate focus on local diversity and locally meaningful ways of doing things. Another study by Barrett, Sahay and Walsham[57] draw on Giddens theory of globalization to examine the introduction of GIS for forestry management. Specifically, they draw on and use Giddens concepts of macro institutional reflexivity in globalization process involving different trust systems and link this to challenges to shifts in identity of Indian foresters who are expected to rely on spatial features embedded in GIS software, but which conflicts with their local ways of knowing and working.

5 Temporality, Human Agency and Organizational Change

The role of temporality and human agency is a very important dimension that has received surprisingly little attention[58] despite its centrality in ICT and organizational change processes. Tsoukas and Chia, like other reviews before them, have shown that the bulk of research on organizational change draws on synoptic accounts of change. That is, change is viewed typically as a stage model in which the entity undergoing change has distinct states at different points in time, along with explanations for the trajectories organizations followed[59]. However, they argue that, by themselves, synoptic accounts cannot capture or do justice to the open-ended micro-processes that underlay the trajectories of change. Performative accounts of organizational change are also needed, which with their focus on situated human agency unfolding in time, offers insights into emergence and accomplishment of change, which are more directly linked to practitioners' lived experiences and actions[60]. However, longitudinal studies include the above performative accounts while following dynamic change processes across time do not necessarily incorporate a theoretic basis for time[61]. To this end, some recent literature has focused on developing a temporally reflective perspective into the analysis of ICT-enabled organizational change through the implementation of an enterprise system, which recognizes both 'linear' and 'non-linear', or socially defined aspects of time.

In other conceptual developments on IS and organizational change, Boudreau and Robey[62] has emphasized the importance of framing agency in temporal terms[63]. Human capacity is simultaneously oriented toward the past, the future, and the present at every given moment. Drawing on similar views of time[64], Barrett and Scott[65] developed a temporal perspective which explicitly integrates the temporal features of structuration, namely reversibility in global time, irreversibility in global time, and institutionalization in global time, with Adam's social theory of time to examine the emergence of electronic trading and the process of globalization in traditional futures markets. Surprisingly few other studies[66] have explicitly developed a temporal perspective drawing on structuration theory to examine IS and organizational change, whereby temporal structures are both constituted by and constitute social practices[67].

6   The Role of Social Influences, Networks and Institutional Forces

In this penultimate section of the chapter, we highlight recent calls in the literature[68] to better recognize that social influences, networks and institutional forces[69] are at play alongside human agency in the enactment of technology use over time. Boudreau and Robey argue that the current focus of the literature on human agency and enactment neglects the importance of the influence of social network and structures on human agency of individual actors. Of particular note, actor network theory approaches[70] and ecological approaches[71] have examined dynamic socio-technical relations between ICTs and organizations. ANT examines the motivations and actions of actors (both human actors and actants such as technological artifacts) who form elements of heterogeneous networks of aligned interests. In understanding change and innovation associated with IS, the theory traces and explains the processes whereby relatively stable networks of aligned interests are created and maintained, or why such networks fail to establish themselves.

A major difference with an ecological analysis is that the latter has much less of a focus on the Machiavellian use of rhetoric and strategms, as is the case with ANT in the construction and maintenance of network allegiances. Rather, the ecological approach aims at allowing for multiple voices to be heard, while also opening up possibilities to "disembed the narratives" contained in ICT development and use and so "unearth" the deeper social structures embedded in the broader organizational context[72]. This perspective therefore considers both the ICT innovation and the process of change as a network of institutional arrangements, ICTs, people and work practices. A good illustration of this ecological approach in the literature is Bowker and Star's study of the WHO's global information system which developed the International Classification of Diseases (ICD). Their work highlights the challenges in (re)constructing the ICD as involving negotiations between public institutions and professional health communities as well as the role of standards, artifacts and various classification systems.

Avgerou[73] highlights the importance of an institutional perspective to connect multiple levels within a historical context in the analysis of IS innovation and organizational change in conditions of globalization. From an institutional point of view, ICT is not seen as a set of material products functioning according to technical rules embedded in their physical components but as products of a social network embedded in social institutions. Early work on institutional theory[74] emphasised social, political, and cultural elements as endogenous institutional forces of organizations that contribute to the formation, continuation, and transformation of institutions. More recent writings on new institutionalism[75] move away from cultural persistence to recognize the role of such elements in processes of de-institutionalization and institutional transformation whereby established meanings and action in an organization are discredited as a result of competing meanings and actions[76].

In addition to endogeneous forces contributing to continuity and transformations of institutions, institutional analysis also emphasizes the importance of interaction between institutions. As organizations tend to be clustered in fields and become similar to each other (process of isomorphism), they respond to coercive or normative pressures or imitate the structures and processes of other organizations considered by others in the field to be successful. Though at a relatively early stage, the value and use of institutional theory for examining ICTs and organizational change is being increasingly recognized[77] as a promising theoretical direction within the IS field.

7 Conclusion

In this chapter, we started out by highlighting how ICTs can potentially facilitate changing organizational forms, both intraorganizationally and interorganziationally. Over the next few years, a whole host of emerging disruptive technologies such as RFID, mobile technologies, and ubiquitous computing have enormous potential to offer new modes of organizing. This promise afforded by the implementation of these technologies, however, needs to be simultaneously attentive to change both as an ongoing, radical process enacted by individuals in the use of technology as well as recognizing the social influences, networks, and institutional forces at play.

We have reviewed a number of important theoretical developments based on structuration theory including: duality of technology, process – context approaches, technological frames, and practice based approaches to highlight the interplay of human agency and structure in the process of ICT and organizational change. We also noted some recent critiques of the practice-based perspective drawing from the organizational becoming literature, which argues for more fully recognizing the reflexivity of change as pervasive and ongoing. IS literature consonant with this perspective of reflexivity and change has drawn on Giddens' theory of reflexive modernization, namely the ICTs and globalization and ICTs in developing countries literature streams. In addition, we have emphasised the often neglected, yet critical aspect of temporality and human agency in IS and organizational change and highlighted the importance of networks and institutional forces.

We close by suggesting that future directions for research on ICT and organizational change may be fruitfully developed through an increased cross-fertilization of theoretical developments in the organization studies and information systems literatures[78]. Of particular note, the enduring and active debate on the role of human agency and materiality of technology in the IS literature (SJIS 2005) is of critical importance in the ongoing quest to conceptualise the relationship between ICT and organizational change. Additionally, while the IS literature has recently embraced institutional theory there is considerable scope to learn from the developments in this rapidly growing area within organization studies[79]. Similarly, discourse analysis approaches to ICT and organizational change[80] are relatively new in the IS field though there is an emerging body of work developing in this area[81]. Finally, we envisage further developments on emotion in information systems[82] and organization studies literature[83] to complement cognitive approaches in understanding situated change associated with ICTs.

References

1. Yates, J. *Control through Communication: The Rise of System in American Management*, Johns Hopkins University Press, Baltimore, 1989.
2. Fulk, J., G. DeSanctis. Electronic Communication and Changing Organizational Forms. *Organization Science*. 6(4), 1995, pp. 1-13.
3. Monge, P.R., J. Fulk. Global Network Organizations. Paper presented to International Communication Association, Albuquerque, NM, 1995.
4. Nohria, N., J.D. Berkley. In C. Heckscher and A. Donnelon (Eds.), *The Post-Bureaucratic Organization: New Perspectives on Organizational Change*, Sage, Thousand Oaks, CA, 1994, pp. 108-128.
5. Barrett, M., S. Cappleman, G. Shoib, G. Walsham. Learning in Knowledge Communities: Managing Technology and Context. *European Management Journal*. 22(1), 2004, pp. 1-11.
6. Fulk and DeSanctis *Op. Cit.*

7. Daft, R.L., A.Y. Lewin. Where are the 'New' Organizational Forms? *Organization Science*. 4(4), 1993, pp. 513-528.
8. Daft, R.L. *Organization Theory and Design*, West, St Paul, MN, 1986.
9. Fulk and DeSanctis *Op. Cit.*
10. *Ibid.*
11. Zuboff, S. *In the Age of the Smart Machine: The Future of Work and Power*, Oxford University Press, Oxford, 1988.
12. Sahay, S., B. Nicholson, S. Krishna. *Global IT Outsourcing*, Cambridge University Press, Cambridge, 2003.
13. Cash, J.I., F.W. McFarlan, J.L. McKenney, L.M. Applegate. *Corporate Information Systems Management*, Irwin, Boston, 1992.
14. Monge and Fulk *Op. Cit.*
15. Fulk and DeSanctis *Op. Cit.*
16. Reich, R. *The Work of Nations: Preparing Ourselves for 21st Century Capitalism*, Knopf, New York, 1991.
17. Boland, J.R.J., R. Tenkasi. Perspective Making and Perspective Taking in Communities of Knowing. *Organization Science*. 6(4), 1995, pp. 350-372.
18. e.g. AHS as discussed by Cash *et al. Op. Cit.*
19. Davenport, T.H., J.D. Brooks. Enterprise Systems and the supply chain. *Journal of Enterprise Information Management*. 17(1), 2004, pp. 8-19.
20. Malone, T., J. Yates, R.I. Benjamin. Electronic Markets and Electronic Hierarchies. *Communications of the ACM*. 30, 1987, pp. 484-496; and Malone, T., R. Laubacher, M.S. Scott-Morton. *Inventing the Organizations of the 21st Century*, MIT, Cambridge, MA, 2003.
21. e.g. Winter, S.J., S.L. Taylor. The role of IT in the transformation of work: A Comparison of Post-Industrial, Industrial, and Proto-Industrial Organization. *Information Systems Research*. 7(1), 1996, pp. 5-21.
22. Markus, M.L., D. Robey. Information technology and organizational change: causal structure in theory and research. *Management Science*. 34, 1988, pp. 583-598.
23. Jones, M., H. Karsten. Review: Structuration Theory and IS Research. Judge Institute of Management Studies, University of Cambridge. (WP11/2003) 2003.
24. Barley, S.R. Technology as an occasion for structuring: Evidence from observation of CT scanners and the social order of radiology departments. *Administrative Science Quarterly*. 31, 1986, pp. 78-108.
25. Robey, D., S. Sahay. Transforming work through information technology: A comparative case study of geographic information systems in county government. *Information Systems Research*. 7, 1996, pp. 93-110.
26. Barley *Op. Cit.*
27. Orlikowski, W., D. Robey. Information technology and the structuring of organizations. *Information Systems Research*. 2, 1991, pp. 143-169; and Walsham, G. *Interpreting Information Systems in Organizations*, John Wiley, New York, 1993.

28. Orlikowski and Robey *Op.Cit.*
29. Orlikowski, W. The duality of technology: Rethinking the concept of technology in organizations. *Organization Science.* 3, 1992, pp. 398-427.
30. Orlikowski, W.J. CASE tools as organizational change: Investigating incremental and radical changes in systems. *MIS Quarterly.* 17(3), 1993, pp. 309-340.
31. Walsham *Op.Cit.*
32. Pettigrew, A.M. *The Awakening Giant: Continuity and Change in Imperial Chemical Industries*, Blackwell, Oxford, 1985.
33. Walsham *Op. Cit.*
34. Jones and Karsten *Op. Cit.*
35. Karsten, H. Converging paths to Notes: in search of computer-based information systems in a networked company. *Information Technology and People.* 8(1), 1995, pp. 7-34.
36. Crowston, K., S. Sawyer, R. Wigand. Investigating the interplay between structure and information and communications technology in the real estate industry. *Information Technology and People.* 14(2), 2001, pp. 163-183.
37. Orlikowski, W.J., D. Gash. Technology Frames: Making Sense of Information Technology in Organizations. *ACM Transactions on Information Systems.* 12(2), 1994, pp. 174-207.
38. See review by Davidson, E., D. Pai. Making Sense of Technological Frames: Promise, Progress and Potential. In B. Kaplan, D.P. Truex III, D. Wastell, and J. DeGross (Eds.), *Relevant theory and informed practice: looking forward from a 20 year perspective on IS research*, Kluwer, 2004, pp. 473-491.
39. Orlikowski and Gash *Op. Cit.*
40. Barrett, M. Challenges of EDI adoption for electronic trading in the London Insurance Market. *European Journal of Information Systems.* 8(1), 1999, pp. 1-15.
41. Davidson and Pai *Op. Cit.*
42. Davidson, E. Technology Frames and Framing: A Socio-Cognitive Investigation of Requirements Determination. *MIS Quarterly.* 26(4), 2002, pp. 329-358.
43. Davidson, E. Information Technology And Organizational Change: A Technological Frames Perspective. Working Paper, University of Hawaii, 2005.
44. Tsoukas, H., R. Chia. On Organizational Becoming: Rethinking Organizational Change. *Organization Science.* 13(5), 2002, pp. 567-582.
45. Orlikowski, W.J. Using Technology and Constituting Structures: A practice lens for studying technology in organizations. *Organization Science.* 11(4), 2000, pp. 404-428.
46. Giddens, A. *Modernity and Self Identity: Self and Society in the Late Modern Age*, Polity Press, Cambridge, 1991.
47. Giddens, *Ibid*, p. 20.
48. Tsoukas and Chia *Op. Cit.*

49. Orlikowski, W. Improvising organisational transformation overtime: a situated change perspective. *Information Systems Research.* 7, 1996, pp. 63-92.
50. Tsoukas and Chia *Op. Cit.* p. 570.
51. Giddens, A. *The Consequences of Modernity*, Polity Press, Cambridge, 1990.
52. Barrett, M., G. Walsham. Electronic trading and work transformation in the London Insurance Market. *Information Systems Research.* 10(1), 1999, pp. 1-22.
53. Scott, S.V. IT-enabled credit risk modernisation: a revolution under the cloak of normality. *Accounting, Management and Information Technology.* 10(3), 2000, pp. 221-255.
54. Beck, U. *The Risk Society: Towards a New Modernity*, Sage, London, UK, 1992.
55. Nicholson, B., S. Sahay. Some Political and Cultural Issues in the Globalization of Software Development: Case Experience From Britain and India. *Information and Organization.* 11(1), 2001, pp. 25-44.
56. Bada, A. Local Adaptations to Global Trends: A Study of an IT-Based Organizational Change Program in a Nigerian Bank. *The Information Society.* 18, 2002, pp. 77-86.
57. Barrett, M., S. Sahay, G. Walsham. Understanding IT and social transformation: GIS for natural resources management in India. *The Information Society.* 17(1), 2001, pp. 5-20.
58. Lee, H., J. Liebenau. Time in organizational studies: Towards a new research direction. *Organization Studies.* 20(2), 2000, pp. 1035-1058.
59. E.g. Greenwood, R., C.R. Hinings. Understanding Radical Organizational Change: Bringing together the old and the new institutionalism. *Academy of Management Review.* 21(4), 1996, p. 1022.
60. Tsoukas and Chia *Op. Cit.*
61. Sawyer, S., R. Southwick. Temporal Issues in Information and Communication Technology-Enabled Organizational Change: Evidence from an Enterprise Systems Implementation. *The Information Society.* 18(4), 2002, pp. 263-280.
62. Boudreau, M., D. Robey. Enacting Integrated Information Technology: A Human Perspective. *Organization Science.* 16(1), 2005, pp. 3-18.
63. Emirbayer, M., A. Mische. What is agency? *American Journal of Sociology.* 103, 1998, p. 1023.
64. Adam, B. *Timewatch: The Social Analysis of Time*, Polity Press, Cambridge, 1995.
65. Barrett, M., S. Scott. Electronic trading and the process of globalization in traditional futures exchanges: a temporal perspective. *European Journal of Information Systems.* 13(1), 2004, pp. 65-79.
66. Notably Barley, S. On Technology, Time, and Social Order: Technically Induced Change in the Temporal Organization of Radiological Work. In F. Dubinskas (Ed.), *Making Time: Ethnographies of High Technology Organizations*, Temple University Press, Philadelphia, 1988; and Orlikowski, W.J., J. Yates. It's About Time: Temporal Structuring in Organizations. *Organization Science.* 13(6), 2002, p. 684.

67. Orlikowski, W., J. Yates. Its About Time: An Enacted View of Time in Organizations. Working Paper# 4055, MIT Sloan School of Management, 1999.
68. Boudreau and Robey *Op. Cit.*
69. Avgerou, C. *Information Systems and Global Diversity*, Oxford University Press, Oxford, 2002.
70. Hanseth, O., E. Monteiro. Inscribing behaviour in information infrastructure standards. *Accounting, Management and Information Technology.* 7(4), 1997, pp. 183-211.
71. Bowker, G., S.L. Star. *Sorting Things Out — Classification and its Consequences*, Cambridge, MA, 1999.
72. Star, S.L. Infrastructure and ethnographic practice: working on the fringes. *Scandinavian Journal of Information Systems.* 14(2), 2002, p. 110.
73. Avgerou *Op. Cit.*
74. DiMaggio, P.J., W.W. Powell. In *The New Institutionalism in Organizational Analysis*, University of Chicago Press, Chicago, 1991, pp. 1-38.
75. E.g. Greenwood and Hinings *Op. Cit.*
76. Avgerou *Op. Cit.*
77. Boudreau and Robey *Op. Cit.*
78. Orlikowski, W., S. Barley. Technology and institutions: what can research on information technology and research on organizations learn from each other? *Management Information Systems Quarterly.* 25, 2001, pp. 145-165.
79. Scott, W.R. *Institutions and organisation*, Sage Publications, 2001.
80. Heracleous, L., M. Barrett. Organizational change as discourse: communicative actions and deep structures in the context of information technology implementation. *Academy of Management Journal.* 44, 2001, pp. 755-778.
81. Wynn, E., E. Whitley, M. Myers. Placing language in the foreground: themes and methods in information technology discourse. In E. Wynn, E. Whitley, M. Myers and J. DeGross (Eds.), *Global and organizational discourse about information technology*, Kluwer Academic, Boston, 2003, pp. 1-15.
82. Ciborra, C. In need for knowledge: a new study of improvisation. Working paper, London School of Economics, 2001.
83. Fineman, S. *Understanding emotion at Work*, Sage, London, 2003.

CHAPTER 3

Exploring the Virtual Work Environment: A Process Perspective

Katherine M. Chudoba[*]
MIS Department
College of Business
Florida State University
Tallahassee, FL 32306-1110, USA
Email: kchudoba@cob.fsu.edu

Mary Beth Watson-Manheim
Department of Information and Decision Sciences
2426 University Hall, 601 S. Morgan Street MC 294
University of Illinois, Chicago
Chicago, IL 60607-7124, USA
Email: mbwm@uic.edu

1 Introduction

In the 20th century, the use of ICT allowed organizations to stretch themselves in time and space, morphing from primarily a physical form to an electronic or virtual work environment (VWE)[1] entity. Operations have been pushed farther and farther into the realm of communications and away from anything that could be done without a communications network. As companies become increasingly informatted[2] and make use of individual employee's expertise and knowledge, they become more dependent on the individual to adjust direction and adapt to the changing environment. ICTs, therefore, have forced a shift in view even as they facilitate a shift in physical circumstances[3].

While today's organizational designs require adaptive responses to overcome barriers to collaboration[4], much of the research has focused on characterizations of explicit discontinuities in the VWE. Geographic

[*]We gratefully acknowledge the contributions of our collaborators on the three previously published research studies that form the nexus of our analyses in this chapter.

57

dispersion is the single-most commonly referenced discontinuity[5,6,7,8]; others that are frequently noted include time, organization, culture, identity (e.g., team membership), and technology. As understanding has increased, many have come to consider the VWE as a hybrid condition[9], or as a continuum with varying degrees of virtuality[10]. This suggests a more fluid conceptualization of discontinuities in the VWE, rather than a finite set of attributes.

We extend this idea by using discontinuities only as the starting point for our discussion of the VWE. Then, we focus our attention on the process issues that surround them. Drawing from our research in several Fortune 100 companies, all with a strong global presence, we found that the *process* of working in the VWE has a greater impact on performance than simply the presence of one or more discontinuities. For example, communication becomes more complex in the VWE as people find it necessary to be deliberate and conscious of their communication strategies in order to convey accountability that would be obvious in a FTF environment. Redundant ICT-enabled communication such as follow-up emails and cc'ing multiple people is not as necessary in the FTF environment where a passing glance on the way to the water cooler suggests someone is hard at work at her desk. Such redundant communication means increased work for both senders and receivers. By focusing on *how* work happens in the VWE, we highlight the adjustments and adaptations that those in the VWE make.

We begin with a brief discussion of discontinuities commonly associated with the VWE, followed by our observations of the VWE drawn from research. Next, we discuss several overarching process issues that emerged from our examination of discontinuities, and conclude with implications for research and practice.

2 Discontinuities in the VWE

While Gibson and Cohen[11] argue that the defining characteristic of virtual work is that participants are geographically dispersed, other researchers suggest additional dimensions are also relevant in identifying the challenges and opportunities in the VWE. These dimensions have alternatively been labeled boundaries[12,13] and discontinuities[14]. We use the terminology of discontinuities – "a break or gap in the work context" or a "lack of continuity"– because consideration of discontinuities logically calls attention to continuities as an opposing concept. Robey and Boudreau[15] suggest that paying attention to oppositional forces when investigating information technology and organizational change can lead to a more complex understanding of resulting social and behavioral consequences. For example, Watson-Manheim *et al.*[16] found many studies were simultaneously addressing continuities as factors that are in place or that emerge to bridge possible negative consequences of discontinuities. We now briefly review some of the discontinuities more likely to be encountered in the VWE.

As Gibson and Cohen[17] observed, *geographic discontinuity* is the most closely associated characteristic of the VWE. Today, organizations face an ever-changing environment, distinguished by increasing size, diversification, and globalization[18]. They neither can nor want to assemble all employees in a single geographic space to work. The ability to be relatively place-independent benefits both employer and employee. The employer saves substantial dollars by not moving employees when they assume new assignments, and employees can avoid the stress and social costs of uprooting and moving for the sake of the job. In place of collocation, organizational networks bring together people with the appropriate skills and knowledge to react in emergent situations. Frequently, key support functions are distributed worldwide so that people may coordinate daily with team members halfway around the clock from them.

Under conditions of virtuality, *temporal discontinuities* are particularly interesting because time is paradoxical in that it has both objective and subjective components. People are frequently cognizant of time zone differences, yet may not be aware of other temporally related differences. For example, while some people work monochronically and focus on a single task within a given period of time, others engage in polychromic work, or what is typically called multi-tasking[19,20]. People also differ in their perceptions of what is legitimately considered "work time" and what is considered socializing[21]. Some must always be "on task," with a single-minded focus on work. Others believe that socializing is necessary for building relationships, an important aspect of the work environment. In a collocated environment, it is easier to reach a shared sense of timing because of physical cues given by others. Today employees may not even know accurately what time of day it is where their coworkers are, much less be able to sense the "meaning" of time from environmental cues.

The changing form of *organizational functions* suggests another aspect of discontinuity. Instead of remaining within functional hierarchies, many employees work in matrixed organizations where they provide a form of organizational coordination through task forces and teams that represent many business groups. As companies lose some of their traditional organizing structures, the uses of ICT propagate new social networks. For example, inter-organizational alliances and virtual work teams cross functional, organizational, and national boundaries[22,23].

Cultural discontinuity is evident in the myriad forms of socially sanctioned behavior that represents diversity in today's corporate world. In what he suggests is a paradigm shift, Wellman describes people that "work in multiple sets of overlapping relationships, cycling among different networks"[24]. Today's global workforce in the multinational firm is increasingly integrated with respect to skill, training and authority distributed across people from multiple cultural and national origins[25]. Professional work, especially software development, is now distributed around the globe[26].

The VWE would not be possible without ICT, and so *technology discontinuity* is one of the keys to understanding its dynamics. A myriad of technologies are available such as email, audio and video conferencing, IM, web-based repositories, and distributed meeting software that supports shared workspace. Functionality available with these technologies may advance interaction processes, or impede work because of its complexity. In addition, differing access to ICT, either because of availability or access (e.g., joining meetings from office, home, or airport) may make it difficult for some team members to contribute to team efforts[27].

3   Observations of the VWE

We now turn to an examination of the VWE environment using data gleaned from field studies we conducted in four Fortune 100 companies.

First, we consider the environments based on the discontinuities discussed above, and then we consider the process issues that surround the discontinuities to better understand how work is accomplished. The three studies are summarized in Table 1.

3.1 *MTI*

MTI is a division of a Fortune 50 company formed as a joint partnership with an Asian corporation, and responsible for manufacturing industrial technology. In the mid 1990's, the company initiated two strategic alliances, one with a European competitor and the other with a major customer, also located in Europe, in order to enhance its supply chain operations. A team composed of representatives from both companies, and responsible for cross manufacturing products in an OEM arrangement to extend each company's offerings, managed the alliance with the competitor. Representatives from both companies also managed the partnership with the customer. The MTI team leader and a senior engineer served on both teams; other members were unique to their respective teams. This contractual arrangement provided for close coordination between the two companies on requirements for enhanced features on existing products and new products to meet the ongoing needs of the customer. A third team was composed of members of the U.S.-based company and the Asian joint venture partner, and charged with creating a new product line that melded strengths from the existing product lines.

For two of the MTI teams, geographic and cultural discontinuities were essentially the same. In other words, the distributed nature of the team reflected its cross-cultural composition. The third team with the Asian JV partner had MTI members in numerous locations throughout the continental U.S., whereas all Asian team members resided at a single Asian headquarters location. Temporal discontinuities were primarily reflected in the 5 or more time zones that separated team members, making scheduling of synchronous meetings or phone calls challenging. Unlike teams in the other field studies, members of the MTI teams were not observed multi-tasking during meetings, whether FTF or ITC-mediated. Organizational discontinuities were reflected in both functional differences in member background across the three teams, as well as the fact that members worked for different corporations whose objectives were not always consistent with a team's objectives.

Relative to the other studies, the MTI teams had a basic set of ICT available for their use, including e-mail, telephone, fax, and audio conference calls. Technology discontinuity was reflected in the fact that U.S.-based team members were able to attach documents to their email messages, whereas non-U.S.-based team members were 6-15 months behind their U.S. team members in upgrading their email systems to include this functionality. In the interim, the team resolved the discontinuity by faxing documents such as meeting agendas and status lists to European and Asian members and emailing the documents to U.S.-based members.

3.2 *Intel*

Intel Corporation is a large, distributed multinational corporation that manufactures semiconductor chips, servers, and other high-tech products. Our understanding of the VWE at Intel is drawn from data from a web-based survey of company employees across all job functions and levels in the corporation. The objective of the research was to answer the questions: "How virtual is Intel?" and "What difference does it make?" Data suggest that the company exemplifies a VWE, with extensive geographic, cultural, functional, and temporal discontinuities encountered in employees' work.

About 70% of all employees regularly work with team members at another geographic location, and cope with the consequences of that fact: different time zones, different native languages/dialects, different national and regional cultures, and people they have never met in person. In addition, it is common for people to work at home some part of the workweek. Twenty-one percent of respondents had current team members from more than five sites. In addition to geographical distribution, Intel is increasingly functionally distributed. In many jobs, the company does not require employees to move to a new location when their job changes. Work group membership may span the globe and remote reporting relationships are becoming more common (13% overall remote reporting rate for the company). Employees do not typically work on inter-organizational teams.

3.3 *MyCo and IntOrg*

MyCo and IntOrg are the sales divisions of two Fortune 100 companies in the IT industry. Both sales divisions were located in the mid-western United States. The headquarters for each company was at a distant location in the United States. Both companies also had global operations. The two sales divisions were relatively similar in terms of job roles and responsibilities in the units, level of geographical distribution, and ICT used by employees. Within each division, there were multiple supervisory work units all of whom reported to a division manager. There were approximately 100 employees in the MyCo sales division and 80 employees in the IntOrg sales division. The researchers conducted interviews with 36 employees (18 at each site) to understand how multiple media were used at each site and how usage practices differed across the two sites.

The primary responsibilities for both sales divisions were to identify sales opportunities, develop technical solutions, and manage post-sales service (this was larger responsibility at IntOrg than at MyCo). All employees were members of work unit teams; membership on these teams was permanent and involved a formal reporting relationship to the manager of the team. They were also members of multiple project teams where membership was dependent on the specific project requirements, e.g., technology solution required by customer. Infrequently, team membership included members from other locations of each company including international locations. There was little functional, organizational, or national discontinuity in the work environment.

The teams in the work units experienced geographic discontinuity, MyCo more so than IntOrg. Both sales divisions had a central office location where most employees could work. Employees also worked at customer locations. IntOrg had dedicated offices for all employees, while MyCo has non-dedicated offices for many job functions (hoteling) and dedicated for remainder. Both companies allow telecommuting but with different usage (.6 days/week at IntOrg and 2.6 days/week at MyCo).

4 Process Issues in the VWE

4.1 *Increased structure*

Across all studies there was evidence that a combination of geographical and temporal discontinuities was linked to more structured processes, in particular scheduled communication interactions taking place on a regular or rhythmic fashion. The presence of geographic discontinuities in teams meant that there was little chance interaction would occur unless it was scheduled. Temporal discontinuities meant that finding a suitable time was complicated for global teams at MTI and also, although to a lesser extent, for the less virtual teams at MyCo and IntOrg.

At MTI, effective global virtual teams developed a rhythm of interactions that reinforced relationships and routines within the teams. Scheduled communication interactions (via conference calls and FTF meetings) provided commonly understood mechanisms for pacing the work of the teams. For example, FTF meetings were used to communicate the most complex messages and engage in the highest-level decision processes. Team members then had a common understanding of when this type of decision would be addressed and developed work patterns based on this. Less effective teams were not able to develop predictable rhythms of work and did not have established mechanisms for addressing problems as they arose.

In comparing communication modes used for different work purposes in MyCo and IntOrg, Watson-Manheim & Belanger[28] find that more virtual teams at MyCo reported much more use of scheduled and predictable (e.g., monthly, weekly) meetings using synchronous media (both telephone and FTF) than less virtual teams at IntOrg, who reported more ad hoc FTF meetings. In addition, it was necessary to plan ahead to have meetings. In particular, FTF meetings were difficult to schedule and used less frequently as they often caused team members to disrupt an entire day to participate.

While teams can develop structured processes to more effectively manage communication in a distributed environment, jobs can also be characterized by the degree of structure involved. Highly structured tasks have known procedures and methods of performance[29] while less predictable jobs do not have such clearly defined procedures and require more intensive and explicit communication with team members[30,31]. So for example, a mortgage loan officer's job, while similar in some respects, is more predictable than a venture capitalist's job. Although both are lending money, the procedures for determining when to make a mortgage loan, e.g., what collateral is needed and how to assess the risk of the loan, are fairly clear and predictable, while the procedures for determining when to invest venture capital in a project vary depending on the specifics of the particular project under consideration. Information needed for less structured jobs is often unpredictable, as is the time frame in which it will be needed. Therefore, less structured jobs usually require more ad hoc communication[32].

Not surprisingly, Chudoba and her colleagues[33] found a significant positive relationship between job predictability and performance in the VWE at Intel. More structured jobs appear better suited for the virtual environment, although this question needs further investigation. In addition, technical discontinuities may increase the difficulty of performing less predictable work effectively. The ability to find unpredictable information, or people with the information, in a timely manner has not been the focus of most information systems design. In a search for new information, employees may need to investigate multiple database or knowledge base systems, or scour their network of contacts in an ad hoc fashion. Intel is currently investigating technology solutions to this problem. Tools such as instant messaging, which allow quick impromptu interactions and show availability[34], also may fill this void.

4.2 Shared practices

The concurrent presence of multiple discontinuities supports the importance for those in the VWE to develop a continuity of shared practices in order to operate most effectively. For example, 64% of respondents to the Intel survey work with teams that have differing ways of tracking their work and 55% work with people who use different technologies. The confluence of organizational and technology discontinuities can create process disconnects as one moves from interacting with members of one team to work on another project with a different set of team members. Indeed, Chudoba *et al.*[35] found that people with established and predictable procedures and processes have better perceptions of team performance. It is not necessarily the presence of a single type of discontinuity but the interaction and process impediments that come from the interaction of multiple discontinuities that highlight the need to develop shared practices in the VWE.

Following from the prior discussion of the importance of structured processes, shared practices implies the presence of established and predictable procedures in one's approach to work activities. Likewise, the MTI team composed entirely of engineers in the cross-organizational alliance was the most effective of the three teams Maznevski and Chudoba[36] studied. They suggested one factor contributing to the higher performance was that, by virtue of training, engineers shared common problem-solving processes and thus, approached issues facing the group from a similar perspective. While not possible or desirable to insist on common problem-solving processes and work procedures across teams, there are opportunities to help those working on less structured tasks by providing a coherent toolset that supports shared practices.

Similarly, Watson-Manheim and Belanger[37] introduce the notion of communication mode repertoires, socially developed norms of communication media usage for specific communication purposes. In comparing reported preferences for communication media usage at MyCo and IntOrg, they found differences in repertoires across the two companies but commonalities within the divisions of the companies. The existence of repertoires provided a structure for guiding communication across multiple teams within the two divisions.

The employees at MyCo and IntOrg were members of multiple teams but were relatively less virtual than those at MTI and Intel, with team members typically from the same functional, national and organizational background. At Intel, results indicated that more virtual teams faced more variety of practices, e.g., use of different technologies for different purposes across different teams.

The first step in supporting shared practices in a VWE is to provide a sense of organization by reducing uncertainty in the general tools environment. This suggests continued emphasis on application integration – common interfaces, updating across documents and embedded applications and support for certain core collaboration infrastructures. These include simple workflow tools for less complex projects, streamlined meeting management, visibility of timelines and others' progress for better coordination, basic Bayesian search and social networking tools, and the ability to work on a common document or application synchronously or asynchronously.

4.3 *Membership in multiple teams*

Observations across all three studies suggest that the same technologies that have made it easier to collaborate across geographic and temporal discontinuities have also enabled extensive multi-teaming. As the prevalence of teams in organizations has increased over the past 20 years[38], ICT allows people to more easily participate in teams beyond a single place of work, crossing organizational and functional discontinuities. As we have come to assume that meetings do not require FTF interactions, geographic constraints limiting one's concurrent participation on different teams have been minimized.

All three studies found members were on multiple teams concurrently. Maznevski and Chudoba[39] studied three specific teams but point out that employees were members of other teams besides those being studied. In addition, two senior MTI employees were members of two of the teams that were studied. Watson-Manheim and Bélanger[40,41] found that all employees were members of work unit teams with formal reporting relationships and similar work responsibilities. Employees also reported membership on multiple project teams where members had different responsibilities and membership was based on skills necessary for achieving project outcomes. Employees also sometimes reported membership on task force teams such as quality teams, which were usually formed to supplement normal work structures. These teams had clearly defined objectives and adhered to structured processes, forming continuities in the face of discontinuities of geography and organization.

The prevalence of multi-teaming is an important insight into the reality of networked organizations that to our knowledge has not been widely documented before. Although probably not a new phenomenon, multi-teaming is likely to be more prevalent today partially because ICT makes it easier to connect across discontinuities, and partly because of the emergence of networked organizational forms. In our experience, people do not explicitly reflect on their membership in multiple teams. Rather, they recognize the condition when it is described to them. Similarly, most academic research has focused on intact teams without accounting for the possibility of multi-teaming[42].

Multi-teaming makes it easier for people to follow new trends within the organization and expand their social networks[43,44], speeding the spread of information through informal contacts[45]. In addition to promoting knowledge sharing across teams, a common knowledge management objective[46], larger knowledge networks may provide employees with a more robust social network, which facilitates lateral moves and provides personal insurance against downsizing. Participating on multiple teams with varying membership can also help reduce the isolation felt by a distant worker by providing a stronger connection and identification with the organization. Thus, in general, multi-teaming appears to benefit both the organization and individual even as it brings complications of coordinating across multiple responsibilities and possible cognitive overload from persistent boundary spanning activities[47].

While there is less initial cost to form teams across discontinuities of geography, organization, and so forth, working across multiple teams has costs for the individuals involved. For example, the Intel study found a negative relationship between performance and the number of teams to which an employee belonged. It is plausible that the negative impacts on performance stem from an inability to develop the continuity of shared practices across teams.

5   Implications for Research and Practice

New organizational forms, and virtuality, most often assume a stretching of the organization across space and time. Surprisingly, working across multiple discontinuities, i.e., work on distributed teams in different time zones and with different nationalities, does not appear to have a direct negative effect on performance. This contradicts the conclusions of many studies that characterize distance itself as a significant and almost impassable hurdle to effective team communication, coordination and productivity[48]. Instead, our examination of four VWEs, each with varying degrees of virtuality, suggests that the effect of the discontinuities in the work environment, either singly or bundled, is not necessarily with the discontinuities themselves, but with the processes that surround them.

Consistency across work practices can compensate for other discontinuities and provide a basis for common expectations. With inconsistent practices, there are no boundary spanning tools with which to resolve either uncertainties or ambiguities[49]. This reinforces the role that employee education modules and performance reviews play in creating consistent work practices. A strong corporate vocabulary for routine situations is an important success factor[50]. Management policies that support consistent use of tools and repeatable processes through more disciplined information and document sharing within teams is important so that personnel changes do not interrupt the continuity of team work processes.

Similarly, the VWE appears to be linked to increased structure. Even less virtual teams, at least MyCo, report preference for more structured and predictable processes for at least some aspects of communication. Likewise, effective teams at MTI developed a predictable rhythm of communication in their interactions. On the other hand, more explicit communication and less tacit communication may have an impact on knowledge creation[51]. Some forms of structure may be helpful and necessary in the VWE, whereas others may stifle inventiveness. Excessive standardization may impede creativity, innovation, and responsiveness, all necessary to maintain competitiveness. Additional research is needed to tease out these relationships. It is also important to identify other process issues around discontinuities in the VWE. Our research at Intel was explicitly designed to use discontinuities framework to investigate virtuality while we have characterized the MTI and MyCo/IntOrg studies in a post hoc fashion to compare findings.

For practitioners embarking on or managing distance work, there is a critical need to assess actual virtual teaming practices (how many teams are employees members of at any one time, how often does the membership of a team change, etc.) and to evaluate the ICT available for employees in light of importance of developing shared practices across teams. Practitioners can use the discontinuities framework to assess the extent of virtuality and to identify potential problem areas. For example, distributed teams have become so commonplace that many firms are unaware of the number of concurrent teams that employees work on, and how many of those teams are geographically distributed or experience other discontinuities. Employees are often adaptable but may also be engaging in unnecessary or inefficient work practices in order to cope with the complexity of the environment. In addition, there is a need for more fine-grained understanding of technology-supported teaming practices in order to develop effective collaboration support. This is especially true as the use of ICT becomes more integrated into work practices or processes, regardless of whether a team is geographically distributed or not.

Table 1. 3 Studies of Virtuality

	More Virtual MTI[52]	More Virtual Intel[53]	Less Virtual MyCo & IntOrg[54,55]
Research Methodology	Longitudinal study of 3 teams for 21 months	Web-based survey	Case study of sales divisions in two organizations in same industry
Data Sources	Interviews, observations, communications log	1269 responses from employees, representing all job types and regions (Americas, Greater Asia, Greater Europe)	Interviews with 36 employees, observations of workplace and technology applications, organizational documentation
Sample Characteristics (Teams)			
Type	Product development, sales and marketing	N/A	Sales and marketing of information technology products and solutions
Purpose	Co-develop new products with major competitor Sales / marketing plan with major customer Develop new product line with Asian JV partner		Identify sales opportunity Develop technical solution Manage post sale service

Table 1. (*Continued*)

Geographic Discontinuity	2 teams had members from U.S. (1 location) and 2-4 Western European countries. 1 team had members from U.S. (multiple locations) and Asia (1 location)	Equal representation of employees across 3 regions: Americas, Greater Europe, Greater Asia Approximately 70% of Intel employees collaborate without meeting FTF About 16% regularly work while traveling or work at multiple Intel sites	Sales divisions in both companies have central office where most employees can work. Employees also work at customer locations IntOrg has dedicated offices for all employees MyCo has non-dedicated offices for many job functions (hoteling) and dedicated for remainder Both companies allow telecommuting but with different usage (.6 days/week at IntOrg and 2.6 days/week at MyCo)
Temporal Discontinuity	Membership on teams crossed 5 or more time zones. 2 teams had quarterly FTF meetings that also included time for socializing, especially around shared meals. No indication of multi-tasking during FTF or ICT-mediated meetings	About half of the employees regularly extend their workdays at home, work at home occasionally or regularly during normal business hours, and/or work with mobile devices such as notebooks, PDAs, or mobile phones 69% collaborate with people in different time zones on a regular basis	Different temporal expectations between IntOrg and MyCo, e.g., expected email response at IntOrg – 24 hours, expected email response at MyCo – 4 hours

Table 1. (*Continued*)

Organizational Discontinuity	All 3 teams had development engineers and marketing representatives, although members of 2 teams were all trained and "thought" as engineers. One team also had manufacturing representatives Cross-organizational membership (strategic partners – 2 teams or joint-venture partner – 1 team)	Only Intel employees surveyed Respondents represented all job types and functional areas in proportion to company demographics Job functions themselves are distributed, rather than co-located at geographic divisions. Remote reporting relationships are common, especially in the service areas of Finance, IT and HR (around 25% for these areas, with a 13% overall remote reporting rate for the company, per internal unpublished communication) Membership on the teams is fluid. Nearly half of the respondents regularly work on teams with changing team members	Intra-organizational teams Team members relatively homogeneous, e.g., same organization, functional area
Cultural Discontinuity	All teams had 3 or more national cultures represented. 2 teams had some members who were not fluent in English	71% collaborate with people who speak different languages	Little cross-nationality

Table 1. (*Continued*)

Technology Used	E-mail, telephone, fax, audio bridge	E-mail, telephone, teleconference, calendaring software, web-based repositories, shared workspace software	E-mail, telephone, teleconference, pagers, project tracking software, calendaring software, cellular telephones, intranet
Discontinuity	Early in study, some non-U.S. based team members did not have email systems compatible with systems of U.S.-based members. Fax was used frequently to overcome or supplement shortcomings of email	55% work with people who use different technologies A separate study at Intel found that, for the purpose of project status tracking, the group of 34 study participants reported use of 18 different tools, and for document management, they reported 20 tools	Different perceptions of ICT capabilities found when comparing MyCo and IntOrg, e.g., email suitable for knowledge sharing at MyCo but not at IntOrg Dysfunctional use of email found at IntOrg due to lack of interpersonal trust in work unit, e.g., redundant messages and use of multiple media to send messages
Extent of Virtuality	2 teams had quarterly FTF meetings. 1 team never met FTF	70% collaborate in non-FTF mode with global coworkers	FTF interaction relatively easy to bring about in both firms IntOrg reported much more FTF than MyCo, which was comparatively more physically distributed
	Sr. Manager + Lead Engineer were members of 2 teams	60% reported concurrent membership on 2-10 teams	All employees members of multiple teams concurrently, one work unit team and multiple project teams

References

1. Boudreau, M.-C., K.D. Loch, D. Robey & D. Straub. Going Global: Using Information Technology to Advance the Competitiveness of the Virtual Transnational Organization. *Academy of Management Executive*, 12 (4), 1998, pp. 120–128.
2. Zuboff, S. *In the Age of the Smart Machine: The Future of Work and Power*. Basic Books, New York, 1984.
3. Silver, M., L. Markus & C. Beath. The Information Technology Interaction Model: A Foundation for the MBA Core Course. *MIS Quarterly*, 19 (3), 1995, pp. 361–390.
4. DeSanctis, G. & P. Monge. Introduction to the Special Issue: Communication Processes for Virtual Organizations. *Organization Science*, 10 (6), 1999, pp. 693–703.
5. Espinosa, J.A., J.N. Cummings, J.M. Wilson & B.M. Pearce. Team Boundary Issues across Multiple Global Firms. *Journal of Management Information Systems*, 19 (4), 2003, pp. 157–190.
6. Gibson, C. & S. Cohen. *Virtual Teams That Work*. Jossey-Bass, San Francisco, CA, 2003.
7. Orlikowski, W.J. Knowing in Practice: Enacting a Collective Capability in Distributed Organizing. *Organization Science*, 13 (3), 2002, pp. 249–273.
8. Watson-Manheim, M.B., K. Chudoba & K. Crowston. Discontinuities and Continuities: A New Way to Understand Virtual Work. *Information, Technology and People*, 15 (3), 2002, pp. 191–209.
9. Griffith, T.L., J.E. Sawyer & M.A. Neale. Virtualness and Knowledge in Teams: Managing the Love Triangle of Organizations, Individuals, and Teams. *MIS Quarterly*, 27 (3), 2003, pp. 265–287.
10. Gibson and Cohen, *Op. Cit.*
11. *Ibid.*
12. Espinosa *et al.*, *Op. Cit.*
13. Orlikowski, *Op. Cit.*
14. Watson-Manheim *et al.*, *Op. Cit.*
15. Robey, D. & M.C. Boudreau. Accounting for the Contradictory Organizational Consequences of Information Technology: Theoretical Directions and Methodological Implications. *Information Systems Research*, 10 (2), 1999, pp. 167–185.
16. Watson-Manheim *et al.*, *Op. Cit.*
17. Gibson and Cohen, *Op. Cit.*
18. Castells, M. *The Rise of the Network Society*. Blackwell, Oxford, UK, 1996.
19. Ancona, D.G., P.S. Goodman, B.S. Lawrence & M.L. Tushman. Time: A New Research Lens. *Academy of Management Review*, 26 (4), 2001, pp. 645–663.
20. Lee, H. & J. Liebenau. Time in Organizational Studies: Towards a New Research Direction. *Organization Studies*, 20 (6), 1999, pp. 1035–1058.
21. *Ibid.*

22. Nardi, B., S. Whittaker & H. Schwarz. Networkers and Their Activity In Intensional Networks. *Journal of Computer-supported Cooperative Work*, 11 (1-2), 2002, pp. 205–242.
23. Wellman, B. Designing the Internet for a Networked Society. *Communications of the ACM*, 45 (5), 2002, pp. 91–96.
24. Wellman, *Op. Cit.*, p. 91.
25. Waters, M. *Globalization*. Routledge, London, 1995.
26. Carmel, E. *Global Software Teams*. Prentice-Hall, Upper Saddle River, NJ, 1999.
27. Duarte, D. & N. Snyder. *Mastering Virtual Teams*. Jossey-Bass Inc., San Francisco, CA, 1999.
28. Watson-Manheim, M.B. & F. Belanger. Communication Mode Repertoires: Dealing with the Multiplicity of Media Choices, working paper, 2005.
29. Perrow, C.A. Comparative Analysis of Organizations. *American Sociological Review*, 32, 1967, pp. 194–208.
30. Kraut, R.E. & L. Streeter. Coordination in Software Development. *Communications of the ACM*, 38 (3), 1995, pp. 69–81.
31. Van De Ven, A., A. Delbecq & R. Koenig. Determinants of Coordination Modes within Organizations. *American Sociological Review*, 41, 1976, pp. 322–338.
32. *Ibid.*
33. Chudoba, K., E. Wynn, M. Lu & M.B. Watson-Manheim. How Virtual are We? Measuring Virtuality and Understanding Its Impact in a Global Organization. *Information Systems Research*, 15, 2005, pp. 279–306.
34. Rennecker, J. & L. Godwin. Theorizing the Unintended Consequences of Instant Messaging (IM) Use, Presentation at the Academy of Management, Seattle, WA, 2003.
35. Chudoba *et al.*, *Op. Cit.*
36. Maznevski, M. & K. Chudoba. Bridging Space over Time: Global Virtual Team Dynamics and Effectiveness. *Organization Science*, 11 (5), 2000, pp. 473–492.
37. Watson-Manheim and Belanger, *Op. Cit.*
38. *cf.* Arrow, H., J. McGrath & J. Berdahl. *Small Groups as Complex Systems*. Sage Publications, Thousand Oaks, CA, 2000.
39. Maznevski and Chudoba, *Op. Cit.*
40. Watson-Manheim, M.B. & F. Belanger. Support for Communication-based Work Processes in Virtual Work. *e-Services Quarterly*, 1 (3), 2002, pp. 61–82.
41. Watson-Manheim and Belanger, 2005, *Op. Cit.*
42. Watson-Manheim and Belanger, 2002, *Op. Cit.*
43. Griffith *et al.*, *Op. Cit.*
44. Orlikowski, *Op. Cit.*
45. Stohl, C. *Connectedness in Action*. Sage Publications, Thousand Oaks, CA, 1995.

46. Alavi, M. & D. Leidner. Review: Knowledge Management and Knowledge Management Systems: Conceptual Foundations and Research Issues. *MIS Quarterly*, 25 (1), 2001, pp. 107–136.
47. Carlile, P. A Pragmatic View of Knowledge and Boundaries: Boundary Objects in New Product Development. *Organization Science*, 13 (4), 2002, pp. 442–455.
48. Olson, G. & J. Olson. Distance matters. *Human-Computer Interaction*, 15, 2002, pp. 139–178.
49. Carlile, *Op. Cit.*
50. Garbarro, J. The Development of Working Relationships. In J. Galegher, R. Krant and C. Egido (Eds.), *Intellectual Teamwork*. Lawrence Erlbaum Associates, Hillsdale, NJ, 1990, pp. 79–110.
51. Griffith *et al.*, *Op. Cit.*
52. Maznevski and Chudoba, *Op. Cit.*
53. Chudoba *et al.*, *Op. Cit.*
54. Watson-Manheim and Belanger, 2002, *Op. Cit.*
55. Watson-Manheim and Belanger, 2005, *Op. Cit.*

CHAPTER 4

Organizational Implementation and Integration of Information Technology

J. David Johnson and Kevin Real
College of Communications and Information Studies
105 Grehan Building
University of Kentucky
Lexington, KY 40506-0042, USA
Email: jdj@pop.uky.edu; kreal@uky.edu

1 Introduction

The social reality of technology implementation is highly complex. Different technologies are brought into different social settings for distinct reasons, often with opposite effects and thus complex theories recognizing the emergent and socially constructed nature of technology are needed[1].

Contemporary organizations must constantly adapt to meet evolving environmental conditions to survive in today's rapidly changing, complex and technologically sophisticated economies[2,3]. Innovative organizations are able to respond faster and are more likely to expand their resources by creating joint programs with others in consortia, often relying on the underlying medium of electronic markets, thereby increasing their resources[4]. The significance of information technology (IT) integration cannot be understated. Organizations undertake large investments in IT and these outlays come with considerable risks and benefits. Effective IT integration can be a source of competitive advantage by linking information technologies to organizational goals, enhancing performance and increasing efficiency. However, integration and implementation of IT are not uniform across organizations or even innovations, and the degree of organizational involvement in electronic markets can influence these processes as well. Moreover, one overlooked and important component of IT innovation integration is the role of brokers.

1.1 *Definitions and distinctions*

Organizational integration will be defined here in terms of its various types; with implementation one type of integration. Although implementation is extensively discussed, there are few widely-accepted conceptualizations of IT implementation[5]. We will distinguish broad categories of integration and their relationship to key organizational characteristics.

At a fundamental level, technology may be defined as organizational actions employed to transfer inputs into outputs[6]. Information technology has a central and pervasive effect on organizational functioning, since it often needs to be implemented on a system-wide basis, which makes it qualitatively different than other types of innovation[7]. Information itself is distinct from physical commodities and IT requires organizational members to be trained to meet increasing levels of technological complexity.

Organizations use IT in electronic markets as a way of achieving efficiencies and cost-savings. IT allows organizations to identify, record, connect, and utilize valuable organizational knowledge, by preserving it in ways that make it easily available for use by different groups. This may include mundane knowledge such as customer databases, problems that have occurred with products, and so on, but can also be used to preserve expertise from employees or knowledge about who experts are in an organization[8] or to link suppliers and organizations in electronic markets.

1.2 *Innovation*

Innovation is a social process of information seeking and sharing of ideas perceived as new[9]. The nature of the information transmitted concerning an innovation can be grouped into three general categories: (1) information concerning the innovation; (2) information related to influence and power; and (3) information concerning operationalizing the innovation[10]. The centrality of communication becomes even more pronounced when innovation occurs in the operation of electronic markets that have additional informal, coordination pressures not found in conventional organizations; thus, introducing the critical role of brokers in IT integration.

There is a rich literature on the organizational integration of new information technologies as innovations. This is not surprising given its importance in terms of: level of financial investment; its role in strategy and developing competitive advantage; the possibility of disruptive innovations changing industries overnight; the relatively high failure rate; and its relation to a digital society. Unfortunately there has not been much agreement about the types of integration that are possible or a synthetic framework that can be used to organize this literature. Similarly the interrelationships between technology and work organization has been the focus of several major perspectives that share little in common[1] with the literature on technology and structure relationships characterized by a bewildering array of confusing and contradictory findings[11]. We focus on differing types of integration and the critical role of brokers in attempting to bring some clarity and focus to these diverse perspectives.

1.3 *Electronic markets*

Malone, Yates, and Benjamin[12] and Bakos[13] assert that organizations involved in electronic markets will reduce their transaction costs associated with the search for competing suppliers and this will result in shifts from hierarchies toward market forms of organizations. In markets, it is possible to change relationships with suppliers, competition is open, and information is more readily available than in hierarchies, which are characterized by organizations controlling a vertically integrated supply chain (see Salazar in this volume for a more extended discussion).

A market approach shares much with both network and formal approaches and rests on economic and exchange assumptions[14]. "Markets are arrangements which coordinate the actions of large numbers of people automatically, and on a lateral basis, through the operation of the price mechanism, without infringing their freedom or requiring inequalities of status"[15] (p. 136). While markets have been viewed as occurring outside the context of formal organizations, they have been recognized as containing many authority properties found in organizations, and organizations with complex, multidivisional structures take on market characteristics[16]. "The internal operations of real-world firms are controlled by a blend of authority and market-like mechanisms"[17] (p. 66).

Nohria and Eccles[14] suggest that several factors related to new technologies make entirely new organizational forms, such as networked organizations, possible. First, they increase possibilities for control and decrease needs for vertical processing of information. Second, new technologies facilitate communication across time and space. Third, they increase external communication thus blurring traditional lines of authority (and associated transaction costs) within the firm. These factors are highlighted in the operation of electronic markets and are dependent on the manner of IT integration.

2   Types of Integration

Historically the innovation literature has focused on binary adopt not-adopt decisions, but implementation and integration are really a continuum of different types of IT integration where uncertainty management, not reduction is the critical issue. We develop a classification scheme for types of integration within organizations: outsourcing, turn-key, reinvention, implementation, and assimilation. We then discuss how each of these types involve different levels of alignment, organizational learning, skills, impacts on work processes, structural change, transaction costs, and their impact on electronic markets (see Table 1). The ideal outcome of all of the types is the optimal handling of a critical organizational function in the context of transaction costs. What we are proposing here is not a stage theory, but separate types, or taxonomies as in earlier work in this area[7]. Organizations within electronic markets may start anyplace on the continuum or move back and forth along it.

Outsourcing and turn-key approaches may be ways of escaping internal problems by disengaging from them, whereas reinvention, implementation, and assimilation involve more full scale engagement. While ITs have objective characteristics, how they are instantiated in a particular context often depends on their interactions with implementers and how they are modified in use by the demands of a particular situation. As a result, implementation and integration processes become critical to understanding IT innovation processes[18].

Table 1. Relationship between Types of Integration and Key Organizational Dimensions

Dimensions	Types of Integration				
	Outsourcing	Turn-Key	Reinvention	Implemen-tation	Assimilation
Alignment	Limited	Minimal	Conscious Action	Contested	Taken for Granted
Organizational Learning	Abandoned	Compart-mentalized	Generalizing to Context	Mindful	Complete
Employee Skills	Low	Low	Critical Thinking	Translation	New Level
Work Processes	Low	Black Box	Recognition	Surprise	Compatible
Structural Change	Cast Off	Minimal	Possible	Unantici-pated	Compatible
Uncertainty	Lose Control	Ceded to Another	Removed	Heightened	Tacitly Managed
Resistance/ Readiness to Change	Political	Minimal	In Principal	Activity-based	Acceptance
Transaction Costs	Increasing	Moderate	Planning	Heightened	Not an Issue
Electronic Markets	Limited	Shared Platform	Designed for Explicitly	Tested	New Medium

2.1 *Outsourcing*

Outsourcing involves increasing transaction costs by transferring organizational operations (e.g., accounting) to external entities. As Table 1 reveals, in an associated manner, this can cause increased uncertainty because of loss of control of key organizational functions, it deskills organizational employees in affected areas, and abandons organizational learning. On the other hand, these potentially negative outcomes can also be interpreted as positives, since an organization can focus its attention on more central strategic concerns, reduce internal complexity and internal work interdependence, and reduce the need to track often rapidly changing, specialized IT. This type of integration can involve varying degrees of cooperation with external vendors in development of operations, something particularly important in IT innovations[7], especially related to the medium within which electronic market exchanges occur and how they are embedded in networks.

2.2 *Turn-key*

Turn-key or traditional off-the shelf acquisition of an externally developed IT involves purchasing a system from outside the organization[7]. Turn-key, as is, with minimal impact on existing operations, is a functional substitute for existing technology (see Table 1). While the technology becomes part of organizational operations, there is only moderate alignment, compartmentalized organizational learning and enhanced employee skills. The organizational may also become quite vulnerable to the vendor. The structural change and impact on work processes is minimal. However, uncertainty management is essentially ceded to the software developer, minimizing transaction costs, and the assumption exists that external collaborators in electronic markets have adopted the same technology. The costs of this approach are somewhat hidden and involve mindful engagement and optimal organizational adaptation to the technology.

2.3 *Reinvention*

Research involving adaptive structuration theory[19] (also Salazar this volume), mutual adaptation[20] and fidelity of implementation[20,21] indicate reinvention, or the conscious modification of an existing innovation to fit the requirements of a new organizational context, may occur with many innovations. It involves a higher level of alignment, an ability to relate to other things an organization has learned and some critical thinking skills on the part of an organization's employees. Since it is recognized that an innovation has to 'fit in' there is awareness that it relates to other work processes and that structural change might be required. The planning process tries to reduce uncertainty and anticipate a readiness to change that can overcome potential points of resistance. Transaction costs can be planned for and electronic markets are designed for explicitly in the reinvention process.

2.4 *Implementation*

Successful implementation of an innovation can be conceived of as the routinization, incorporation, and stabilization of the innovation into the ongoing work activity of an organizational unit. For organizations, "the bottom line is implementation (including its institutionalization), and not just the adoption *decision*"[22] (p. 79, italics in original). Relatively fewer studies focus on what happens to the innovation after it has been adopted[5,23], yet implementation is often a great challenge since alignment can become contested, organizational learning is very mindful until new routines kick in, and employees need skills in translating the new to the old and making it meaningful in an existing context. There are often surprises involving unexpected relationships to existing work processes and structures; as such uncertainty is often heightened resulting in resistance to change. Electronic markets are tested and the higher levels of transaction costs may raise questions as to whether outsourcing and turn-key options should be reexamined.

2.5 *Assimilation*

Assimilation, or institutionalization in Rogers' terms or refreezing in Lewin's classic description of organizational change, is the end-state of organizational integration. This is the "payoff" stage of innovation process[24]. Here people are no longer mindful of the IT innovation, it becomes part of the flow of work in the organization. Employee skills are now matched to the new IT, their learning is complete and alignment is taken for granted. Uncertainty no longer needs to be actively managed, since compatibility with existing work processes and structural change has been achieved. There is acceptance of the innovation and its transaction costs are no longer contested. Electronic markets and the new IT have become the medium in which the organization's work is accomplished, creating powerful inertial forces.

3 Brokers

Recent years have seen an explosion of interest in network analysis in a range of disciplines[25]. Historically a variety of network factors have been positively associated with innovation processes including multiplexity, centrality, and network roles[3,26]. Here we emphasize human agents, brokers, who overcome the incompleteness of organizational design to achieve the various types of IT integration. Knowledge brokers address the following problems: conversion of tacit to explicit knowledge; addressing individual cynicism and resistance to change; disruptions of work relationships; internal political and cultural barriers; familiarity with industry standards and professional norms; and broader extraorganizational trends. Unfortunately, perhaps because of this long-list of problems, these are difficult roles to fill[25] and in the natural course of events their bridging linkages may decay quite rapidly[27]. This focus on individuals acting as agents of change also dovetails quite nicely with a contemporary focus on markets, individual incentives and the increasingly complex issue of organization boundary management and horizontal relationships in electronic markets[28]. It also relates to the need to have individual agents who can facilitate technology-use mediation, often by changing contextual elements, throughout the implementation process[29]. Indeed, there is a growing recognition that knowledge networks "require a human hub or switch, whose function is as much to know who knows what as to know what is known"[30] (p. 225). In a somewhat piecemeal fashion aspects of these roles have been described as opinion leaders, boundary spanners, liaisons, and structural hole brokers in the literature[26].

These different designations often reflect different types of linkages, key problems addressed, and critical roles required for each type of integration (see Table 2). Individuals may also alternate between different organizational roles in response to shifting organizational demands[31]. In outsourcing, turn-key, and reinvention types, the broker encompasses much of the traditional boundary spanning roles operating as contractor, purchasing agent, and environmental scanner respectively. In the implementation and assimilation types the focus is more on internal operations, with the broker acting as opinion leader for change in the implementation stage. Interestingly, in the assimilation stage the broker assumes more of a background role, monitoring ongoing operations of IT yet mindful of other alternatives that may need to cause an unfreezing of now comfortable organizational arrangements.

Brokers in each stage of integration have different critical roles and associated incentives that address the "what's in it for me" question for individuals (see Table 2). In outsourcing brokers act as liaison with suppliers of services and can either garner a commission or enhanced visibility both within and outside the organization and associated prestige. In turn-key operations they select from an array of alternatives and exercise expert power as a result within the organization. While selection is also a part of reinvention, the translation of the innovation to internal operations is much more mindful, requiring developed translation skills which could anticipate the latent impacts on power relationships within the organization. The role of change agent involves many of the incentives associated with being the innovation champion. One of the problematic aspects of assimilation is many of the incentives for brokers have been exhausted, which then encourages people in such roles to constantly churn the organization, much as more unscrupulous investment advisors do with stock trades.

Table 2. Relationship between Types of Integration and Brokerage

Dimensions	Types of Integration				
	Outsourcing	Turn-Key	Reinvention	Implementation	Assimilation
Key Problem	Contracting	Purchasing	Scanning	Opinion Leadership	Monitoring
Critical Role	Liaison	Selector	Translator	Change Agent	In Background
Incentive	Go Between	Expertise	Power Broker	Champion	Satiated
Homophily	Lowest	Discounted	Evaluated	Emphasized	Tacit
Trust	Vigilance	Verified	Monitored	Tested	Taken for Granted
Shared Interests/ Threats	Contracted	Exchanged	Weighted	Contested	Shared Interests Assumed
Differentiation/ Integration	Specialization	Integration Assumed	Weighted	Problematic	Balanced

Johnson[25] identified four key sets of variables that have traditionally been identified in the literature as important in determining brokerage: homophily, trust, shared interests/threats, and differentiation/integration. A systems model developed for examining communication factors related to closer ties between entities that has been empirically tested in intercultural research[32–34] may be usefully extended to the context of the operation of consortia and electronic markets. The fundamental premises of the model are based on the notion that, in a classic systems framework, perceived value/attitudinal similarities lead to behavioral intentions, particularly those related to future communication behaviors and relational ties, linked to the social distance between two communicators. This model stresses the balance between shared interests and threats that emerge in relationships with other groups. It also links these factors to homophily, a key feature of modern organizational demographic theory[8], as well as a continuing foundational factor in communication theory[9]. Central to both systems theory and structuralist[3] explanations of problems that develop in intergroup relationships is the balance between differentiation and integration. Finally, market-driven approaches stress that trust is the most important factor in knowledge brokering and managing risks[35,36], with electronic markets both increasing ways of monitoring trust and diminishing the needs for interpersonal contact that have been its traditional basis[37].

In terms of homophily, one of the features of outsourcing and turn-key is an explicit recognition of difference and a focus on limited exchange relationships. The remaining types see more explicit recognitions of fit issues in the reinvention stage, a recognition that IT innovations can be rejected because of incompatibility and, finally, a tacit acceptance of fit in assimilation (see Table 2). Trust also ranges from explicitly insured in contractual relationships to taken-for-granted across the types; potential threats are more salient in outsourcing and turn-key types, while shared interests take on increasing weight across the remaining types. One of the things that leads to outsourcing is the high transaction costs associated with the increased specialization characteristic of modern high technology organizations. Achieving the appropriate balance between integration and differentiation is an ongoing struggle that finally reaches a balance in assimilation.

3.1 *Implications for practitioners and policy makers*

While optimists wait for the next generation of computer software and hardware, realists are increasingly looking at the organization itself, especially its culture and structures, as the major impediment to improved information processing. It has almost become a cliché that the reason IT systems fail is that they do not consider the needs of users[38] with estimates of failure rates of thirty percent attributable to nontechnical factors[38]. Brokers historically are individuals who profit from satisfying the needs of the various parties they bring together. Thus, they can be the generative motors of success in the integration of IT. While computerization can result in deskilling, it also can overload the capacity of key decision makers[39] and these conditions make the role of brokers as human agents even more critical.

3.2 *Implications for future research*

In recent years there has been much discussion of differing research approaches to integration of IT (Salazar, this volume). Variance approaches assume clear operationalizations with solid sets of criteria, whereas process approaches often see integration as a moving target[5]. Both approaches need clearly defined typologies, such as the one developed here, to advance. They also need more creative approaches, such as a focus on brokers who represent human agents who bridge different groups, to the problems of levels analysis (see also Salazar, this volume).

3.3 *Implications for everyday life, working life and community*

Innovativeness in organization can impact perceptions of overall climate, members' satisfaction, and the likelihood of members initiating innovations[26]. Adoption of new technologies, especially those that facilitate and enrich the work, can play a key role in motivating the new knowledge worker[40]. Learning new technologies also entails socialization of workers to the firm[41] (and to the electronic market in which the firm is embedded).

At times technologies are used to reify existing structures, further reinforcing existing relationships[8]. So, if relationships are only possible with existing contractors in an electronic market, this further reinforces a firm's existing dependency on them. As Burkhardt and Brass[42] cogently observed, technologies can be used as tools by savvy individuals, such as brokers, to both change and solidify power relationships within organizations.

While reliable communication may deepen disputes when parties truly understand the disparity of their positions, it is still a critical condition for further inquiry that may be the only hope of adjustments leading to successful implementation. Too often managers do not listen to "back talk," assuming that individuals are willfully denying their arguments (they just don't understand)[43]. Thus, a failure to engage each other in dialogue may be the ultimate denial of the pluralistic world of contemporary organizations and electronic markets (see also Salazar, this volume) that is often splintered into specialized functional groupings and "occupational communities"[3]. Each group has its own view of what is of value in electronic markets. However, understanding the interplay of these factors can result in more effective individual and institutional change strategies[44]. There are also real organizational costs to innovations: wasting resources on inappropriate technology, constant uncertainty resulting from perpetual change, lowered morale from unsuccessful adoption efforts, to name but a few. Implicit in most IT and electronic markets approaches is a return to a more optimistic view of the impacts of innovations on organizations and societies[45]. In turn, this understanding can considerably increase the currently low odds of successful implementation of IT. Brokers can play a key role in facilitating dialogue within an organization and outside of it.

4 Conclusions

Markets are central to global economies, facilitating the exchange of commerce, information, and trust, and IT plays a major role in supporting organizations in electronic markets, as Salazar highlights. The ability to successfully integrate and implement technology in organizations has provided organizations with a competitive advantage by helping them reduce transaction costs. However, electronic markets underscore the need to account for network structures and environmental factors when utilizing transaction costs approaches. Electronic markets can obscure boundaries between organizations, suppliers, and others while technology reduces the cost of preparing and monitoring agreements, thus introducing elements unforeseen by Coase[46]. Second, human agency in IT integration cannot be understated, as people need help in deciding on and adjusting to new technology. Brokers provide the human side of technology integration in social networks (see also Salazar in this volume). Third, communication technologies have captured increasing attention over the last decade because communication plays a unique role in the successful integration of IT, which requires buy-in from organizational members and communication is vital to this process. Finally, we would be remiss if we did not discuss the need for clarity and multi-level approaches to IT integration-implementation research[5]. Brokers have a role in understanding and negotiating electronic markets. They focus our attention on the often neglected role of human agents in their development.

References

1. Liker, J. K., Haddad, C. J. & Karlin, J. Perspectives on technology and work organization. *Annual Review of Sociology*, 25, 1999, pp. 575-596.
2. Foray, D. Continuities and Ruptures in Knowledge Management Practices. In J. de la Mothe and D. Foray (eds.), *Knowledge management in the innovation process* (pp. 43-52). Boston, MA: Kluwer Academic Publishers, 2001.
3. Johnson, J. D. *Organizational communication structure*. Norwood, NJ: ABLEX, 1993.
4. Hage, J. & Aiken, M. *Social Change in Complex Organizations*. New York, NY: Random House, 1970.
5. Real, K. & Poole, M. S. Innovation implementation: Conceptualization and measurement in organizational research. In R. W. Woodman and W. A. Pasmore (eds.), *Research in Organizational Change and Development*, Vol. 15 (pp. 63-135). Oxford, UK: Elsevier, 2005.
6. Woodward, J. *Industrial Organization: Theory and Practice*. London: Oxford University Press, 1965.
7. Sabherwal, R. & Robey, D. An empirical taxonomy of implementation processes based on sequences of events in information system development. *Organization Science*, 4, 1993, pp. 548-576.
8. Monge, P. R. & Contractor, N. S. *Theories of communication networks*. New York: Oxford University Press, 2003.
9. Rogers, E. M. *Diffusion of innovations*, 5th ed. New York, NY: Free Press, 2003.
10. Fidler, L. A. & Johnson, J. D. Communication and innovation implementation. *Academy of Management Review*, 9, 1984, pp. 704-711.
11. Miller, C. C., Glick, W. H., Wang, Y. & Huber, G. P. Understanding technology-structure relationships: Theory development and meta-analytic theory testing. *Academy of Management Journal*, 34, 1991, pp. 370-399.

12. Malone, T. W., Yates, J. & Benjamin, R. I. Electronic markets and electronic hierarchies. *Communications of the ACM*, 30, 1987, pp. 484-497.
13. Bakos, J. Y. Information links and electronic marketplaces: The role of interorganizational information systems in vertical market. *Journal of Management Information Systems*, 8, 1991, pp. 31-52.
14. Nohria, N. & Eccles, R. G. (Eds.) *Networks and organizations: Structure, form, and action.* Boston: Harvard Business School Press, 1992.
15. Beetham, D. *Bureaucracy.* Milton Keynes, UK: Open University Press, 1987.
16. Eccles, R. & White, H. Price and authority in inter-profit center transactions. *American Journal of Sociology*, 94, 1988, pp. S17-S51.
17. McGuinness, T. Markets and managerial hierarchies. In G. Thompson, J. Frances, R. Levacic and J. Mitchell (eds.), *Markets, hierarchies, and networks: The coordination of social life* (pp. 66-81). Newbury Park, CA: Sage, 1991.
18. McKinney, M. M., Barnsley, J. M. & Kaluzny, A. D. Organizing for cancer control: The diffusion of a dynamic innovation in a community cancer network. *International Journal of Technology Assessment in Health Care*, 8, 1992, pp. 268-288.
19. Poole, M. S. & DeSanctis, G. Understanding the use of group decision support systems: The theory of adaptive structuration. In J. Fulk and C. Steinfield (eds.), *Organizations and communication technology* (pp. 175-195). Newbury Park, CA: Sage, 1990.
20. Leonard-Barton, D. Implementation as mutual adaptation of technology and organization. *Research Policy*, 17, 1988, pp. 251-267.
21. Lewis, L. K. & Seibold, D. R. Innovation modification during interorganizational adoption. *Academy of Management Review*, 18, 1993, pp. 322-354.
22. Rogers, E. M. & Adhikayra, R. Diffusion of innovations: An up-to-date review and commentary. In D. Nimmo (ed.), *Communication Yearbook 3* (pp. 67-81). New Brunswick, NJ: Transaction Books, 1979.
23. Klein, K. J. & Ralls, R. S. The organizational dynamics of computerized technology implementation: A review of the empirical literature. In L. R. Gomez-Mejia and M. W. Lawless (eds.), *Implementation management in high technology* (pp. 31-79). Greenwich, CT: JAI Press, 1995.
24. Nord, W. R. & Tucker, S. *Implementing routine and radical innovations.* Lexington, MA: Lexington Books, 1987.
25. Johnson, J. D. The emergence, maintenance, and dissolution of structural hole brokerage within consortia. *Communication Theory*, 14, 2004, pp. 212-236.
26. Johnson, J. D. *Innovation and knowledge management: The Cancer Information Science Research Consortium.* Cheltenham, UK: Edward Elgar, 2005.
27. Burt, R. S. Bridge decay. *Social Networks*, 24, 2002, pp. 333-363.
28. Zhu, K. Information transparency in electronic marketplaces: Why data transparency may hinder the adoption of B2B exchanges. *Electronic Markets*, 12, 2002, pp. 92-99.

29. Orlikowski, W. J., Yates, J., Okamura, K. & Fujimoto, M. Shaping electronic communication: The metastructuring of technology in the context of use. *Organization Science*, 6, 1995, pp. 423-444.
30. Earl, M. Knowledge management strategies: Toward a taxonomy. *Journal of Management Information Systems*, 18, 2001, pp. 215-233.
31. Johnson, J. D. & Chang, H. J. Internal and external communication, boundary spanning, innovation adoption: An over-time comparison of three explanations of internal and external innovation communication in new organization form. *Journal of Business Communication*, 37, 2000, pp. 238-263.
32. Johnson, J. D. & Oliveira, O. S. Communication factors related to closer international ties: An extension of a model in Brazil. *The International Journal of Conflict Management*, 3, 1992, pp. 267-284.
33. Johnson, J. D., Oliveira, O. S. & Barnett, G. A. Communication factors related to closer international ties: An extension of a model in Belize. *International Journal of Intercultural Relations*, 13, 1989, pp. 1-18.
34. Johnson, J. D. & Tims, A. R. Communication factors related to closer international ties. *Human Communication Research*, 12, 1985, pp. 259-273.
35. Dai, Q. & Kauffman, R. J. B2B e-commerce revisited: Leading perspectives on the key issues and research directions. *Electronic Markets*, 12, 2002, pp. 67-83.
36. Davenport, T. H. & Prusak, L. *Working knowledge: How organizations manage what they know.* Boston: Harvard Business School Press, 1998.
37. Kliest, V. F. A transaction cost model of electronic trust: Transactional return, incentives for network security and optimal risk in the digital economy. *Electronic Commerce Research*, 4, 2004, pp. 41-57.
38. Johnson, J. D. *Information seeking: An organizational dilemma.* Westport, CT: Quorum Books, 1996.
39. Bennet, D. & Bennet, A. The rise of the knowledge organization. In C. Holsapple (ed.), *Handbook on Knowledge Management 1: Knowledge matters* (pp. 5-20). New York, NY: Springer-Verlag, 2003.
40. Downing, J. R. "It's easier to ask someone I know": Call center technicians' adoption of knowledge management tools. *Journal of Business Communication*, 41, 2004, pp. 166-191.
41. Waldeck, J. H., Seibold, D. R. & Flanagin, A. J. Organizational assimilation and communication technology use. *Communication Monographs*, 71, 2004, pp. 161-183.
42. Burkhardt, M. E. & Brass, D. J. Changing patterns of change: The effects of a change in technology on social network structure and power. *Administrative Science Quarterly*, 35, 1990, pp. 104-127.
43. Schon, D. A. & Rein, M. *Frame Reflection: Toward the Resolution of Intractable Policy Controversies.* New York: Basic Books, 1994.

44. Eisenberg, E. M., Murphy, A. & Andrews, L. Openness and decision making in the search for a university provost. *Communication Monographs*, 65, 1998, pp. 1-23.
45. MacMorrow, N. Knowledge management: An introduction. *Annual Review of Information Science and Technology*, 35, 2001, pp. 381-422.
46. Coase, R. H. The nature of the firm. *Economica*, IV, 1937, pp. 386-405.

CHAPTER 5

Implementing Enterprise Systems:
A Review of Critical Success Factors

John Loonam and Joe McDonagh
School of Business Studies
University of Dublin, Trinity College, Dublin 2, Ireland
Email: loonamj@tcd.ie; joe.mcdonagh@tcd.ie

1 Introduction

The objective of this paper is to provide a review of critical success factors deployed for the implementation of enterprise systems (ES). A brief historical tour of these systems is provided before moving on to discuss their implementation in organisations. This review highlights factors deemed critical to the successful implementation of enterprise systems. Critical success factors from the past decade are compiled and ranked. For illustration purposes the ten most highly critical success factors are then discussed in greater detail. Finally, questions are asked about ES implementations, with a more thorough examination of critical success factors called for.

2 A Historical Tour

From a historical overview of information systems, it becomes clear that organisations, and invariably information systems, have been looking to create a more integrated and seamless working environment. Enterprise systems, therefore, have been heralded as systems by which such 'seamless integration'[1] can be achieved. While ES packages are a relatively recent phenomenon, i.e., only featuring seriously in business and academic press from the late 1990s, they do have a past. It has been suggested that ES packages are an extension of Material Requirements Planning (MRP) and Manufacturing Resource Planning (MRPII) packages, with enhanced and greater functionality[2,3]. These systems were 'some of the earliest computerised information systems for operations management'[2] (p. 259). In addressing such systems, we find that MRP packages date back to the 1960s[4]. In simplest terms, MRP systems involved the calculation of quantities of materials and the times they were required in order to improve operations within manufacturing organisations[5]. MRPII systems were to extend upon this concept during the 1970s, and encompassed new functionality like sales planning, capacity management and scheduling[6]. However, during the 1980s companies began to realise that profitability and customer satisfaction were objectives for the entire enterprise, extending beyond manufacturing, and encompassing functions such as finance, sales and distribution, and human resources. This gave rise to the concept of computer integrated manufacturing (CIM), which is regarded as the next evolutionary step on the road towards ES[6] (p. 144). By the early 1990s, with continued growth in package functionality and the need for greater organisational integration, ES packages began to emerge.

These systems are the internal technological hub of the enterprise, allowing data from different business functions, mainly from manufacturing, logistics, finance, sales & marketing, and human resources, to be manipulated and processed by a single software package such as SAP, PeopleSoft, Baan, or J.D. Edwards. Enterprise systems are able to simplify, accelerate, and automate much of the data transfers that must take place in organisations to guarantee the proper execution of operational tasks[7]. As Davenport[1] purports 'a good ES is a technological tour de force. At its core is a single comprehensive database. The database collects data from and feeds data into modular applications supporting virtually all of a company's business activities-across functions, across business units, across the world' (p. 123). Figure 1 below provides an illustration of the anatomy of an enterprise system.

In understanding what these enterprise systems are and what they do, Hirt & Swanson[8] see them as 'software that is designed to model and automate many of the basic processes of a company, from finance to the shop floor, with the goal of integrating information across the company and eliminating complex, expensive links between computer systems that were never meant to talk to one another' (p. 246). According to Nah *et al.*[9], an enterprise system is a packaged business software system that enables a company to manage the efficient and effective use of resources (materials, human resources, finance etc) by providing a total, integrated solution for the organisation's information processing needs. It supports a process-oriented view of business as well as business processes standardised across the enterprise (p. 285). According to Davenport, (see Figure 1) an ES package is comprised of four primary functional areas, i.e. financials, human resources, operations and logistics, and sales and marketing.

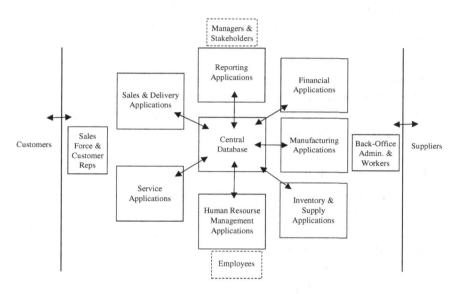

Figure 1. Anatomy of an ES

Source: Davenport, 1998: 124.

3 Enterprise Systems Implementation

From the late 1990s onwards enterprise systems continued to experience massive growth in organisational uptake. By 1998, for example, approximately 40% of companies with annual revenues greater than $1 billion had already implemented an ES[10]. In a survey by AMR Research, results showed that from 800 U.S companies queried, 43% of the companies' application budgets were spent on ES packages, while over half of these companies had installed an ES. While according to

Akkermans *et al.*, 'a recent survey by Fortune magazine revealed that seven out of the top ten global pharmaceutical and petroleum companies, nine out of the top ten global computer companies, and all of the top ten global chemical companies are using SAP's R/3 package'[11] (p. 288).

Unlike their prehistoric ancestors, enterprise systems were fast becoming a core part of everyday IS investments. These systems were breaking traditional manufacturing links, and soon represented a new 'IS integration' alternative for many organisations. With the promise of seamless integration[1], organisations were able to justify ES investments, believing that these systems were the answer to all their IS integration problems. In response, software companies provided a myriad of application tools (e.g. SAP, JD Edwards, and Oracle) that promised enterprise integration of all kinds and for every company. Organisations began to implement these systems to remove legacy system challenges and to obtain greater enterprise-wide competitive advantages.

4 The Utopian Dream

Since enterprise systems burst onto the marketplace, their promise has been to 'seamlessly integrate'[1] the organisations business processes. These systems have been the culmination of decades of aspirations by the IS function. According to Stefanou[12], enterprise systems adoption is now more important than ever due to global-wide phenomena such as outsourcing, joint ventures and alliances, and partnership across the value chain, which have formulated a new form of organisation described as the 'virtual enterprise'. Monolithic and stand-alone business information systems are giving way to more flexible, integrated and modular systems that support business operations across the value-chain from the supplier to the customer (p. 800). Al-Mashari *et al.*[4] informs us that the need 'to increase visibility in corporate data, create new or improve current business processes, improve responsiveness to customers, obtain tighter integration between systems, standardise computer platforms, increase flexibility, share information globally, and improve business performance' as reasons for the adoption of an ES. Davenport also believes that overcapacity and reengineering, globalisation, and dealing with constant change are some of the prime reasons many organisations are implementing enterprise systems into their organisations. Similarly, Markus & Tanis[13] note that there are a number of distinct technical and business reasons for adopting enterprise systems today, most notably these include; the reduction of data duplication, improving IS architecture, reducing software maintenance, and integrating applications cross functionally. From a business perspective, reasons include; reducing business operation and administrative expenses, cleaning up informal and ad hoc business processes, standardising procedures across different locations, and reducing inventory carrying costs.

The adoption of these systems is also expected to bring significant financial benefits to the organisation. The case literature illustrates this point, with the Toro Co., saving $10 million annually due to inventory reductions, while Owens Corning claims that their ES software helped it to save $50 million in logistics, materials management, and sourcing. Similarly, other cases reveal large savings in costs and increased levels of organisational effectiveness after ES implementation. Companies such as Geneva Pharmaceuticals[14], Lucent Technologies[15], Farmland Industries[16], and Digital Equipment Corporation[17], have had significant reductions in costs and increased organisational performance as a result of ES adoptions.

5 A Reality Check

Yet, despite their perceived benefits, these systems remain complex and expensive to implement[18]. Kirkpatrick, for example, states that the average Fortune 500 company can spend $30 million in license fees and $200 million in consulting fees, with additional millions spent on computers and networks (1998). Similarly, the Standish Group report that 'ES implementations were on average 178% over budget, took 2.5 times longer than anticipated and delivered only 30% of the promised benefits' (cited in Krumbholz & Maiden[19]).

Other studies report similar poor performances after ES implementations. According to a survey conducted in December 2000 called "ES post implementation issues and best practices", where 117 firms across 17 countries were surveyed on their satisfaction with ES implementation projects, only 34% of the organisations were 'very satisfied' with their ES investments (cited in McNurlin[20]). Sammon *et al.*[21] believe that over 90% of ES implementations are late or more costly than first anticipated. According to Crowe *et al.*[22], further research conducted by the Standish Group International revealed that 40% of all ES installations achieved only partial implementation, nearly 28% were scrapped as total failures or never implemented, while only 25% were completed on time and within budget.

Further studies also support these findings, even among the ES 'extensions' technologies. For example in an in-depth study among 145 European companies carried out by Cap Gemini Ernst & Young, they found that 68% of companies surveyed could not provide any evidence of expected Returns on Investment from their CRM investments (FT Precision Marketing, Nov. 2001). Similarly in SCM, the number of failure rates has been up to 60%, where supply chains are not returning any investments for the organisations[23].

Examples from the case literature also reveal poor ES outcomes. Whirlpool experienced delays in shipments of appliances to distributors and retailers. Allied Waste Industries Incorporated, found SAP too expensive and too complicated to operate, while Waste Management Incorporated aborted its SAP implementation after it had spent $45 million. Similarly, Chen[24] reports on other case outcomes. For example, FoxMeyer Drug, a $5 billion pharmaceutical company, filled for bankruptcy after major problems were generated by a failed ES system. Dell Computers spent millions of dollars on an ES package before scraping it because the system was too rigid for their expanding global operations. Other cases with ES failures include, Boeing, Dow Chemical, Mobil Europe, Applied Materials, Hershey, and Kellogg's.

6   Flaws in the System!

It, therefore, becomes important to ask; why are ES implementations delivering such poor performances, and in some cases complete failure. According to Sammon *et al.*[21] 'the main implementation risks associated with ES projects are related to change management and the business reengineering that results from integrating an organisation' (p. 2). This point is also consistent with supply chain management (SCM) systems, where according to Vokurka *et al.*[25], the greatest implementation problems come about because of 'the cultural resistance to change, and lack of top management understanding and commitment' (p. 5). Similarly, with customer relationship management (CRM) projects the focus should not just be centred upon technological integration, but should centre upon people and processes[26]. According to a study by Deloitte & Touche[27], the main reasons for poor ES performance after implementation range from people obstacles (which according to the study contributed to 68% of the problem), to business processes (which were at 16%), and information systems issues (which were at 12%)[22]. Some of the more notably challenges and limitations of ES implementation are now provided below.

- *Financial costs & risks:* Financial costs of ES packages can be enormous. According to Scheer & Habermann 'Baan, Peoplesoft as well as SAP calculate that customers spend between three and seven times more money on ES implementation and associated services compared to the purchase of the software license'[28]. The authors believe that the ratio is somewhere around 5:1 between ES implementation efforts and the cost of software licenses. The reasons they give for such costs are due to the scale of business process reengineering (BPR) and change management issues involved in the implementation of the software. Stewart reinforces this point suggesting that ES implementations fail because of poor organisational attention in dealing with the issues of risk orientation and user involvement. They maintain that system implementations are fundamentally agents for organisational change and such change requires effective leadership practices.
- *Technical aspects:* Excessive focus on technical aspects to the detriment of business aspects has been identified as a leading factor for many ES failures[29,30]. As Umble *et al.* state 'unfortunately, many chief executives view ES as simply a software system and the implementation of ES as primarily a technological challenge' (p. 245). Sarker believes that a significant amount of projects fail because human aspects are often 'overlooked' or 'remain to be

resolved', hence the focus is on technology and not the organisation (p. 414). Esteves & Pastor[31] also believe that failure occurs because 'too often, project managers focus on the technical and financial aspects of a project and neglect to take into account the non technical issues'.

- *Competitive advantage:* Sor states that using an ES package can rob an organisation of its competitive advantage[32]. This point is further supported by Porter, who states that if everyone in a particular industry sector or niche market are to adopt these packages, then everyone will have the same set of best practices as determined by the software vendor and ES package. This will, invariably, result in a lack of competition between organisations.

- *Organisational inflexibility:* ES packages can be structured, systematic packages that make the organisation 'fit' the software rather than the software fit to the needs of the enterprise. This level of inflexibility can prohibit organisational change and business process growth (Sor, 1999: 229-230). The organisation ends up forcing its business processes into the new system and adopting 'best practices' that may not be required (Markus, 2000c).

- *Integration:* Dong[33] indicates that the challenge for ES implementation lies in the nature of the system, i.e. they are generic solutions reflecting a vendor's rather than a customer's assumptions about what organisational best practices are. It pushes companies toward full integration, and changes various business processes into generic ones even if the company wants to customise some of these business processes. Therefore, the real paradox facing organisations implementing ES projects is rooted in their ability to seamlessly integrate all business processes across the enterprise. The fewer changes made to these systems, the greater the level of integration and realised benefits for the implementing organisation (Dong, 2001: 243). However, accepting the generic nature of an ES package means companies are accepting vendor integration not company specific integration, this in turn may not achieve the desired integration sought by adopting companies.

- *Cultural misfit:* Soh et al.[34] talk about the problem of 'misfits' with ES packages, i.e. the gaps between the functionality offered by the package and that required by the adopting organisation. Due to the fact that these implementations are more complex and larger than other packaged software implementations, the 'misfit' problem is exacerbated when implemented in a non-generic type organisation. In other words, ES packages are designed by western vendors for western type organisations. Countries such as Japan often find the implementation of such packages particularly difficult, as there is a problem with the systems cultural identity. In short, Soh *et al.* point to 'cultural misfits' with this software, particularly when it is implemented outside of North America and Europe.

- *Size & complexity:* Smyth[35] believes that ES implementation disappointments can be largely attributed to the great size and complexity of the packages and the associated problems in customisation and organisational change. These systems affect every part of the organisation, their implementation therefore remains complex and challenging. Another flaw in the ES character is the cost of workarounds and upgrades in specific modules, particularly when an organisation is customising the package to suit organisational business needs. With add-ons or bolt-on technologies the cost and maintenance of the project increases dramatically.

- *External assimilations:* Sasovova *et al.*[36] believe that limitations to ES packages arise when mergers, acquisitions, and divestitures are going to take place within the implementing company. Such occurrences cause huge external and internal changes, and make the process of both system and business process integration all the more difficult, particularly if new business processes and old legacy systems have to be integrated from the new companies into the central ES package.

- *ES dependency:* Markus & Tanis[37] tell us about the over-reliance or dependence on software vendors. Reliance on a single-vendor can weaken the organisations ability to be technologically independent forcing the enterprise to go into an appeasement mode with the software vendor. This is also true of external advisors. Many companies implementing an ES system depend on external consultants to assist with knowledge generation and the provision of expertise[38].

However, these systems continue to be important, primarily because of the opportunities afforded to organisations that successfully install them. As a consequence, and in an effort to reduce the number of poor implementation performances, scholarly work over the past decade has focused on issues important to ES implementation. In particular, studies have focused on issues that contribute to the successful implementation of an enterprise system. These issues are referred to as critical success factors. The identification of such factors aim to assist organisations with the successful implementation of their enterprise systems.

7 A Critical Matter

Implementation of an ES package is an expensive, lengthy and complex process, typically measured in millions of dollars. The investment is both in the software and in related services such as consulting, training, and system integration[39]. Despite millions being spent on such implementations, the evidence from the case literature and empirical studies above reveals that many implementations are not successful. These poor performances and inability to make a return on investment have resulted in the study of factors critical to successful ES implementation. These factors have, in turn, given rise over the last decade to a plethora of ES critical success factors (CSF) studies[40–48].

Daniel (1961) is remarked to be one of the first to discuss the concept of 'success factors' in the management literature (cited in Soliman *et al.*[49] and Trimmer *et al.*[50]), however it was Rockart[51] who popularised the approach. Rockart defined CSFs as the limited number of areas where things must go right for the business to flourish. He argued that managers need appropriate information in order to manage and that management performances should be measured continually in order to assist executives to identify their information needs. According to Trimmer *et al.*, 'when CSFs are appropriately identified they represent areas in which excellent performance is essential to continued organisational success...where monitoring CSFs is a form of 'management by objective', monitoring those objectives or activities that have been identified as being essential to the continued well-being of the entity' (p. 114). Many ES studies have similarly adopted CSFs to highlight 'those few critical areas where things must go right'[52] (p. 292). Figure 2.4[1] provides an illustration of the ES studies that have used CSFs to explain issues necessary to implementation.

However, criticisms of critical success factors were also highlighted. Davis, in response to Rockart's proposition, criticised the CSF approach because it relied on manager's responses, which could be incorrect, incomplete, or insufficient and constrained by human behaviour. In other words, Davis[53] felt that CSFs would 'elicit the information that executives feel they need and not the information that executives actually do need'. The pursuit of listing critical success factors, therefore, becomes almost a wish list, where executives end up labelling factors that are not relevant or available within their organisation. Similarly, according to Robey *et al.*, studies[54] of ES critical success factors offer few surprises. They believe that 'findings which point to the necessity of ES success factors such as top management support are not substantially different from factors that are critical to the success of most IS projects and to organisational change of other kinds'.

In an effort to overcome these CSF challenges, Boynton & Zmud[55] concluded from their study, that the weaknesses identified by Davis that may occur using the CSF method can be largely overcome through careful application of the technique. The authors propose a number of guidelines to assist researchers in conducting CSF studies, in particular 'CSF criticisms can be overcome by interviewing managers across a diagonal slice of the organisation'. In fact, in the defence of critical success factors, Robey *et al.* state that 'it is important to begin ES research somewhere, and the factors identified are certainly likely areas of concern' (p. 8). Within the ES literature, critical success factors have also been widely recognised as a powerful enabler for identifying key issues for organisational attention prior to and during project implementation. In an effort to review the most important critical success factors, this paper presents Table 1. This table uses Somers and Nelson's[56] list of critical success factors to outline the importance other studies attributed to similar factors. After a detailed review of the

---

[1]Somers & Nelson's (2001a) CSF list is used to benchmark all other studies.

Table 1. CSF Studies

Critical Success Factors (Somers & Nelson, 2001a)	Top Management Support	Project Team Competence	Cooperation	Clear Goals & Objectives	Project Management	Communication	Management of Expectations	Project Champion	Ongoing Vendor Support	Careful F/S selection	Data Analysis & Conversion	Dedicate Resources	Steering Committee	User Training & Involvement	Education	Business Process Reengineering	Minimal Customisation	Define Architecture	Change Management	Vendor/Customer Partnership	Use of vendor tools	Use of Consultants
1 Soliman & Clegg, 2001	X			X	X	X		X		X	X	X		X	X	X	X	X	X	X		
2 Al-Mashari et al, 2003	X	X	X	X	X	X				X	X	X		X	X	X	X	X	X		X	
3 Umble et al, 2003	X	X	X	X	X	X	X		X	X	X	X	X	X	X	X	X	X	X	X	X	X
4 Somers & Nelson, 2001a	X	X		X	X	X	X	X	X	X	X	X		X	X	X	X	X	X	X	X	X
5 Esteves & Pastor, 2000	X				X	X	X		X	X				X					X			
6 Al-Mashari & Zairi, 1999	X	X																				
7 Bingi et al, 1999	X							X	X							X						
8 Sumner, 1999	X	X				X	X							X		X						X
9 Holland et al, 1999b	X				X	X						X								X		X
10 Sedera et al, 2001	X				X	X	X															
11 Stefanou, 1999	X			X	X	X						X		X								
12 Nah et al, 2001	X				X	X	X															
13 Holland & Light, 1999a	X				X	X								X				X	X			
14 Esteves & Pastor, 2001	X	X		X	X	X	X	X	X	X	X			X		X	X	X	X	X		X
15 Rosemann et al, 2001	X				X	X								X								
16 Buckhout et al, 1999	X	X		X					X							X				X		X
17 Jarrar et al, 2000	X	X	X		X	X	X										X	X	X			
18 Wee, 2000	X	X		X	X	X					X			X		X	X	X	X	X		
19 Al-Mudimigh, 2002	X	X		X	X	X	X			X	X					X	X	X	X			
20 Akkermans & Helden, 2002	X	X		X	X		X		X					X								

Source: Author, 2005.

literature, Somers & Nelson's list of critical success factors were selected to describe in detail the ES implementation process. Similarly, Akkermans & van Helden[48] for their study, employ Somers & Nelson's critical success factor list, finding them to be 'a very useful and well-grounded ranked list of CSFs for ES implementation' (p. 35). The authors state that their choice was 'strongly influenced by the sound literature study underlying Somers & Nelson's ranked list' (Akkermans & van Helden, 2002: 36). The list is comprised of 22 critical success factors, ranked in order of preference from Somers & Nelson's study findings. It must be stated, however, that this list does not intend to represent a definitive categorisation of ES critical success factors; it is merely used as a tool for explanatory purposes.

In an effort to understand the contribution such critical success factors have made towards ES implementations, this paper now presents ten of the most frequently cited CSFs. These success factors are taken from the results of the studies above:

- *Top management support:* Sustained top management support is one of the most often cited CSFs within the ES literature[3,41,57–59]. Sarker & Lee[60] state that 'ES implementations can be successful only if there is strong and committed leadership guiding the initiative' (p. 416). 'Top management must be involved at every step of the ES implementation. They must be willing to allow for a mindset change by accepting that a lot of learning has to be done at all levels, including themselves'[58] (p. 218). According to Holland & Light[45], they must be willing to allocate valuable organisational resources and must have the credibility to 'build strong/strategic partnerships with functional areas'[61] (p. 35). Sumner[40] says that a 'lack of senior management commitment, and a lack of agreement on a set of project goals and objectives and aligning these with business objectives as reasons for project failure' (p. 318). Dong[33] also notes that a 'lack of shared IS vision, shared understanding between senior business officers and senior IS officers about an IS innovation and its contributions to organisational competitive advantage' (p. 245) as three critical issues within top management support for IS innovations. Al-Mashari *et al.*[4] sum up the importance of top management support stating, 'a review of successful ES implementations has shown that leadership and top management support are the most critical factors in organisations embarking on ES implementations' (2003: 356).

- *Communication:* While, communication is recognised as an imperative for ensuring successful ES outcomes[4,9,41,62], Welti[63] argues that it can often be one of the most challenging and difficult tasks for any ES project. Communication is essential within the project team and between the project team and the rest of the organisation, or as Somers & Nelson stated 'communication is the oil that keeps everything working properly'. Sedera *et al.*[30] further support the need for communication stating that 'structured communication and feedback... is one of the most important factors for success'. This point is further enhanced by Sarker and Lee[60] consider that ES implementation can only be successful if there is open and honest communication among stakeholders. Sumner notes that communication should cover the scope, objectives, and tasks of the ES implementation project, while Holland *et al.*[44] state that communication should include the promotion of project teams and the advertisement of project progress to the rest of the organisation. Finally, Al-Mashari *et al.*[4] consider that the communication plan has to detail the rationale for the ES implementation, details of the business process management change, demonstration of applicable software modules, briefings of change management strategies and tactics and establishment of contact points.

- *Project management:* Project management activities span the life of the project from initiation to completion (Somers & Nelson, 2001a). Kraemmergaard & Moller tend to see the role of project management as incorporating several CSFs, stating that it involves effective project planning, effective change control, business justification, and compatibility of skills with the skill set needed for project requirements. Esteves & Pastor consider that proper management of scope is critical to clarify the goals and ensure they run in tandem with the overall organisational mission and strategy, otherwise poor project management can result in greater costs, extended schedules, and the constant altering of the projects scope. Umble *et al.*[3] also support a clear definition of project objectives in order to 'avoid the all-too-common 'scope creep' which can strain an ES budget, jeopardise project progress, and complicate project implementation. Instead the project scope must be clearly defined at the outset and should identify the modules selected for implementation as well as the affected business processes'. Nah *et al.* found that the role of project management was to avoid schedule and budget overruns, forcing the project team to stick to planned events and cost targets, while delivering early measures of success to the organisation.

- *End user training:* Inadequate user training and the failure to understand how enterprise systems change the organisations business processes, frequently appears as a reason for implementation challenges and outright project failure. Bingi *et al.* believe that training employees is often a hidden cost during project implementation, with Volwer[72] telling us that by reserving 10-15% of the budget for training, it gives the organisation an 80% chance of implementation success. Similarly, Umble *et al.* state that 'training is probably one of the most widely recognised critical success factors, because user understanding and buy-in is essential'. Stefanou points out that user training assists in overcoming organisational fear, fear associated with the loss of job security, prestige and general fear of organisational change.

- *Business process reengineering (BPR):* An EIS system on its own cannot improve organisational performance unless an organisation aligns its core business processes to the system[64,65]. One way of aligning the core business processes of an organisation to the new EIS package is through the re-engineering or redesign of the business processes, or as Davenport and Short coined it, through 'business process re-engineering' (BPR). According to Hammer & Champy, BPR is defined as 'the fundamental rethinking and radical redesign of business processes to achieve dramatic improvements in critical, contemporary measures of performance, such as cost, quality, service and speed'. BPR allows organisations to align their business processes with the enterprise information system, therefore customising the company's business process needs to the new system.

- *Change management:* Enterprise information systems introduce large-scale change that can cause resistance, confusion, redundancies, and errors[47]. In terms of the implementation of an EIS, Al-Mashari[66] refers to change management as involving all human, social-related and cultural change techniques needed by management to ease the transition to, and minimise organisational resistance, for the new system. Change management receives a lot of intention within the EIS literature[67]. According to Brown & Vessey pre-planned communications and training are vital considering the amount of organisational learning associated with the implementation of an EIS. Al-Mashari considers that effective communication, revising reward and motivation systems, empowerment, human involvement, training and education, creating an effective culture for organisational change, and stimulating the organisation's receptiveness to change are the core elements necessary for a successful change management strategy.

- *Project champion:* Much of the literature suggest that a project champion is important to drive project implementation. The project champion often plays a fundamental role in change management efforts throughout the implementation life-cycle. Sumner further suggests that the champion should be a business leader in order to offer the project a constant business perspective.

- *Project team competence:* Davenport[1] talks about how it is the goal of the ES project team to promote the project but also to transfer the skills and knowledge they have to other users throughout the organisation. Willcocks & Sykes believe that successful ES implementation requires a balanced multifunctional team that is composed of members with a variety of skills from different areas. The project team should have access to an individual who is a 'business analyst', possessing knowledge of the business and the technology. Davenport believes that this individual should come from the business realm but have a strong grounding in technology, hence they will be able to transfer their knowledge to all users, and perhaps more importantly to top management and project investors. In another study, Sumner found that instead of 200 programmers with average skills, 20 'business analysts' who have specialised expertise, the ability to learn quickly, and effective communication abilities, to be much more productive for the implementation process. Wee[73] states that a cross-functional project team is required, where 'the team should have a mix of consultants and internal staff where the internal staff can develop the necessary technical skills for design and implementation'. Project team competence is, therefore, a crucial element for ensuring ES implementation success.

- *Defining the architecture:* While successful ES implementation is often determined by business and organisational changes, architecture choices also deserve thorough consideration. According to Esteves & Pastor previous legacy systems, which encapsulate the existing business processes, organisation structure, culture and information systems, should have an influence in determining the new systems architecture. Architectural concerns should include centralisation or decentralisation, i.e. mainframe or client/server, compatibility of existing tools within the enterprise with the new ES software, i.e. vanilla or customised installation, and identification of bolt-ons, i.e. linking the value chain at the front (CRM) and back (SCM) ends and the need for web-based tools[68]. However, Sumner warns of 'technological bottlenecks' in building bridges between legacy systems and the new ES software, with significant costs and time delays added to project implementation. It is, therefore, important for top management and the project management team to consider these points themselves and not allow ES vendors dictate architectural hypothesis to them.

- *Clear goals and objectives:* According to Somers & Nelson the initial phase of any project should begin with a conceptualisation of the goals and possible ways to accomplish the projects objectives. In order for the ES implementation to have any chance of success, a clear and concise strategy outlining project scope, time and costs is imperative. Attention to these factors allows the project implementation team to get on with the task at hand, while top management are able to set aside particular resources required for the project. Umble *et al.* believe that 'there must be clear definitions of goals, expectations, and deliverables, in order to get organisational buy-in'. A clear strategy from the outset allows the organisation to understand the value of the new system, outlining how the company will support and integrate the ES vision across the enterprise.

8   Calling for Deeper Inquiry

Yet, despite empirical interest in listing CSFs for ES implementations, Robey *et al.* note that 'these research studies, which focus on critical success factors, are not embedded in rich conceptual or theoretical frameworks. Neglecting theory is a serious omission because there is little general explanation of why the factors identified are critical to success'. In other words, much of the research on CSFs, has focused on 'describing factors that are important for implementation, but have failed to develop an explanation as to what these factors are or how they are enacted'. Aladwani[67] furthers this point stating, 'although critical success factor research is valuable for advancing our understanding of ES implementation success, it adopts a rather static view, which limits its adequacy in explaining the dynamics of the implementation process'. Similarly, other studies support Robey *et al.*'s[54] suggestions, calling for greater inquiry into ES post-implementation issues[69,70]. Markus, for example, makes a call for deeper and richer ES research, while Davenport notes that much of the ES research, because of the length of time required to implement these systems, is still limited to providing descriptions for the field.

To this end, and with the continued escalation in ES implementations, and indeed equally poor outcomes[71], greater attention is required. Such empirical attention must seek to explain, rather than describe. Granted, current critical factor studies may be excused because of the relatively recent introduction of enterprise systems into many organisations, particularly in light of the length of time and extent of implementation required for these systems. However, it has almost been a decade now since such systems first started to appear within organisations, therefore scholarly inquiry must seek to delve deeper. Descriptions of ES implementations will only prolong poor performances; academics must, therefore, seek to explain, and hence build solid theoretical foundations, within this area. Enterprise systems continue to be hugely important; in fact many vendors are assimilating emerging technologies so that these systems will remain a core feature for future organisational implementations and integrations.

Deeper investigation of critical success factors will explain *what* factors are required for ES implementation and *how* such factors can best be implemented. For example, top management support, which was identified by all studies as an imperative for ensuring successful ES outcomes, needs further inquiry. Questions such as the following need to be addressed; what is the role of top management in supporting the ES initiative? Who in top management needs to be involved? At what stages do top management need to be involved in the project? What is the relationship between top managers and the project champion/implementation team? What form of leadership is best for such projects? Are there specific personality traits and styles that would assist top managers in implementing such an initiative? Similar questions could be asked of the project champion. For example, what is the role of the project champion? Who should the project champion be? What is the relationship of the project champion to the implementation team/top management? How much responsibility/project ownership rests with the champion? Are there specific personality traits such individuals need for the job? Is it best to nominate external/internal champions? How will the champion relate to external advisors/internal staff?

Similarly, other questions can be asked of remaining critical success factors. These questions seek to explain each success factor in detail, and invariably create greater depth around each topic. From a holistic perspective, such inquiry will remove the current 'descriptive' bias in investigations and replace it with an 'explanatory' focus. A deep explanatory focus will assist in grounding the topic, affording researchers with an opportunity to develop solid theoretical foundations for the field. Without this attention, enterprise systems investigations will continue to rely on other fields of inquiry, which invariably reduces the field to one of dependence. ES investigators are now presented with an opportunity.

9   Conclusion

Enterprise systems promise to seamlessly integrate business processes throughout the organisation. Prior to such systems, organisations were faced with the constant challenge of aligning information systems to the needs of the business. The result was often a form of 'spaghetti integration' (Slee & Slovin, 1997), where disparate legacy systems were connected in an ad hoc manner. With the emergence of enterprise systems, however, organisations were able to integrate business processes throughout the company. Yet, significant challenges have arisen with the implementation of these systems. In particular, organisations often find themselves investing huge resources but yielding a limited return. Empirical investigations of such challenges reveal that greater attention needs to be paid to factors critical to success. However, critical success factor studies, while valuable in determining what the firm requires for successful ES implementation, now need to focus on the 'how' question. In other words, researchers need to move away from merely 'describing' what is required for success and explain, in a theoretical manner, how such factors are carried out. Future ES packages will extend the integration challenge to embrace inter-enterprise integration. It is, therefore, vital that we ground current knowledge before extending the horizon.

References

1. Davenport, Thomas H. "Putting the Enterprise Into The Enterprise System." *Harvard Business Review* 76(4), 1998, pp. 121-131.
2. Helm, S., Hall, M. and Hall, C. "Pre-implementation attitudes and organisational readiness for implementing an ERP system." *European Journal of Operational Research* 146, 2003, pp. 258-273.
3. Umble, E. J., Haft, R. and Umble, M. "Enterprise Resource Planning: Implementation procedures and critical success factors." *European Journal of Operational Research* 146, 2003, pp. 241-257.
4. Al-Mashari, Majed, Al-Mudimigh, A. and Zairi, M. "Enterprise Resource Planning: A taxonomy of critical factors." *European Journal of Operational Research* 146, 2003, pp. 352-364.
5. Light, B. and Holland, C. Enterprise Resource Planning Systems: Impacts and Future Directions. In *Systems Engineering for Business Process Change*, P. Henderson (ed.). London: Springer: 117-126. 2000.

6. Klaus, Helmut, Roseman, Michael and Gable, Guy G. "What is Enterprise Resource Planning?" *Information Systems Frontiers*, Special Issue on The Future of Enterprise Resource Planning Systems 2(2), 2000, pp. 141-162.

7. Adam, F. and O'Doherty, P. "Lessons from Enterprise Resource Planning Implementation in Ireland — Towards Smaller and Shorter ERP Projects." *Journal of Information Technology* 15(4), 2000, pp. 305-316.

8. Hirt, Sabine Gabriele and Swanson, E. Burton. "Adopting SAP at Siemens Power Corporation." *Journal of Information Technology* 14, 1999, pp. 243-251.

9. Nah, F. H., Lee-Shang Lau, J. and Kuang, Jinghua. "Critical factors for successful implementation of enterprise systems." *Business Process Management Journal* 7(3), 2001, pp. 285-296.

10. Caldwell, B. and Stein, T. "New IT agenda." *Information Week* November 30, 1998, pp. 30-38.

11. Akkermans, H., Bogerd, P., Yucesan, E. and van Wassenhove, L. "The impact of ERP on supply chain management: Exploratory findings from a European Delphi Study." *European Journal of Operational Research* 146, 2003, pp. 284-301.

12. Stefanou, C. Supply Chain Management (SCM) and Organizational Key Factors for Successful Implementation of Enterprise Resource Planning (ERP) Systems. Americas Conference on Information Systems AMCIS, Milwaukee, USA, 1999.

13. Markus, M. Lynne and Tanis, Cornelis. The Enterprise Systems Experience — From Adoption to Success. In *Framing the Domains of IT Research: Glimpsing the Future Through the Past*, R. W. Zmud (ed.). Cincinnati, OH: Pinnaflex Educational Resources, Inc: 173-207. 2000c.

14. Bhattacherjee, A. "Beginning SAP R/3 implementation at Geneva Pharmaceuticals." *Communications of the AIS* 4(2), 2000, pp. 1-38.

15. Francesconi, T. "Transforming Lucent's CFO." *Management Accounting* 80(1), 1998, pp. 22-30.

16. Jesitus, J. "Even farmers get SAPed." *Industry Week* 247(5), 1998, pp. 32-36.

17. Bancroft, N., Seip, H. and Sprengel, A. *Implementing SAP R/3: How to introduce a large system into a large organisation.* Greenwich, CT, USA: Manning Publications. 1998.

18. King, W. "Ensuring ERP Implementation Success." *Information Systems Management* 22(3), 2005, pp. 83-84.

19. Krumbholz, M. and Maiden, N. "The implementation of enterprise resource planning packages in different organisational and national cultures." *Information Systems* 26, 2001, pp. 185-204.

20. McNurlin, B. "Will users of ERP stay satisfied?" *MIT Sloan Management Review* 42(2), 2001, p. 13.

21. Sammon, David, Adam, Frederic and Higgins, Kevin. Preparing for ERP-Generic Recipes will not be enough. In *BIT 2001*. Cork: Executive Systems Research Centre, UCC. 2001a.

22. Crowe, T. J., Zayas-Castro, J. L. and Vanichsenee, S. Readiness Assessment for Enterprise Resource Planning. IAMOT2002, The 11th International Conference on Management of Technology. 2002.

23. Larsen, T. S. "Supply Chain Management: A new challenge for researchers and managers in logistics." *International Journal of Logistics Management* 10(2), 1999, pp. 41-54.

24. Chen, I. "Planning for ERP systems: analysis and future trend." *Business Process Management Journal* 7(5), 2001, pp. 374-386.

25. Vokurka, R. J. and Lummus, R. R. "The role of just-in-time in supply chain management." *International Journal of Logistics Management* 11(1), 2000, pp. 89-98.

26. Karimi, J., Somers, T. M. and Gupta, Y. P. "Impact of Information Technology Management Practices on Customer Service." *Journal of Management Information Systems* 17(4), 2001, pp. 125-158.

27. Deloitte&Touche. Value for Money audit of the Irish Health System. Government of Ireland, June, 2001.

28. Scheer, August-Wilhelm and Habermann, Frank. "Making ERP a success." *Communications of the ACM* 43(4), 2000, pp. 57-61.

29. Kraemmergaard, P. and Moller, C. A Research Framework for studying the Implementation of Enterprise Resource Planning (ERP) Systems. IRIS 23. Laboratorium for Interaction Technology, University of Trollhattan Uddevalla. 2000.

30. Sedera, W., Rosemann, M. and Gable, G. Process Modelling for Enterprise Systems: Factors Critical to Success. Twelfth Australasian Conference on Information Systems. 2001.

31. Esteves, J. and Pastor, J. Analysis of Critical Success Factors Relevance along SAP implementation phases. Seventh Americas Conference on Information Systems. 2001.

32. Sor, R. Management Reflections in Relation to Enterprise Wide Systems Projects. Americas Conference on Information Systems AMCIS, Milwaukee, USA. 1999.

33. Dong, Linying. "Modeling Top Management Influence on ES Implementation." *Business Process Management Journal* 7(3), 2001, pp. 243-250.

34. Soh, Christina, Kien, Sia Siew and Tay-Yap, Joanne. "Cultural fits and misfits: Is ERP a universal solution?" *Communications of the ACM* 43(4), 2000, pp. 47-51.

35. Smyth, R. W. Challenges to Successful ERP Use: Research in Progress. European Conference on Information Systems, Bled, Slovenia. 2001.

36. Sasovova, Z., Heng, M. S. and Newman, M. Limits to using ERP systems. Seventh Americas Conference on Information Systems. 2001.

37. Markus, M. Lynne and Tanis, Cornelis. The Enterprise Systems Experience — From Adoption to Success. In *Framing the Domains of IT Research: Glimpsing the Future Through the Past*, R. W. Zmud (ed.). Cincinnati, OH: Pinnaflex Educational Resources, Inc: 173-207. 2000c.

38. Caldas, M. P. and Wood, T. How consultants can help organisations survive the ERP frenzy. Paper submitted to the Managerial Consultation Division of the Academy of Management. Chicago. 1999.

39. Parr, Anne, Shanks, Graham and Darke, P. The Identification of Necessary Factors for Successful Implementation of ERP Systems. In *New Information Technologies in Organisational Process: Field Studies and Theoretical Reflections on the Future of Work*, O. Ngwenyama, L. D. Introna, M. D. Myers and J. I. DeCross (eds.). Boston: Kluwer: 99-119. 1999.

40. Sumner, M. Critical Success Factors in Enterprise Wide Information Management Systems Projects. Americas Conference on Information Systems AMCIS, Milwaukee, USA. 1999.

41. Bingi, P., Sharma, M. K. and Godla, J. "Critical Issues Affecting an ERP Implementation." *Information Systems Management* 16(3), 1999, pp. 7-14.

42. Al-Mashari, Majed and Zairi, Mohamed. "BPR implementation process: an analysis of key success and failure factors." *Business Process Management Journal* 5(1), 1999, pp. 87-107.

43. Holland, C., Light, Ben and Gibson, N. Global ERP implementation. In *Proceedings of the Americas Conference on Information Systems*, Baltimore, August 14-16. 1998.

44. Holland, Christopher P., Light, Ben and Gibson, N. Critical Success Factors Model For ERP Implementations. In *Proceedings of the Seventh European Conference on Information Systems (ECIS)*, Vol. 1, pp. 273-297. 1999.

45. Holland, Christopher P. and Light, Ben. "A Critical Success Factors Model For ERP Implementation." *IEEE Software* May/June, 1999, pp. 30-36.

46. Rosemann, M., Sedera, W. and Gable, G. Critical Success factors of Process Modeling for Enterprise Systems. Seventh Americas Conference on Information Systems, August 3-5, Boston. 2001.

47. Somers, T. M. and Nelson, K. G. Organisations and ERP systems: Conceptualising the Fit. Production and Operations Management Society, Orlando, FL. 2001b.

48. Akkermans, H. and VanHelden, K. "Vicious and virtuous cycles in ERP implementation: A case study of interrelations between critical success factors." *European Journal of Information Systems* 11, 2002, pp. 35-46.

49. Soliman, F., Clegg, S. and Tantoush, T. "Critical success factors for integration of CAD/CAM systems with ERP systems." *International Journal of Operations & Production Management* 21(5/6), 2001, pp. 609-629.

50. Trimmer, K., Pumphrey, L. and Wiggins, C. "ERP Implementation in rural Healthcare." *Journal of Management in Medicine* 16(2/3), 2002, pp. 113-132.

51. Rockart, J. F. "Chief executives define their own data needs." *Harvard Business Review* (March-April), 1979, pp. 81-93.

52. Parr, Anne and Shanks, G. "A model of ERP project implementation." *Journal of Information Technology* 15, 2000b, pp. 289-303.

53. Davis, G. "Comments on the critical success factors method for obtaining management requirements in article by John F. Rockart, 'Chief executives define their own data needs'." *Harvard Business Review* 57(2), 1979, pp. 81-93.

54. Robey, Daniel, Ross, Jeanne W. and Boudreau, Marie-Claude. *Learning to Implement Enterprise Systems: An Exploratory Study of the Dialectics of Change.* Georgia State University and MIT Center for Information Systems Research: 1-45. 2000.

55. Boynton, A. C. and Zmud, R. W. "An assessment of critical success factors." *Sloan Management Review* (Summer), 1984, pp. 17-27.

56. Somers, T. and Nelson, K. The Impact of Critical Success Factors across the Stages of Enterprise Resource Planning Implementations. Hawaii International Conference on Systems Sciences. 2001a.

57. Brown, Carol V. and Vessey, Iris. ERP Implementation Approaches: Toward a Contingency Framework. International Conference on Information Systems (ICIS), Charlotte, North Carolina. 1999.

58. Al-Mudimigh, A., Zairi, M. and Al-Mashari, Majed. "ERP software implementation: an integrative framework." *European Journal of Information Systems* 10, 2001, pp. 216-226.

59. Esteves, J. and Pastor, J. Towards the Unification of Critical Success Factors for ERP Implementations. 10th Annual BIT conference, Manchester, UK. 2000.

60. Sarker, S. and Lee, A. Using a Case Study to Test the Role of Three Key Social Enablers in ERP Implementations. International Conference on Information Systems ICIS, Brisbane, Australia. 2000.

61. Willcocks, Leslie P. and Stykes, Richard. "The role of the CIO and IT function in ERP." *Communications of the ACM* 43(4), 2000, pp. 32-38.

62. Davenport, Thomas H. *Mission Critical: Realizing the Promise of Enterprise Systems.* Boston, Massachusetts: Harvard Business School Press. 2000.

63. Welti, N. *Successful SAP R/3 Implementation: Practical Management of ERP projects.* Reading, MA: Addison Wesley. 1999.

64. Koch, Christopher. "BPR and ERP: realising a vision of process with IT." *Business Process Management Journal* 7(3), 2001a, pp. 258-265.

65. Norris, G., Hurley, J. R., Hartley, K. M., Dunleavy, J. R. and Balls, J. D. *E-Business and ERP - Transforming the Enterprise.* Chichester, England: John Wiley & Sons. 2000.

66. Al-Mashari, Majed. Constructs of Process Change Management in ERP Context: A Focus on SAP R/3. Americas Conference on Information Systems, Long Beach, California. 2000.

67. Aladwani, Adel M. "Change management strategies for successful ERP implementation." *Business Process Management Journal* 7(3), 2001, pp. 266-275.

68. Callaway, E. *ERP - the Next Generation.* CTRC Computer Technology Research Corporation. 2000.

69. Pan, S. L., Newell, S., Huang, J. C. and Cheung, A. W. Knowledge Integration as a key problem in an ERP implementation. International Conference on Information Systems. 2001.

70. Themistocleous, Marinos and Irani, Zahir. "ERP and application integration: Exploratory Study." *Business Process Management Journal* 7(3), 2001, pp. 195-204.

71. O'Regan, E. "Enterprise Resource Planning-IT Supplement." *The Sunday Business Post* March 27, 2005.

72. Volwer, J. "Learning in the play pit." *Computer Weekly* 27, 1999, p. 35.

73. Wee, S. "Juggling toward ERP success: Keep key success factors high." *ERP News* February (www.erpnews.com/erpnews/erp904/02get.html). 2000.

CHAPTER 6

An Interdisciplinary Research Framework to Investigate Electronic Business Models

Adamantia Pateli and George Giaglis
ELTRUN - The eBusiness Center
Department of Management Science & Technology
Athens University of Economics and Business
47A Evelpidon Str. & 33 Leukados
T.K. 113 62 Athens, Greece
Email: pateli@eltrun.gr; giaglis@aueb.gr

1 Introduction

The impact of advanced information and communications technologies (e.g. ERPs, Internet Commerce, etc) on the current way of doing business has raised the interest of researchers on describing and analyzing the new internet-enabled business logic. This interest has been intensified by the great number of e-venture failures, which are mostly caused by firms' inability to incorporate Internet into their business and manage change[1]. Research in the area of information technology management has made it explicit that the introduction of advanced IT technologies is a complex issue, and as such it should be examined not only from the IT infrastructure viewpoint, but mainly in terms of organizational strategy, structure and operation. The business model is thus conceived as a focusing device that mediates between technology development and organizational value creation[2].

The term 'business model' was then introduced to include an ample space of business concepts, in order to communicate in a simplified and structured manner the way firms 'think' and 'operate' in an IT-enabled economy. In most research studies, the term has been defined to denote the organizations' mission, core competence, operations, customer service and internal (organizational) and external (inter-organizational) business structure[2,3,4]. In some research works, the term was even amplified to refer not only to the internal parameters of an organization transformation but also to the external context that has driven or enabled this transformation, including mainly the technology and the regulatory framework, the market structure and dynamics[5].

The 'business model' term is not always used to describe the same concept in the same context. The perspective researchers adopt to refer to business models is mainly determined by their interest for a specific aspect of business transformation, whether this is the change on the information infrastructure of the firms, its business processes, the internal and external integration of its functions, or the industrial and social environment in which the organization operates.

This chapter aims to review research on business models under a multi-perspective approach. Towards this direction, the chapter applies a theoretical framework, including eight domains, to describe research on business models and examine work conducted in each domain using a technology (IT/IS) and a management perspective. The chapter concludes by identifying a four-layered scheme for categorizing business models, and consequently research on them, taking into consideration the diversity of stakeholders' interests and the abstraction level in which analysis is conducted.

2 Studying Business Models under an Interdisciplinary Approach

This section comprises a comprehensive review of research on business models structured under eight domains; 1) Definitions, 2) Components, 3) Conceptual Models, 4) Design Methods and Tools, 5) Taxonomies, 6) Adoption Factors, 7) Evaluation of Models, and 8) Change Methodologies. The methodology followed for the business model literature review as well as the identification and validation of the aforementioned eight domains is thoroughly discussed by Pateli and Giaglis[6].

The following paragraphs present a review of work conducted under each domain with the aim of facilitating discussion on the interdisciplinary nature of business model research, and mainly indicating the difference between the two primary perspectives (technology versus managerial) in the way they handle the 'business model' concept.

2.1 *Definitions*

Although defining a business model has naturally been amongst the first tasks of early researchers in the area, the concepts surrounding the definition of a business model have been subject to intense debate. The definitions range from quite simplistic statements of the meaning of business models to more complex ones, based on the term's focus and scope.

As such, we have met some quite short but explicit definitions, given under the management perspective, on business models; such as Linder and Cantrell's definition as "the organization's core logic for creating value"[7] and Magretta's definition as a "story that explains how an enterprise works"[8]. Magretta goes one step further in her research to discriminate the business model concept from the strategy concept. Thus, she explains that business models describe, as a system, how the pieces of a business fit together, but do not factor in one critical dimension of performance, usually competition, as strategy does.

Researchers of the strategic management field have worked on defining business models in more broad terms including liaisons between the strategic, the tactical and the operational level. Drawing from theory on transaction costs, Amit and Zott state that; "a business model depicts the content, structure, and governance of transactions designed as to create value through the exploitation of business opportunities..."[9]. Under the strategic management perspective, and with the aim of using business models to link strategy with business processes, Osterwalder and Pigneur define a business model as "a description of the value a company offers to one or several segments of customers and the architecture of the firm and its network of partners for creating, marketing and delivering this value and relationship capital, in order to generate profitable and sustainable revenues streams"[10].

A quite simple but less inclusive, and thus more focused, definition of business models is given under the technology (IT/IS) perspective. IT/IS researchers consider a business model as a "theoretical statement of business requirements for an information system" and face the development of a business model as a software design issue[11]. In a similar vein, Applegate defines a business model as "a description of a complex business that enables study of its structure, the relationships among its elements, and how it responds to the real world"[12]. In this case, the graphical design of a business model gives rise to the specification of an information system's data and functional requirements.

2.2 *Components*

Along with research on defining the scope and focus of business models, a quite great part of research in the area is focusing on decomposing business models into their structural elements. In essence, studies referring to business model components adopt a simplistic approach of partitioning business models and then examining their elements in isolation.

From a management perspective, Rayport and Jaworski argue that a 'new economy' business model requires four choices[13]: 1) a value proposition for targeted customers; 2) a scope of marketspace offering, which could be a product, service, information, or all three; 3) a unique, defendable resource system; and 4) a financial model, which includes a firm's revenue model, shareholders' value models, and future growth models. Moreover, Osterwalder suggests four pillars and nine building blocks as components framework for describing business models. The four pillars are[14]; Product Innovation (Innovation and Learning Perspective), Customer Relationship (Customer Perspective), Infrastructure Management (Internal Business Perspective) and Financial Aspects (Financial Perspective).

2.3 *Conceptual models*

The primary purpose of a conceptual model is to specify dimensions of business model analysis, identify the main components that are relevant to each dimension, and provide an illustration for each level. The literature review has spotted two general streams of research in this domain.

In the first stream, researchers from the IT/IS field work on developing a business model *ontology*, which encompasses the concepts, relationships, and terms used when describing a business model[15]. From the studies analyzed in the literature review, Gordijn *et al.* provide the most rigorous conceptual modeling approach, which they call e^3-value ontology[16]. This ontology includes specification of actors, market segment, value offering, value exchanges, value activities, value objects, value ports and value interfaces.

Following a similar approach, Osterwalder and Pigneur propose the *eBusiness model ontology* (e-BMO) that formalizes the elements, relationships, vocabulary, and semantics of a business model[10]. The ultimate purpose of both studies is describing a business models in terms of structural elements and processes, which can later provide input for a design or simulation software tool.

In the second stream of research, Hedman and Kalling propose a conceptual business model that integrates diverse aspects of the management perspective; strategy (e.g. market level), organizational theory (e.g. resource level), and IT management (e.g. the activity and organizational level)[17]. The inter-relationships between business models and strategy are also conceptualized and discussed by Winter[18], who distinguishes two types of models, the business network model and the business strategy model, each of which employs a different modeling technique for its illustration.

2.4 *Design methods and tools*

Building methods and developing tools for designing business models has been of intense interest basically for Information Systems researchers, since the embryonic stages of business model investigations. The major stream of research in this sub-domain has historically derived from the technology (IT/IS) perspective, which addresses business models as process models. Under this perspective, a number of process and simulation tools can be applied to design internal business models, aiming at: 1) redesigning existing organizational processes, 2) inventing new organizational processes that take advantage of information technology, and 3) sharing ideas about organizational practices[19].

In conjunction with parallel work on conceptual models, as well as in the standardization of modeling methods and tools (e.g. the Unified Modeling Language[20]), a great deal of technology (IT/IS) research has focused on designing methods and tools for formulating conceptual models and automating the design task. In an earlier study, Chen-Berger developed a knowledge-based support tool for business modeling with IBM's Business System Development Method (BSDM)[21]. Also, a research team from the Ecole des HEC (Université de Lausanne) has constructed an XML schema, called eBML, consisting of elements that represent the vocabulary of a model and the relationships between the elements[22]. This XML schema was later transformed to an improved version, referred to as BM^2L (Business Model Modeling Language), which was used to transfer the Osterwalder's Business Model Ontology from the conceptual to the implementation level[14].

2.5 *Taxonomies*

A great deal of research has been devoted towards developing taxonomies of business models using a set of criteria, such as pricing policy or customer relationship model. Taxonomy frameworks are basically differentiated from the classification criteria applied.

Based on the technology that enables the transformation of the current business logic, and thus under the technology perspective, business models may be discerned into e-business models[4], Web business models[23], mobile[24,25] and wireless business models[26] and even collaborative (i.e. groupware, e-market) business models[27,28].

However the most sophisticated taxonomies are made under the management perspective, where we can see taxonomies of business models based on revenue and position in the value chain[23], functional integration and degree of innovation[27], core activities and price-value balance[7], economic control and value integration[29], and sourcing parameters[30].

2.6 *Adoption factors*

Research on factors that can positively or negatively influence the business model adoption is multi-disciplinary by nature, since it includes a wide range of stakeholders (organizations, customers, employees, society) having different requirements and behavior. By adopting a holistic approach, a group of researchers from the information systems and management perspective have proposed a framework consisting of key factors that promote or inhibit eBusiness model adoption: technology-related (e.g. system integration, service performance), organizational (e.g. product characteristics, resources and capabilities), industry-related (e.g. type of industry, degree of competition), individual (e.g. education, demographic), and societal (e.g. location, culture). The proposed framework considers the above factors as complementary perspectives, drawing from established theories, such as the value chain analysis, the resource-based view of the firm, the innovation theory, the strategic network theory, and the transaction cost economics theory[31,32]. While the research is focusing on eBusiness models, the specified parameters can as well apply to other type of technology-enabled business models, such as mobile business models.

2.7 *Evaluation of models*

While research on adoption factors aims at providing criteria for *ex ante* analysis of business models, research on evaluation of business models focuses on *ex post* analyses and thus aims to assess, rather than guide, business model implementation. The definition of assessment criteria is naturally dependent on the purpose of evaluation, whether it is benchmarking among competitors, choice among alternatives models, risk identification of the model or assessment of the model's feasibility and profitability.

Drawing on concepts under the management perspective, Hamel identified four factors that determine a business model's wealth potential: efficiency in which customer benefits are delivered, uniqueness of the business concept, fit among the elements of the business concept, and profit boosters (increasing returns, competitor lock-out, strategic economies, strategic flexibility)[3]. Further research on each of these parameters implies investigation of several theories, such as the network economics, the resource-based view of the firm, and the strategic positioning theory.

In a similar vein, Afuah and Tucci focus their evaluation research on financial parameters, such as measures of profitability and profitability prediction[33].

In a narrower evaluation sense, Gordijn *et al.*, researchers of the technology (IT/IS) perspective focus on assessing the economic feasibility of a business model, based on assessment of incoming and outgoing value (benefits vs. costs and risks) for each actor involved in the IT-automated business process[16].

2.8 *Change methodologies*

The research works in this domain vary considerably based on the theoretical perspective adopted, which implies a different driver of change (technology, market, organizational factors) as well as a different level in which changes are anticipated (firm vs. industry level). Research in this domain aims at satisfying the practical business need for guidelines towards transforming current organizational or inter-organizational business model under the light of developing or commercializing a technology innovation[34].

Adopting a technology (IT/IS) perspective, Papakiriakopoulos *et al.* propose a step-by-step methodology for transforming a business model, responding to the need for introducing a technology innovation[35]. Again, the utility is restricted in the sense that it applies only to technology-driven business model change, as opposed to change driven by a new market or business opportunity. The analysis is also focused on industry level, which means that it investigates changes on the firms' relationships and value flows with other actors of the same industry rather than changes in the internal organizational level.

Under a management perspective, the Evolaris eBusiness Competence Center[36] has developed a methodology for changing business models based on three learning stages identified by literature on Organizational Learning[37], as well as a number of system theories, such as System Dynamics, Thinking in Networks and Action Research. The analysis is also focused on firm level, which means that the incurred changes concern the company-specific business model.

Moreover, under the same perspective, Linder and Cantrell provide a general framework that defines a set of change models, classified based on the level of change introduced by the new business model: realization, renewal, extension, and journey models[7]. The identification of four types of change models serves the organizations' need for first identifying its strategy for change (e.g. new markets, new products, new technology infrastructure), and thus the change model, they want to introduce and then building the organizational machinery required for executing their change model. Researchers in the strategy area have also worked on another business model transformation, which concerns the shift from organizational to inter-organizational business configurations. Specifically, Tapscott *et al.* have identified six steps for changing an organization's business model to a b-web model[29].

3 Abstraction Levels of Business Models

From the literature review on business model research, we have reached the conclusion that the 'business model' concept has raised the interest of researchers from several different theoretical backgrounds (disciplines) with diverse motivations for research on specific business model aspects (domains). That is why the term 'business model' is widely considered as one of the mostly discussed business concepts within the last five years[5,38]. Table 1 cross-tabulates the set of reviewed research studies with the eight identified domains under the two principal theoretical perspectives (technology versus management) to which they refer.

Table 1. Key Theoretical Perspectives of Business Model Research

Theoretical Perspectives	Domains	References
Management	Definitions	7,8,9,10
	Components	13,14
	Conceptual Models	17,18
	Taxonomies	23,27,7,29,30
	Adoption Factors	31,32
	Evaluation of Models	3,33
	Change Methodologies	7,29,36
Technology (IT/IS)	Definitions	11,12
	Conceptual Models	16,10,17
	Design Methods & Tools	20,21,22
	Taxonomies	4,24,26,28
	Adoption Factors	31
	Evaluation of Models	16
	Change Methodologies	34,35

The intrinsic multi-disciplinary and multi-aspect nature of business model investigations also derives from the different abstraction level that each study assumes for the object or the concept that is modeled. Based on the scope of the modeled object, we can develop a scale of business models. At the narrowest, least abstract, end of this scale, we can identify models of an organization's structural elements and workflows (for example, UML models), which can feed an information design process. At the broadest, most abstract, end of the scale, we may position models that refer to the industrial and social dimension of organizations' business behavior. Figure 1 illustrates the four analysis and abstraction levels to which the term 'business model' may refer.

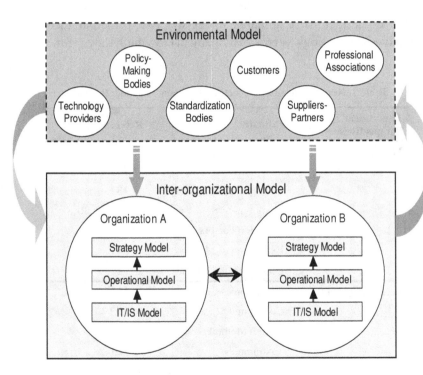

Figure 1. Abstraction Levels of Business Models

3.1 *IT/IS models (data models, ontologies)*

In a quite narrow sense, business models are used in the analysis phase of the software development cycle to communicate the main business requirements for the design of an information system. As such, an IT/IS model depicts the key actors of the business environment, the principal and secondary business concepts (entities), and their logical inter-connections (relationships). Typical instances of these models include those described under an ontology[16], business patterns illustrated with the use of a modeling language, such as UML[20], as well as data models defined with the use of an XML schema[22].

Research studies on IT/IS models are of interest for information systems analysts and programmers, since they draw on principles from the information systems discipline and focus on either providing a conceptual model or developing a software-based tool for expressing in a pictorial way the business requirements for developing an information system.

3.2 *Operational models (process models, simulation models)*

In a rather broader level of analysis, we can find models of the organizations' daily operation, including internal actors (employees and departments), organizational functions and operations as well as processes that aim at integrating or transacting with third parties (customers, partners and suppliers). Typical instances of these models include process, workflow and simulation models, usually applied for illustrating existing and inventing new organizational processes, communicating business practices among the organization's stakeholders, and testing the efficiency of the current or new process model[19]. Investigations on Operational Models concern business analysts, operational and tactical managers. Such research studies can be found in the technology (IT/IS) fields and mainly focus on providing design tools for modeling the business logic of an organization in an operational, rather than strategic, level.

3.3 *Organizational/inter-organizational models (firm models, network models)*

Proceeding to a more abstract level of analysis, we can position two types of models; organizational models, including specification and analysis of a set of organizational management concepts (e.g. mission, resources, capabilities, revenue model, customers), and inter-organizational models, focusing on describing the business configurations (network structures) that enable the delivery of business, customer and network value. In this analysis level, we can identify models mentioned as company value creation models[2], strategy models[18], value network models[39,29], collaborative and e-marketplace models[27], to which most recent studies focus.

Both organizational and inter-organizational models meet the practical interest of managers for understanding, analyzing, communicating and even changing their corporate and competitive strategy. As such, models in this group are described drawing on several strategy and management theories (e.g. transaction costs, organizational learning, resource-based view). As the analysis level becomes broader, the number of investigated domains increases. Thus, researchers of organizational and inter-organizational models work on defining them[27,7,8], conceptualizing them[17,18], decomposing them[14,13], classifying them[23,7,29,30], evaluating them[3,33] and changing them[29,34,36].

3.4 *Environmental models (industry reference models, market models)*

At the highest abstraction level, we position models that illustrate a set of actors being either individuals or organizations or coalitions, and their interactions in a given market, industry or social setting. Representative examples of such models include industrial models, such as the exhibition industry model presented by Pateli and Giaglis[34], market models, such as the mobile markets models presented by Mylonopoulos *et al.*[40], the electronic market models discussed by Timmers[27], and the Industrial Age model defined by Applegate[12].

Research in this quite abstract level includes studies on investigating the technology-driven evolution of market and industry models[35] and studies on defining the factors that affect individuals' and organizations' behavior towards new business model adoption[41,31]. Such studies are based on strategy and management theories (e.g. reasoned action, planned behavior). Individuals or legal bodies in the role of policy makers are mostly interested in this research stream.

4 Conclusions and Further Research

This chapter has provided a critical review of research on business models within an IT-enabled business environment. In doing so, the chapter presented a theoretical framework, including eight domains, for classifying current research on business models. Each domain was discussed and analyzed drawing on concepts and principles of two primary theoretical perspectives; the management perspective, and the technology (IT/IS) perspective.

Prior reviews and frameworks have examined and synthesized extant research in the business models field under one of these perspectives, usually denoted by the interests and position of the researcher, whether he/she is an information systems analyst, an operational, tactical or strategic manager, or a policy maker. The present literature review framework addresses the limitations of prior review efforts by adopting a 2X8 (2 perspectives, 8 domains) approach to analyze different objects of analysis (business model domains) with the aid of diverse theoretical lenses (business model perspectives). The ultimate purpose of the chapter has been not just to leverage the multi-disciplinary nature of existing research, but also to present an opportunity for future research synergies by identifying issues where the intersection of diverse theoretical perspectives is likely to produce progress in the study of IT-enabled business models.

Another goal of the chapter has been to advance current understanding about business models by classifying them in an order of abstraction. The level of abstraction is primarily determined by the focus and detail entailed in the unit of analysis. Thus, while we proceed from the IT/IS models to operational, then to (inter)-organizational and finally to environmental models, the focus is shifting from a very specific technology-based construct to a process and workflow illustration, then to a codification of key organizational and strategy concepts, and finally to a generic modelling of the market, industrial or social environment. This classification scheme aims to facilitate future researchers in positioning their research interests and outcomes in a certain analysis level, and thus identifying the scope of their investigated business model, the concepts that it should comprise, the perspective that should be adopted, and consequently the theories on which they should draw for building new knowledge in the area.

References

1. Auer, C., and Follack, M. Using Action Research for Gaining Competitive Advantage out of the Internet's Impact on Existing Business Models, In the *Proceedings of the 15th Bled Electronic Commerce Conference – eReality: Constructing the eEconomy*, Bled, Slovenia, June 17–19, 767-784. 2002.
2. Chesbrough, H., and Rosenbloom, R. S. *The Role of the business model in capturing value from Innovation: Evidence from XEROX Corporation's Technology Spinoff Companies*, 2002. Available online at: http://www.hbs.edu/dor/papers2/0001/01-002.pdf (Last Accessed on: 27/02/2002).
3. Hamel, G. *Leading the Revolution*, Harvard Business School Press, Boston. 2000.
4. Weill, P., and Vitale, M. R. *Place to Space: Migrating to ebusiness models*, Harvard Business School Press, Boston. 2001.
5. Alt, R., and Zimmermann, H. Introduction to Special Section – Business Models, *Electronic Markets*, 11(1), 2001, pp. 3-9.
6. Pateli, A., and Giaglis, G. A research framework for analyzing eBusiness Models, *European Journal of Information Systems*, 13, 2004, pp. 302-314.
7. Linder, J. C., and Cantrell, S. Changing business models: Surveying the Landscape, Working Paper, Accenture Institute for Strategic Change. 2000.
8. Magretta, J. Why business models matter, *Harvard Business Review*, May, 2002, pp. 86-92.
9. Amit, R., and Zott, C. Value Creation in eBusiness, *Strategic Management Journal*, 22(6-7), 2001, pp. 493-520.
10. Osterwalder, A., and Pigneur, Y. An ebusiness model Ontology for Modeling eBusiness, In the *Proceedings of the 15th Bled Electronic Commerce Conference – eReality: Constructing the eEconomy*, Bled, Slovenia, June 17–19, 75-91. 2002.
11. Gordijn, J., and Van Vliet, J. C. On the Interaction between Business Models and Software Architecture in Electronic Commerce, In M. Lemoine (eds.), *Addendum to the proceedings of the 7th European Software Engineering Conference/Foundations of Software Engineering*, Toulouse, 1999.

12. Applegate, L. M. E-business Models: Making sense of the Internet business landscape, In G. Dickson, W. Gary, and G. DeSanctis (Eds.), *Information Technology and the future enterprise: New models for managers*, Prentice Hall, Upper Saddle River, N.J. 2001.

13. Rayport, J. F., and Jaworski, B. J. *E-Commerce*, McGraw-Hill/Irwin, New York. 2001.

14. Osterwalder, A. The Business Model Ontology – A Proposition in a Design Science Approach. PhD Thesis, Ecole des Hautes Etudes Commerciales, Universite de Lausanne. 2004.

15. Jasper, R., and Uschold, M. A framework for understanding and classifying ontology applications, In B. Gaines, R. Cremer and M. Musen (Eds.), *Proceedings of 12th International Workshop on Knowledge Acquisition, Modelling, and Management KAW'99*, SRDG Publications, Banff, Alberta, pp. 4–9–1 — 4–9–20. 1999.

16. Gordijn, J., Akkermans, J. M., Van Vliet, J. Designing and Evaluating EBusiness models, *IEEE Intelligent Systems*, 16(4), 2001, pp. 11-17.

17. Hedman, J., and Kalling, T. The business model concept: theoretical underpinnings and empirical illustrations, *European Journal of Information Systems*, 12(1), 2003, pp. 49-59.

18. Winter, R. Conceptual Modeling of Business Networks and Business Strategies, In the *Proceedings of 16th Bled eCommerce Conference – eTransformation*, Bled, June 9–11 (CD-ROM Proceedings). 2003.

19. Malone, T. W., Crowston, K., Lee, J., Pentland, B., Dellarocas, C., Wyner, G., Quimby, J., Osborn, C., Bern-stein, A., Herman, G., Klein, M., O'Donnell, E. Tools for inventing organizations: toward a handbook of organizational processes, *Management Science*, 45(3), 1999, pp. 425-443.

20. Eriksson, H., and Penker, M. *Business modeling with UML – Business Patterns at Work*, John-Wiley & Sons, New York. 2000.

21. Chen-Berger, Y. KBST: A Support Tool for business modeling in BSMD. Master Thesis, Department of Artificial Intelligence, The University of Edinburgh, September, 1994.

22. Ben-Lagha, S., Osterwalder, A., Pigneur, Y. Modeling eBusiness with eBML, In the *Proceedings of 5th International Conference on Management of Networked Enterprises (CIMRE)*, Mahdia, October 25-26, 2001.

23. Rappa, M. *Managing the digital enterprise – Business models on the Web*, 2003. Available online at: http://ecommerce.ncsu.edu/business_models.html (Last Accessed on: 27/01/2003).

24. Tsalgatidou, A., and Pitoura, E. Business models and transactions in mobile electronic commerce: requirements and properties, *Computer Networks*, 37, 2001, pp. 221-236.

25. Panis, S., Morphis, N., Felt, E., Reufenheuser, B., Bohm, A., Nitz, J., Saarlo, P. Mobile Commerce Service Scenarios and related Business Models, In the *Proceedings of the First International Conference of Mobile Business*, Athens, Greece, July 8-9, 2002.

26. Rao, B., and Parikh, M. A. Wireless broadband drivers and their social implications, *Technology in Society*, 25, 2003, pp. 477-489.

27. Timmers, P. Business models for Electronic Markets, *Electronic Markets*, 8(2), 1998, pp. 3-8.

28. Rehfeldt, M., and Turowski, K. Business Models for coordinating next generation enterprises, In the *Proceedings of Academia/Industry Working Conference on Research Challenges (AIWORC'00)*, Buffalo, New York, USA, April 27-29, 2000.

29. Tapscott, D., Lowi, A., Ticoll, D. *Digital Capital – Harnessing the Power of Business Webs*, Harvard Business School Press, Boston. 2000.

30. Kaplan, S., and Sawhney, M. E-hubs: The New B2B Marketplaces, *Harvard Business Review*, 70(1), 2000, pp. 71-79.

31. Pouloudi, A., Vassilopoulou, K., Ziouvelou, X. A Societal Perspective on E-Business Adoption, *Journal of Information, Communication and Ethics in Society*, 1(3), 2003, pp. 149-165.

32. Vassilopoulou, K., Ziouvelou, X., Pateli, A., Pouloudi, N. Examining EBusiness models: Applying a Holistic Approach in the Mobile Environment, In the *Proceedings of 11th European Conference on Information Systems (ECIS) – New Paradigms in Organizations, Markets and Society*, Naples, June 16-21, 2003.

33. Afuah, A., and Tucci, C. *Internet business models and Strategies*, McGraw-Hill International Editions, New York. 2001.

34. Pateli, A., and Giaglis, G. Technology Innovation-Induced Business Model Change: A Contingency Approach, *Journal of Organizational Change and Management*, Special Issue on Organizational Transformation and E-Business, 18(2), 2005, pp. 167-183.

35. Papakiriakopoulos, D., Poulymenakou, A., Doukidis, G. Building eBusiness models: An Analytical Framework and Development Guidelines, In the *Proceedings of 14th Bled Electronic Commerce Conference*, Bled, Slovenia, June 25-26, 2001.

36. Petrovic, O., Kittl, C., Teksten, R. D. Developing business models for eBusiness, In the *Proceedings of International Conference on Electronic Commerce 2001*, Vienna, Austria, October 31–November 4, 2001.

37. Senge, P. M., and Sterman, J. D. System Thinking and Organizational Learning: Acting Locally and Thinking Globally in the Organization of the Future, In J.D. Morecroft and J.D. Sterman (eds.), *Modeling for Learning Organizations*, Productivity Press, Portland, 1994, pp. 195-216.

38. Seddon, P. B., and Lewis, G. P. Strategy and Business Models: What's the Difference? In the *Proceedings of the 7th Pacific Asia Conference on Information Systems*, Adelaide, South Australia, July 10-13, 2003.

39. Applegate, L. M., and Collura, M. Emerging Networked Business models: lessons from the field. *Harvard Business School No. 9-801-172*, Harvard Business School, Boston. 2001.

40. Mylonopoulos, N., Sideris, I., Fouskas, K., Pateli, A. *Emerging Market Dynamics in the Mobile Services Industry*, IST-MobiCom Project White Paper, IST-MobiCom Project, 2002. Available online at: http://www.eltrun.gr/whitepapers/#1st (Last Accessed on: 20/03/2005).

41. McGann, S., and Lyytinen, K. Capturing the Dynamics of eBusiness Models: The eBusiness Analysis Framework and the Electronic Trading Infrastructure, In the *Proceedings of 15th Bled Electronic Commerce Conference - eReality: Constructing the eEconomy*, Bled, Slovenia, June 17–19, 2002.

CHAPTER 7

Emerging Virtual Infrastructures in Service Delivery: Scenarios for Health Care

Ann Seror
Faculty of Administrative Sciences
Laval University
Quebec City, QC G1K 7P4
Canada
Email: ann.seror@mng.ulaval.ca

1 Introduction

Information and telecommunications technologies, including the Internet and grid computing are transforming global consumer markets and the delivery of products and services. While there is a vast literature on the contributions of information technology to organization structure and process, little research has focused on the interorganizational system level of analysis in service delivery[1-4]. For example, many studies in health care services are designed to evaluate specific information technology applications such as electronic patient records[5], but few studies consider the larger service delivery system as an integrated entity. The objective of this paper is to build on earlier work in organization science, economics, and telecommunications to consider further how new information technologies, the Internet and grid computing shape ideologically diverse service delivery systems in the context of health care[6-9].

Health care is a system of services for the public good defined as the preservation of mental and physical health by prevention or treatment of illness through services offered by the health professions.[1] A health care system is a dynamic set of interconnected individuals, institutions,

---

[1]See WordNet 2.0, 2003, Princeton University at www.wordreference.com (accessed on December 20, 2004).

organizations, and projects offering services in health care markets[10]. The boundaries of such systems are increasingly difficult to identify as subsystems may also be defined by overlapping corporate, professional, or other social entities. In this study we consider national health care systems as defined by the World Health Organization[11].

Within the service delivery system, virtual infrastructures refer to (a) an environment characterized by overlapping distribution networks, systems brokerage functions, and the adoption of a software perspective emphasizing the devices and channels through which information is processed and distributed, as well as (b) a layer of abstraction between the computing, storage and networking hardware, and the software technologies that allow multiple operating systems to run on the same processor. This layer of abstraction leads to standardization and the support of legacy operating systems and applications on current hardware and software platforms. These infrastructures in turn are accessible through Internet websites and gateways designed to facilitate integrated use of the resources offered through virtual infrastructures. The adjective "virtual" thus describes any web-based product, service, organization or institution arising from the technical infrastructure defined above[2].

In this paper we will examine how emerging virtual infrastructures in service delivery express market ideologies in their unique organizational configurations. First we define the research problem in the health care sector. Then we explore by scenario analysis how dominant market dynamics and control processes affect emerging virtual infrastructures in the health care sector. From this analysis we formulate general conclusions and recommendations for future research and managerial practice.

2 Research Problem

Research on economics and health care services has shown that national system quality is not directly related to GNP, but rather a function of variables describing rate of investment in public health as well as

---

[2]The author would like to thank an anonymous reviewer for this definition.

mechanisms for the equitable distribution of wealth[12]. Health care systems deliver widely differing services in terms of overall performance and per capita cost[13]. Thus institutional and organizational configurations based on diverse ideologies are hypothesized to account for some of this variance. Ideology is the body of integrated assertions, theories and aims that constitute a coherent socio-political system. Health care system ideology is expressed as the extent or manner of government and other stakeholders' involvement in the financing, administration and regulation of health care[14-17]. Indicators of such involvement include investment in health care, oversight and control of health care services, as well as ownership and governance of the health care system.

Research on the association between ideology and health care system structures, processes, and performance remain inconclusive[18-24]. Recent qualitative case studies conducted in China[25], South Africa[26], and countries in transition from communism[27] present mixed results. Health standards in China have improved under communist rule, while the transition from communism in Russia and Eastern Europe has resulted in short-term regression in such standards with some signs of improvements to come in the future. The South African democracy has seen significant regression in health indicators due to other factors related to the AIDS pandemic as well as the high rate of violence in the country. The conclusions of these studies suggest that a more detailed analysis of the configurations of health care systems is required to understand dimensions affecting their internal coherence.

Consistent with Sen[12], Franco *et al.*[19] found that democracy was more strongly associated with life expectancy, infant mortality, and maternal mortality than was gross national product. Sen has pointed out that national health care system effectiveness measured on public health indicators such as life expectancy is not directly correlated with gross national product, but rather this relation is mediated through variables related to public investment in health care as well as mechanisms for the redistribution of wealth. This economic analysis is validated in the rankings of general effectiveness of national health care systems developed by the World Health Organization[13]. For example, the general performance of the U.S. health care system is ranked 37th while total healthcare expenditure per capita is estimated at US$3724. The level of expenditure in the U.S., highest among OECD member countries, is not reflected in health care system performance measured as life expectancy among OECD nations[28]. This diverse evidence for the association between health care system effectiveness and ideology is also the result of the wide variety of descriptive as well as quantitative methods used in the studies and the lack of a systematic approach to meta-analysis[29]. However, it is also important to consider the complexity of health care systems and the proposition that system performance may be better explained by the internal coherence of the system, including the fit between system configurations and market ideologies as well as their integration in global networks and their adaptability to rapidly changing political and economic environments.

While patterns of expenditure in national health care systems seem to show decreasing variation, the particular professional activities and patterns of usage within each system show significant divergence[18]. This diversity responds to the particular characteristics of local health care services markets. According to evolutionary economic theory, the transformation of organizational systems must be examined within their social and institutional contexts. This transformation emerges through the "co-evolution of physical and social technologies"[30], where social technologies include institutions and their network configurations. Collaboration and partnership at the national and international levels are critical for the creation of extended health care systems[31] as are local cultures in the appropriation of new technologies[32-34], and the diversity of paths for technological development. Decentralisation of health care management to the local level promotes integration of new and traditional technologies and political culture for local participation in governance as well as equitable resource allocation shaped by local priorities. Locally collected public health and clinical data enable evidence based health care system management as well as locally relevant experimentation and innovation in delivery of services[35,36].

While in traditional organizational structures and processes, decentralization of authority and decision making may compromise the benefits of large system economies, information technologies including computational grid infrastructures enable decentralized information systems while at the same time extending economies of scale and scope in allocation of system resources. These complex changes raise important questions concerning the evolution of diverse health care systems, such as the convergence hypothesis. Theory in sociology suggests that over time organizations may tend to resemble one another through processes of isomorphism that divert them from objectives of optimization or efficiency towards legitimacy in inter-organizational relations[37,38]. Information technologies including grids and virtual institutions add another level of analysis to be considered with respect to this hypothesis.

3 Scenario Methodology

The qualitative research methodology used in this study is scenario analysis of virtual health care system infrastructures and their ideologies This holistic methodology integrates both inductive and deductive logics to identify dimensions of uncertainty affecting future development within a well-defined domain and to construct a scaffolding of meaning to explain a logically coherent system of constructs[39,40]. Uncertainty dimensions serve as a basis for identification of critical contingencies or discontinuities and their effects on system configurations. Scenario analysis takes into account the external political, social, economic and technological environment as well as the internal characteristics of rapidly evolving institutional systems. Although applications of scenario analysis vary among academic disciplines, in the health care sector, this methodology offers tools for systematic construction of logical stories describing alternative institutional arrangements[8]. The steps of this methodology are:

- The first step is description of the current state of the system and identification of axes of uncertainty as well as structural dimensions underlying that description. These dimensions serve to distinguish alternative scenarios in the analysis.
- The next step is the definition of evolutionary trends apparent in the system which will be subject to the structural dimensions of the first step.

- Scenario logics are then created to distinguish the scenarios. These are the scaffolding of the analysis integrating variation on the structural dimensions. These logics express the internal consistency of each alternative scenario.
- Each scenario is elaborated from the dimensions identified in step one to operationalize a distinct scenario logic.
- Comparative analysis identifies the unique characteristics of each scenario.
- Each scenario represents a unique configuration of characteristics within an institutional and market context derived by pattern analysis of the distinguishing structural dimensions. The scenario analysis is based on an extensive review of the literature and published research reports as well as websites of health care sector organizations shown as examples.

4 Analysis and Discussion

4.1 *Health care system infrastructures: Evolutionary trends*

Complex technological change challenges institutional capacities for adaptation, particularly in coordinating and controlling integrated health care services and in educating service providers and caregivers in emerging disciplines including medical informatics and bioinformatics. These tendencies contribute to development of virtual infrastructures integrating specialized information and computing services, online software applications, and database management[10,41]. Convergence among WANs, LANs, other networks and Internet contributes to development of Web services offered through the Internet. Outsourcing management of services delivered over the Internet reduces both human resources and technology infrastructure costs including hardware and software while creating opportunities to extend services beyond the boundaries of the system. The exponential growth of computational power requirements in health care systems including service delivery, research and education is addressed by grid computing. The grid is defined as a distributed computing infrastructure providing direct access to computing power and software with "coordinated resource sharing and problem solving in dynamic, multi-institutional virtual organizations"[41].

These infrastructures may be classified according to their functions as computational, data, and collaborative grids. Computational grids create a virtual supercomputer by aggregating the computing power of a large number of individual computers to derive a platform for advanced high-performance applications. Data grids focus on sharing vast quantities of data while information and knowledge grids extend these capabilities by supporting data mining and analysis, information discovery and ontologies. These grid infrastructures offer data gathering, processing and presentation with an interactive interface for translation of information into complex knowledge, planning, management, and raw data exploration through simulation. Collaborative grids enable virtual environments supporting individuals or groups in pursuit of shared objectives. These grids may support virtual laboratories as well as remote control of medical technologies for medical imaging and sensing[42]. While these grid functions may be distinguished, it is important to note that they are increasingly integrated in extensive national and regional infrastructures, particularly in the United Kingdom and the European Union.

Such collaborative problem solving and resource brokering also defines the nature of the virtual organization[43]. Grid computing technology addresses the challenges of heterogeneous computing environments, management of decentralized systems and resources, as well as high IT infrastructure costs. Grid environments rely on connectivity, resource and coordination protocols for communication, resource allocation and system integration. The multi-level virtualization of resources means that the same abstractions and mechanisms can support collaboration across organizational domains and within hosting environments of a single domain spanning multiple system tiers. Ideology is expressed in these infrastructures as differences in visibility and accessibility controlled by resource ownership rather than interaction mechanisms[10,44]. Grid infrastructures may be understood according to types of ownership and market dynamics of the communities they serve[44,45]:

- Private grids are managed by a corporate or professional owner to mobilize the computing capacity of idle desktop computers or unused servers within the corporate entity. Such capacity may also be outsourced for computing on demand. An example is the Archimedes model of diabetes disease processes and treatments powered by a United Devices enterprise grid solution owned by Kaiser Permanente and the American Diabetes Association.

- National or regional grids create large collaboratories serving communities based on institutional membership or citizenship. There are many initiatives in this category contributing to development of the eScience infrastructures in the United Kingdom and the European Union; examples of these include *Géant*[3], *DataTAG*[4], and *EGEE(Enabling Grids for E-science in Europe)*[5]
- Virtual grids serve communities of researchers and professionals requiring specific resources such as instrumentation for research, medical imaging and diagnostics. Examples in health care include the *Hydra Project (UK)*[6], *Telemedicine on the Grid (UK),*[7] and *Mammogrid (EU).*[8]
- Public grids emerge from markets for computational resources guided by consumer groups as well as specialized service providers. Such markets depend on effective commoditization of computing resources. Examples include *Find-a-Drug (UK),*[9] *Grid.org (US),*[10] and the *World Community Grid (US).*[11]

These infrastructures support a variety of market dynamics for integration of health care services including research and education. Centralized local IT environments are thus transformed by market pressures inducing collaboration, data sharing, research, and clinical as well as managerial decision making founded on distributed resources. These evolutionary tendencies shift the focus to management of complex

---

[3]See the Géant project website at http://www.geant.net/server.php?show=nav.007
[4]See the DataTAG website at http://datatag.web.cern.ch/datatag/project.html
[5]See the EGEE website at http://egee-intranet.web.cern.ch/egee-intranet/gateway.html
[6]See the Hydra project website at http://www.informatics.leeds.ac.uk/pages/hydra/
[7]See the Telemedicine on the Grid website at
http://www.escience.cam.ac.uk/projects/telemed/
[8]See the Mammogrid website at http://mammogrid.vitamib.com/
[9]See the Find-a-Drug website at http://www.find-a-drug.org.uk/
[10]See the Grid.org website at www.grid.org
[11]See the World Community Grid website at www.worldcommunitygrid.org

interconnections within and across institutional systems through technology - intelligent networks, switching devices, caching services, appliance servers, storage systems, or storage area network management systems – as well as through organizational designs such as outsourcing IT services to Internet or other service providers[10,41].

Both internal and external factors affect the evolution of institutions linked in health care networks and markets to facilitate integration and interoperability. Local medical data banks and expert protocols for clinical and local best practice decision making are increasingly integrated through local area network (LAN) interconnection. To leverage collaborative and computing capacity through emerging grid infrastructures, markup languages such as SGML and XML as well as object oriented system architectures and meta-data structures permit construction of ontological relations among diverse information entities[46]. These developments respond to system requirements for extended integration of linguistically, culturally, and ideologically diverse subsystems.

The enterprise extranet has contributed to trends in network design and usage including the shift from 'point-to-point' and 'hub and spoke' models to a 'many-to-many' or 'extranet' model, disappearance of the clear ideological distinctions and technical boundaries between private and public networks as well as LANs and WANs, and abstraction of services including applications and messaging from the underlying network[47,48]. An extranet is a private network that uses the Internet protocols and the public telecommunication system to share enterprise information, data or operations with external suppliers, vendors or customers. An extranet can be viewed as the external part of a company's Intranet. These trends give rise to a continuum of choices reflecting integration of public and private networking heterarchies such as consumer or business oriented service providers, 'Virtual Private Networks' (VPNs) providing a secure overlay on the Internet, industry extranets linking many providers to many clients, and private extranets connecting a single firm to its clients.

Beyond the diminished boundaries between public and private networks, the powerful open source software movement is effectively challenging the logic of proprietary information systems as well as the ideologies motivating such systems and the products and services they produce. For example, the open source model is being considered in "open source drug discovery" to significantly reduce the cost of discovering, developing and manufacturing cures for tropical diseases. Large numbers of scientists could be offered a practical way to donate urgently need skills, expertise, and research contributions. Such open source discoveries would not be patented, but production contracts would be granted to the lowest bidder and competition from generic drug makers would control manufacturing prices. Application of an "open source drug discovery" model could promote drug development for diseases affecting large populations in the developing world[49]. This application of the open source model suggests a process of isomorphism linking infrastructures and the activities they support. The open source software movement also contributes to the commoditization of health care services as well as the virtual infrastructures serving in their delivery[50].

In addition to the structure and ownership of networks and software, ideological context particularly affects the social and hierarchical relationships among service delivery professionals and consumers as well as the emphasis on individual choice with respect to collective or institutional interests and priorities[8]. Free health care market dynamics promote deprofessionalization of health care services and information symmetry among physicians, patients, and other health care services market actors[51]. On the other hand, a more social medicine model of health care delivery creates powerful centralized government institutions[52,53].

Increased empowerment of patients to assume responsibility and ownership of their own health care is based on scientific understanding of medicine and related disciplines. Such knowledge enables informed decision making and choice of appropriate treatments in consultation with health care service providers[51]. Patient responsibility and ownership facilitates risk sharing in service outcomes as well as rationalization of services in light of health care resource constraints[54]. Consumer information with participative decision making including patients and their families may reduce demand for expensive medical procedures such as surgery and end-of-life care[55]. An important constraint on these benefits of patient empowerment is the general level of health literacy. For example, recent research by the Educational Testing Service has reported that 17% of the general US adult population and almost half of those over 65 years of age are functionally illiterate with respect to health-related literacy skills[56].

Interdisciplinary integration of research, education, products and services is another important trend affecting virtual infrastructures. In health care systems around the world efforts are being deployed to identify, evaluate and integrate traditional medical knowledge and practice through research and evidence-based practice. Traditional medicine often offers less invasive and lower cost treatment alternatives to patients with limited resources making complex choices. The Indian case is an example where modern and traditional medicine are practiced in distinct systems and where many citizens choose traditional medicine because of the perception of its stronger human dimension as well as its local availability and lower cost[57,58].

Another interdisciplinary area is genomic medicine, a field that may revolutionize the future practice of medicine. Basic research revealing the human genome promises to offer individualized disease diagnostics and treatment based on unique genetic information developed from an understanding of the molecular basis of complex diseases[59]. This area of research also requires immense computing power, and bioinformatics is joining medical informatics in the design of integrated technologies. Methods used would integrate all levels of information, including the molecule, cell, tissue, organ, and the patient as well as the relevant population[42,60,61]. Genomic medicine brings a new focus on basic research and its critical importance to health care services, while the discipline of biomedical informatics produces technologies to support integration of research in genomic medicine in health care delivery systems.

The most important evolutionary trends affecting health care service delivery systems include integration of ideologically diverse networks, the emergence of grid infrastructures, and pervasiveness of the open source software movement. Deprofessionalization of health care services coevolves with increased interdisciplinary integration of biomedical informatics and greater emphasis on basic research into the human genome. As system, disciplinary and professional boundaries diminish across global service markets, ideological diversity of health care services is challenged. The next section of the paper presents a scenario analysis to suggest the future role of virtual infrastructures in diverse health care service ideologies.

4.2 *Scenarios*

The model dimensions describing dominant market dynamics (supply and demand) and control processes (clans, hierarchies, and heterarchies) are identified as the defining dimensions of health care systems, while the distinguishing characteristics differentiating the scenarios include network architectures, gateways, system integration, access control, authority and centralization, certification and quality control, and types of grid infrastructures. Four scenarios are identified according to the above dimensions as shown in Figure 1: Professional Covenants, National Constitutions, Free Markets, and Business Contracts.

4.2.1 *Control structures and processes*

Telecommunications infrastructures and the Internet contribute to control mechanisms of health care management systems through network structures and transaction services offered directly on the Internet. The classic concepts of clans and hierarchies in economics and organizational theory are useful to the understanding of control processes in virtual infrastructures[62]. Clan control is expressed through norms and standards emergent in behaviour on the Internet. Examples of clan control include codes of professional conduct and codes of ethics governing cyberbehavior as well as norms for presentation of Web content and criteria for consumer evaluation of electronic information. On the other hand, grid technologies, telecommunications networks and the Internet may give rise to institutional hierarchies of control[7]. Technological control mechanisms may effectively control access to health care services and ensure social or business contract security, confidentiality and integrity. For example, diverse physical databases may be integrated into a single federated unit. Federation enables unified access to any digital information, in any format, structured or unstructured, among such diverse databases appearing as a single resource[43].

While these infrastructures may in some cases replace traditional institutional networks, they may also extend or complement existing structures and enhance federative system integration or serve as vehicles for clan control processes[63]. In the case of clan control, autonomous and distributive multi-agent architectures contribute to associative system assembly and integration as well as commoditization of health care services in response to consumer demand, particularly in the Free Market model. Hierarchical control in the National Constitution and Business Contract models yields structural or process integration through federation architectures[64].

4.2.2 *Market dynamics and ideologies*

Supply and demand in health care markets are governed by dynamics of interaction among market actors: information and service providers and consumers, health care professionals, patients, and the public at large. Free market dynamics promote deprofessionalization of health care and information symmetry among physicians, patients, and other health care services market actors. On the other hand, a social medicine model of health care delivery creates powerful centralized government institutions[52,53]. Information and service supply express medical and other professional expertise mediated through institutional and telecommunications infrastructures or interaction among autonomous network actors as in the National Constitution and the Professional Covenants models. While all of the scenarios emphasize consumer participation and demand, system ideology affects the form of this participation and how resources are distributed among stakeholders. Grid infrastructures for example express ideological orientations supporting public research and development projects integrated in national and regional grid systems as in the case of the NHS in the European Union context, while enterprise grids support proprietary research and practice such as in the case of United Devices grid applications at Kaiser Permanente[65-68]. Ideology is also expressed in degree of commoditization of health care as well as computing resources.

The emergence of telecommunications infrastructures serving health care product and service delivery contribute to centralized National Constitution and Business Contract models of social medicine or managed care with structural control mechanisms enhanced by technology. As in the example of the British NHS, institutional network affiliation certifies information and service quality and controls individual access and institutional affiliation with the NHS WAN, while in the case of managed health care organizations such as Kaiser Permanente in the United States, quality control is accomplished by government oversight and independent accreditation agencies as well as internal quality control mechanisms.

On the other hand, free market dynamics among autonomous actors and entities on the Internet governed by consumer demand gives rise to grid infrastructures and networks driven by consumer choice to diversify, deprofessionalize, and delocalize health care services. While the services offered by Kaiser Permanente are anchored in regional structures according to the localization of the patient member, HealthAllies[12] (also a California Based Enterprise) has designed a system to empower the consumer to select health care service providers in the US or abroad based on evaluation standards unrelated to geographical location. The standards applied to treatments and procedures in such a system presage the commoditization of health care services assembled by consumers according to their individual criteria. While diversity and deprofessionalization challenge quality control, review is increasingly ensured by independent evaluators and enterprises such as HealthAllies certifying products, services and information in the consumer interest. Free markets encourage active consumer participation and information symmetry among consumers, professional and institutional actors. Such information symmetry in turn contributes to consumer empowerment and risk-sharing with professional health care service providers. The scenarios illustrated in Figure 1 are not mutually exclusive, but show alternative market dynamics delivering health care services. These systems may overlap or co-evolve in patterns of interdependency or heterarchy linking ideologically diverse entities[69].

---

[12]See the California HealthAllies (US) website at www.healthallies.com

		Control Mechanisms : CLANS
MARKET DYNAMICS : HEALTH CARE PRODUCTS AND SERVICES	SUPPLY-**PUSH** : PROFESSIONALS	**PROFESSIONAL COVENANTS** *PROPRIETARY NETWORK STRUCTURE (WAN/LAN). *Distributive multi-agent system architecture. *Subject gateways. *Associative clinical process integration. (medical specialties) *Access controlled by healthcare professionals. *Decentralized professional authority. *Professional criteria for presentation of Web content and other electronic health care information. *Professional certification of health care workers, services and institutions. *Virtual grids: American Diabetes Association (US) PROFESSIONAL VALUES Example: American Medical Association PRINCIPLE: Professional norms, Hippocratic oath.
	DEMAND-**PULL** : CONSUMERS	**FREE MARKETS** *OPEN INTERNET NETWORK STRUCTURE. *Mixed architectures with autonomous agent systems. *Search engines. *Dynamic associative integration. *Access controlled by individual consumer choices and availability of products and services in the market. *Decentralized and deprofessionalized authority with individual consumer participation. *Certification of products and services by independent evaluators. *Criteria for individual consumer evaluation of web content and other electronic information developed with consumer participation. *Public grids: Grid.org, World Community Grid, Global Grid Exchange – West Virginia CONSUMER VALUES Example: Health Allies PRINCIPLE: Responsible self-regulation. Emergent norms.

Figure 1. Comparative Scenario Analysis[7,8]

		Control Mechanisms : HIERARCHIES

MARKET DYNAMICS : HEALTH CARE PRODUCTS AND SERVICES	**SUPPLY-PUSH : PROFESSIONALS**	**NATIONAL CONSTITUTIONS**
		
		*PROPRIETARY NETWORK STRUCTURE (WAN/LAN).
		*Federation architectures.
		*Institutional gateways.
		*Federative structural integration.
		*Access controlled by institutional and telecommunications network
		   structures.
		*Centralized national and regional hierarchies.
		*Institutional standards for presentation of Web content and other
		   electronic health care information.
		*Institutional certification by network affiliation.
		*National/regional grids: eScience (UK-EU)
		
		CITIZENSHIP VALUES
		Example : British National Health PRINCIPLE : System performance
		   effectiveness: Universal service and citizen equality. Social contract.

	DEMAND-PULL : CONSUMERS	**BUSINESS CONTRACTS**
		
		*PROPRIETARY NETWORK STRUCTURES (WAN/LAN).
		*Federation architectures.
		*Corporate gateways.
		*Federative business process integration. (business transactions)
		*Access controlled by collective choices and network structures.
		*Managerial authority with enterprise hierarchies governing institutions
		   and consumer organizations.
		*Certification of products and services by institutional evaluators,
		   consumer organizations, and accreditation agencies.
		*Criteria for collective consumer evaluation of web content and other
		   electronic information by accreditation agencies.
		*Private grids: Kaiser Permanente: Archimedes (US)
		
		MANAGERIAL VALUES
		Example: Kaiser Permanente:
		PRINCIPLE: Consumer contract efficiency.(cost/benefit).

Figure 1. (*Continued*)

5 Conclusions and Recommendations

This scenario analysis has suggested how grid computing, telecommunications and the Internet may contribute to virtual service delivery infrastructures in health care markets depending upon forms of control, market dynamics of supply and demand and corresponding system ideologies. Information is the foundation of future health care management systems including genomic science and evidence based medical practice, global public health watch and research governance. The analysis suggests alternative paths to health care service delivery motivated by professional, citizenship, consumer and managerial values expressing ideological diversity among institutional systems.

Grid computing is emerging in health care markets to address exponential increases in computing power requirements according to market dynamics: virtual, public, enterprise, and national or regional grids offer extended virtual health care infrastructures.

- Interdisciplinary integration, particularly genomic medicine and bioinformatics are refocusing attention on basic research at the foundation of medical practice. Bioinformatics and medical informatics create information systems and infrastructures to bring vaste amounts of evidence to shape clinical practice.
- While health care systems are motivated by professional, citizenship, managerial and consumer values, health care websites and portals more frequently offer integrated services for all health care stakeholders including physicians, other health care service providers, patients, their families, and the general public. For example, websites founded by professional associations such as the American Medical Association, business corporations such as WebMD, national health care systems such as the British National Health Service and public agencies such as the US Centers for Disease Control and Prevention propose specialized services responding to the needs of these stakeholders. Such integration creates synergies by creating markets and linking health care providers with consumers of their services.
- The open source software movement is influencing the software industry and the emergence of grid computing in the health care

sector, particularly in the National Constitution scenario of the UK
and European Union. The open source movement contributes not
only to the commoditization of software and grid infrastructure
components, but also to the commoditization of health care services
delivered through such technologies.

- The scenario analysis reveals the complexity of health care systems
  and their underlying ideologies. The ideology of Free Markets
  guided by individual and collective consumer choice suggests
  decomposition and commoditization of health care services on
  industry markets with reassembly of such services according to
  consumer needs and evaluation criteria as shown in the case of
  California HealthAllies. On the other hand, centralized National
  Constitution models such as the NHS and other European systems
  offer universal service and access through federated national and
  regional infrastructures integrating research and education.
- Grid computing facilitates management of resources to integrate the
  benefits of economies of scale and scope in decentralized service
  delivery systems.

These conclusions suggest significant questions for future research on
virtual infrastructures in service delivery systems:

- How will the commoditization of computing resources affect system
  ideologies and configuration of service delivery?
- What patterns of isomorphism will characterize grid infrastructures
  in services such as health care?
- How will the layers of grid infrastructures be commoditized and
  what will be the consequences for the convergence hypothesis on
  service delivery infrastructures?
- How will the ideologies of infrastructures affect service delivery?
  For example, will the open source model in the software industry be
  extended to development of health care products and services?

The National Constitution service delivery scenario expresses the values
of equity and universal access to health care services as well as system
integration exemplified in the regional European Union context.
National and regional grid infrastructures emerging in the European

Union facilitate integration of research, access to federated data grids, education and health care service delivery, while fragmented proprietary grids emerging in North America may create barriers to such broad integration[70]. Research exploring the above questions will contribute to an understanding of the effects of ideological diversity on service delivery systems for public goods such as health care and how such diversity should be managed to protect the integrity of system contributions to global services markets.

References

1. C. Hipp and H. Grupp, "Innovation in the Service Sector: The Demand for Service-Specific Innovation Measurement Concepts and Typologies," *Research Policy*, 34, 2005, pp. 517-535.
2. R. Landi and M. Raisinghani, "Global Service Provider Strategies and Networking Alternatives," *Information Resources Management Journal*, 17, 2004, pp. 19-36.
3. J. Tan, H. Wen, and N. Awad, "Health Care and Services Delivery Systems as Complex Adaptive Systems," *Communications of the ACM*, 48, 2005, pp. 36-44.
4. M. Wasko and R. Teigland, "Public Goods or Virtual Commons? Applying Theories of Public Goods, Social Dilemmas, and Collective Action to Electronic Networks of Practice," *Journal of Information Technology Theory and Application*, 6, 2004, pp. 25-41.
5. P. Basch, "Electronic Health Records and the National Health Information Network," *Annals of Internal Medicine*, 143, 2005, pp. 227-228.
6. A. Séror, "Integrating Virtual Infrastructures: A Sociometry of the Cuban National Healthcare System," in Academy of Management Meetings. Seattle, 2003.
7. A. Séror, "Internet Infrastructures and Health Care Systems: a Qualitative Comparative Analysis on Networks and Markets in the British National Health Service and Kaiser Permanente," *Journal of Medical Internet Research*, 4, 2002. Available at http://www.jmir.org/2002/3/e21/index.htm
8. A. Séror, "The Internet, Global Healthcare Management Systems and Sustainable Development: Future Scenarios," *The Electronic Journal on Information Systems in Developing Countries*, 5, 2001. Available at http://new.ejisdc.org/ojs/index.php
9. A. Séror and J.-M. Fach Arteaga, "Telecommunications Technology Transfer and the Development of Institutional Infrastructure: The Case of Cuba," *Telecommunications Policy*, 24, 2000, pp. 203-221.
10. I. Foster, C. Kesselman, J. Nick, and S. Tuecke, "The Physiology of the Grid: An Open Grid Services Architecture for Distributed Systems Integration," The Globus Project, Overview paper 2002. Available at http://www.globus.org/alliance/publications/papers.php

11. World Health Organization, "The World Health Report: Changing History," Geneva, 2004. Available at http://www.who.int/whr/2004/en/

12. A. Sen, "Economics and Health," *The Lancet*, 354, 1999, p. 20.

13. WHO-World Health Organization, "World Health Report-Health Systems: Improving Performance," Geneva, 2000. Available at http://www.who.int/whr2001/2001/archives/2000/en/index.htm

14. D. Mechanic, "The Comparative Study of Health Care Delivery Systems," *Annual Review of Sociology*, 1, 1975, pp. 43-65.

15. D. Mechanic, "Ideology, medical technology, and health care organization in modern nations," *American Journal of Public Health*, 65, 1975, pp. 241-247. Available at http://www.ajph.org

16. J. Mistry, "A Conceptual Framework for the Role of Government in Bridging the Digital Divide," *Journal of Global Information Technology Management*, 8, 2005, pp. 28-46.

17. F. Martin-Sanchez, V. Maojo, and G. Lopez-Campos, "Integrating genomics into health information systems," *Methods of Information in Medicine*, 41, 2002, pp. 25-30.

18. E. J. Castilla, "Organizing Health Care: A Comparative Analysis of National Institutions and Inequality Over Time," *International Sociology*, 19, 2004, pp. 403-435.

19. A. Franco, C. Alvarez-Dardet, and M. T. Ruiz, "Effect of democracy on health: ecological study," *British Medical Journal*, 329, 2004, pp. 1421-1423.

20. D. A. Lake and M. A. Baum, "The Invisible Hand of Democracy: Political Control and the Provision of Public Services," *Comparative Political Studies*, 34, 2001, pp. 587-621.

21. F. E. Baum and A. M. Ziersch, "Social capital," *Journal of Epidemiology and Community Health*, 57, 2003, pp. 320-323. Available at http://jech.bmjjournals.com/cgi/content/abstract/57/5/320

22. C. C. Kelleher, "How exactly do politics play a part in determining health? New perspectives on an age old issue," *Journal of Epidemiology and Community Health*, 56, 2002, p. 726.

23. K. Kizer, "Establishing Health Care Performance Standards in an Era of Consumerism," *Journal of the American Medical Association*, 286, 2001, pp. 1213-805.

24. R. G. Wilkinson, "Socioeconomic determinants of health: Health inequalities: relative or absolute material standards?" *British Medical Journal*, 314, 1997, pp. 1724-1727.

25. T. Hesketh and W. X. Zhu, "Effect of restricted freedom on health in China," *British Medical Journal*, 329, 2004, p. 1427.

26. D. J. Ncayiyana, "Is democracy good for people's health? A South African perspective," *British Medical Journal*, 329, 2004, pp. 1425-1426.

27. M. McKee and E. Nolte, "Lessons from health during the transition from communism," *British Medical Journal*, 329, 2004, pp. 1428-1429.

28. M. Friedman, "How to Cure Health Care," *The Public Interest*, 2001. Available at http://www.webcitation.org/query?snapshotid=4462

29. P. Hussey, G. Anderson, R. Osborn, C. Feek, *et al.*, "How Does The Quality Of Care Compare In Five Countries?" *Health Affaires*, 23, 2004, pp. 89-99.

30. R. R. Nelson and B. Sampat, "Making Sense of Institutions as a Factor Shaping Economic Performance," *Journal of Economic Behavior & Organization*, 44, 2001, pp. 31-54.

31. F. Godlee, R. Horton, and R. Smith, "Global Information Flow," *British Medical Journal*, 321, 2000, pp. 776-777. Available at
http://bmj.com/cgi/reprint/321/7264/776

32. S. Atkinson, "Political Cultures, Health Systems and Health Policy," *Social Science and Medicine*, 55, 2002, pp. 113-124.

33. S. Atkinson, R. Rolim Medeiros, P. Lima Oliveira, and R. Dias de Almeida, "Going Down to the Local: Incorporating Social Organisation and Political Culture into Assessments of Decentralised Health Care," *Social Science & Medicine*, 51, 2000, pp. 619-636.

34. C. Clancy and K. Cronin, "Evidence-Based Decision Making: Global Evidence, Local Decisions," *Health Affairs*, 24, 2005, pp. 151-162.

35. T. J. Bossert and J. C. Beauvais, "Decentralization of health systems in Ghana, Zambia, Uganda and the Philippines: a comparative analysis of decision space," *Health Policy and Planning*, 17, 2002, pp. 14-31. Available at
http://heapol.oupjournals.org/cgi/reprint/17/1/14.pdf

36. P. Hutchinson, "Health Care in Uganda - Selected Issues," World Bank, Discussion Paper WDP404, 1999.

37. P. DiMaggio and W. Powell, "The Iron Cage revisited: Institutional Isomorphism and Collective Rationality in Organizational Fields," *American Sociological Review*, 48, 1983, pp. 147-160.

38. D. Hunter, "Culture War," *Texas Law Review*, 83, 2005, pp. 1105-1136.

39. J. Morrison and I. Wilson, "The Strategic Management Response to the Challenge of Global Change," in *Future Vision, Ideas, Insights, and Strategies*, H. Didsbury (Ed.), Bethesda, Md.: The World Future Society, 1996.

40. K. Van der Heijden, "Scenarios, Strategies and the Strategy Process," Center for Organizational Learning and Change, Nyenrode University, 1997. Available at http://www.library.nijenrode.nl/NL/publicaties/NIJREP/nijrep/1997-01/1997-01.html

41. I. Foster, C. Kesselman, S. Tuecke, "The Anatomy of the Grid: Enabling Scalable Virtual Organizations," *International Journal of Supercomputer Applications*, 15, 2001. Available at http://www.globus.org/alliance/publications/papers.php

42. Healthgrid, "From Grid to Healthgrid: Prospects and Requirements," White paper, 2004. Available at http://www.healthgrid.org

43. M. Hyatt and R. Vrablik, "The Information Grid: Secure Access to Any Information, Anywhere, Over Any Network," DeveloperWorks, White Paper, 13 January 2004. Available at http://www-106.ibm.com/developerworks/library/gr-infogrid.html

44. I. Foster and C. Kesselman, "Computational Grids," in *The Grid: Blueprint for a New Computing Infrastructure*, I. Foster and C. Kesselman (Eds.), New York: Morgan Kaufmann, 1998.

45. L. Loewe, "Global Computing for Bioinformatics," *Briefings in Bioinformatics*, 3, 2002, pp. 377-388.

46. W. Stead, R. A. Miller, M. A. Musen, and W. R. Hersh, "Integration and Beyond: Linking Information from Disparate Sources and into Workflow," *Journal of the American Medical Informatics Association*, 7, 2000, pp. 135-145.

47. B. Carley, "The implications of the financial services extranet: Metcalfe's Law, and Carley's Corollary," in *Handbook of World Stock, Derivative & Commodity Exchanges*, H. Skeete (Ed.), Herts, UK: Mondo Visione, 2002.

48. C.-M. Smoot, "Computing Commoditization," TIC Consulting, White Paper, 2004. Available at http://www.tic.com/whitepapers/computer_commodization.pdf

49. S. Maurer, A. Rai, and A. Sali, "Finding Cures for Tropical Diseases: Is Open Source an Answer," *PLoS Medicine*, 1, 2004, pp. 180-183. Available at http://salilab.org/pdf/136_MaurerBIOESSAYS2004.pdf

50. L. Harrison, "Traditional Health Care: Going Once, Twice.Gone? Say Hello to a Consumer-Driven Global Market Laden with Competition and Commoditization," *Urology Times*, 2004. Available at http://ut.adv100.com/urologytimes/article/articleDetail.jsp?id=129165

51. S. Woolf, E. Chan, R. Harris, S. Sheridan, C. Braddock, R. Kaplan, A. Krist, A. O'Connor, and S. Tunis, "Promoting Informed Choice: Transforming Health Care to Dispense Knowledge for Decision Making," *Annals of Internal Medicine*, 143, 2005, pp. 293-300.

52. National Health Service Information Authority, "The NHS Plan," Department of Health, London The Command Paper 4818 - 1, 2000. Available at http://www.nhsia.nhs.uk/nhsplan/

53. National Health Service Information Authority, "Building the Information Core-Implementing the NHS Plan," Department of Health, London, 2001. Available at http://www.nhsia.nhs.uk/def/pages/info_core/overview.asp

54. A. Rai, "Reflective Choice in Health Care: Using Information Technology to Present Allocation Options," *American Journal of Law and Medicine*, 25, 1998, pp. 387-402.

55. D. Pencheon, "Matching Demand and Supply Fairly and Efficiently," *British Medical Journal*, 316, 1998, pp. 1665-1667.

56. R. Rudd, I. Kirsch, and K. Yamamoto, "Literacy and Health in America," Educational Testing Service, Princeton, N.J., Policy Information Report, 2004.

57. Government of India - Ministry of Health and Family Welfare, "National Policy on Indian Systems of Medicine & Homoeopathy," Department of AYUSH, New Delhi, 2002. Available at http://indianmedicine.nic.in/html/news/draftnat.pdf
58. R. Wilder, "Protection of traditional medicine," Indian Council for Research on International Economic Relations, New Delhi, Working Paper, June, 2001.
59. R. C. Bast, Jr. and G. N. Hortobagyi, "Individualized Care for Patients with Cancer — A Work in Progress," *New England Journal of Medicine*, 351, 2004, pp. 2865-2867.
60. V. Maojo, I. Iakovidis, F. Martin-Sanchez, J. Crespo, and C. Kulikowski, "Medical Informatics and Bioinformatics: European Efforts to Facilitate Synergy," *Journal of Biomedical Informatics*, 34(6), 2001, pp. 423-427.
61. F. Martin-Sanchez, I. Iakovidis, S. Norager, *et al.*, "Synergy between Medical Informatics and Bioinformatics: Facilitating Genomic Medicine for Future Health Care," *Journal of Biomedical Informatics*, 37, 2004, pp. 30-42.
62. O. Williamson, *Markets and Hierarchies: Analysis and Antitrust Implications*. New York: The Free Press, 1975.
63. F. Riggins and H. Rhee, "Developing the Learning Network Using Extranets," *International Journal of Electronic Commerce*, 4, 1999, pp. 65-84. Available at http://ids.csom.umn.edu/Faculty/friggins/papers/learning.html
64. W. Shen, "Virtual Organizations in Collaborative Design and Manufacturing Systems," *Journal of Organizational Virtualness*, 2, 2000, pp. 43-58.
65. American Diabetes Association Consensus Panel, "Guidelines for Computer Modeling of Diabetes and Its Complications," *Diabetes Care*, 27, 2004, pp. 2262-2265. Available at http://care.diabetesjournals.org
66. D. M. Eddy and L. Schlessinger, "Archimedes: A trial-validated model of diabetes," *Diabetes Care*, 26, 2003, pp. 3093-3101. Available at http://care.diabetesjournals.org
67. D. M. Eddy and L. Schlessinger, "Validation of the Archimedes Diabetes Model," *Diabetes Care*, 26, 2003, pp. 3102-3110. Available at http://care.diabetesjournals.org
68. R. Kahn, "Dealing With Complexity in Clinical Diabetes: The value of Archimedes," *Diabetes Care*, 26, 2003, pp. 3168-3171. Available at http://care.diabetesjournals.org
69. D. Stark, "Heterarchy: Distributing Authority and Organizing Diversity," in *The Biology of Business: Decoding the Natural Laws of Enterprise*, J. Clippinger (Ed.), New York: Jossey-Bass, pp. 153-179, 1999.
70. S. Schoenbaum, A.-M. Audet, and K. Davis, "Obtaining greater value from health care: The roles of the U.S. government," *Health Affairs*, 22, 2003, pp. 183-193.

CHAPTER 8

Knowledge Transfer in Global Organizations: The Case of Siemens

Sven C. Voelpel[1]
International University Bremen
College Ring 2
D-28759, Bremen, Germany

Malte Dous, Walter Brenner and Lutz Kolbe
University of St. Gallen
Institute of Information Management
Mueller-Friedberg-Strasse 8
CH-9000 St. Gallen, Switzerland

1 Introduction

During the late 1990s Knowledge Management as a topic had been widely discussed in management theory. Consequently, the majority of global companies were attempting to put at least some of the most promising concepts into practice at the turn of the millennium. Although a number of approaches have proven to be successful, many of these initiatives failed because they did not consider the particular organizational environment or knowledge culture necessary to embed the initiative effectively.

An outstanding example of an organization successfully enabling the global transfer of knowledge is that of Siemens AG. Siemens, one of the world's largest private organizations[2] with 415,000 employees in 196 countries, is on its way to transforming into a knowledge-networked company. An important building block in the transformation process was the implementation of ShareNet, a global knowledge-sharing network.

In this case study we describe how ShareNet was established as a system with which to share knowledge globally within Siemens ICN

---

[1]Corresponding author: Email: s.voelpel@iu-bremen.de
[2]Siemens is one of the largest private organizations in terms of number of employees.

(Information and Communication Networks), a major division within the company with 33,000 employees[1]. Subsequent to the ShareNet case description we derive key recommendations for the edification of global companies wishing to learn from Siemens' experiences with the ShareNet implementation. Although the technical reliability and usability of a knowledge-sharing system are basic prerequisites for its success, this contribution focuses on how Siemens dealt with organizational and cultural particularities of the initiative.

A seven-year research study involving in-depth expert interviews with leading authorities in knowledge-intensive companies from which we identified Siemens ShareNet as a best practice knowledge management system fashioned the first stage of the research approach that we used to derive conclusions and insights from the Siemens ShareNet case[3]. From this research we identified Siemens ShareNet as a best practice knowledge management system[2]. In the second stage we focused predominantly on Siemens ShareNet, exploring its implementation process and global establishment in detail. Between 2001 and 2004 we conducted 23 semi-structured interviews on global knowledge management with executives, general managers, and line managers within different Siemens units worldwide. We also used participant and direct observation as a primary data source. Secondary data such as internal documents, project manuals, presentations, annual reports, and internal company presentations were revised to support our research.

2   A Global Knowledge Network Solution: Siemens ShareNet

In 1998 the telecommunications industry shifted significantly. The deregulation of that industry, especially in Germany, Siemens' core market, confronted Siemens with fierce competition and the challenge to transform from a "simple" product-oriented manufacturer to a complex, customer-oriented organization that could provide customized solutions

---

[3]The companies we investigated are headquartered in North America (including Accenture, The Boston Consulting Group, Cap Gemini Ernst & Young, DHL, McKinsey), Europe (Bayer, DaimlerChrysler, Infineon, Novartis, Roche, Siemens) and Asia (Motorola, NTT DoCoMo, Sony).

and service globally. New competencies had to be established and this impelled Siemens to carry out a comprehensive restructuring. As part of this restructuring, Information and Communication Networks (ICN) was one of the newly named groups which united Siemens' telecom networks' carrier and the enterprise branches. The new group encompassed the Wireline Networks Group, Communications on Air, IP/Data Networks, Transport Networks, Manufacturing and Logistics, and Service and Carrier Networks. In 1999, ICN had 65,000 employees – of which 17,000 were sales and marketing personnel – in more than 84 countries[3]. As a long-time leader in this industry, the group understood that it needed to locate, share and leverage its large number of employees' expertise in order to put their comprehensive knowledge to work.

3 Conceptualizing a Knowledge-Sharing Initiative Beyond that of a Mere Data Repository

The President of Group Strategy at Siemens ICN, Joachim Döring, and his team decided to establish a knowledge initiative for ICN's Sales and Marketing organization. A knowledge management system that would connect the 17,000 sales and marketing staff had to be developed. This would enable a Sales and Marketing team in a local company to capitalize on an ICN team in another country or region's experience whenever the local team encountered a similar deal. The goal was to increase the speed and quality of the knowledge-receiving team's bid.

According to Donald Tsusaki, Head of IT Knowledge Management Platforms, Siemens ICN, the concept of creating a knowledge management system was nothing extraordinary, but most of the existing systems dealt only with codified or explicit knowledge and thus resembled data repositories. Döring's idea was to create a system that was able to handle not only explicit, but also help externalize the individuals' tacit knowledge. Such a solution is also referred to as a "codification" strategy. With a codification strategy, the firm's knowledge is organized into reusable assets that are stored in a formal KMS and knowledge is shared through the reuse of these assets[4]. A codification strategy is best suited to organizations that reuse the same knowledge repeatedly and therefore require a scalable knowledge-sharing approach that enables efficient knowledge transfer[5].

Subsequently, Döring assembled ICN's most successful sales persons to outline the solution-selling process that covered everything from general business development to the preparation of individual bids as well as the creation of specific solutions. This team had to analyze and determine the broad classifications of knowledge as well as the questions relevant to each step in order to establish a structure for organizing the knowledge content (see Figure 1).

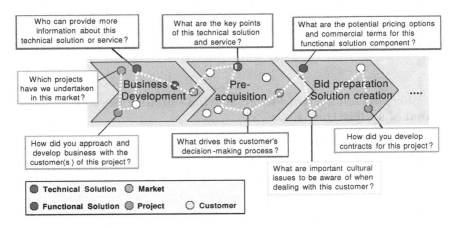

Figure 1. Solution-Selling Process and Examples of Questions

Source: Siemens ICN.

The design of the new system had to integrate components such as a knowledge library, a forum for urgent requests, and platforms for knowledge sharing that would allow the knowledge transmission channels to accommodate a higher degree of "richness" than that of traditional, repository-based knowledge management systems. The platforms had to comprise community news bulletin boards, discussion groups for certain topics and live chat rooms. The resulting product was called ShareNet.

The knowledge library would be the heart of the initiative and be comprised of knowledge bids constructed so that they would categorize the experience gained from ongoing and completed projects. Project team participants would enter the details of each bid by means of web-based entry forms. The questionnaire-type design was important; Andreas Manuth, ShareNet manager at ICN, remarked: "We knew we needed to capture some of the 'tacit' knowledge managers had in their heads – the 'real life' tested pros and cons of a solution. We had to ask questions that managers wouldn't necessarily think about after just completing a bid or project document."

The "urgent request" platform would offer an opportunity to enter urgent questions for answer by other users who would regularly scan through this forum to check if they had answers to questions such as: "Does anyone have a list of recent network projects by this competitor?", or "My customer needs a business case to implement this new router technology by next Thursday. Can anyone help?" In practice this component revealed its value when, for example, for insurance purposes an ICN project manager in South America tried to ascertain the problems associated with the laying of cables in the Amazon rainforest. He posted an urgent request asking help from anyone with a similar project in a similar environment. A project manager in Senegal responded almost immediately. Obtaining the right information before the cables went underground saved Siemens a considerable amount of money.

The initial gathering of the ShareNet initiators was followed by ten more meetings before the end of 1998. Döring used this time to gather competent and motivated members for his ShareNet core team who would map out the detailed plan of how the system's technological and managerial processes would operate.

Pilot projects were subsequently conducted in Australia, China, Malaysia, and Portugal from April to August 1999. The projects provided insights from those users who were far from the Siemens headquarters in Munich and would have to rely on the system the most. The ShareNet team therefore wanted to avoid the usual, and not always successful, Siemens practice of rolling out initiatives from Munich to the rest of the company across the globe.

In July 1999 Döring gathered 60 managers - from every country in which ICN was represented - in a boot camp to elaborate on the operational procedure that they would have to follow. A ShareNet committee of 11 members - mainly users from different regions, but one from ICN's board, and two from ICN's Group Strategy board - was responsible for ShareNet's further strategic direction. The opportunity to consider the views of both the managers and employees from all the countries where ShareNet would be launched proved to be crucial to the subsequent global launch of the initiative.

4 Launching a Knowledge Initiative in a Globally Dispersed Organization

When the first version of ShareNet was released in 39 countries, the first challenge was to get people to use the system. As Manuth said: "The only way the urgent request concept would succeed was if we had a high number of users on board. At first the core ShareNet team fielded these problems themselves. They combed their personal networks of contacts to find solutions to posted urgent requests. They then connected their contact with the question poser themselves, sometimes offline. The system had no value until the database was populated and urgent requests were answered."

The central challenge, which was closely related to the issue of getting enough users on board, was how to tackle ShareNet's global character. The ShareNet team's Munich-based headquarters could definitely not manage the launch and the supervision that ShareNet would thereafter require in all 39 countries on their own. Siemens decided to address the global integration and local responsiveness as follows: While the headquarters and the local branches would jointly define ShareNet's strategic direction, it would be centrally maintained at the Munich headquarters. The joint definition and the system's central strategic maintenance would then revert to the local companies. ShareNet managers were therefore appointed to the local subsidiaries to help the initiative access the culturally embedded knowledge there.

Andreas Manuth described this approach to diffusing ShareNet to ICN's worldwide subsidiaries as follows: "To jump-start the network, we held two- to three-day workshops in the local countries to get each local company on board, to get them used to the system and interface, and to convince them of its value. We had an exercise we'd run at every workshop. At the beginning of the sessions, we'd ask them: 'You must have some problem that isn't solved – that you left sitting on your desk before you came here. Put that up on the system as an urgent request.' Without fail, by the end of the day, that posting would get at least one reply, and inevitably, the effect was that the person who had posted it would be stunned. And everyone else in the room would see the effect too. So they'd go home convinced."

Additionally, those ShareNet managers who would represent their local company and promote the initiative within their regions were handpicked. These were people who were intrinsically motivated by the idea that a knowledge-sharing system would be beneficial. They were responsible for supervising local level usage, but also handled many of the urgent requests at the start of the initiative. This international group of ShareNet managers was a major cornerstone for implementing the knowledge-sharing idea globally. They served as the nucleus in their local organizations to convince people who did not recognize the value of sharing their knowledge.

Bringing together the expertise and cultural assumptions of both headquartered and local ShareNet managers emerged as an appropriate way of handling the rollout cross-culturally. According to Holden, the interaction and shared experience between individuals with specific cultural knowledge gives rise to active (implementational) know-how, informs participative competence and stimulates cross-cultural collaborative learning[6].

During the following months the attention to detail and strenuous efforts prior to the start of the project began to pay off. Every local workshop was followed by an increase in the urgent request postings from that country and introduced a flow of knowledge bids. As anticipated, the benefits became obvious almost immediately, especially in ICN's more remote regions. Towards the end of 1999 ShareNet had about 4,000 registered users. Manuth remembered, "For example, we had an official hotline for engineers in the field to call in to get technical help for one of our switches. If someone in Vietnam had a problem with the switch, they were supposed to call the hotline. Over and over again, we heard 'No one ever calls me back. We're too small.' But with urgent requests, ShareNet gave them access to other people struggling with switch problems out in the field – people who would call them back or at least drop them an email."

Important to note is that the ICN headquarters fully funded the ShareNet initiative. ICN's product divisions and local companies offered the service for free therefore users could simply log on and start utilizing the system. Manuth noticed the immense benefits of this approach: "Nobody has to obtain a signature to spend money to use ShareNet. For example, in Brunei there is just one technical sales person. Via ShareNet, he is connected to all the other ICN technical sales people, which would not be possible if we billed him for system use."

5 Getting People to Collaborate by Using Incentives Judiciously

Motivating Siemens people to cooperate with one another, and thus to continually contribute to and rely on ShareNet for solutions, was a significant challenge. The ShareNet management team injected energy and resources into getting people to use the system. They soon realized that Siemens needed to substantially change its organizational and individual knowledge-sharing culture if the exercise were to be a resounding success. Siemens' corporate structure could not be used as a foundation for this change, as the single business units were separated instead of networked and the leading paradigm regarding governance mainly relied on hierarchy instead of cross-unit collaboration, says Volker Gieseke, Head of Competence Management at Siemens ICN.

The Director of the Center of Competence Europe and Middle East at ICN Carrier Sales, Gerhard Hirschler, who was one of ShareNet's first chosen managers, recalled that "[…] there were always excuses. People said, 'I don't have the time to spend on this.' Others were reluctant to share. The network consultants, for example, said 'Sure, we have knowledge, but it's for sale, it's not for free.' Still others said 'Everyone has certain clarity about their own projects in their heads, but it won't translate well for others.'" The ShareNet team was also concerned about managing people's expectations - employees might be disappointed with their first interactions and not use ShareNet. This also implied the need to change people's opinion regarding the negative perception of "re-use" by actively encouraging them to use – or copy – the knowledge that was offered by ShareNet.

De Long and Fahey also observed such phenomena in their research on 50 companies pursuing knowledge management projects. They assert that a corporation's knowledge-culture in terms of interactivity, collaboration and attitude towards reusing existing knowledge dictates what knowledge belongs to the organization and what knowledge remains in control of the individual. This is a distinction that becomes obvious when management tries to convince individuals to share their knowledge. Companies should therefore examine whether their organizational culture enhances or hinders knowledge-sharing behavior and thereafter derive appropriate measures to foster trust, sharing and teaching, as well as collaboration among their employees[7].

In order to achieve a quick motivational boost in participation, the ShareNet team decided to introduce incentives that would motivate the employees to use the virtual knowledge network. The first system was called "Bonus-On-Top". It provided incentives for local country managers, and rewarded a country's overall participation in knowledge sharing. If a country's sales team managed to secure a certain amount of business with the help of international knowledge sharing, they received a bonus. The bonus was applicable to both the country that had contributed the knowledge and the country that used it[8]. By introducing this kind of incentive, Siemens made a significant investment in ShareNet. Nevertheless, although a considerable number of country managers did receive the bonus, there was no guarantee that ShareNet would ultimately benefit from this reward system. ShareNet managers recognized that direct recognition of how much their daily job is appreciated motivates employees far more than receiving some reward. The managers consequently decided to focus more on the users themselves. This was realized by means of a web-based incentive system in early 2000. Users received ShareNet "shares", which were, in fact, bonus points as in an airline mileage system, for a valuable contribution. Contributors gained shares for entering knowledge bids into the library, for reusing knowledge, for responding to urgent requests and for appraising one another's contributions. Users earned, for example, ten shares for technology, market or customer bids. For a project, technical solution or service, or a functional solution component as well as for contributing a success story, twice the number of shares was allocated. For answering an urgent request they gained three shares. Later an award system was introduced in which shares could be redeemed for various gifts and prizes, such as textbooks, Siemens mobile phones, or even trips to knowledge exchange partners.

Even though the scheme had accelerated the growth in quantity of contributions significantly, quality problems started to occur, which compelled the ShareNet team to establish a rating method. This meant that the users had to evaluate the contributions, with the number of stars allocated reflecting the contributions' usefulness. The rating of contributions was also rewarded with shares to encourage users to evaluate the bids that they had utilized. Moreover, whenever a user wanted to redeem his shares, members of the ShareNet team would first approve his contributions and ratings before authorizing an appropriate award.

The effect of the ShareNet "Shares" program was that during July 2001, more than 2,000 contributions were posted in contrast with the slightly more than 600 the previous October. Likewise, around four times more shares were gained in this month compared to the 20,000 the previous October. Despite accumulating large numbers of shares, however, few users ever converted them into prizes. ShareNet managers speculated that the knowledge had become its own reward, and that users did not want to relinquish the status associated with having a high share total by redeeming them. Ardichvili *et al.* made a similar observation in their study on motivation in knowledge-sharing communities of practice[9]. They too confirmed the insight that employees feel the need to establish themselves as experts, e.g., by gaining formal expert status by contributing to the community, or by gaining informal recognition through multiple postings and contributions to the community.

Before the end of 2001, ShareNet had 18,200 registered users. These users would, in an average month, answer many hundreds of urgent requests, in addition to posting approximately 300-400 new knowledge bids. Success stories started to emerge and accumulate, signifying the system's value. In Switzerland, e.g., although certain managers' bid was 30 percent above a competitor's, they landed a contract to build a telecommunications network for two hospitals. This was possible because ShareNet colleagues in the Netherlands had provided technical data that supported the sales representatives' contention that the network Siemens offered would be more reliable. Another example is provided by a project to build a pilot broadband network in Malaysia that was obtained with the help of ShareNet. In their bid, the local team was required to provide a reference customer. Via ShareNet they found a team in Denmark that had accomplished a similar undertaking. With the help of the Danish group's experience, the team in Malaysia obtained the contract.

6 Transferring a Successful Initiative to Further Domains

At ICN the success of knowledge sharing via a virtual platform had extended beyond the marketing and sales department by 2001. Like Joachim Döring a few years before, the head of the Wireline Network Development Group at Siemens ICN, Jürgen Klunker, recognized ShareNet's potential and introduced the idea of using the system in his research and development (R&D) division as well.

The Wireline Network product development was run by 3,000 employees at Siemens' headquarters in Munich. The unit focused on developing core platforms for telephony and data network switching systems. At Regional Development Centers (RDC) these platforms were adapted to local market needs for each of 300 customers in more than 100 countries. Situated in countries such as Belgium, Brazil, Greece, Hungary, India, Portugal, Russia, Slovenia, South Africa, and Thailand, these RDCs employed approximately 460 employees, mostly regional engineers.

For its introduction at ICN R&D, ShareNet was adapted from its original Sales and Marketing version. The structure of the knowledge library architecture remained almost unchanged, although it had to be adapted to mirror a knowledge base appropriate for R&D, which mainly meant a change in the relevant criteria and parameters when contributing a knowledge object. This adaptation acknowledged the fact that R&D knowledge is more specific and complex than that in other organizational units, which is also a reason for its more problematic transfer ability[10].

When the inaugural version of R&D ShareNet was launched in February 2002, there had been no prior marketing campaign, as the R&D ShareNet team wanted to proceed carefully. The team was therefore simultaneously presented with the major challenge of encouraging people to contribute to this 'little known' system. The results were dismal - by May 2002 only 50 knowledge bids had been posted. A more intense effort would be required to encourage contributions. The scant participation might have been due to the lack of marketing effort, but was more probably due to the ShareNet team being confronted with a different context in the R&D department. This issue is also known in theory, with the literature explaining that protectiveness and "shielding mechanisms" by the source of knowledge can hinder the knowledge flow between different R&D units[11].

The ShareNet team furthermore had to cope with an organizational culture at ICN R&D that was less supportive of knowledge sharing than at the Sales and Marketing department. It was more or less a question of lack of "care" within the R&D organization; "care", according to von Krogh, consists of values like trust, empathy, help, lenient judgment and courage that will allow a knowledge-friendly organizational culture to evolve[12].

At the R&D division, these cultural barriers within the organization were harder to overcome than geographical or language barriers. The most important object to achieve was to get the knowledge that was concentrated in the headquarters in Munich to those engineers who needed that knowledge. The people in the labs – in Klunker's group, for example – already had their own informal information networks established and already belonged to communities of experts. The ShareNet team had to communicate knowledge-oriented cultural values, such as openness and trust, as well as the personal benefit that could be achieved through knowledge sharing to ICN R&D's engineers. Klunker argued: "The developers are the owners of the knowledge, and, for the most part, they are not aware that others might need some part of this knowledge. We had to convince them that even though writing an answer to a question doesn't seem to yield any immediate return, it's worth to participate and to be part of the community. This is not an advantage that counts in the next quarter of an hour, but it will definitely pay off after a certain length of time."

Remarkable, however, is that the engineers located outside the Munich headquarters recognized the system's strengths far better. They depended on knowledge from outside and therefore had to be less intensively convinced to use the system than the engineers in Munich. In the end, this observation contributed to the insight that there is hardly any better incentive to bring knowledge transfer into action than its value for the knowledge receiver.

7 Implications for Knowledge Management Practitioners

The ShareNet case study we described in this contribution illustrates how Siemens managed to address the various aspects and challenges of an organizational and knowledge-sharing culture when establishing a global knowledge-sharing system. The development of ShareNet is closely associated with the six key insights that are summarized in Table 1 and outlined below. These insights regarding organizational issues that influenced the knowledge-sharing culture at Siemens could serve as a guideline for other companies that intend to establish a knowledge-sharing system in a global environment.

Table 1. Managerial Implications for Knowledge-Sharing Initiatives

How to overcome barriers and increase knowledge-sharing
▪ Choose a fertile ground in which to start knowledge-sharing initiatives
▪ Integrate the needs of the addressees
▪ Employ a creative leader and driver for change
▪ Pool knowledge resources globally while preserving local strengths
▪ Install an incentive system that fosters peer motivation for knowledge sharing
▪ Consider different knowledge-sharing cultures within the organization

- Choose a fertile ground in which to start knowledge-sharing initiatives. In departments such as sales and marketing the results from knowledge-sharing become immediately visible in the form of a gained customer, or an avoided mistake when moving into unknown markets. These "quick wins" are needed to promote the system within the organization.

- Integrate the needs of the addressees. Significant for ShareNet's success was the inclusion of the views of managers and employees in all the countries where ShareNet would be launched. Siemens realized that global user acceptance of the system required a global procedure for its development. In a strongly headquarter-centered organizational culture like Siemens, it was perceived as a signal that different views and opinions from global subsidiaries were taken serious and resulted in a joint approach.
- Employ a creative leader and driver for change. At ShareNet, Joachim Döring and his management team possessed the enthusiasm that was necessary to serve as the project's nucleus. An initiative whose success and benefit is hard to predict and to quantify requires a creative leader that will convince those responsible for budget allocations, the project team as well as the heads of departments in which the implementation will be piloted, of the project's potential value from the very beginning.
- Pool knowledge resources globally while preserving local strengths. At Siemens, a decentralized solution with elements such as the local ShareNet managers or local training takes cultural particularities and attitudes towards knowledge sharing into consideration. Above all it was the ShareNet managers' personal contribution that served as "glue", thus helping the company to better access context-specific knowledge worldwide and to actually take the system to its users. Regular global meetings between the Munich-based ShareNet team and the local ShareNet managers help to supervise the strategic direction and keep the personal contact between the dispersed organizations alive.
- Install an incentive system that fosters peer motivation for knowledge sharing. Having seen the first incentive program "Bonus-On-Top" fail because it only rewarded the local company heads with abstract premiums, Siemens introduced the ShareNet Shares scheme to reward knowledge contributors individually. The program itself, however, only reached its full potential in combination with a rating system that ensured the contributions' quality. The main observation regarding the "shares" incentive program, however, was the comparatively small number of shares redeemed for premiums. The

insight was that peer comparison and recognition may be far better motivators than material rewards. Furthermore, transparency regarding the number and quality of contributions can reveal contributors' "expert status", thus putting peer motivation to work.

- Consider different knowledge-sharing cultures. At Siemens, the R&D unit responded differently to knowledge sharing than the marketing department, and required other terminologies. Taking the differing contexts into consideration was not only necessary on a semantic level of terms and definitions, but also in a cultural sense. In fact, in R&D the knowledge-sharing culture was far less strong than in other departments like marketing and was characterized by protectiveness and "shielding mechanisms". On introducing ShareNet, it took far more effort to convince the R&D workers that sharing their knowledge would benefit them more than protecting it. Marketing efforts at the R&D department turned out to be a very personal business, with many meetings and workshops. Moreover, the use of successful cases as well as the good reputation that ShareNet had gained during its inauguration in the marketing and sales department helped to promote the initiative at R&D.

Of course, knowledge management practitioners intending to start a ShareNet-like project have to keep in mind that the environmental conditions with which a knowledge-sharing initiative is confronted play an important role. It is obvious that the launch of an entirely new project would have been difficult to accomplish during economically bad times. In fact, the knowledge management "hype" at the end of the 1990s provided ShareNet with favorable times during which it was comparatively easy to dedicate resources to boost the system. The learning here is that profiting from such an enabling context and anchoring the system within the organization are necessary actions if an initiative is to survive when contrary winds are encountered. Without references and success cases that demonstrate the value of a knowledge-sharing initiative, its survival might be endangered as well. However, if substance can be achieved, the chances that those responsible for budgets will be willing to maintain the initiative until times turn more favorable are considerably enhanced.

8 Limitations and Future Challenges

While some authors have argued that an IT-based knowledge-sharing strategy cannot improve performance[13], others argue that the just in time delivery of context specific knowledge can significantly improve performance[14]. The Siemens case supports the second view as it reveals that a thoughtful implementation of a knowledge-sharing system enhances the transfer of knowledge within a global organization and can therefore create value. However, a system like ShareNet also has certain limitations that are hard to overcome. On the financial side, maintaining a knowledge-sharing system will remain a significant cost, as the supervision can only be automated to a certain degree. This means that personnel resources have to be dedicated. At Siemens ShareNet's global editors still have to do content management manually. Some automated solutions have already been implemented, but the current state of technology still makes maintaining consistent terminology and overall quality within a global knowledge-sharing system an extensive task.

Another insight from the ShareNet case is that virtual media have limitations when it comes to the sharing of tacit knowledge. Alavi and Leidner assert that "the institutionalization of best practices by embedding them into IT might facilitate efficient handling of routine, predictable situations during stable and incrementally changing environments. When change is radical or discontinuous, however, there is persistent need for continual renewal of the basic premises underlying the practices achieved in the knowledge repositories."[15] For transferring specific, contextual (i.e. "sticky") knowledge for product or business model innovation, rich mechanisms, like face-to-face contact, are required[16].

The personal interaction that might be necessary for the knowledge receiver to understand the knowledge source's context can only be promoted by a system, but not guaranteed. The personal interaction that might be necessary for the knowledge receiver to understand the knowledge source's context can only be promoted by a system, but not guaranteed. Tacit knowledge, however, is one of the most important drivers of innovation, as is demonstrated by various academic concepts[17]. Approaches to tackling the problem of enhancing innovation through global knowledge transfer and creation have been introduced in the management literature, some of which can already be found in practice[18]. Hansen points out that the limitation of virtual knowledge platforms is that they only enable "weak ties" within the organization, since their lack of media richness does not provide an enabling context for creating "strong ties"[19]. Hansen's findings suggest that weak interunit ties help a project team search for useful knowledge in other subunits, but impede the transfer of complex knowledge, which tends to require a strong tie between two parties. He therefore proposes the introduction of personal "knowledge networks" to provide a rich mechanism for strong ties and thus for the transfer of complex, context-specific knowledge.

Fostering the dissemination of tacit knowledge, and thereby enabling collaboration and innovation, is another of Siemens' objectives. The company is currently developing PeopleShareNet, a system that will serve as a virtual expert marketplace for worldwide project staffing. This system will in turn act as enabling technology for teams that are formed according to each member's specific knowledge and competency. Such interdisciplinary teams or "knowledge networks" may help to foster the "social glue" that is necessary to anchor knowledge management within the organization, thereby bringing a knowledge-sharing corporate culture to its people.

References

1. Siemens AG, *Siemens Annual Report 2003 – Go for Profit and Growth*, Berlin, Muenchen, 2004.
2. Davenport, T. and Voelpel, S., The Rise of Knowledge Management towards Attention Management. *Journal of Knowledge Management*, 5(3), 2001, pp. 212-221.
3. Siemens AG, *Siemens Annual Report 1999 – Count on us...*, Berlin, Muenchen, 2000.
4. Hansen, M.T., Nohria, N. and Terney, T., What's your Strategy for Managing Knowledge? *Harvard Business Review*, March-April, 1999, pp. 106-116.
5. Zack, M.H., Managing codified knowledge. *Sloan Management Review*, Summer, 1999, pp. 45-58; Markus, M.L., Toward a Theory of Knowledge Reuse: Types of Knowledge Reuse Situations and Factors in Reuse Success. *Journal of Management Information Systems*, 18(1), 2001, pp. 57-93.

6. Holden, N. J., *Cross-Cultural Management: A Knowledge Management Perspective.* Harlow: Financial Times/Prentice Hall, 2002.

7. De Long, D.W. and Fahey, L., Diagnosing cultural barriers to knowledge management. *Academy of Management Executive*, 14(4), 2000, pp. 113-127.

8. Voelpel, S., Kugler, P. and Gibbert, M., Siemens Premium-on-Top: Measuring knowledge management with a bonus system for fostering innovation. University of St. Gallen Case, European Case Clearing House 902-012-1: 14, 2002.

9. Archdivili, A., Page, V. and Wentling, T., Motivation and barriers to participation in knowledge-sharing communities of practice. *Journal of Knowledge Management*, 7(1), 2003, pp. 64-77.

10. Simonin, B.L., Ambiguity and the process of knowledge transfer in strategic alliances. *Strategic Management Journal*, 20, 1999, pp. 595-623.

11. Simonin, B.L., Ambiguity and the process of knowledge transfer in strategic alliances. *Strategic Management Journal*, 20, 1999, pp. 595-623.

12. Von Krogh, G., Care in Knowledge Creation. *California Management Review*, 40(3), 1998, pp. 133-153.

13. McDermott, R., Why Information Technology Inspired But Cannot Deliver Knowledge Management. *California Management Review*, 41(4), 1999, pp. 103-117.

14. Davenport, T.H. and Glasser, J., Just-in-Time Delivery Comes to Knowledge Management. *Harvard Business Review*, July, 2002, pp. 5-9.

15. Alavi, M. and Leidner, D.E., Review: Knowledge Management and Knowledge Management Systems: Conceptual Foundations and Research Issues. *MIS Quarterly*, 25(1), 2001, pp. 107-136.

16. Subramaniam, M. and Venkatraman, N., Determinants of Transnational New Product Development Capability: Testing the Influence of Transferring and Deploying Tacit Overseas Knowledge. *Strategic Management Journal*, 22, 2001, pp. 359-378.

17. Nonaka, I., A Dynamic Theory of Organizational Knowledge Creation. *Organization Science*, 5(1), 1994, pp. 14-37; Davenport, T. and Prusak, L., *Working Knowledge.* Boston: Harvard Business School Press, 1998; Von Krogh, G., Ichijo, K. and Nonaka, I., *Enabling Knowledge Creation.* New York: Oxford University Press, 2000.

18. Von Krogh, G., Ichijo, K. and Nonaka, I., *Enabling Knowledge Creation.* New York: Oxford University Press, 2000.

19. Hansen, M.T., Knowledge Networks: Explaining Effective Knowledge Sharing in Multiunit Companies. *Organization Science*, 13(3), 2002, pp. 232-248.

CHAPTER 9

Organizational Transformation by Activating Knowledge: The Mediating Role of Collaboration Technologies

Sajda Qureshi
Department of Information Systems and Quantitative Analysis
College of Information Science & Technology
University of Nebraska-Omaha
Omaha, NE 68182-0392, USA
Email: squreshi@mail.unomaha.edu

Peter Keen
Department of Information and Communication Technology
Faculty of Technology, Policy, and Management
Delft University of Technology
P.O. Box 5015, 2600 GA Delft, The Netherlands
Email: peter@peterkeen.com

1 Introduction

Research has produced evidence to suggest that knowledge sharing is problematic. In her empirical research of engineers, technicians and assemblers on a production floor, Bechky[1] identified difficulties in sharing knowledge due to differences in language, the locus of their practice, and their conceptualization of the product. Reasons for this, Bechky suggests are that as certain expressions could potentially signify multiple contents, an expression could mean something different to the receiver than it does to the communicator. Cramton's study[2] of geographically distributed collaboration by members of 13 teams, analyzed 1,649 emails, online chats, team logs and 26 analysis papers and identified five types of problems constituting failures of mutual knowledge which is knowledge that people share and know that they share: failure to communicate and retain contextual information, unevenly distributed information, difficulty in understanding and sharing the salience of information, differences in speed of access to information, and difficulty in interpreting the meaning of silence.

Occupational communities within and in between organizations can have difficulty sharing different domains of knowledge that are dispersed across different individuals. A case to point is that US intelligence agencies have difficulty sharing knowledge among themselves as well as in between different agencies investigating the similar problems. According to the 9/11 Commission report "The FBI did not have the capability to link the collective knowledge of agents in the field to national priorities"[3] (p.10). It suggests that "Management should have ensured that information was shared and duties were clearly assigned across agencies, and across the foreign-domestic divide" (p.11). The 9/11 commission sites loss of power as a reason for not sharing mission critical information.

Practical efforts to stimulate knowledge sharing and management have largely concentrated on codifying or explicating knowledge. Infrastructures are proposed for storing explicit knowledge as well as refining, managing and distributing it[4,5]. While these efforts are valuable in themselves, practical considerations such as motivating employees to add to such databases and use them in their "knowledge work" have thwarted the success of such codification strategies. Ruppel and Harrington[6] suggest that resistance to intranets as a knowledge sharing environment is a management and corporate issue rather than a technology issue. There is a sense that as people and organizations do business and work with each other over the web, the need for collaborative technologies, processes and structures will become necessary[7,8]. There is agreement that in order to be able to provide customized goods and services, the effective performance and growth of organizations requires integrating and sharing highly distributed knowledge[4,9,10]. Despite the best efforts in IT implementations and knowledge management, a key questions looms high: Why are knowledge management efforts problematical? This paper suggests that a paradox exists in that the building and sharing of knowledge is one of the highest sources of advantage for an organization, but also the most guarded resource. Restated the paradox is "If the payoffs from knowledge management are so immense why is it so difficult to get results?"

Two of the most frequent explanations of these barriers are (1) the lack of incentives to share knowledge and often strong reasons to protect and hoard it[11] and (2) the lack of mechanisms to make it easy to organize and access knowledge resources[1,6]. A major challenge remains one of harnessing the power of these "knowledge" networks of distributed knowledge[12,13]. The challenge is deep-rooted, dating back to Barnard's conception of the organization as driven by the need to build and share intelligence[14,15], with a long tradition of research on organizational learning[16,17], and intellectual capital[18]. By leveraging the creation and use of this key resource, new levels of organizational effectiveness can be attained[9,10,19]. Such organizational effectiveness is illustrated in a case study reported by Qureshi and Vogel[20], the Central and Eastern European node within a Multinational oil company's European Oil Products Retail Network had to be managed as a whole and investment plans had to be proposed for the entire Central and Eastern European node. Qureshi and Vogel found that the use of collaborative technologies actually enabled more effective face-to-face negotiations. The decision-making process relied on a network of people from different geographical locations and expertise to work together. This network was composed of a core team for all retail activities established in Budapest, and an extended team of planners, engineers, and other staff located throughout the region.

While the challenge is to mobilize hidden manpower[21], there is a recognition that electronic collaboration has the potential to leverage this key resource[22,23]. However, it is as yet unclear as to how electronic collaboration can leverage knowledge resources. The contribution of this paper is two fold: first it identifies the reason why current knowledge management and Information Technology implementations remain problematical and second it provides concepts by which electronic collaboration can be used to harness and use knowledge resources towards joint effect. The first contribution is developed as a theoretical framework for the activation of knowledge. This framework provides the lens through which we examine how people in a multinational organization use and shape their use of collaborative technologies for knowledge sharing and use. The second contribution are findings from a case study of a multinational organization conducted to investigate this framework. These findings are "activation effects" and a mediating role for collaborative technologies that can be used to guide IT implementations to support knowledge management. The paper concludes with implications for practice and directions for future research.

2 A Framework for Knowledge Activation: Knowledge-as-Identity

Knowledge activation is the conversion of knowledge into action. Activating knowledge is about finding people with relevant knowledge and using it effectively through their willingness to provide, access and share it as and when needed. Activation, explains Galaskeiwicz[24], is being at the centre of resource networks. This gave people in the organisations that he studied, access to a greater number of other organisations that could provide them with the necessary resources. Because the likelihood of mobilizing resources is much greater for actors in the centre of social networks, they could more confidently engage the political process - the process of influencing other actors and mobilizing resources for collaborative initiatives. In addition, Knoke and Kulksinki[25] found that by cultivating diversified ties to large numbers of community organisations capable of supplying resources, a group's dependence on a single source can be significantly reduced. This suggests that activating knowledge can reduce an organization's dependence on a single set of experts or extend the organization's access to expertise from other organizations or communities.

The role of meaning, particularly the creation of shared meaning in organizations, takes us a long way towards understanding the translation of knowledge to purposeful action – hence activation. Theories of changing perceptions of stimuli[26], theories of personal knowledge creation[10] based upon tacit and explicit knowledge[27], and the processes of how to deal with these types of knowledge[28] suggest that there are multiple dimensions of knowledge. According to Duncan and Weiss[29] organizational learning consists of producing communicable, consensual and integrated knowledge. Organizational learning is often seen as an emergent, holistic process of sensemaking through the creation of mental models[17,30] or a distinct dynamic spiral[16]. Duncan and Weiss[29] suggest that although the individual is the only entity in the organization that can learn, this must be viewed as part of a system of learning with exchanges of what is learned among individuals. While these views do not make the identity of the individual explicit, they suggest that knowledge is perceptual and is created through the individual.

In this sense it is useful to visualize organizations as Lockean inquiring systems. Courtney *et al.*[31] suggest that inquiring organizations are learning organizations modeled on the theories of inquiring systems. They add that collective action in organizations needs to be based on valid knowledge. However, while an inquiring organization should ensure that its actions are based on valid knowledge, in many cases, the only reasonable guarantor is a Lockean type of consensus among its members. Interaction among individuals that are open to and may be influenced by external information brings about shared understanding. This shared meaning may lead to consensus and collective purposeful action. While these views do not make the identity of the individual explicit, they suggest that knowledge is perceptual and is created through the individual. This paper takes this notion a step further and suggests that learning is shaped by individual knowledge identities: this can be accountable and part of individuals' professional life, or discretionary that is theirs to share voluntarily, or autonomous knowledge that forms their private experience. The following Figure 1, illustrates the theoretical framework of Knowledge Activation that we investigate in this paper.

Knowledge is activated through networks of people. Such activation networks emerge through communities of practice[32], industrial networks[24] and social relationships[30] where knowledge, expertise and experiences are activated as and when needed. Knowledge produced by individuals is used when it becomes exchanged and accepted by others. This is *knowledge in action*. Knowledge in action is determined by the knowledge identities of individuals and the network in which their knowledge — tacit or explicit — is activated. In order to activate knowledge, there has to be a demand for it in the form of a request placed within an activation network. Once demand for action has been communicated, collaboration activates the knowledge identities needed for knowledge to be used in action. The three types of knowledge identities can be activated through collaboration.

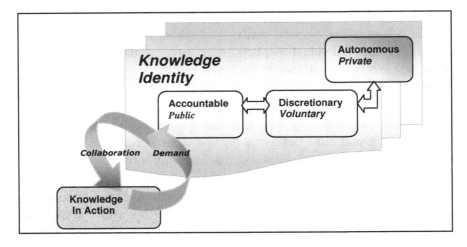

Figure 1. Theoretical Framework of Knowledge Activation

Accountable Knowledge is knowledge that is part of the public identity and responsibility of an individual, group or profession. Professionals are accountable for the building, use and sharing of knowledge, either as part of their professional identity or their formal position and role in the organization. Accountable knowledge is both role and domain-specific: A CPA, professor, or sales manager is accountable to the communities who recognize and draw on their public identity. Theories of organizational learning suggest various ways in which this knowledge identity may be enacted. According to Duncan and Weiss[29] organizational learning consists of producing communicable, consensual and integrated knowledge. Organizational learning is often seen as an emergent, holistic process of sensemaking through the creation of mental models[17,30] or a distinct dynamic spiral[16]. This builds upon Daft and Weick's[26] model of organizations as interpretation systems. Duncan and Weiss[29] suggest that although the individual is the only entity in the organization that can learn, this must be viewed as part of a system of learning with exchanges of what is learned among individuals.

Discretionary Knowledge is considered a gift to be presented voluntarily as there is no accountable responsibility to share it. The individual announces a willingness to do so and thus opens up his or her private identity and makes the knowledge part of public identity. The decision to contribute to a virtual community requiring discretionary knowledge is voluntary. It is activated through activation networks emerge through communities of practice[32,33], industrial networks[24] and social relationships[30] through which Lockean inquiring systems where knowledge, expertise and experiences are activated as and when needed.

Autonomous Knowledge is part of an individual's private identity and is not easily shared. This knowledge is both tacit and experiential and a decision to share it is highly personal. As it is core to one's sense of self and not easily recognized, it is depicted on the outer edge of Figure 1. It is mobilized – made active – in personal relationships, including friendships and mentoring, and in particular types of communities. The role of meaning, particularly the creation of shared meaning through communication of autonomous knowledge takes us a long way towards understanding the translation of knowledge to purposeful action – hence activation. Theories of changing perceptions of stimuli[26], theories of personal knowledge creation[10] based upon tacit and explicit knowledge[27], and the processes of how to deal with this type of knowledge. In addition, Boisot[34] suggests that there are multiple dimensions of such personal knowledge.

Collaboration is purposeful joint action through the construction of relevant meanings that are shared by members. Collaboration is needed to 1) determine what action is required and is relevant, 2) determine what knowledge is required to carry out the required action and 3) initiate demand for action. Together, these three aspects enable activation or the use of knowledge to create a joint product or service. In order for collaboration to take place, relevant knowledge must be communicated by members who take part in the networks. In order to support communication it is necessary not only to have proper media with which to communicate, but also a social network or "community of minds" whose members know one another and speak the same language[31]. Holsapple and Winston[35] add that as organizations will be increasingly regarded as joint human-computer knowledge processing systems, they will be viewed as societies of knowledge workers who are interconnected by computerized infrastructures.

Demand for action is the trigger that brings about the activation of knowledge. Activation of knowledge on demand depends upon the power of a particular request. Acquiring power through corporate networks is very much akin to Rosabeth Moss Kanter's[36] studies that illustrate how mobility of certain individuals between parts of organisations and to other organisations serves as a mechanism for building up the power of certain groups and individuals. Elements of cohesion within a network relative to that of another may provide an indication of the extent to which power and control is potentially exercised over the collective resources of a particular network. Sometimes, looking at the positions on the network may provide an indication of the type and level of authority that actors occupying certain positions possess. This suggests that demand for action has to be coupled with the authority to initiate activation or a legitimacy recognized by other members in the network.

In the following sections, an interpretive approach is used to investigate this framework of knowledge activation. Within this approach a case study is conducted to examine the above knowledge identities and the ways in which knowledge is activated. Data is collected in a multinational organization that relies on the knowledge of its employees to produce customized services for its customers. This data is analyzed using grounded theory techniques to uncover concepts within the three categories of knowledge identity.

3 Research Approach

This research follows an interpretivist approach to uncovering the phenomenon in question: knowledge activation. According to Klein and Myers[37] Information Systems (IS) research can be classified as interpretive if it is assumed that our knowledge of reality is gained through social constructions such a language, consciousness, shared meanings, documents, tools, and other artifacts. Interpretive methods of research in IS are "aimed at producing an understanding of the context of the information system, and the process whereby the information system influences and is influenced by the context"[38]. While there is a debate as to the extent to which the researcher should begin without any a priori understanding of the phenomenon being investigated, this research follows Klein and Myers's view that it is better to have some principles than none at all, since the absence of any criteria increases the risk that interpretive work will continue to be judged inappropriately. Strauss and Corbin[39] suggest that theoretical sensitivity is required to enable the researcher to interpret and define data and thus develop a theory that is grounded, conceptually dense and well integrated. Sources of theoretical sensitivity are the literature, professional and personal experience – all of which we draw upon in developing the knowledge activation framework. In building upon interpretive research, Orlikowski[40] provides a lens to examine how people, as they interact with technology, shape their use of that technology. We use the framework of knowledge activation as a lens to examine how people interact with collaborative technologies and shape their use of the technology.

Within this interpretive research approach, a case study was carried out to collect data. Our case study strategy followed a combination of Eisenhardt's theory building[41] and Weick's sensemaking[30] methods. We began with: 1) a definition of the knowledge activation concepts we wanted to research (as described above), 2) selected a case in which dispersed knowledge was activated to achieve joint objectives, 3) developed multiple data collection techniques, 4) entered the field and collected the data, 5) analyzed the data, 6) shaped our concepts, and 7) compared our results with similar literature to sharpen the concepts. This was an iterative process that was tightly linked to the data. Data was gathered through interviews, observations and electronic transcripts of newsgroup and community interaction. In order to triangulate our data, a usability survey was also conducted to evaluate the users of collaborative technologies for knowledge sharing. This survey evaluated employee satisfaction with respect to information provision, the communication and collaboration facilities available through the company's intranet.

The transcript and interview data was analyzed using grounded theory techniques developed by Strauss and Corbin[39]. Theoretical sampling was used to select the transcript and interview data. Theoretical sampling is sampling of data on the basis of concepts that have proven theoretical relevance to the evolving theory. The concepts with proven theoretical relevance were identified in the interviews and transcripts of electronic collaboration using the open coding technique. Open coding is conceptualizing raw data by naming and categorizing the phenomena through close examination of the data. During open coding, data were broken down into discrete parts, closely examined and compared for similarities and differences. Events, happenings, actions and interactions that were found to be conceptually similar in nature or related in meaning were grouped under abstract concepts. We termed these abstract concepts "activation effects". The activation effects were classified into the thee categories of knowledge identity. The following sections describe the background and findings from the case study, the activation effects within the knowledge identity categories and the relationships that were discovered. The analysis also includes comparisons with similar literature to sharpen the concepts.

4   Case Study: Knowledge Activation at Galaxy Corporation

The case chosen to investigate Knowledge Activation is a multi-national information technology and business services organization that is the result of a merger. In order to protect its privacy, we call this merged company Galaxy Corporation and its two separate merged entities Starnet and Global Consultancy. The concept of an intelligent enterprise rings true to Galaxy Corporation as it provides customized services by selling the skills and intellects of its key professionals. The merged organization, Galaxy Corporation is referred to in the rest of this paper as Galaxy. By June of 2001 Galaxy had close to 60,000 employees across the world and had a significant presence in 20 countries in Europe, the USA and in Asia. Its businesses included management consulting, information technology consulting, systems integration, software development, outsourcing and training.

This case is particularly appropriate for a study of knowledge activation through the use of electronic collaboration because an elaborate suite of collaborative technologies have been made available on the company's intranet for the purpose of sharing knowledge. The information and communication facilities available on Galaxy's intranet are the Knowledgebank, which is a database of documents and other information, email, newsgroups and homepages relating to various functions, units and training programs. This is not a standard intranet application as more sophisticated tools are available, such as the Knowledge Marketplace, Virtual Rooms, and My Galaxy. In addition, Sibylle is a sophisticated natural language query tool available to all the Galaxy Corporation consultants. Consultants can make My Galaxy fit their personal information and communication needs by customizing every function that is available on My Galaxy. The appropriation of this technology leads to the emergence of very personalized workspaces. Consultants make their own selection of on line newspapers (a few are standard), own newsgroups, Internet and Intranet sites and choice of communication and collaboration tools. Once consultants have configured My Galaxy, they can work at any place, at any time, on any computer in the world (an Internet connection is all that is needed to find their galaxy). The configuration of each personalized workspace is stored on the My Galaxy central server.

5 Findings

The results are derived from data collected just prior to and after the merger of Starnet and Global Consultancy into Galaxy Corporation; the data was collected over a period of one and a half years. The results reported here derive from open interviews, observations and transcripts of electronic collaboration. A usability survey conducted in by Galaxy, prior to the merger with Global Consultancy is used to triangulate our findings. At the time our data was collected, 40% of the organization's budget had been spent on the IT infrastructure described above and the organization was facing the knowledge paradox. This illustrated in the following quote from an open interview with a consultant and project coordinator at Galaxy Corporation:

> The biggest [knowledge management] problem has to do with the resistance in the organization to share knowledge. This is because knowledge sharing is about putting a price on knowledge. A consultant who leaves to work for a competitor, takes to the competitor important and sensitive information. There is also resistance because consultants are paid according to their performance. Putting a price to their knowledge means that other consultants can have the benefit of this acquired

knowledge and turn it around so that they can earn more money at the cost of the consultant who created the knowledge. This means that we need a more appropriate performance appraisal structure. [...] The next problem is to make time after a successful project to share the acquired knowledge. Time needs to be given and taken to make the knowledge explicit and to file into the knowledgebank.

In order to examine this knowledge paradox using the knowledge activation framework, the data collected was organized into conceptual categories and further refined using open coding. The main types of collaborative effort that emerged from coding the transcripts are categorized into activation effects. These are the existence of *shared spaces* and *support* for the activation of accountable knowledge, *reciprocity* and *relationship* are needed to activate discretionary knowledge and the existence of *trust* and *personalization* are required to activate autonomous knowledge. The following sections describe these results by providing direct quotes to support the theoretical categories described and provide comparisons with similar literature to refine them.

5.1 *Activation of accountable knowledge*

Accountable knowledge is activated because there is demand for action. Consultants within Galaxy Corporation have to develop and deliver customized solutions for clients problems. The development of such products or solutions takes place in teams with members from different disciplines that bring to bear their experiential and explicit knowledge for which they are accountable. Such teams may often include people from the client organization. In order to deliver customized products and solutions, the consultants of Galaxy Corporation must be able to work with each other as well as with the employees of their clients. This is consistent with Ruppel and Harrington's findings[6] that suggest that organizational culture and work practices are a factor in the adoption and implementation of intranets. The advantage of using such network technologies is that they allow new knowledge to be combined with existing information to generate and systematize knowledge throughout the organization[10].

Within My Galaxy is the Virtual Project Room. This is a tool for electronic collaboration which enables accountable knowledge to be activated every time there is demand for action. The following example illustrates this: Alan is working in a project for a client organization. There is demand for his action as software developed within this project will be used in five other organizations also involved in this project. The project members from Galaxy Corporation are working from several different places and hold information and knowledge relevant and critical to the success of this project. Their knowledge needs to be activated through communication and collaboration. The Virtual Project Room is used to activate, share and develop knowledge on this project. Figure 2 illustrates how accountable knowledge is activated by Alan who is working at home using the Virtual Project Room.

Alan is working at home today because he has to write a final report. When he starts in the morning he logs in at his Virtual Project Room to check the latest news and download a draft of the final report he started on yesterday. He finds the latest news on the program dashboard and finds his document in the developing work stream. He downloads the document on which his colleagues have been working and begins finalizing it. At the beginning of the afternoon he has some queries about the data in the report and he posts these in a note on his work stream. Within half an hour one of his colleagues responds with a review of the data in a new note. Alan does not understand the review and starts a NetMeeting session with this colleague. On-line the consultants discuss the data, the review and come to a solution. At the end of the afternoon Alan puts the finalized document back in the virtual office so that the other members of the project can read and review the document. It is especially important that the project members who are part of the client organization read it. In this way, Alan feels that he has been able to work more effectively at a distance.

Figure 2. Activation of Accountable Knowledge

In the space provided by the Virtual Project Room information on projects and status is shared. Consultants and the members of Galaxy Corporation's client organization can use different levels of functionality within the Virtual Project site. The project manager or consultant responsible for the project ensures that all the necessary information is visible at the top project level. In order to activate accountable knowledge shared spaces and support are needed. These are described in the following sections.

5.1.1 *Shared spaces*

In order to activate accountable knowledge, shared spaces are needed through which different project members can communicate and create shared understanding. Virtual Office (VO) is an electronic shared space used by Galaxy's professionals who work on large projects that span a number of different sites. VO is a web-enabled communication tool accessible at the project level and is combined with My Galaxy. The VO contains several levels of information relating to the project(s) being undertaken, work-packages or work-streams, and personal information relating to participants within projects. A special project administrator compiles a list of members on the project. These may be Galaxy's professionals and also members of the Galaxy's client organizations. They all receive an identification and a password in order to access this facility through the intranet and post information. The results of the usability survey suggest that 78% of the respondents agreed that the intranet "is a good means of communication". The rest of the respondents did not agree with this statement: 10% of the respondents said they were unsure and 12.4% disagreed. It is interesting to note that about 30% of the respondents had been employed for less than two years. The following quotes from a newsgroup discussion illustrates the use of shared spaces at Galaxy: Such shared spaces form the boundary objects that mediate differences between the consultants. Qureshi *et al.*[42] found that such electronic spaces enable the accommodation of different perspectives to take place. This is consistent with Inkpen and Dinur's findings[43] in that intranets facilitate communication and interaction and create a *knowledge connection.*

5.1.2 *Support*

A person's accountable knowledge can be activated by a number of different people, or organizations demanding action. The exchange of information and social support took place through the newsgroups, among other face to face and phone interactions. However, the newsgroups were used by 44.6% of the respondents to communicate needs and share information. According to the usability survey, 78% of the respondents said they preferred to search for the information that they need (using Sibylle) and read the newspages/newsfeeds. This suggests that updating accountable knowledge had high priority. Information exchange was seen to support the work of geographically dispersed employees. It is interesting to note that only 8% of the employees stated that they used the Knowledgebank. The electronic news desk, the FTP site and the division and unit pages rate higher (average 6.8 out of 10) than the other information and communication tools. Accountable knowledge is updated through several information ordering tools known as news, notes, files/documents, events, activity/to do list and forums. These findings are consistent with El-Shinnawy and Markus[44] in that media features of functionality, usability and ease of use were found to have a major influence on media choice. Blanchard and Markus[45] suggest a feeling of belonging is important in a virtual community. They found that while support was an important part of the community, it was informational and not social (and emotional) support that was considered most important. It appears that it is informational support that enables accountable knowledge to remain updated.

5.2 *Activation of discretionary knowledge*

When accountable knowledge is not sufficient to satisfy a demand for action, discretionary knowledge is activated. This is why the division and unit homepages are more often accessed in comparison to the other facilities. According to a survey carried out of Galaxy's employees, 70% of the respondents use the homepages frequently compared to 61.5% use email frequently, 44.6% use the newsgroups frequently and only 19.8% used the Knowledgebank frequently. Only 10% of the employees stated that they had trouble sharing knowledge. The rest did so regularly in various ways. One popular site for sharing knowledge (not available at the time of Starnet's survey) was the Knowledge Marketplace where consultants would put up a question relating to a specific problem they experienced in the project that they were working on. Often the answer to such problems lie in experiential, and personalized knowledge held by various members of the organization but not necessarily related to their job description. The Knowledge Marketplace was a site on Galaxy corporation's intranet that contained spaces marked by icons that looked like stalls. Each stall was facilitated by one or two consultants in their area on interest but not necessarily expertise. An example of such a stall was "data dictionaries". As expertise was not evenly distributed in the organization, people needed to tap into each other's expertise that was distributed across the organization. While the existence of this social network was known, it was not clear who should be contacted for particular questions not answered through known experts. The Knowledge Marketplace harnessed this social network and enabled it to be activated. This tool mediated the knowledge sharing activities by connecting people with their world of objects/expertise and also with other people (Sherry and Meyers 1998, Engeström *et al.* 1995). A shared vocabulary emerged on this tool and interaction was mediated through a set of norms and rules.

Activation of discretionary knowledge through the Knowledge Marketplace took place as consultants would post questions specific to the topic of the stall. The answer would be given by any consultant, at their own discretion, who was able to provide an answer to the question. When someone posted a question or an answer was put on the market spot, the consultant whose market spot had been queried then received an email notification. An example is Martin, a Galaxy consultant, who working at a client site, is looking for a search engine for searching in directories and CD Roms for special documents. To find an answer he logs in through the Internet to the Galaxy Corporation's Knowledge Marketplace and asks his question. Figure 3 illustrates how the Knowledge Marketplace is used to activate discretionary knowledge.

As a result of the above interaction on the Knowledge Marketplace, Martin decides to contact Janis by telephone. They discuss the matter, the options available to him and possible courses of action he can take. In the end Martin is able to follow an informed course of action based on his assessment of the information exchange that has taken place. The activation effects that were identified from such interactions on the Knowledge Marketplace are discussed in the following sections.

> Martin: "I am looking for a standard software component with which you can search through documents with several formats (Word, Powerpoint, etc.). The documents are on a CD Rom so the search engine must be server independent. It must be simple and straightforward."
>
> Alan: "You can use Alta Vista, freeware for searching and indexing documents. Works specially for Word and Powerpoint. Within our group we have very good experience with the tool."
>
> Peter: "You can use MS Index Server for building an automatic index"
>
> Janis: "MS Index Server does not work with cd-rom. You have to think about ActiveX control as a plug in , in your browser for making an index. That is a lot of work. Other possibilities you find on www.progressivelogic.se, www.netresults-search.com or www.astaware.com."
>
> Sandra: "MS Index server can not be used with cd-rom. Another solution is verity, but that is very expensive. "

Figure 3. Activation of Discretionary Knowledge in the Knowledge Marketplace

5.2.1 *Reciprocity*

Participants who had received answers to their queries through the knowledge marketplace were required to reciprocate when they had answers to or knew how to arrive at answers to questions posted on the market spot from which they had received assistance. The knowledge market place was seen to be a serious space on which no idle chats were allowed. The shared spaces on the knowledge market place were divided into consultant-defined subjects known as "market spots." A consultant known as the "midwife" was the facilitator responsible for managing their assigned market spot or "the maternity ward." This facilitator is responsible for ensuring that the facility is used to share relevant information. In addition, expectations of almost immediate response have also become a reality.

This pattern of interaction is consistent with Burgoon *et al.*[46] who found that successful outcomes in computer mediated group communication were related to higher levels of interactivity. They found processes of mutuality and involvement to be significant in effecting task outcomes. Partners perceived as more involved were judged as more credible and attractive to work with. Mutuality was also positively associated with credibility and attraction. The more participants felt that their partners were similar to them, the more they rated the partner as reliable, useful, friendly, dominant, trustworthy and attractive to work with. This suggests that in order to activate discretionary knowledge, reciprocal collaborative relationships need to be facilitated by fostering involvement and mutuality. In addition, virtual teams benefit from the presence of caretakers whose sole contribution is to support regular, detailed and prompt communication, as well as identifying individual role relationship and responsibilities[47].

5.2.2 *Relationship*

There was an extent to which the creation of relationships among participants had become an integral part of the practice. The activation network was particularly powerful: consultants from very different parts of Galaxy corporation found out about each other through interacting on the Knowledge Marketplace. As a result, they were able to work together on projects that they would otherwise have not been able to. The activation network developed as a result of interactions using the collaborative technologies has meant that consultants had free access to each others' expertise. They were no longer bound by organizational walls (departments, divisions) and or restricted to working on projects that fell within their own departments. As the identities of the participants in the Knowledge Marketplace was defined by their action, short biodatas of the facilitators of each stall were described in each market spot.

The consultants who shared their experiential and often tacit knowledge at their discretion with strangers within their organization, tended to meet up with each other in a café or over the phone hence developing relationships with each other. Powell *et al.*[47] suggest that if it is feasible for members to meet physically meet, these should focus on relationship building. Otherwise facilitating socialization through chat sessions or increased social communication can stimulate relationship building. Robey *et al.*[48] found that electronic communication improved social and emotional relations among workers in remote locations. They even found that a degree of intimacy was achieved with remote communication that spanned functional, geographic and cultural divides.

It appears that even though relationships tend to develop through the initial activation of discretionary during electronic collaboration, activation of discretionary knowledge also requires the existence of more ongoing relationships.

5.3 *Activation of autonomous knowledge*

Working with clients requires a great deal of personal input. In order to work well with their clients consultants need to draw upon their personal experiences often delving into their private identities. The key mediating tools for activating autonomous knowledge were email, mobile phone and the newsgroups on the intranet. Collaboration with clients was seen to be a legitimate way of working while the extent to which there was collaboration among employees varied between units. From the transcripts of interactions in the Newsgroups, it is clear that a repertoire of technical jargon used in the consultants' work environments was also being used in the electronic spaces. Shared communication was mostly related to software and technical system development issues. In this process, private autonomous knowledge was brought into the collaborative arena. The use of collaborative technologies did enable conversations with new kinds of properties to emerge (Schrage 1990). Ideas that would have remained part of an individual's personal repertoire of knowledge, became both external and manipulatable. People were able to create icons and textual imagery to represent ideas and concepts which others could modify or manipulate until they become both community property and a visual part of the conversation. According to Blanchard and Markus[45], the affective bonds that differentiate between neighborhoods and true communities is "sense of community". In their study of a virtual community, Blanchard and Markus[45] found three processes by which sense of community was reinforced: 1) exchange of information and socio-emotional support, 2) creating identities for themselves and creating identifications of others and 3) the production of trust. This suggests that activating autonomous knowledge implies a sense of community. This creation of sense of community is illustrated in the following Figure 4:

JM: Who can help me find a product comparison of UML Modeling tools?

WL: Have you looked on the Gartner Group (www.gartner.com ?) site and searched Sibylle ?

PH: Some good alternatives are GDPro reviewed by SD Magazine. http://www.sdmagazine.com/articles/2000/0002/0002j/0002j.htm Or TogetherJ, which you can try at: http://www.togethersoft.com/together/togetherJ.html

DS: Has anyone got templates of procedure handbooks for the management of Intranet content (BBCM)? Any information on the set up and management of content ?

EL: At Warp11 we are busy putting together a handbook. Come and see us at our office and you can browse through a draft version.

Figure 4. Activating Autonomous Knowledge in the Newsgroups

Activating autonomous knowledge in the newsgroups was done by posting questions in exchange for information or support. Identities emerged through interactions on the newsgroups. Given the amount of personal knowledge that was being exchanged, it appears that trust was in the making. Such virtual interactions have expanded to off-line interactions and have become part of the life of the community. The activation effects identified for activating autonomous knowledge are discussed in the following sections.

5.3.1 *Trust*

Community members expose their personal feelings and share private knowledge if they trust other members of their community. The collaborative technologies were set up to support that principle by stimulating two way communication rather than top-down communication. However, according to the survey results, only 25% of the employees felt that through My Galaxy they are "masters of their own destiny". Although the organizational culture at Galaxy Corporation is open, consultants do like to keep important knowledge and information to themselves. The reason for this is if particular business development or information system development techniques are made available electronically, the main concern is, how will they be used? The integrity of information and appropriate use by other consultants are seen to be very important.

There is however, sharing of knowledge on the newsgroups and knowledge marketplace. It has been suggested that high levels of trust and cohesiveness reduce barriers to communication in virtual teams and are instrumental in promoting cooperation[49]. Perceptions of members' benevolence and integrity are important in the development and maintenance of trust. It follows that the perception of trust has an important effect in activating autonomous knowledge.

5.3.2 *Personalization*

Flexibility in the use of collaborative and information technologies to personalize individual work environments is important not only for activating autonomous knowledge but also for bringing it into the collaborative arena. Because of the merger, Galaxy Corporation's accepted work practices were in a state of dynamic redefinition. Collaboration through discussion groups, face to face team working and even simple telephone conversations are seen to be paramount. Individual consultants would personalize a project site for themselves where they would put personal activities, files, their personal address book and links to sites and newsgroups they used. In this way all project members were able to manage their own projects and could still be part of several projects. Different consultants worked in one or several work streams at the same time, and had access to the work streams in which they participated and to all the related information modules, contained in files, notes, news for their own stream. They would activate each others' knowledge and develop it using various discussion tools and email. In developing upon each other's ideas, consultants were able to be more creative and apply themselves to more innovative types of projects. The following quote from an interview with a consultant and project coordinator illustrates this:

> Knowledge (tacit) is created within the units/divisions, from research or experiences with clients. This knowledge is spread within the unit informally as "real knowledge can be found at

the coffee corner". If this knowledge has proven to have sufficient value, it is used in projects carried out at clients.

Situated learning or learning by doing takes place in communities of practice where a sense of belonging and common interests have developed over time[33]. A community that develops is own organizational memory, serves the organization by encouraging learning and creativity without stifling emergent ideas[50]. This suggests that personalized work environments are conducive to the activation of autonomous knowledge as they enable knowledge to be channeled towards more creative and innovative projects.

6 Analysis: Processes of Knowledge Activation

From the above analysis it appears that electronic collaboration has a *mediating effect* in the activation of knowledge. Collaborative technologies mediate activities carried out by different people with different levels of expertise and understanding who work in very different contexts. The process of collaborating electronically spans multiple boundaries[51] and activities[52]. The use of electronic collaboration technologies has made it possible in this study to harness intellectual resources across space and time. Yet the technology is only a part of the development and maintenance of the activation networks. These powerful networks are social and community based. As stated by one consultant "You cannot do everything through this contraption [My Galaxy and the Virtual Project Room] !!". Consultants feel that even though they may not relay on the collaborative technologies, electronic collaboration has meant that they can move through the organization more freely and innovative hybrid projects have become more commonplace. We know that the role of electronic communications to leverage networks of people in decision-making and innovation is a growing theme in research[53,54] and practice[23,55]. We have found as a result of this research that electronic collaboration mediates the activation of knowledge identities. This is illustrated in the following Figure 5:

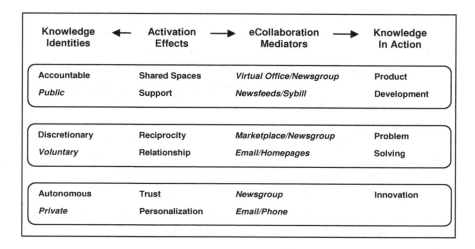

Figure 5. Processes by which Knowledge is Activated

The case studied in this paper illustrates that the activation of knowledge identities and their appropriate activation effects, the knowledge paradox can be overcome. In this, the role of electronic collaboration is to bridge boundaries through mediating collaborative technologies. For accountable knowledge to be exchanged, the meanings have to be the same in the minds of the receiver and communicator. Shared spaces that enable different perceptions of meaning to be exchanged are required. Electronic collaboration technologies such as the Virtual Office provides the spaces upon which shared understanding can develop and accountable knowledge activated on demand. But it is information support provided by the electronic media that enables accountable knowledge to remain updated. Once activated through these effects, mediated by the Virtual Office suite, news feeds and intelligent searches, accountable knowledge is best suited to actions in which the deliverables are distinct such as the development of products.

Discretionary knowledge is exchanged and activated through voluntary participation. The activation effects needed to activate discretionary knowledge are reciprocity in interactions mediated not only through technology but also a facilitator who sets and moderates rules of engagement. Collaborative tools for reciprocity are those that develop interactivity by fostering involvement and mutuality such as the Knowledge Marketplace described in this paper. The emergence of relationships through electronic collaboration appears to be an outcome of the activation of discretionary knowledge. Yet the activation of discretionary knowledge also requires relationship building to be successful. The discussion boards on the Knowledge Marketplace and homepages can enable relationships to built upon the identification of individual interests. Discretionary knowledge appears to best serve action where multiple alternatives are discussed in problem solving situations.

Autonomous knowledge forms the private and personal identity of an individual. The activation effects for bringing autonomous knowledge into action are the existence of trust whereby the risk of sharing aspects of one's private identity with the community is minimal. The flexibility with which collaborative technologies may be used to share aspects of an individual's personal identity effects the extent to which autonomous knowledge can be activated. It appears that the personalization of work environments and the flexibility with which collaborative technologies support this, enable autonomous knowledge to be activated in creative interactions. Together with the learning that may take place in communities of practice, these activation effects suggest that autonomous knowledge is particularly valuable in hybrid projects that entail innovation.

7 Implications for IT Transformation in Organizations

This chapter suggests that the knowledge paradox can be overcome if knowledge identities and their activation conditions are matched with appropriate collaboration technology infrastructures. The opportunity for traditional practice is a focus on accountable knowledge through the creation of shared spaces that are structured according to the skills sets being supported. Here, any effort to codify knowledge will have organizational legitimacy and personal validity. The implications of this research for knowledge management practice attempted to harness tacit and personalized knowledge are that any effort to "package" knowledge resources and access tools is likely to fail in mobilizing the precious and personally valued discretionary and autonomous knowledge. Our analysis points to the view that building knowledge communities should be the primary basis for management but adds an additional dimension; within any community, "knowledge" is not homogenous. Individuals have their own implicit sense of personal identity. In our view, the highly public nature of most tools for electronic collaboration overlook this; they build an open and generic forum for communication and assume that the members of the targeted community will make use of it. In view of this, we provide the following guidelines for overcoming the knowledge paradox:

1. *Develop reliable structures and consistent protocols to support accountable knowledge.* These communication protocols are needed when developing business processes and technology infrastructures.
2. *Support multiple skill sets within well structured closed spaces that are shared.* The key to activating accountable knowledge is in structuring rich content and ease of use. It should be easy to enter a shared space and be supported – knowledge is shared power.
3. *Provide mechanisms to make it convenient to engage in activation networks.* It should be possible to meet one's responsibility via an activation network that provides the technical, informational and social support. Accountable knowledge mainly requires activation networks that change the marginal economics of effort in offering and using knowledge. The decision to be part of an activation network is a decision about how much of one's private identity to make part of a public identity.
4. *Design for reciprocity and interactivity to support discretionary knowledge.* A collaboration system enables community to emerge if there is demand and supply for knowledge or any of its products.
5. *Provide formal and informal incentives for mobilizing discretionary knowledge.* Relationship building is needed before intranets can be used by experts who are normally unwilling to become a free help desk for colleagues with lesser skills and experience. The personal costs of effort and time to keep the knowledge resource base updated is too high to make it worthwhile.

6. *Provide individual toolkits and allow personalized spaces to evolve.*
Autonomous knowledge can be brought into the collaborative space
if there is flexibility and independence from authority. Incorporate
personal tools open spaces and use new media to provide more
choices in the design of spaces.

Our perspective on knowledge-as-identity has the following implications
for overcoming the knowledge paradox: First and perhaps most
importantly it defines knowledge as part of the person and thus highly
situational. Second, the knowledge management challenge is to activate
knowledge via networks. Third, knowledge management will move
towards achieving its goals by recognizing the need for multiple
activation networks based on the link between knowledge identities and
"signing up" as a member. All of us have accountable, discretionary and
autonomous knowledge. The very same knowledge may have entirely
different activation features depending on one's identity. Finally, *people*
determine knowledge in action.

8 Conclusions, Lessons Learned and Future Directions

This research defines and develops a theoretical framework of knowledge
activation. This adds to the knowledge management literature by
developing a notion of knowledge-as-identity that is brought into action
through activation effects. The mediating role of electronic collaboration in
activating knowledge is an important one. The analysis of the case studied
in this paper suggests that by mediating the activation effects needed
to bring knowledge into action, electronic collaboration enables the
knowledge paradox to be overcome. By mediating the existence of
shared spaces and information support, electronic collaboration enables
accountable knowledge to be activated. By capturing communities of
practice in which reciprocity and relationships develop, electronic
collaboration enables discretionary knowledge to be activated. Electronic
collaboration may also enable the personalization of work environments
and the maintenance of trust. When the activation effects are in place,
autonomous knowledge can be brought into action in creative hybrid
projects. This perspective of electronic collaboration has implications for

the activation of dispersed knowledge for the creation of customised, goods and services. Collaborative technology support must match the activation effects if it is to mediate the activation of knowledge into action.

Lessons learned from this research are that collaborative technology mediators cannot be matched directly to the activation effects discussed in this paper. This is because the same technology, such as the newsgroups, can be used to activate more than one knowledge identity. It appears that it is the demand for action and cohesion of the groups using a particular technology that determine its success in activating knowledge. Further research in the field should be carried out to assess the activation effects using multiple collaborative technologies.

References

1. Bechky, B. Sharing meaning Across Occupational Communities: The Transformation of Understanding on a Production Floor. *Organization Science*, 14(3), 2003, pp. 312-330.
2. Cramton, C.D. The mutual knowledge problem and its consequences for dispersed collaboration. *Organization Science*, 12(3), 2001, pp. 346-371.
3. Kean, T.H., Hamilton, L.H., Ben-Veniste, R., Kerrey, B., Fielding, F.F., Lehman, J. F., Gorelick, J.S., Roemer, T.J., Gorton, S. and Thompson, J.R. Final Report of the National Commission on Terrorist Attacks Upon the United States executive summary. http://www.gpoaccess.gov/911/index.html. July 22, 2004.
4. Zack, M. Managing Codified Knowledge. *Sloan Management Review*, 40(4), 1999, pp. 45-58.
5. Hansen, M.T., Nohria, N. and Tierney, T. What's your Strategy for Managing Knowledge? *Harvard Business Review*, March-April, 1999, pp. 106-116.
6. Ruppel, C.P. and Harrington, S. Sharing Knowledge Through Intranets: A Study of Organizational Culture and Intranet Implementation. *IEEE Transactions on Professional Communication*, 4(1), 2001, pp. 37-52.
7. Kownslar, S. Collaborative Commerce. *ACM Ubiquity*. Retrieved 23 February 2004. http://www.acm.org/ubiquity/views/s_kownslar_1.html
8. Alexander, S. Collaborative Commerce. *ComputerWorld*. July 2000. http://www.computerworld.com/softwaretopics/software/story/0,10801,46547,00.html
9. Quinn, J.B. *Intelligent Enterprise*. Free Press. New York. 1992.
10. Nonaka, I. and Takeuchi, H. *The Knowledge Creating Company*. Oxford University Press. Oxford. 1995.
11. Hibbard, J. and Carillo, K.M. Knowledge Revolution – Getting employees to share what they know is no longer a technology challenge – it's a corporate culture challenge. *InformationWeek*, 663, 1998, pp. 49-54.

12. Davenport, T.H., Jarvenpaa, S.L. and Beers, M. Improving Knowledge Work Processes. *Sloan Management Review*, Summer, 1996, pp. 53-65.

13. Powell, W.W. Neither market nor hierarchy: network forms of organization. In: G. Thompson, J. Frances, R. Levacic and J. Mitchell (Eds.), *Markets, Hierarchies and Networks: The Coordination of Social Life*. Sage. London. 1991.

14. Barnard, C. *The Function of the Executive*. Harvard University Press. Cambridge. 1938.

15. Williamson, O. *Organization Theory*. Oxford University Press. 1995.

16. Argyris, C.D. and Schoen, D.A. *Organizational Learning: A Theory of Action Perspective*. Addison-Wesley. London. 1978.

17. Senge, P.M. *The Fifth Discipline: The Age and Practice of the Learning Organization*. Century Business. London. 1990.

18. Stewart, T.A. *Intellectual Capital: The New Wealth of Organizations*. Currency Doubleday. 1997.

19. Drucker, P. The Coming of the New Organisation. *Harvard Business Review*, January-February, 1988, pp. 45-53.

20. Qureshi, S. and Vogel, D. Organizational Adaptiveness in Virtual Teams. *Group Decision and Negotiation*, 10(1), 2001, pp. 27-46.

21. Eom, B.S. and Lee, C.K. Virtual Teams: An Information Age Opportunity for Mobilizing Hidden Manpower. *SAM Advanced Management Journal*, Spring, 1999, pp. 12-15.

22. Schrage, M. *Shared Minds: The New Technologies of Collaboration*. Random House. New York. 1990.

23. Lea, M., O'Shea, T. and Fung, P. Constructing the Network Organization: Content and Context in the Development of Electronic Communications. *Organization Science*, 6(4), 1995, pp. 462-478.

24. Galaskiewicz, J. *Exchange Networks and Community Politics*. Sage Publications. London. 1979.

25. Knoke, D. and Kulksinki, J.H. Network Analysis: Basic Concepts. In: G. Thompson, J. Frances, R. Levacic and J. Mitchell (Eds.), *Markets, Hierarchies and Networks: The Coordination of Social Life*. Sage. London. 1991.

26. Daft, R.L. and Weick, K.E. Toward a model of organizations as interpretation systems. *Academy of Management Review*, 9, 1984, pp. 284-295.

27. Polanyi, M. *The Tacit Dimension*. Routledge and Kegan Paul. London. 1966.

28. Boisot, M. *Knowledge Assets*. Oxford University Press. Oxford. 1998.

29. Duncan, R. and Weiss, A. Organizational learning: Implications for organizational design. In: B. Straw, L.L. Cummings (Eds.), *Research in Organizational Behavior*, Vol. 1, pp. 75-132. JAI. Greenwich. 1979.

30. Weick, K.E. Theory Building as Disciplined Imagination. *Academy of Management Review*, 14(2), 1989, pp. 516-531.

31. Courtney, J.F., Croasdell, D.T. and Paradice, D.B. Inquiring Organizations. *Australian Journal of Information Systems*, 6(1), 1998, pp. 3-15.

32. Wenger, E. *Communities of Practice: Learning, Meaning and Identity.* Cambridge University Press. Cambridge. 1998.

33. Lave, J. and Wenger, E. *Situated Learning. Legitimate Peripheral Participation.* Cambridge University Press. Cambridge. 1991.

34. Boisot, M. *Knowledge Assets.* Oxford University Press. Oxford. 1998.

35. Holsapple, C.W. and Whinston, A.B. Knowledge-based Organizations. *Information Society*, 2, 1987, pp. 77-89.

36. Kanter, R.M. *The Change Masters.* Unwin. New York. 1983.

37. Klein, H.K. and Myers, Michael D. A Set of Principles for Conducting and Evaluating Interpretive Field Studies in Information Systems. *MIS Quarterly, Special Issue on Intensive Research*, 23(1), 1999, pp. 67-93.

38. Walsham, G. The Emergence of Intrepretism in IS Research. *Information Systems Research*, 6(4), 1995, pp. 376-394.

39. Strauss, A. and Corbin, J. *Basics of Qualitative Research: Techniques and Procedures for Developing Grounded Theory.* Sage. Thousand Oaks, London. 1990.

40. Orlikowski, W.J. Using Technology and Constituting Structures: A Practice Lens for Studying Technology in Organizations. *Organization Science*, 11(4), 2000, pp. 404-428.

41. Eisenhardt, K. Building Theories from Case Study Research. *Academy of Management Review*, 14(4), 1989, pp. 532-550.

42. Qureshi, S., Bogenrieder, I. and Kumar, K. Managing Participative Diversity in Virtual Teams: Requirement for Collaborative Technology Support. In: R. Sprague and J. Nunamaker (Eds.), *The Thirty Third Hawaii International Conference in Systems Sciences.* IEEE Computer Society Press. 2000.

43. Inkpen, A.C. and Dinur, A. Knowledge Management Processes and International Joint Ventures. *Organization Science*, 9(4), 1998, pp. 454-468.

44. El-Shinnawy, M. and Markus, L. Acceptance of Communications Media in Organizations: Richness or Features? *IEEE Transactions on Professional Communication*, 41(4), 1998, pp. 242-253.

45. Blanchard, A.L. and Markus, M.L. The Experienced "Sense" of a Virtual Community: Characteristics and Processes. *The DATA BASE for Advances in Information Systems*, 35(1), 2004, pp. 65-79.

46. Burgoon, J., Bonito, J.A., Bengtsson, B., Ramirez, A., Dunbar, N. and Miczo, N. Testing the Interactivity Model: Communication Processes, Partner Assessments, and the Quality of Collaborative Work. *Journal of Management Information Systems*, 16(3), 2000, pp. 33-56.

47. Powell, A., Piccoli, G. and Ives, B. Virtual Teams: A Review of Current Literature and Directions for Future Research. *The Database for Advances in Information Systems*, 35(1), 2004, pp. 6-36.

48. Robey, D., Khoo, H.M. and Powers, C. Situated Learning in Cross Functional Virtual Teams. *IEEE Transactions on Professional Communication*, 42(1), 2000, pp. 51-66.

49. Jarvenpaa, S., Knoll, K. and Leidner, D. Antecedents of Trust in Global Teams. *Journal of MIS*, 14(4), 1998, pp. 29-64.

50. Morrison, J., Morrison, M. and Vogel, D. Software to Support Business Teams. *Group Decision and Negotiation*, September, 1992, pp. 91-115.

51. Engeström, Y., Engeström, R. and Kärkkäinen, M. Polycontextuality and Boundary Crossing in Expert Cognition: Learning and Problem Solving in Complex Work Activities. *Learning and Instruction*, 5, 1995, pp. 319-336.

52. Sherry, L. and Myers, K. The Dynamics of Collaborative Design. *IEEE Transactions on Professional Communication*, 41(2), 1998, pp. 123-139.

53. Fulk, J. and DeSanctis, G. Electronic Communication for Changing Organizational Forms. *Organisation Science*, 6(4), 1995, pp. 337-349.

54. DeSanctis, G. and Monge, P. Communication processes for virtual organizations. *Journal of Computer Mediated Communication*, 3(4), 1998, pp. 1-21.

55. Charan, R. How Networks Reshape Organizations for Results. *Harvard Business Review*, September-October, 1991, pp. 104-115.

CHAPTER 10

Ecological Models of Inter-Organizational Routines in Electronic Commerce

Brian T. Pentland
Department of Accounting and Information Systems
Michigan State University
E. Lansing, Michigan 48824-1122, USA
Email: pentland@bus.msu.edu

1 Introduction

Using organizational ecology as a starting point, this paper outlines a framework for studying the ecology of inter-organizational routines in e-commerce. From this perspective, the adoption of e-commerce technology can be viewed as a population level phenomenon, rather than a firm level phenomenon. This framework provides an alternative vocabulary for explaining the prevalence and impact of net-based technologies, such as electronic auctions and web services, that are intended to facilitate the "net enabled" firm.[1] Net-enabled organizations use net-based technologies to support internal operations, as well as their relationships and transactions with customers, suppliers, and other organizations. Net-based technologies are distinctive because they require integration with the systems of *other* organizations, as well as one's own internal systems.[2]

It makes sense to study technology adoption at the firm level for technologies whose impact is limited to the boundaries of the firm. But for technologies ranging from EDI to ebXML and beyond, the main goal is to facilitate inter-organizational relationships.[3] For these kinds of technologies, I argue that it is better understood as a *population* level phenomenon. Thus, to understand the dynamics and adoption of inter-organizational technologies, an ecological framework is required. Ecological theory has been applied at the level of firms.[4] In this paper, I explore the possibility of applying ecological analysis to populations of inter-organizational routines.[5]

I focus on routines because the adoption of technology is embedded in organizational routines – repetitive, recognizable patterns of interdependent actions carried out by multiple actors.[6] To the extent that these routines involve the creation and maintenance of inter-organizational relationships, we can think of them as inter-organizational routines. This paper outlines a framework for the study of populations of inter-organizational routines and discusses its implications for future research.

2   Why an Ecology of Routines?

Several well-known factors affect the adoption of technology across multiple firms, especially in the case of technology that supports inter-organizational relationships. For example, network effects can have a tremendous influence on the adoption of new technology when the returns to investment are positively associated with the number of current and future adopters[7] FAX and email provide prominent examples, as do HTML, HTTP and the growing number of XML standards. When a technology achieves "critical mass," adoption takes off.[8]

Technical standardization can also foster adoption of standard technology, even in the absence of strong network externalities. In some cases, these are open standards, such as TCP/IP. In other cases, such as credit card payment systems or 3rd party logistics systems, the standards are created and enforced by the service provider (e.g., VISA, FedEx, etc.).

Mimetic pressures (as identified in institutional theory) can drive the adoption of a routine even when there is no technological imperative. Legitimacy depends on meeting expectations of customers and business partners, and firms tend to adopt organizational forms and routines that enhance their legitimacy.[9] Legal and regulatory requirements also enforce conformity on inter-organizational relationships. Procedures for issuing debt and equity, for example, are highly regulated.

There are two key points to draw from these observations. First, the adoption of net-enabling technology is not just a decision made by individual, isolated firms. It is enmeshed in an on-going social and technological context that is distributed across some set of firms. In the discussion that follows, we will pay particular attention to the social network aspects of the phenomenon.

Second, focusing on the technology per se also tends to misrepresent the phenomenon. Like any significant information system, the adoption of net-enabling technology involves significant changes to organizational procedures and practices; it is never just a question of putting some new hardware in the rack, or installing a new software package.[10] As Zahra and George argue, a wide range of organizational and managerial factors affect the ability of firms to absorb and utilize the technology.[11] What is adopted can be thought of as a complex bundle of technology, work practices and social relationships. To the extent that many of these practices and relationships involve actors from multiple organizations, they can be called inter-organizational routines. In the case of inter-organizational routines, the participants engaged in the routine are distributed among different formal organizations. Payment systems, logistics systems, and other supply chain support systems are obvious examples of routines that are carried out by members of different formal organizations.

Inter-organizational routines can also be seen as creating or sustaining network ties. I use the term "network tie" as it is used in the study of social networks.[12] While sociologists have operationalized this concept in many different ways, I refer here to behavioral interaction and transfer of material resources. So, when two firms are engaged in a net-enabled transaction (e.g., automatic inventory replenishment), we can view them as having a tie in an appropriately defined social network. Just being plugged into the Internet does not create such a tie – it is the joint participation in the inter-organizational routine that defines the tie. Thus, inter-organizational routines are particularly relevant to our concept of net-enabled and "virtual" organizations, who may participate in extensive inter-organizational networks.

I have argued elsewhere that there is a duality between network ties (defined as behavioral interaction) and ties based on patterns of action, such as routines.[13] Each tie reflects an instance of a routine and vice versa. Thus, a set of network ties represents a population of inter-organizational routines, and vice versa.

To make this duality rigorous, we must recognize that there are different kinds of routines, and therefore different kinds of ties. Each kind of tie reflects a different aspect of the relationship between the entities in the network. For example, "automatic inventory replenishment" is different than "purchasing." Social ties can be multiplex: they can indicate more than one kind of relationship between two entities.[14] In a supply chain network, many firms would have multiplex ties, including purchasing, inventory replenishment, product development, and more. In mapping such a network, one needs to specify which ties (or combinations of ties) are included. The duality between network ties and routines will prove helpful when we consider how to operationalize the ecological perspective in empirical research.

3 Definitions of Key Ecological Concepts

The ecological perspective shifts the level of analysis from single firms (or routines), to populations of competing firms (or routines). Rather than studying the properties of a particular individual, an ecological perspective considers the viability of entire populations of individuals as they compete with other populations for scarce resources. Rather than asking, "What factors led brewery X to begin brewing small batches?" organizational ecologists ask, "What led to the rise of microbreweries as an organizational form?" Similarly, in the realm of net-enabling technology, we can ask firm-level questions, such as "When should firm A adopt technology X?" or "How can firm A gain competitive advantage from technology X?" These are important questions, and can provide valuable guides to managerial practice. But the ecological perspective shifts the level of analysis and the time scale to questions like, "Why has technology X transformed (or failed to transform) certain sectors of the economy?" Steinfield poses this question in his discussion of structure and impact (or lack of impact) of B2B markets,[15] but researchers in ICT have lacked empirical tools to study this kind of industry level phenomenon.

Empirically, ecological analysis focuses on so-called "vital rates": founding rates (or birth rates), transformation rates, and morbidity rates.[16] These vital rates are a function of the interaction between the focal species, the environment, and other species that may be present. These rates are estimated using hazard models, as demonstrated by Kauffman, McAndrews, and Wang in their study of ATM network sharing.[17] These rates reflect the likelihood of foundings, mortality, and other events of interest in a given time period. The ecological perspective allows us to estimate hazard rates as a function of co-variates, such as population density and other environmental factors. In the sections that follow, I will lay out some of the problems involved in defining and studying the ecology of inter-organizational routines.

To operationalize the ecological framework, we must define the core concepts. At a minimum, we need to identify species, populations, and niches. I will use analogies to organizational ecology to help motivate these definitions. Like the analogy between biological organisms and organizations, the analogy between organizations and routines is not perfect or complete. In particular, the potential for complementarity between routines (Galunic and Weeks, 2002; Milgrom and Roberts, 1995) and their embeddedness in inter-firm social networks complicates the analogy considerably.

3.1 *Species*

Hannan and Freeman identify four "core features" of organizational forms that "serve as the organizational ecologists analogue to the biological ecologist's species." These include: 1) mission (or goal); 2) form of authority or governance (e.g., formal or informal); 3) basic technology; and 4) marketing strategy.[18]

So, for example, one can identify fast food restaurants as an organization form with the following core features (1) a food service mission; (2) formal governance; (3) standardized food preparation technology and (4) convenience-oriented mass marketing. In addition, there are "peripheral features" that may further differentiate organizations within a population (e.g., selling tacos versus selling hamburgers).

Unlike most biological species, firms can be polymorphic: they can have more than one mission, more than one core technology and so on. This is particularly true of multi-divisional firms. Furthermore, unlike biological species firms can be transformed from one species to another. For example, they can change their mission or replace their core technology. While transformations are relatively rare and usually quite tumultuous, they are certainly possible. Polymorphism and transformation are two possibilities we need to allow for in species of organizational routines, as well.

To identify species of routines, the four core features identified by Hannan and Carroll provide a reasonable starting point. At the minimum, we could identify species of routines based on (1) their goal and (2) their core technology. It may also make sense to include "governance" (informal vs. formal), but it is harder to see a meaningful analogy to "marketing strategy." Functional or goal-based classification is probably the most common approach to classifying organizational work processes. *The MIT Process Handbook*, for example, uses a functional classification for a wide variety of business processes.[19] *The MIT Process Handbook* also includes classifications based on core technology ("Sell-how"). We can define a species of inter-organizational routine as all instances of a routine that have the same function (goal) and same core technology.

In other words, a species of routine can be defined by the ends and the means. A taxonomy of inter-organizational routines based on these two dimensions (goal and core technology) would be relatively straightforward. For example, some high–level categories are fairly well established, such as "purchasing" and "sales." To the extent that we are interested in "net-enabled" technology, we might start by dividing the core technology into two categories ("net" or "not"). Further refinements (EDI, ebXML, etc.) are certainly possible. As discussed below, the appropriate structure of additional sub-categories should be a topic of empirical research.

3.2 *Populations*

Organizational populations are defined as "specific time-and-space instances of organizational forms."[20] A population consists of all members of a species who inhabit a particular niche or environment. In biological organisms, we might have a population of raccoons in the countryside, and a different population of raccoons in the city. They are all the same species, but it makes sense to study them as separate populations. Similarly, we might want to distinguish fast food restaurants in a distinct geographical location (e.g., California vs. New York) as two different populations of the same species of organization. Indeed, studies in organizational ecology are often geographically bounded (e.g., hotels in Manhattan).

A population of routines is analogous to a population of organizations: "specific time-and-space instances of organizational routines." So, one might include all of the sales routines in a particular segment of firms. In the sociological literature, there are some examples of research on populations of routines. For example, Anne Miner studied changes in the population of formal job descriptions.[21] Consistent with the ecological framework, she examined variation and selective retention of jobs within a population. Martin Shultz looked at populations of rules within particular organizations (such as a German bank and an American university).[22] He studies the vital rates for this population of rules: foundings (new rules), transformation (rule changes), and mortality (rule suspensions). These studies exemplify the idea of applying ecological concepts to organizational routines, but there are few studies of *inter*-organizational routines per se.[23]

The social network literature, however, is filled with studies of various kinds of inter-organizational ties.[24] These ties reflect the presence of underlying inter-organizational routines. We can define a population of inter-organizational routines as the set of specific time-and-space instances of a given species. A population of inter-organizational routines can be operationalized as a set of ties in an appropriately defined social network.

The phrase "appropriately defined" reflects the need to define what kind of tie is being graphed in the network. Each species of routine implies a different set of ties. This makes sense because each species of routine should have a distinct population. Networks of multiplex ties provide a convenient way to show multiple species of routines simultaneously.

3.3 *Niches*

Carroll and Hannan state that "the fundamental niche of an organizational form consists of the social, economic and political conditions that can sustain the functioning of organizations that embody a particular form."[25] Niches are important because they define the sphere of competition. The ecological similarity between two species can be defined as the extent of overlap in their fundamental niches. They go on to say:

> In general, the potential for two populations to compete is proportional to the intersection of their fundamental niches. Two populations compete if and only if their fundamental niches intersect.[26]

When two populations compete, each one will only occupy a portion of their fundamental niche that is called their "realized" niche, which is roughly analogous to an aggregate market share for all members of a population. In general, only the realized niche for a population can be observed. By analogy to the biological world, a niche is defined to have a carrying capacity, which is the number of members it can sustain.

For a firm, a niche consists of the economic, physical and social resources required to survive. A routine needs all of that, plus it often has fairly specific requirements in terms of inputs and outputs, especially when supported by ICT. Inter-organizational systems, from EDI to ebXML, all require the use of standardized data and document formats.

Interdependence arises because routines are closely enmeshed in other routines.[27] Process interdependence arises from the flow of material or information between processes. Malone *et al.* identify three kinds of interdependence: flow, shared resources and common output. Flow dependencies occur when the input of one process is the output of another. Shared resources occur when two processes require the same inputs (e.g., same operating system). Common output occurs when two processes have to produce results that go together in some way.[28]

Interdependencies between routines are critical factors in defining a niche because a routine cannot survive unless these dependency constraints are met. Process interdependence enforces powerful constraints on the choice of technologies and inter-organizational routines. Flow dependencies are most important between organizations: you have to conform to the standard. Shared resource dependencies are likely to be important within the adopting organization. We can define a niche as the set of economic, physical, social conditions and interdependencies required by a species of routine.

It is important to realize that interdependence arises in the context of particular firms – between instances of a routine. Thus, it makes the most sense to operationalize a niche in terms of an appropriately defined social network of specific firms (suppliers, buyers, etc). The social network transcends immediate boundaries of geography and industry. For this reason, it can capture the set of places within which a given species of inter-organizational routine could be survive.

3.4 *Competition and complementarity*

Competition between species occurs within niches. In my yard, for example, grass competes with weeds. Galunic and Weeks argue that routines can be viewed as competing with each other:

> Routine competition is present whenever there is risk to the survival of one routine because of the presence of another. The endgame is usually the supplanting of one routine by another, as one routine fulfills the same objectives but with greater effectiveness, efficiency, or legitimacy, or the dominant routine simply devours scarce resources leaving no life support for others. In turn, the losing routine may face inattention, relegation to some less significant use, or death.[29]

Competition implies that routines would be considered substitutes or alternatives. For example, there may be alternative ways of recruiting new personnel, such as newspaper advertisements, campus interviews, and web-based services. At some point, web-based acquisition of candidates may come to replace the alternatives. Alternative payment mechanisms provide another example. Cash and personal checks are increasingly being replaced by credit cards, but other forms of electronic payment have not been particularly successful.

Unlike grass and weeds, routines may also be complementary with other routines. "Routines are complemented by another if the other's presence contributes to the focal routine's efficacy, development, and, ultimately, survival."[30] Milgrom and Roberts define complementarity in terms of marginal returns: doing more of one thing increases the returns for doing more of another.[31] In practice, complementarity seems to manifest itself as bundles that are self-reinforcing. In biological terms, complementarity might be roughly analogous to symbiosis.

Like interdependence, complementarity implies a specific organizational context. The statement "X complements Y" only makes sense in the context of a particular firm. X does not complement Y if they occur in different firms. This reinforces the need to treat the ecology of inter-organizational routines as a network phenomenon, so that the co-presence of particular instances of competing or complementary species within particular firms is explicitly represented.

4 Example

In an extensive study of the non-ferrous metal recycling industry, Adelaar studied the adoption of various technologies for e-business.[32] Non-ferrous metal recycling is a global industry; large lots of aluminum, copper and other kinds of scrap metal are sent to and from facilities all over the world. Adelaar hypothesized that this industry would conform to the Electronic Market Hypothesis, which predicts the adoption of e-business tools such as auctions.[33] In ecological language, e-business auctions are a species of inter-organizational routine; they employ a particular technology to perform the task of price discovery. The Electronic Markets Hypothesis predicts that auctions will become the dominant species in a wide variety of conditions. Metals recycling seems like a good candidate for e-business innovation because of high search and transaction costs.

Adelaar discovered, however, that participants in the industry generally restricted themselves to email, fax and telephone. They had experimented with auctions, but only a few continued using it to auction off highly specific scrap metals. A majority of the firms found that auctions were not a good fit with industry routines and practices, including negotiation, inventory management and problem-solving routines. Email was especially popular because of the ability to attach digital images of the scrap materials. In ecological terms, the use of email for negotiations is a particular species of inter-organizational routines. Contrary to the prediction of the Electronic Markets Hypothesis, Adelaar found that this routine was dominant.

It is important to note that this is not simply an issue of critical mass. Every significant participant in the market had all of the necessary technology to adopt and participate in auctions, and some had done so. They preferred email because it was a better fit with their way of doing business.

5   Research Issues

The framework presented here embodies a significant departure from the more familiar economic or managerial view that is typically applied to this domain. It raises a number of interesting questions.

The first issue in carrying out research using this framework would be the classification of species. *The MIT Process Handbook* provides an interesting model, but may be more elaborate than necessary. It might be that in early empirical work, a much simpler taxonomy would be adequate. The function of the routine (e.g., "purchasing") provides the basic classification for the purposes of defining the population and the niche within which competition occurs. For the core technology, one might ask whether the routine is based on (a) face-to-face; (b) "traditional" technologies (paper, US Mail); (c) telephonic technologies (phone, FAX); or (d) net-enabled technologies.

Inter-organizational routines can be seen as creating or reproducing network ties between organizations. Thus, population dynamics in inter-organizational routines is directly connected to network dynamics. Vital rates for inter-organizational routines translate directly into network dynamics. Foundings (new routines) correspond to the initiation of new network ties. Transformations correspond to changing from one kind of tie to another (for example, when a purchasing process converts from FAX to EDI). Mortality corresponds to the termination of network ties.

The example of the metals recycling industry suggests that we must think of these processes in the context of the work practices and routines of the industry as a whole. The "niche" for a particular kind of routine, such as an auction or a reverse auction, depends on how well the routine complements related routines, not just the economics of the routine itself. Furthermore, it depends on the preferences of the trading partners who must carry out their half of the routine.

6 Conclusion

The ecological framework provides a valuable counter-point to traditional firm-level perspectives because it places emphasis on interdependence and complementarity within the population of routines. These factors constrain and enable the growth rates of certain "species" of routines. The ecological perspective does translate very readily into prescriptions for managerial action. Species thrive (or go extinct) based on the availability of suitable niches. Traditional managerial variables, such as the costs and benefits of adopting a particular technology in a particular firm, are of secondary importance. As a result, managerial action is not a significant explanatory variable in ecological theory.[34] But unlike firm level models, ecological theory has the potential to explain the transformation (or lack thereof) of whole industries and ways of doing business.

References

1. Coyle, F. P. *XML, Web Services and the Data Revolution.* Addison-Wesley, 2002; Wheeler, B. C. NEDIC: A dynamic capabilities theory for assessing net enablement. *Information Systems Research*, 13, 2002, pp. 125-146.
2. Riggins, F. J., Kriebel, C. H. and Mukhopadyay, T. The growth of inter-organizational systems in the presence of network externalities. *Management Science*, 40, 1994, pp. 984-998.
3. Kauffman, R. J., McAndrews, J. J. and Wang, Y. M. Opening the "black box" of network externalities in network adoption. *Information Systems Research*, 11, 2000, pp. 61-82.

4. Hannan, M. T. and Carroll, G. R. An introduction to organizational ecology, in G. R. Carroll and M. T. Hannan (Eds.), *Organizations in Industry: Strategy, Structure and Selection*. New York: Oxford University Press, 1995, pp. 37-58; Hannan, M. T. and Freeman, J. R. Structural Inertia and Organizational Change. *American Sociological Review*, 29, 1983, pp. 149-164; Aldrich, Howard. *Organizations Evolving*. London: Sage Publications, 1999.

5. Powell, Walter W. Learning from collaboration: Knowledge and networks in the biotechnology and pharmaceutical industries. *California Management Review*, 40, 1998, pp. 228-240; Adelaar, Thomas. Explaining variations in the use of the internet to support inter-organizational exchange: The case of the recycling industry. Unpublished PhD dissertation, Department of Telecommunications, Information Studies and Media, Michigan State University, 2005.

6. Feldman, M. S. and Pentland, B. T. Organizational Routines: Towards a Practice-based Theory of Routines, Flexibility and Change. *Administrative Science Quarterly*, 48, 2003, pp. 94-118.

7. Economides, N. The economics of networks. *International Journal of Industrial Organization*, 14, 1996, pp. 673-699; Katz, M. L. and Shapiro, C. Technology adoption in the presence of network extemalities. *Journal of Political Economy*, 94, 1986, pp. 822-841; Kauffman, R. J., McAndrews, J. J. and Wang, Y. M. *Op. Cit.*

8. Markus, M. Lynne. Toward a 'Critical Mass' Theory of Interactive Media: Universal Access, Interdependence, and Diffusion. *Communications Research*, 14, 1987, pp. 491-511.

9. Hannan, M. T. and Freeman, J. R. Structural Inertia and Organizational Change. *American Sociological Review*, 29, 1983, pp. 149-164.

10. Zmud, R. W. and Apple, L. E. Measuring Technology Incorporation/Infusion. *Journal of Product Innovation Management*, 9, 1992, pp. 148-155; Cooper, R. and Zmud, R. Information Technology Implementation Research: A Technological Diffusion Approach. *Management Science*, 36, 1990, pp. 123-139.

11. Zahra, S. A. and George, G. The net-enabled business cycle and the evolution of dynamic capabilities. *Information Systems Research*, 13, 2002, pp. 147-150.

12. Wasserman, S. and Faust, K. *Social Network Analysis: Methods and Applications*. New York: Cambridge University Press, 1994.

13. Pentland, B. T. Organizations as Networks of Action, in J. Baum and B. McKelvey (Eds.), *Variations in Organization Science: In Honor of Donald T. Campbell*. Thousand Oaks, CA: Sage, 1999, pp. 237-253.

14. Wasserman, S. and Faust, K. *Op. Cit.*

15. Steinfield, C. Conceptualizing the role of collaborative e-commerce in geographically defined business clusters. Presented to the workshop on The Ambivalent Relationship Between IT and Social Capital, Vrije Universiteit Amsterdam, The Netherlands, May 27-28, 2002.

16. Hannan, M. T. and Carroll, G. R. *Op. Cit.*

17. Kauffman, R. J., McAndrews, J. J. and Wang, Y. M. *Op. Cit.*
18. Hannan, M. T. and Freeman, J. R. *Op. Cit.*
19. Malone, T. W., Crowston, K. G., Lee, J., Pentland, B., Dellarocas, C., Wyner, G., Quimby, J., Osborn, C. S., Bernstein, A., Herman, G., Klein, M. and O'Donnell, E. Tools for inventing organizations: Toward a handbook of organizational processes. *Management Science*, 45, 1999, pp. 425-443.
20. Hannan, M. T. and Freeman, J. R. *Op. Cit.*
21. Miner, A. Organizational Evolution and the Social Ecology of Jobs. *American Sociological Review*, 56, 1991, pp. 772-785.
22. Schulz, M. Limits to bureaucratic growth: The density dependence of organizational rule births. *Administrative Science Quarterly*, 43, 1998, pp. 845-876.
23. Powell, Walter W. *Op. Cit.*; Adelaar, Thomas, *Op Cit.*
24. Gulati, R. and Gargiulo, M. Where do interorganizational networks come from? *American Journal of Sociology*, 104, 1999, pp. 1439-1493.
25. Hannan, M. T. and Carroll, G. R. *Op. Cit.*
26. *Ibid.*
27. Feldman, M. S. and Pentland, B. T. *Op. Cit.*
28. Malone *et al.*, *Op. Cit.*
29. Galunic, C. and Weeks, J. R. Intraorganizational Ecology, in J. Baum (Ed.), *A Companion to Organizations*. Oxford: Blackwell, 2001, p. 81.
30. *Ibid*, p. 82.
31. Milgrom, P. and Roberts, J. Complementarities and fit: Strategy, structure, and organizational change in manufacturing. *Journal of Accounting and Economics*, 19, 1995, pp. 179-208.
32. Adelaar, Thomas. Explaining variations in the use of the internet to support inter-organizational exchange: The case of the recycling industry. Unpublished PhD dissertation, Department of Telecommunications, Information Studies and Media, Michigan State University, 2005.
33. Malone, T., Yates, J. and Benjamin, R. Electronic markets and hierarchies. *Communications of the ACM*, 30, 1987, pp. 484-497.
34. Aldrich, Howard. *Organizations Evolving*. London: Sage Publications, 1999.

CHAPTER 11

Alliance Networks, Inter-Firm Learning and Communication: A Search for New Insights

Nadine Roijakkers, Geert Duysters and Gaby Sadowski-Rasters

ECIS and Department of Organization Science and Marketing
Faculty of Technology Management
Eindhoven University of Technology
P.O. Box 513, 5600 MB Eindhoven, The Netherlands
Email: a.h.w.m.roijakkers@tm.tue.nl; g.m.duijsters@tm.tue.nl;
g.rasters@tm.tue.nl

1 Introduction

In the past decades, we have witnessed an enormous increase in alliance and networking activity where the traditionally independent, self-contained knowledge-intensive company has evolved into a networked firm that is largely dependent on external partners for its internal, technological knowledge development[1,2,3]. While many sectors of industry have experienced an increase in alliance activity, this increase is . particularly important in knowledge-intensive industries, such as internet and biotechnology, where learning, tacit knowledge transfer, and innovation is of crucial importance for the competitive position of firms[3]. With a few notable exceptions agreements have been studied from a dyadic or firm-level perspective[4]. In this chapter we will argue, however, that the true value of strategic alliances can only be assessed by also examining the overall structure of the network in which a firm is embedded. Knoke and Kuklinski (p. 13), for example, noted that "the structure of relations among actors and the location of individual actors in the network have important behavioral, perceptual, and attitudinal consequences both for the individual units and for the system as a whole". Therefore the evaluation of the power, identity and competitive position in a in a network requires an extensive analysis of an organization's position in the network and its connection to other

223

players. The existing networking literature has mainly studied learning within networked, knowledge-intensive companies in relation to particular characteristics of the alliance network to which these firms belong, such as their networking position, the overall network density, and the strength of their ties (see literature overview in Section 2). While alliance networks can in fact be seen as collections of geographically dispersed groups of collaborating employees that share tacit knowledge and technical information, the alliance and networking literature has paid little or no attention to the role of the underlying, personal communication network linking these employees in facilitating their knowledge sharing. Alliances often can be seen as the context in which individual employees work with each other. It is the overarching structure that facilitates companies to work together. Most alliance literature considers alliances as a black box in which inter-personal communication remains undiscussed. We argue that the relationship between CMC and alliances is important because while employees involved in international learning alliances are likely to meet each other in a face-to-face setting on a regular basis, a large part of their long-distance communication is likely to occur through computer-mediated communication (CMC), such as e-mail, video conferencing, and groupware. In the communication literature, which is largely grounded in experimental research, relevant insights have been gained regarding the role of both face-to-face communication and CMC in learning, knowledge transfer, and communication within groups of employees that are not always geographically close, i.e. virtual teams (see literature overview in Section 3). Although communication research has not tested its assertions within the context of real-life settings, such as international alliance networks, we believe that some of its insights might be highly relevant for alliance networks as well. A typical example of the use of CMC in a knowledge-based, networked alliance is for instance the use of Virtual A-labs in the Aeronautical industry brought together in the Advance case. The Advance project, launched in 1999 and partly funded by the European Commission, was a significant attempt to improve the conditions for collaboration in the European aerospace industry.

Advance project would have to make European aeronautical product development more efficient by shortening time-to-market and reducing the costs of data management, conversion, and transmission. Within this dispersed network a precondition for the collaboration was the usage of CMC to support communication[5]. Different CMC tools were used to support knowledge sharing within this complex network, for instance the use of e-mail, virtual labs, videoconferencing and electronic workflow databases. Specifically, our understanding of collective learning in groups of networked, geographically distributed, knowledge-intensive companies could benefit to a large degree from applying insights regarding the effectiveness of face-to-face communication and CMC in virtual teams to this alliance setting.

The use of CMC in an alliance setting has been relatively ignored in the existing literature. There is abundant literature on the use of CMC for virtual teams and in within-company settings but there are almost no studies that focus on the relationship between CMC use and strategic alliances. In order to fill this void, we will provide an integrative overview for the use of CMC in an alliance setting. More insight into this specific issue might lead to a more efficient use of CMC in international alliance setting.

While we emphasize the international dimension of alliances, we want to elaborate on the interactions between the international scope of an alliance and its reliance of CMC. "The global nature of alliances teams fosters a discussion of possible cross-cultural differences in collaborative behaviors"[6]. We have reason to assume that given differences in culture between formed alliances, the usage of CMC influences alliance outcomes.

The aim of this chapter is to make a first attempt at identifying insights from the communication literature that may also have important value for theory building within the alliance and network literature. In Section 2, we first describe the existing views on learning, technological knowledge transfer, and innovation within knowledge-intensive firms and their international alliance networks. More in particular, we focus on how the current alliance and networking literature has related learning and innovation within knowledge-intensive companies to overall characteristics of the alliance networks in which these firms are embedded. In Section 3, we examine the existing body of communication literature regarding the role of face-to-face communication and CMC in virtual teams with the aim of gaining relevant insights for alliance and network research. In our concluding section, we evaluate these insights and we give some suggestions for future research building on combined views from the alliance and communication literatures.

2   Learning within Networks: An Examination of the Alliance and Network Literature

2.1   *Learning and innovation: From firm to network*

More than any other type of industry, knowledge-intensive industries, such as internet and biotechnology, are characterized by rapid scientific and technological developments where knowledge is so broadly distributed that no single firm possesses all relevant information for successful learning and innovation[1,2]. Many groups of competing firms are likely to be working on the same or somewhat similar technologies and those firms that are able to swiftly prepare their new technology for commercialization are the ones that reap critical first-mover benefits. In the existing alliance and network literature, basic differences in the ability of knowledge-intensive companies to successfully innovate and the speed with which these companies are able to learn are argued to be the result of differences in both their ability to access external knowledge and their capacity to use and build on this knowledge internally[7,8,9].

Internal learning and knowledge creation within the firm occur when firm scientists engage in in-house research and distribute newly found technological knowledge within the boundaries of the firm. Internal capability development enables companies to build up skills and exercise routines that facilitate a rapid evaluation and successful integration of state-of-the art research conducted outside[10,11]. While some researchers argue that internal learning, skills, and routines allow firms to have a hand in research and stay current with respect to the latest technological developments in their rapidly moving field, others have pointed at the negative consequences of the organizational context for learning and innovation[12]. Specifically, authors in this tradition have expressed the view that the firm with all its bureaucratic rigidities and static, tightly bound routines is in fact a rather poor vehicle for learning and innovation. A company's technological knowledge base is grounded in many years of costly, dedicated research and it is therefore very difficult to change the technological foundation of a firm. Technological knowledge created by internal learning and in-house research is embedded in organizational routines and it has an important cumulative and tacit, non-codified dimension, indicating that it cannot be easily articulated or changed[8,13,14,15].

Research in alliances and networks has suggested that inter-firm alliance networks facilitate learning, innovation, and the creation of new knowledge within companies[16]. These alliance networks are argued to be an important part of an external learning process in which knowledge-intensive companies learn about new opportunities and obtain access to new tacit knowledge through interacting with other network participants. By linking firms, universities, research laboratories, buyers, and suppliers together, an international network setting of evolving alliances and dynamic relations provides a flexible learning structure that overcomes the shortcomings of formal, routinized organizational structures[17,18,19,20]. The degree to which knowledge-intensive companies learn about new technological opportunities and the speed with which they integrate and commercialize externally acquired knowledge depend both on the extent to which they participate in the alliance network and the level of their internal skills[12,21]. Coleman[22] has argued that being part of a closely knit group of familiar partners is beneficial because it stimulates trust and cooperation among its members. Therefore firms often engage in so-called local search for partners as a result of their social capital[23] and embeddedness[24,25]. Actors who maintain cohesive ties among eachother are more likely to have increased absorptive capacity and will increasingly act "similarly, to share information, to develop similar preferences, or to act in concert"[26] (p. 56).

2.2 *Inter-firm learning and tacit knowledge transfer in alliance networks: Centrality, density and tie strength*

In Section 2.1, we have outlined part of the alliance and networking literature where an assessment of the shortcomings of organizational routines has led to a joint emphasis on both the routinized learning environment within knowledge-intensive firms and the flexible innovative conditions within international alliance networks. Over the past decades, the traditionally independent, inward-directed, knowledge-intensive company seems to have evolved into a firm that replaces part of its internal innovative activity by learning through alliances and knowledge networks. Rather than constantly building on their internal skills, most of these knowledge-intensive companies thrive on large numbers of external relationships with other firms (see Figure 1). In the majority of knowledge-intensive sectors, such as the internet industry, the large growth in the formation of these learning alliances has led to the emergence of dense, inter-organizational knowledge networks (see Figure 2).

In a number of important contributions to the alliance and network literature, researchers have related learning and innovation within knowledge-intensive companies to their position in international alliance networks or other characteristics of the network, such as density and tie strength[27-38].

2.2.1 *Network position*

Some researchers have pointed out that knowledge-intensive companies in high-status, highly central network positions have maneuvered themselves in such a way that they can learn from a variety of international network participants and, as such, successfully innovate[23,35,37]. Centrality in networks is associated with the importance of a specific organization for the overall structure of the network. Central firms are said to be in the "thick of things". They can often be seen as central sources of information, at least in terms of the number of partners they have alliances with. Firms can generally move into central positions by teaming up with a large number of partners. In the case these partners are powerful players in the network, they gain a high status.

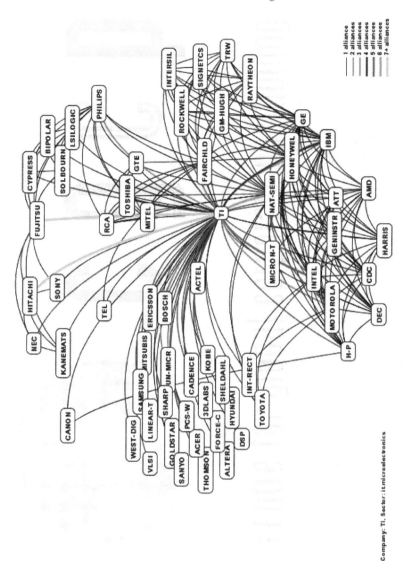

Figure 1. The Alliance Network of Texas Instruments

Source: CGCP (www.cgcp.nl).

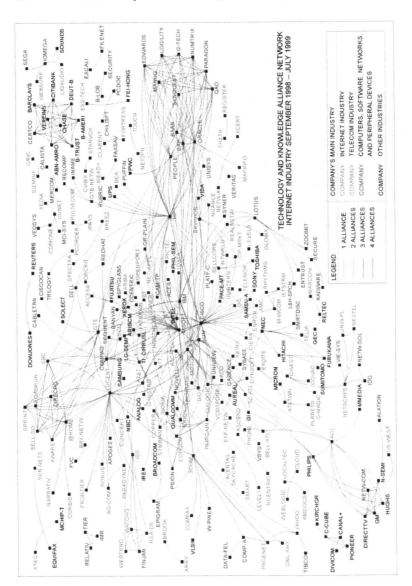

Figure 2. The Alliance Network in the Internet Industry

Source: CGCP (www.cgcp.nl), September 1988-July 1999.

A knowledge-intensive company holding such a central position within an alliance network is understood to have information about both the positioning of other network participants and their tacit knowledge flows, which enables it to use its centrality to successfully choose future partners. Furthermore, a central network position shapes a firm's reputation as a skilled, experienced, and knowledgeable network participant that make it an attractive partner for other participants[29]. Knowledge-intensive firms with a central network position in between other network participants are argued to be able to use their visible, powerful position, their high-status reputation, and their attractiveness to other companies to continuously search for new international partners and thus ensure their timely, easy access to the latest technological knowledge.

Alternatively, other researchers have expressed the view that a peripheral network position rather than a central one is beneficial for creating access to new technological knowledge and innovation[4,34]. Specifically, it is argued that knowledge-intensive companies at the periphery of the international alliance network are more flexible and less bound by shared codes and routines than companies in the network core. Centrally positioned firms often form the center of dense research cliques where partners are connected through long-term, routinized learning alliances and the exchange of tacit technological knowledge occurs within a learned and shared code[34,39]. Moreover, central, high-status companies are likely to have invested large amounts of resources in the technology from which they have derived their central status and they are thus more likely to benefit from the cumulative improvement of this technology than from innovation. As knowledge-intensive firms operating in more dynamic, peripheral parts of the international network suffer less from routines, social commitment, and attachment to existing technologies, these firms are more inclined than central firms to engage in experimental learning and generate new innovations.

2.2.2 *Density and tie strength*

In his 1988 seminal article, Coleman has argued that a dense or closed alliance network based on strong, redundant relationships, i.e.

relationships that provide knowledge-intensive companies with technological knowledge to which they already have access through their existing alliances, presents these firms with the most optimal context for learning and innovation. He points out that such a closed alliance network facilitates the development of shared social codes, routines, and inter-organizational trust between international alliance partners, which stimulate the sharing of tacit, non-codified technological knowledge through long-term, repeated learning alliances and reduce the chances of opportunistic behavior on the part of partners to these alliances. In support of this view, Hagedoorn and Duysters[40] have argued that in knowledge-intensive industries, companies with dense, local alliance networks based on quasi-redundant relationships are more innovative than their competitors with a clear preference for highly efficient networks with many non-redundant relationships. Ahuja[41], in his 2000 ASQ piece, has analyzed the extent to which closed and open alliance networks contribute to learning and innovation within knowledge-intensive firms. His results show that there is a strong, negative relationship between the existence of structural holes in international alliance networks and the innovative performance of knowledge-intensive companies when inter-organizational trust and overcoming opportunistic behavior are important determinants of learning and innovative success.

In an opposing view, Burt[23,42] and Granovetter[24] have described the international alliance network of knowledge-intensive companies in terms of more dynamic, non-redundant relationships or 'structural holes'. According to Burt[23], it is not very efficient for knowledge-intensive companies to increase the density or closure of their local alliance network as an increased number of learning alliances enlarges the chances of these alliances being redundant relationships. Instead, knowledge-intensive firms should focus on creating and maintaining more flexible, bridging alliances that connect structural holes and maximize the non-redundancy of their relationships[23]. This line of reasoning is related to the argument of Granovetter[24] who points out that establishing weak, non-redundant relationships offers knowledge-intensive companies the possibility to partner with new, distant network participants and provides them with the opportunity to gain access to a broad, diversified technological knowledge base. In similar vein other researchers have proposed that the innovative success of knowledge-intensive companies is highly dependent on the extent to which they have access to new, tacit, technological knowledge developed in a wide number of technical areas[43,44]. When quick access to a heterogeneous knowledge base (e.g., explorative learning) is a critical antecedent of learning and innovation, an international alliance network rich in structural holes and weak relationships is likely to be preferable. Such a dynamic network connects participants with distinct technological know-how and consequently provides knowledge-intensive companies with flexible access to a broad range of novel technological knowledge[27,33,41,47].

Overall, we might argue that closed networks thrive in situations in which trust is important for facilitating the transfer of tacit information. Furthermore, there is some empirical evidence in the literature that a firm benefits most from redundant ties in a network when its main objective is to refine its existing technology base and competencies, while non-redundant ties are more instrumental in explorative learning. Therefore, we can say that the importance of network closure arguments as put forward by Coleman[22] and the importance of the structural hole theory of social capital[23] is contingent on the specific type of organizational learning.

2.3 *Sharing tacit, non-codified technological knowledge at a distance: A need for insights from the communication literature*

In this section, we have described the transformation of isolated, inward-directed, knowledge-intensive companies into highly networked firms that thrive on their international learning alliances with others. Furthermore, we have provided an extensive outline of the dominant alliance and network literature that has mainly studied learning, innovation, and tacit, non-codified information sharing between knowledge-intensive companies in the context of a number of general, overall characteristics of the alliance networks these firms are part of. Specifically, effective learning and technological knowledge transfer between knowledge-intensive companies have been linked to higher-level network variables, such as centrality, tie strength, and density.

While the strength of the above-mentioned alliance and network research lies in its thorough analysis of high-level network characteristics, this literature has paid little or no attention to the organizational changes that have to come about when knowledge-intensive companies become part of international alliance networks and engage in inter-firm learning. Internal capability development and distribution of tacit technological knowledge within these firms are likely to be supported by inter-personal communication between their scientists and a large number of face-to-face meetings where these employees articulate their know-how. By contrast, the personal communication network underlying an alliance network is likely to be very different as employees involved in international learning alliances may not often have the chance to meet each other in face-to-face settings. Consequently, a large part of their tacit knowledge sharing and communication efforts is bound to be facilitated by computer-mediated communication (CMC), such as e-mail, video conferencing, and groupware.

Surprisingly, most studies of alliances and networks do not include an evaluation of this lower-level communication network through which tacit technical knowledge has to be transferred and new technologies have to be learned into their analysis of the effectiveness of inter-firm learning. In our view, the specific workings of the personal communication network supporting the international alliance network may to a large degree determine the extent to which collaborating employees can learn from each other and thus the effectiveness of learning within alliances. The communication literature, largely grounded in experimental studies of virtual teams (see Section 3 for an overview of this literature), has developed important insights regarding the effectiveness of face-to-face communication and computer-mediated communication. We believe that such insights may significantly improve our understanding of the effectiveness of learning and technological knowledge transfer within networked, globally dispersed, knowledge-intensive companies.

In the next section, we examine an important part of the communication literature and review its treatment of the role of face-to-face communication and CMC in learning, tacit knowledge transfer, and communication within virtual teams. By describing this research tradition and views in favor and against the use of CMC in virtual teams, we aim to demonstrate the value of communication insights for better understanding inter-firm learning within alliance networks.

3 The Effectiveness of Face-to-Face Communication and CMC in Learning: Media Richness Theory and Beyond

3.1 *Traditional media richness theory (MRT)*

The oldest research tradition within the communication literature, i.e. Media Richness Theory or MRT, can be traced back to the early seminal work of Karl Weick[70] on complex tasks, information processing requirements, and the formation of effectively functioning teams within knowledge-intensive companies. In his important 1979 contribution, Weick argues that the effectiveness of teams performing complex tasks, such as the sharing of tacit, non-codified technical knowledge, can only be ensured when team members engage in direct communication and interact with each other in face-to-face settings.

In a similar manner, researchers within the MRT tradition adhere to the view that the personal communication network underlying virtual teams should for a large part be based on face-to-face communication when team members have to collaborate with each other and share each others' knowledge. According to these authors, the role of CMC, such as e-mail, should remain limited in geographically spread teams that face the complex tasks of inter-personal learning and the sharing of tacit know-how that is embedded in individual team members[48-60].

In most of these experimental studies, it is argued that virtual teams carry out their complex tasks most effectively when geographically distributed team members can interact and communicate with each other in a real-time environment that allows for the exchange of all types of (non)verbal cues and signals, such as speech, tone of voice, and physical gestures. By reading and interpreting these different kinds of signals, team members are able to reduce part of the uncertainty and complexity associated with sharing tacit knowledge. Hence, virtual teams are able to effectively conduct their complex tasks at hand. While both face-to-face communication and CMC enable real-time interaction amongst team members, the capacity of the latter communication form to provide for the transmission of nonverbal cues is very limited. A number of more recent articles within MRT (see, for example, Kraut, Fussell, Brennan, and Siegel, 2002; Olson, Teasley, Covi, and Olson, 2002; Weisband, 2002) have shown that virtual teams carrying out their complex tasks solely on the basis of CMC perform substantially worse than teams depending on a combination of CMC and face-to-face communication for their interaction and communication. As such, the prevailing view within the MRT tradition is that face-to-face communication and its ability to transmit nonverbal cues are crucial for effective learning within geographically spread teams and this important role cannot be replaced by computer-mediated forms of communication[61-64].

3.2 *New views refuting MRT*

In Section 3.1, we have outlined an important research tradition within communication theory, i.e. MRT, which states that face-to-face communication plays a highly significant role in inter-personal learning and effective tacit knowledge transfer within virtual teams. This crucial role for face-to-face communication in team member interaction is generally related to its ability to provide for the exchange of nonverbal cues amongst geographically distributed team members. Research within MRT has pointed out that CMC, as this form of communication generally lacks the capacity to transmit nonverbal signals, could never function as a substitute type of interaction within virtual teams.

In more recent years, an important strand of research has come into existence that, although it acknowledges the importance of face-to-face communication for the effective functioning of virtual teams, argues against some of the main assumptions underlying MRT. Specifically, a number of important contributions within this view have stressed that MRT has largely ignored to incorporate the influence of the latest technological advances in CMC, such as groupware and videoconferencing, into its analysis of geographically spread teams[62-69].

These authors claim that virtual teams are very capable of carrying out complex tasks, such as tacit, technical knowledge sharing, by relying largely on CMC for their interaction and communication. Especially in the case when there is a shared technological base that facilitates a better understanding of each others technology, there is an increased chance that CMC is very effective. When absorptive capacity (a shared technology base) is high among firms technological knowledge can be assimilated and transferred more easily among alliance partners (Lane and Lubatkin, 1998). Furthermore, their experimental research shows that the effectiveness of such CMC-based teams is equal to and often higher than the performance of teams functioning for the most part within face-to-face settings[65,67,68]. By and large, these researchers have related their findings to improvements in technology and enhanced attributes of CMC that provide team members with benefits they do not usually experience in face-to-face interactions. Examples of such qualities inherent to CMC are: the ability to reach several team members simultaneously; the possibility to share knowledge, exchange ideas, and learn from more than one team member at any given place and time; the ability to archive and document knowledge flows amongst team members; and, finally, the capacity to electronically search this knowledge base for previous discussions, ideas, and thoughts.

It is sometimes argued that the greater the team member diversity, the more time will be required for team members to form strong bonds. On the other hand, some teams may develop strong bonds and trust despite heterogeneity and short time spans whereas others may not. In order to examine the influence that CMC might have on alliances-based work, it is essential to understand the character of culture that is suitable in the alliance context. This is not an easy task, and more research is needed in the field of describing the culture of alliance. Jarvenpaa and Leidner[6] noted that "while there is a wealth of research on computer-mediated communication and research on cross-cultural communication, there is a paucity of research on cross-cultural computer-mediated communication." Jarvenpaa and Leidner have proposed a few hypotheses which have to be researched in relation to the specific alliance setting. We will highlight a few of their assumptions and leave it to future research. It is common knowledge that members from different (organizational) cultures vary in terms of their communication and group behaviours. Jarvenpaa and Leidner suggest individuals from individualistic (organizational) cultures tend to be less concerned with self-categorizing, are less influenced by group membership, have greater skills in entering and leaving new groups, and engage in more open and precise communication than individuals from collectivist cultures. This might have implications for alliances finding partners to enter the alliance network and using CMC to communicate. CMC leaves room for flexible interactions between members, but also is notable for "swift" team membership. These assumptions suggest that members from individualistic (organizational) cultures might be more ready to engage in (virtual) cooperation than individual members from collectivist cultures in computer mediated environments. Using CMC in an alliance setting sometimes caused trouble in understanding the partner from another organizational culture (due to the lack in visible cues). Research from Wiseman, Hammer, & Nishida has shown that previous cultural exposure is an important factor influencing communication behavior. "People with high confidence in the knowledge of other cultures tend to be more willing to explore cultural topics. This might suggest that people who are more culturally experienced might seek and disclose individuating information more than those who are not. The social dialog in turn might help develop trust on the team, at least in the eyes of the culturally experienced person"[6]. These assumptions have to be taken in mind while exploring alliances in a CMC environment.

4   Relevant Insights and Some Suggestions for Further Research

The aim of this chapter is to identify important insights from the communication literature and evaluate their relevance for improving our current understanding of inter-firm learning in international networks of knowledge-intensive companies. It has become clear from our review of the alliance and networking literature in Section 2 that learning and tacit knowledge sharing amongst networked firms have been subsequently analyzed at the level of the firm, the dyad, and the network. While the sharing of technical knowledge and effective inter-firm learning have been related to general characteristics of knowledge networks, such as centrality and tie strength, very few researchers in the networking literature have studied learning in the context of the personal communication network underlying alliance networks. As alliance networks can be seen as collections of geographically distributed groups of employees that share each others' knowledge through both face-to-face communication and CMC, insights from communication theory regarding the effectiveness of these forms of interaction in inter-personal learning might be highly relevant for alliance theory as well. Unfortunately, neither the networking literature nor the existing research body on communication have explored the potential for cross-fertilization between the two fields.

Our elaborate review of the networking literature has shown that the current understanding of effective inter-firm learning and tacit information sharing within international alliance networks is largely based on notions of network centrality and tie strength. Alliance researchers have argued that knowledge-intensive companies in central positions within alliance networks have the ability to tap into many technical knowledge flows and engage in inter-firm learning with numerous other firms[29,37]. Furthermore, relevant alliance research, that is grounded in the views of Coleman[22], has found that knowledge-intensive companies engaging in repeated, trustful relations with international partners are able to learn from these partners and gain access to their tacit knowledge base.

In relation to these findings, we can think of a number of important research question that have, until now, remained largely unanswered: Do knowledge-intensive companies make use of face-to-face communication, CMC, or a combination of both forms of interaction for facilitating inter-firm learning and tacit knowledge sharing within their international alliance networks? What are the specific characteristics of these personal communication networks underlying alliance networks and how do they affect the effectiveness of inter-firm learning? How do characteristics of the overall alliance network interact with specifics of the personal communication network in influencing inter-firm learning? Is a centrally positioned, knowledge-intensive company whose communication network is solely based on CMC less effective at learning from its international partners than a central firm whose communication network depends on a combination of both CMC and face-to-face interaction? Important insights from communication theory seem to suggest that effective inter-firm learning and tacit knowledge transfer within international alliance networks hinges upon the presence of well-functioning, personal communication networks that incorporate the benefits of face-to-face interaction, i.e. the transmission of nonverbal cues, and the advantages of CMC, i.e. the electronic documentation of knowledge flows[48,65,67,68]. In order to improve our current understanding of face-to-face communication, CMC, and inter-firm learning within international alliance networks, we urge future researchers to address these interdisciplinary issues as answering such questions will generate valuable insights that will further theory development in both fields of research.

References

1. Hagedoorn, J., Understanding the rationale of strategic technology partnering: inter-organizational modes of cooperation and sectoral differences, *Strategic Management Journal*, 14, 1993, pp. 371-385.
2. Powell, W., Koput, K., and Smith-Doerr, L., Inter-organizational collaboration and the locus of innovation: networks of learning in biotechnology, *Administrative Science Quarterly*, 41, 1996, pp. 116-145.
3. Roijakkers, N. and Hagedoorn, J., Inter-firm R&D partnering in high technology industries-patterns in the international biotechnology industry since 1975, in Dunning, J. and Boyd, G. (eds.), *Alliance capitalism and corporate management: entrepreneurial cooperation in knowledge-based economies*, Edward Elgar, Cheltenham, pp. 63-91, 2003.
4. Duysters, G. and Hagedoorn, J., Do company strategies and structures converge in global markets? Evidence from the computer industry, *Journal of International Business Studies*, 32, 2001, pp. 347-356.
5. Rasters, G., *Communication and Collaboration in Virtual Teams: did we get the message?* Print Partners Ipskamp, 2004.
6. Jarvenpaa, S.L. and Leidner, D.E., Communication and trust in global virtual teams, *Organization Science*, 10(6), 1999, pp. 791-815.
7. Cyert, R. and March, J., *A behavioral theory of the firm*, Prentice-Hall, Englewood Cliffs (NJ), 1963.
8. Nelson, R. and Winter, S., *The evolutionary theory of economic change*, Harvard University Press, Cambridge (MA), 1982.

9. Stinchcombe, A., *Information and organization*, University of California Press, Berkeley, 1990.

10. Cohen, W. and Levinthal, D., Innovation and learning: the two faces of R&D, *Economic Journal*, 99, 1989, pp. 569-596.

11. Cohen, W. and Levinthal, D., Absorptive capacity: a new perspective on learning and innovation, *Administrative Science Quarterly*, 35, 1990, pp. 128-152.

12. Brown, J. and Duguid, P., Organizational learning and communities of practice: toward a unified view of working, learning, and innovation, *Organization Science*, 2, 1991, pp. 40-57.

13. Dosi, G., Sources, procedures, and microeconomic effects of innovation, *Journal of Economic Literature*, 26, 1988, pp. 1120-1171.

14. Fai, F., Technological diversification: implications for the firm, Submission for Nelson and Winter conference, DRUID, Denmark, 2001.

15. Teece, D., Profiting from technological innovation, *Research Policy*, 15, 1986, pp. 285-305.

16. Tsai, W., Social capital, strategic relatedness, and the formation of intra-organizational linkages, *Strategic Management Journal*, 21, 2000, pp. 925-939.

17. Dodgson, M., Organizational learning: a review of some literatures, *Organization Studies*, 14, 1993, pp. 375-394.

18. Hamel, G., Competition for competence and inter-partner learning within international strategic alliances, *Strategic Management Journal*, 12, 1991, pp. 83-103.

19. Powell, W., Neither market nor hierarchy: Network forms of organization, in Cummings, L. and Staw, B. (eds.), *Research in organizational behaviour*, JAI Press, Greenwich, pp. 295-336, 1990.

20. Powell, W. and Brantley, P., Competitive cooperation in biotechnology: Learning through networks?, in Nohria, N. and Eccles, R. (eds.), *Networks and organizations: Structure, form, and action*, HBS Press, Boston, pp. 366-394, 1992.

21. Levinthal, D. and March, J., The myopia of learning, *Strategic Management Journal*, 14, 1994, pp. 95-112.

22. Coleman, J., Social capital in the creation of human capital, *American Journal of Sociology*, 94, 1988, pp. 95-120.

23. Burt, R., *Structural holes*, Harvard University Press, Cambridge, 1992.

24. Granovetter, M., Problems of explanation in economic sociology, in Nohria, N. and Eccles, R. (eds.), *Networks and organizations: Structure, form, and action*, HBS Press, Boston, pp. 25-56, 1992.

25. Gulati, R., Nohria, N., and Zaheer, A., Strategic networks, *Strategic Management Journal*, 21, 2000, pp. 203-215.

26. Knoke, D. and Kuklinski, J.H., *Network Analysis*, Sage, 1992.

27. Ahuja, G. and Katila, R., Technological acquisitions and the innovation performance of acquiring firms: a longitudinal study, *Strategic Management Journal*, 22, 2001, pp. 197-220.

28. Aldrich, H. and Fiol, M., Fools rush in: the institutional context of industry creation, *Academy of Management Review*, 19, 1994, pp. 645-670.

29. Brass, D., Butterfield, K., and Skaggs, B., Relationships and unethical behavior: a social network perspective, *Academy of Management Review*, 23, 1998, pp. 14-31.

30. Gargiulo, M. and Benassi, M., Trapped in your own net? Network cohesion, structural holes, and the adaptations of social capital, *Organization Science*, 11, 2000, pp. 183-196.

31. Granovetter, M., The strength of weak ties, *American Journal of Sociology*, 78, 1973, pp. 1360-1380.

32. Gulati, R., Alliances and Networks, *Strategic Management Journal*, 19, 1998, pp. 293-317.

33. Henderson, R. and Cockburn, I., Measuring competence? Exploring firm effects in pharmaceutical research, *Strategic Management Journal*, 15, 1994, pp. 63-84.

34. Madhavan, R., Koka, B., and Prescott, J., Networks in transition: How industry events (re)shape inter-firm relationships, *Strategic Management Journal*, 19, 1998, pp. 439-459.

35. Podolny, J. and Stuart, T., A role-based ecology of technological change, *American Journal of Sociology*, 5, 1995, pp. 1224-1260.

36. Rowley, T., Behrens, D., and Krackhardt, D., Redundant governance structures: an analysis of structural and relational embeddedness in the steel and semiconductor industries, *Strategic Management Journal*, 21, 2000, pp. 369-386.

37. Stuart, T., Producer network positions and propensities to collaborate: An investigation of strategic alliance formations in a high-technology industry, *Administrative Science Quarterly*, 43, 1998, pp. 668-698.

38. Stuart, T. and Podolny, J., Local search and the evolution of technological capabilities, *Strategic Management Journal*, 17, 1996, pp. 21-38.

39. Von Hippel, E., *Sources of innovation*, Oxford University Press, New York, 1988.

40. Hagedoorn, J. and Duysters, G., Learning in dynamic inter-firm networks: the efficacy of multiple contacts, *Organization Studies*, 23, 2002, pp. 525-548.

41. Ahuja, G., Collaboration networks, structural holes, and innovation: a longitudinal study, *Administrative Science Quarterly*, 45, 2000, pp. 425-455.

42. Burt, R., Structural holes versus network closure as social capital, in Lin, N., Cook, K., and Burt, R. (eds.), *Social capital: theory and research*, Walter de Gruyter, New York, pp. 31-56, 2001.

43. Eisenhardt, K. and Martin, J., Dynamic capabilities: what are they?, *Strategic Management Journal*, 21, 2000, pp. 1105-1121.

44. Granstrand, O., Patel, P., and Pavitt, K., Multi-technology corporations: why they have distributed rather than distinctive core competences, *California Management Review*, 39, 1997, pp. 8-25.

45. Bierly, P. and Chakrabarti, A., Generic knowledge strategies in the U.S. pharmaceutical industry, *Strategic Management Journal*, 17, 1996, pp. 123-135.

46. Reed, R. and DeFillipi, R., Causal ambiguity, barriers to imitation, and sustainable competitive advantage, *Academy of Management Review*, 15, 1990, pp. 88-102.

47. Volberda, H., Toward the flexible form: how to remain vital in hypercompetitive environments, *Organization Science*, 7, 1996, pp. 359-374.

48. Daft, R. and Lengel, R., Information richness: a new approach to managerial behavior and organizational design, in Cumming, L. and Staw, B. (eds.), *Research in organizational behavior*, Jai, Greenwich, pp. 191-233, 1984.

49. Daft, R. and Lengel, R., Organizational information requirements, media richness and structural design, *Management Science*, 32, 1986, pp. 554-571.

50. Daft, R. and Wiginton, J., Language and organization, *Academy of Management Review*, 4, 1979, pp. 179-191.

51. Daft, R., Lengel, R., and Trevino, L., Message equivocality, media selection, and manager performance: implications for information systems, *MIS Quarterly*, 11, 1987, pp. 355-366.

52. Dennis, A. and Valacich, J., Rethinking media richness: towards a theory of media synchronicity, in *Proceedings of the 32nd annual Hawaii International Conference on System Sciences*, 1999.

53. Dennis, A., Kinney, S., and Hung, Y., Gender differences in the effects of media richness, *Small Group Research*, 30, 1999, pp. 405-437.

54. Duxbury, L. and Neufeld, D., The impacts of telecommuting on intra-organizational communication, *Journal of Engineering and Technology Management*, 16, 1999, pp. 1-28.

55. Fulk, J., Schmitz, J., and Steinfield, C., A social influence model of technology use, in Fulk, J. and Steinfield, C. (eds.), *Organizations and communication technology*, Sage, Newbury Park (CA), pp. 117-140, 1990.

56. Saunders, C. and Jones, J., Temporal sequences in information acquisition for decision making: A focus on source and medium, *Academy of Management Review*, 15, 1990, pp. 29-46.

57. Kock, N., Can communication medium limitations foster better group outcomes? An action research study, *Information & Management*, 34, 1998, pp. 295-305.

58. Short, J., Williams, E., and Christie, B., *The social psychology of telecommunications*, Wiley, London, 1976.

59. Trevino, L., Lengel, R., and Daft, R., Media symbolism, media richness, and media choice in organizations: a symbolic interactionist perspective, *Communication Research*, 14, 1987, pp. 553-574.

60. Yu, R., Information technology and Media Choice of CFO, 1997. http://members.optushome.com.au/raymondyu/pub/thesis/content.htm

61. Baron, N., Letters by phone or speech by other means: the linguistics of e-mail, *Language and Communication*, 18, 1998, pp. 133-170.

62. El-Shinnawy, M. and Markus, M., The poverty of media richness theory: explaining people's choice of electronic mail vs. voice mail, *International Journal of Human-Computer Studies*, 46, 1997, pp. 443-467.

63. Markus, M., Electronic mail as the medium of managerial choice, *Organization Science*, 5, 1994, pp. 502-527.

64. Nohria, N. and Eccles, R., Face-to-face: making network organizations work, in Nohria, N. and Eccles, R. (eds.), *Networks and organizations: structure, form, and action*, HBS Press, Boston, 1992.

65. Adrianson, L., Gender and computer-mediated communication: group processes in problem solving, *Computers in Human Behavior*, 17, 2001, pp. 71-94.

66. Barker, V., Abrams, V., Tiyaamornwong, D., Seibold, A., Duggan, H., Park, M., and Sebastian, M., New contexts for relational communication in groups, *Small Group Research*, 31, 2000, pp. 470-503.

67. Burke, K., Aytes, K., Chidambaram, L., and Johnson, J., A study of partially distributed work groups: the impact of media, location, and time on perceptions and performance, *Small Group Research*, 30, 1999, pp. 453-490.

68. Lipnack, J. and Stamps, J., *Virtual teams: people working across boundaries with technology*, Wiley, London, 2000.

69. Suh, K., Impact of communication medium on task performance and satisfaction: an examination of media richness theory, *Information and Management*, 35, 1999, pp. 295-312.

70. Weick, K., *The social psychology of organizing*, Addison-Wesley, Reading (MA), 1979.

CHAPTER 12

Strategic Planning and Outsourcing

Colin G. Ash

School of Management Information Systems
Edith Cowan University, Perth
WA 6027, Australia
Email: c.ash@ecu.edu.au

1 A Historical Perspective on Strategic Planning

There are many existing models of strategy - designed strategy, emergent strategy, strategy as revolution, and yet few examples of organisations applying these well defined models to secure competitive advantage in the current environment of constant change. Are such strategic models redundant? Beinhocker[1] suggests that what is needed is a model of a world where innovation, change and uncertainty are the natural state of things. In keeping with Moore's view of strategy in the age of *business ecosystems* Lansiti and Levien[2] interpret strategy as ecology, were organisations need to learn the "art of pruning."

Strategy is full of contradictions and dilemmas as evidenced by the Red Queen effect[3]. The Red Queen in Through the Looking Glass remarks "It takes all the running you can do to keep in the same place". In a system of co-evolution, when the predator learns to run faster, the prey starts to climb trees and then the predator develops alternative means of transport and so on. Long term sustainable advantage isn't possible without continual adaptation. A study of the performance of more than 400 organisations over thirty years reveals that companies find it difficult to maintain higher performance levels than their competitors for more than about five years at a time[1].

Driven by such phenomena as the World Wide Web, mass customisation, compressed product life cycles, new distribution channels and new forms of integrated organisations, the most fundamental elements of doing business are changing and a totally new business environment is emerging. This environment variously described as the

Electronic Business Community (EBC)[4], electronic economy[5], electronic market[6], electronic market place or space[7] and virtual market[8] is characterised by new forms of IT-enabled intermediation, virtual supply chains, increasing knowledge and information based business architecture strategies. This new business paradigm can be described as e-Business where core business processes may need to be rethought and redesigned, new organisational forms and inter-organisational forms may need to be developed. Here emphasis for strategic planning is on balancing cooperation and competition (coopetition).

Organizations source their requirements in a variety of ways. Figure 1 illustrates the "Sourcing" classification scheme scoped by this chapter for discussion of the conceptual frameworks on strategic planning. The chapter sections are defined at three levels of abstraction: (i) Sourcing, (ii) In and Outsourcing, and (iii) e-Sourcing. IT outsourcing is a component of Outsourcing.

The first section explores three frameworks where the focus is on generic *Strategic Sourcing*. The next two sections discuss the merits of various *Strategic Outsourcing* and *IT Outsourcing* models. The final section on *e-Sourcing* commends frameworks on strategic sourcing in e-Business, e-Marketplaces and e-Supply Chain. All frameworks are summarized in Table 4.

2 Strategic Sourcing

Most companies can substantially leverage their resources through strategic sourcing as an optimal combination of outsourcing and insourcing. Strategically insourcing by focusing investment and management attention on its core competencies, and strategically outsourcing many other activities where it cannot be or need not be best. There are always some inherent risks in outsourcing, but there are also risks and costs of insourcing. When approached within a genuinely strategic framework, using the variety of outsourcing options available and analyzing the strategic issues, companies can overcome many of the costs and risks[9].

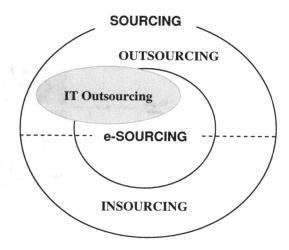

Figure 1. Classification of Sourcing

2.1 A framework for strategic sourcing

Welch and Nayak[10] developed a strategic sourcing model that augments the traditional cost analysis by considering strategic and technological factors. The model examines three dimensions of business activity:

- process technology's role in providing competitive advantage,
- maturity of the process technologies under consideration, and
- competitors' process technology positions.

After following the model's guidelines, the tentative sourcing decision will be one of the following: (a) make, (b) marginal make, (c) develop internal capability, (d) buy, (e) marginal buy, or (f) develop suppliers. Using this framework in conjunction with a cost analysis can help companies make the sourcing decisions that will move them toward best practice. Beyond static cost issues, there are long term strategic considerations intertwined with the make-or-buy decision that are of even greater importance. These strategic issues are the focus of the framework.

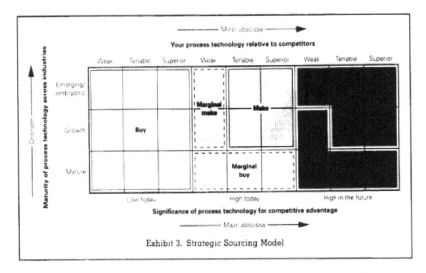

Figure 2. Strategic Sourcing Model

Source: Welch and Nayak (1992: p. 27).

In Figure 2 the authors detail why and how strategic variables should be considered in the course of a make-or-buy decision:

- Process technology and its relationship to competitive advantage
- Maturity of process technology
- Competitors' process technology positions

2.2 *A framework for strategy, structure and performance*

Organizational issues have attracted a great deal of attention in logistics. However, developments such as expanding use of information technology and outsourcing call into question conventional assumptions of past research. Chow *et al.*[11] developed a framework of the core strategic structural properties of logistics organizations, including supply chains.

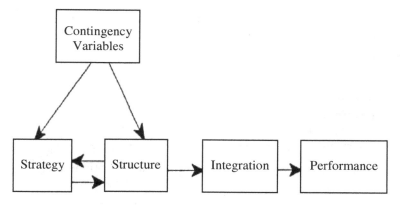

Figure 3. Strategy and Structure Model
Source: Chow *et al.* (1995: p. 287).

Figure 3 represents a framework for logistics research that is focused on strategy, structure and performance. A contingency theory approach is recommended to yield insights into the complex relationships between logistics strategy, organization structure, systems integration and performance. The model could be used in research on the organization of logistics and would facilitate comparability among studies.

2.3 *A framework for strategic capability sourcing*

The question of what functions should be outsourced and which should be left inside under the control of the organization is the fundamental question. What business assets/capabilities should be insourced or outsourced? Gottfredson *et al.*[12] broaden the notion of a company's asset configuration (sourcing of business processes and function; Venkatraman and Henderson[13] embrace the concept of business *capability*).

Gottfredson *et al.*[12] developed a sourcing opportunity map based on a US case study of the 7-Eleven chain of convenience stores. Using their opportunity map (Figure 4) managers can determine which functions have the highest outsourcing potential and which should stay inside the organization. The vertical axis plots how proprietary a capability is for the organization. The horizontal axis measures how common the capability is within or outside an industry. The less proprietary and the more common a function is, the stronger it is as a candidate for outsourcing.

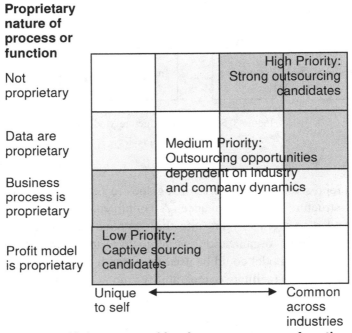

Figure 4. Capability Sourcing Model

Source: Gottfredson *et al.* (2005: p. 138).

The 7-Eleven the strategy issue is no longer about ownership of capabilities that matters "but rather the company's ability to control and make the most of capabilities"[12]. The authors warn that the new era of *capability* sourcing will "trigger organizational redesign and require a new set of managerial skills" (p. 132). This presents a challenge for research into the area of organisational transformation and management of changing roles and new competencies[14].

3 Strategic Outsourcing

Over the last decade, outsourcing has proved to be a relevant strategic option for companies narrowing their operations to focus on core competencies. Quinn and Hilmer[15] analyze the process of outsourcing manufacturing to cost-efficient and innovative suppliers in support of internal resources and capabilities.

3.1 *Outsourcing as part of the strategic plan*

As part of the strategic plan companies can substantially leverage their resources through strategic outsourcing by: (i) developing a few well-selected core competencies of significance to customers and which the company can be the best in the world, (ii) focusing investment and management attention on these core competencies, and (iii) strategically outsourcing many other activities where it cannot be or need not be best.

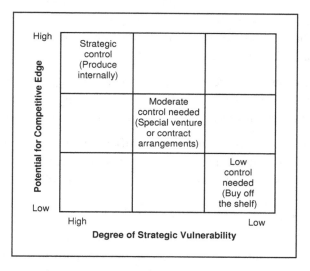

Figure 5. Strategic Outsourcing Model

Source: Quinn and Hilmer (1994: p. 48).

"When approached within a genuinely strategic framework, using the variety of out-sourcing options available and analyzing the strategic issues, companies can overcome many of the unnecessary costs and risks"[15] (p. 50). The model illustrated in Figure 5 is supplemented by two secondary models:

- a range of outsourcing options, from "make" through "buy", and
- a range of potential contract relationships, from full ownership to short term contract. Collectively these three models represent a foundation.

3.1.1 *Reactive and strategic process*

As firms continue to focus on core competencies and outsource non-core products and services to external suppliers, supply chain management is increasingly viewed as a source of competitive advantage. However, if the supply chain is to be a source of competitive advantage, suppliers' performance must be managed and developed to meet the needs of the buying firm. A process model is developed for supplier development. Using this process model as a framework, two approaches buying firms use in supplier development are compared:

- reactive efforts to increase the performance of laggard suppliers, and
- strategic efforts to increase the capabilities of the supply base to enhance the buying firm's long-term competitive advantage.

Strategic efforts were found to significantly increase the buying company's involvement in suppliers' processes, and required greater dedication of resources, personnel, and communication[16].

3.1.2 *Outsourcing manufacturing model*

Momme[17] proposed a scientific reference model founded on manufacturing strategy to help choose the right level of analysis and steer the research process. From this, a system model is developed to enable identification of the production system elements and internal support functions. Finally, a framework that links the six phases of the entire outsourcing process to strategic planning is synthesized. The framework includes a logical sequence of key activities with built-in performance measures and expected output for each of the phases (p. 71). The research methodology combines theory study with case study and action research in Aalborg Industries. The framework has strategic and operational implications for manufacturing in the heavy industrial sector.

3.2 *Value from strategic outsourcing*

The question of where the value will come from, if outsourcing is to create value, is examined. The conventional response to this question has been well worked through in the literature on vertical integration and transaction cost economics[18]. The real cost of buying an output rather than making it must include the costs of identifying suitable providers, communicating needs to them, monitoring their progress and outputs, avoiding predatory behavior by them and so on. Even if one accepts the assumption that outsiders will have scale advantages while insiders will create lower transaction costs, these dimensions do not in themselves provide an adequate framework for assessment.

Other factors important in determining value creation and value appropriation are examined. If outsourcing is to be fully integrated as a valid and respectable management tool, it must be pursued with a clear sense of where and why it leads to enhanced value.

A framework is provided by Dodd and Renterghem[19] to help deal with strategic planning opportunities afforded by adopting outsourcing as well as helping with the inevitable concern regarding quality of the ongoing administration and employee interaction. For service providers, discussion is offered on how to work with plan sponsors to help ensure that outsourcing fulfills their expectations. The answer to meeting both service delivery and overall plan goals lies in properly defined measurements established within the context of a continuous improvement process. By using this framework, a company and its outsourcing partner should be able to develop a strategic partnership aimed at achieving the desired business result.

3.3 *The outsourcing decision*

Building a solid business case is a key activity for a successful outsourcing initiative[20]. Before making a recommendation for outsourcing, managers should first craft a strategic approach to assess both the opportunity and the risk of outsourcing.

The first step is to establish a baseline, outlining current organizational processes and procedures and the affiliated costs. Following this step is the identification of the benefits of outsourcing, other than financial. This includes improved employee satisfaction and retention. Third is the analysis of a status quo approach-must something be done? Fourth, managers must weigh the potential improvements in productivity and cost savings. Lastly, managers should analyze performance metrics to assist in achieving measurable results. The ultimate decision to outsource will hinge on management's ability to demonstrate its worthiness for doing core business. Normally a financial analysis model such as return on investment or net present value is used[2] (p. 11).

3.4 *Outsourcing relationships and partners*

Outsourcing is an increasingly important initiative being pursued by corporations across a wide range of industries in pursuit of improved efficiency. A conceptual framework is provided by Vining and Globerman[21] to assist managers in identifying and implementing outsourcing decisions. In particular, the framework suggests a way for managers to identify the pre- and post-contractual risks associated with outsourcing decisions along with strategies that can be implemented in the pre-contractual stage in order to mitigate those risks. Empirical findings from the transactions cost literature are referenced to illustrate elements of the conceptual framework.

In uncertain economic times, "smart" partnering is used to create effective alliances and partnerships[22]. This approach provides services to human resources and compensation/benefits in an efficient, cost-effective manner, while meeting the needs of the organization, its management and its employees. The Bank of America, one of the world's largest banking institutions, and Exult Inc., a much smaller vendor and supplier of business process outsourcing, have demonstrated how to work together for mutual gain by employing a model for:

- assessing what both organizations want from the partnership,
- exploring their partnership by identifying areas of common interest and mutual benefit,
- initiating projects to build trust and effectiveness within and between organizations, and
- committing partners to a formal relationship and mutual strategic planning.

A high level of partnering intelligence grows out of an understanding of the six key partnering attributes. These are: 1. self-disclosure and feedback, 2. win-win orientation, 3. ability to trust, 4. future orientation, 5. comfort with change, and 6. comfort with interdependence. Smart partnering is not an easy process; it is hard work. However, compensation and benefits professionals stand only to gain from developing an awareness of what is involved in the six partnering attributes.

3.5 *Outsourcing — different industries*

In the pharmaceutical industry, the ability to forge, manage, and sustain strategic outsourcing relationships is increasingly critical to competitive success[23]. A US consulting firm has drawn on its research and experience to develop a strategic outsourcing architecture. A systematic set of practices and frameworks for creating strategic outsourcing arrangements. This architecture, or process, is designed to help companies forge relationships. These relationships will not only cut costs, but they also will allow pharmaceutical companies to join forces with strategic outsourcing partners to find broader, breakthrough benefits in terms of revenue growth, market share gains, and customer service improvements. In short, to become a more "powerful" competitor.

In practice the consulting firm draws upon its outsourcing manual that is designed to help a company's senior executives understand and implement strategic outsourcing arrangements within their organizations.

The architecture comprises six phases: strategy, analytics and selection, co-creation, operational planning, structuring, and management.

Many academic medical centers have significant capacity constraints and limited ability to expand services to meet demand. Health care management should employ strategic thinking to deal with service demands[24]. Their outsourcing approach uses three organizational models to develop a theoretical framework to guide the selection of clinical services for outsourcing.

3.6 *Globalization and offshore outsourcing*

Globalization is fundamentally shifting the status quo of contact centre outsourcing; many firms are now considering outsourcing for the first time as not only an operational efficiency driver, but also a key globalization enabler. Karklins[25] observes the following reasons as:

- Going it alone can prove daunting to firms without an international presence or experience, and the issues are complex,
- Working with an outsourcer allows a firm to tap into an existing operation, and
- Leverage an outsourcer's experience and capital while getting a globalization strategy up and running more quickly.

The result for many has been "speed to market" and the establishment of immediate cost and execution advantages. Robinson and Kalakota[26] provide a phased model of offshoring identifies as; entry, development, and integration process that offshoring companies go through for successful offshore business. The authors identify, at the outset, integration of skills and management practices, management commitment, and organizational culture that encourages and supports effective offshore as elements critical to the success of offshore outsourcing. In clarifying the misconception that all offshoring involve outsourcing, the authors point out that unlike outsource processing, offshored processing can be handed to third-party vendors or remain in-house in a company's remote low-cost location.

The authors give descriptions of numerous offshore outsourcing models based on the dimensions of ownership or relationship structure, and the geographic location of the work. To supplement these models, the authors also describe the models from the perspective of approach as task-oriented (piecemeal) and process-oriented (comprehensive) revenue models. The authors point out that the success of offshoring venture depends on the depth of analysis conducted and time spent to select the right model. For example, offshore outsourcing for American Express has not been as challenging as it has been to Dell.

The authors describe the course taken by Dell as comprehensive approach covering information technology, customer care, finance and accounting, human resource and transaction processing, which was considered to be risky due to the complexity and variation of the business processes landscape covered. The case extensively addresses business process outsourcing (BPO) and information technology outsourcing (ITO) citing lower cost of procurement, reduced management overhead, and familiarity of service provider with client needs as the criteria for offshore outsourcing[27]. The authors suggest companies considering offshoring possibilities address three important questions relating to the competitive advantage that they may have to lose, incremental value they gain to justify the offshoring effort taken, and organizational management control they may have to lose due to offshoring. One major shortcoming is the omission of manufacturing and supply chain processes as components of the comprehensive business process outsourcing[27]. The book can be used as a supplement by academicians teaching courses in operations and production management, and as a reference book by practitioners in the offshoring businesses.

4 Strategic IT Outsourcing

In this section the focus is on IT Outsourcing. There is the assumption is that outsourcing is part of the overall strategic plan and IT outsourcing is part of this outsourcing strategic plan[28].

Studies on determining the degree to which an organisation's IT function should be outsourced became popular when Lacity and Hirschheim[29] studied the various levels of outsourcing. They suggested that organisations should only outsource the portions of their IT function which are not part of the business core. Further studies by Lacity and

Hirschheim[30] brought forward the idea of insourcing as an alternative to conventional IT outsourcing. The selective sourcing approach was introduced by Lacity, Willcocks and Feeny[31]. This outsourcing approach was reiterated by Currie[32].

A framework proposed by Venkatraman and Loh[33] to guide senior managers in answering questions about managing information technology (IT) resources and identifying the best solutions for their information systems (IS) organizations. This framework is predicated on an ongoing IT Study on IT Strategy that examines the strategic role of IT in supporting and shaping business strategies within leading Fortune 500 firms. The vertical dimension in the framework articulates the locus of a firm's IT competencies - ranging from internal to interorganizational (involving an array of external organizations in addition to the user firm). The horizontal dimension deals with the locus of IT decision rights - whether it is concentrated or distributed among a set of managers within the firm. It is advocated that managers consider moving along the diagonal by combining the best of outsourcing and insourcing. It is entirely possible to adopt an insourcing mode for current IS operations while developing a set of inter-firm relationships with external partners for obtaining new IT-based competences for tomorrow.

IT outsourcing is a growth phenomenon in the developed economies. However, it is not often managed as strategically as it should be. Willcocks *et al.*[34] draw on evidence from thirty case histories in the UK, as the basis is presented for a strategic approach.

Six critical factors are identified around which IT outsourcing decisions can be based. A framework is provided by Willcocks *et al.*[34] for decision-making based on organizational experiences of different levels of success, and the additional factors that need to be borne in mind as a reality check, to ensure that the IT outsourcing decision can be delivered upon, are discussed. A more strategic approach to IT outsourcing is argued for and frameworks are provided to enable decision-makers to think through the issues presented by an impending IT sourcing decision.

Outsourcing has been a key method for managing IT and systems (ITS) portfolios of companies since the early 1990s. Earlier research by Kishore[35] developed a framework that classifies client-provider outsourcing relationships into Four Outsourcing Relationship Types (FORT). Outsourcing relationships between client firms and their service providers may change over time. Firms should consider the costs and difficulties of moving from one quadrant to another in determining the direction of movement. Firms can consider multiple movements from one cell to other cells in the matrix through selective outsourcing.

Again, firms must have a clear plan for their future movement within the FORT framework. Outsourcing should be considered more as a total decision about management of relationships with service providers rather than as simple subcontracting for IS commodities[35]. Pollalis[36] in his research on "patterns of co-alignment in information-intensive organizations" has developed a model for business performance through integration strategies. This research suggests, develops and tests a strategic co-alignment model by examining three types of integration that impact the planning process and the overall performance of information-intensive organizations: technological integration (TI), functional integration (FI) and strategic integration (SI). The results of this research yield some useful set of guidelines for theory building for IS, as well as for the business practice aspect of IS: most interesting is the role of consistency (co-alignment) between an organization's business and strategic information systems plans to improve overall firm performance[37]. Other recommendations include; having a high degree of involvement of IS executives in corporate planning, the use of outsourcing services to promote organizational systems integration, and the importance of internal coordination mechanisms to facilitate both systems consistency and lower transaction costs.

Most studies undertaken in the area of IT outsourcing seem to focus only on the customer's perspective leaving a gap in knowledge about the vendor's perspective. The aim of Teo and Chan[38] case study of four Singaporean firms is to correct this deficiency by investigating the views of four organisations providing IT services in Singapore, and comparing this to the current literature base of customer views. The findings showed that the vendor's views about security, contract management and flexibility differed from the customer's point of view. However, two issues, partnerships and vendor inexperience, seem to match the vendor issues found in this study. Additionally, two approaches were found to be used by vendors in the IT outsourcing activities, multiple-team approach and single-team approach (Figures 6a and 6b). A multiple–team approach is likely to be used by vendors having a contract-based relationship and single-team approach is likely to be used by vendors having a partnership-based relationship.

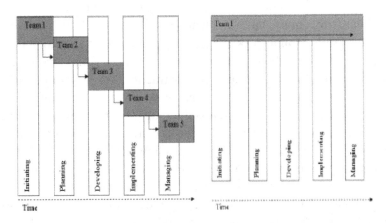

Figure 6a. Multiple-Team Strategy   Figure 6b. Single-Team Strategy

Source: Teo and Chan (2004).

5   Strategic E-Sourcing

5.1   *E-business strategies*

A meta-analysis by Viehland[39] of e-business writings by several authors, proposes six critical success factors for developing an e-business strategy. Table 1 lists learning to outsource to improve e-business performance as the second success factor. For this purpose, a critical success factor is defined as, a factor that is considered critical to the success of the e-business strategy. "Successful performance in this area will assure the success of the strategy and the attainment of the organisation's goals"[40] (p. 4).

Table 1. Six Critical Success Factors for E-Business Strategy

CSF1	Create a consumer/customer-centric strategy
CSF2	Embrace outsourcing to improve business performance
CSF3	Use information management to differentiate your product
CSF4	Be part of an e-business community
CSF5	Act like a new entrant
CSF6	Executive leadership is essential

Source: Viehland (2000: p. 912).

In reference to CSF4, Kalakota and Robinson[41] commend an e-business strategy to adopt partners as part of the extended enterprise. This represents a new generation of outsourcing alliances, beyond contractual relationships. However better coordination of partners and vendors/suppliers is required.

> The goal of the new business designs is to create flexible outsourcing alliances between companies that not only off load costs, but also make customers ecstatic[41] (p. 8).

Learning how to outsource is part of the adoption of the e-business model. Typically, successful organisations will have embraced Enterprise Resource Planning (ERP) systems to integrate e-business processes within the organisation and to underpin the creation of integrated interorganisational systems[42]. This frequently results in new business processes, organisational structures, human resource skill requirements, management roles and knowledge management systems[43]. To be successful in this new climate, however, organisations have to learn new approaches to planning for collaborative systems and to manage e-business enabled cycles of innovation[44,45]. Few studies have explored the dynamics of e-business strategic planning and little information is available on how to implement new paradigms successfully and how to ensure more effective e-business performance as a result[46,47].

5.1.1 *Virtual organizing model*

Venkatraman, and Henderson[13] in "Real Strategies for Virtual Organizing" craft an e-business model for the learning organisation that promotes harmony within three dimensions — customer/market interaction, asset configuration and knowledge leverage — supported by a reboust information communication technology platform. They view this as the virtual organizing model for ICT empowered organisation with ERP as the integrated back-office systems. Asset configuration or *virtual sourcing* (B2B) refers to competency leverage:

- Efficient sourcing of standard components or modules
- Asset leverage in the business network
- Create new competencies through alliances

The VOing model in Table 2 views business at three stages of development, each with performance objectives for greater virtual progression:

Stage 1 - work unit focus on *sourcing modules* for improved operating efficiency.

Stage 2 - organisation focus on *process interdependence* for virtual and economic value adding.

Stage 3 - inter-organisation focus on *resource coalitions* for sustained innovation and growth.

(i) Sourcing Modules

The asset configuration stage is classified as the "sourcing modules." e-ERP system design must allow for the establishing and leveraging of a company's supplier networks[13].

(ii) Process Interdependence

The second stage of asset configuration focuses on the opportunities and challenges in dynamically customising products and services. E-ERP systems must enable companies in responding to competitive markets and rapidly eroding margins by offering customised products and services.

(iii) Resource Coalitions

The third stage of asset configuration is about "the establishment of a resource network." e-ERP systems must enable companies to effectively link business partners and competitors into dynamic resource coalition. This signals a shift towards balancing competition with cooperation.

In Table 2 multiple case studies were used to assess how certain components of products and services are virtually sourced for; improved operating efficiency, customization, and gaining market position due to superior resource networks. Baldwin and Clarke[48] argue that in a new age of modularity, the value-adding role of a corporation is less in the manufacture of a critical component than in the creation of a product or service system.

Table 2. Descriptors of VOing for Each Dimension at Each Stage

	Stages of Development of Asset Configuration		
	Stage 1	Stage 2	Stage 3
Virtual Sourcing	Sourcing Modules EDI Efficiency Procurement networks Sourcing logic revision	Process Interdependence Process outsourcing Asset utilisation IT affects business scope	Resource Coalitions Dependent on relationships for assembling capabilities *Balance your strengths by competition v cooperation
Business Focus	Work-unit	Organisation	Inter-organisation
Examples	Customer service, purchasing, product development	Assemble and coordinate assets; creating value through use of digital info.	Business network to design and leverage interdependent e-communities
Outcomes & Performance gains	Improved operating efficiency (ROI)	Virtual and economic value added (EVA)	Sustained innovation and growth (SIG)

Details and key issues (*) were extracted from Venkatraman and Henderson (1998:34).

5.1.2 *Dynamic planning model*

Planning for such systems has to encompass capabilities for managing, measuring and evaluating organisational abilities to create value across the network of alliances and hence requires evolutionary approaches which can be tailored to organisational needs at different stages of e-business growth[14,44]. This whole process is sometimes described as IT governance, including strategic planning processes, change management processes and accountability and return on investment[47,49]. Planning cannot take place in isolation and must encompass all aspects of the emergent learning organisation in virtual networks of value alliances.

The changing strategic focus across the stages of the dynamic planning model are classified in Table 3, and viewed as interdependent and supportive of each other. This is especially so in the area of *outcomes and performances objectives* where *efficiency* through employee self-service and *effectiveness* through empowerment in customer care is used to support *value adding* activities for sustained competitive advantage. Value includes complementary benefits realized for all network partners across the virtual supply chain. The interplay between strategy, e-business, change management and evaluation is crucial to the creation of dynamic capabilities and will enable organisations to gain sustainable competitive advantage[45].

At stage one of the extended enterprise, the focus is very much internal with top-down planning and an emphasis on training employees to become proficient in self-service to improve operating efficiencies and increase returns on investment. The first shift comes when the enterprise extends its relationships across the full supply chain for products or services. At this stage, the focus is on empowerment and self-learning through bottom up planning within the organisation. There is also a realignment of business objectives to include external alliances across the supply chain. Finally, the focus will be directed towards re-engineering the supply chain though collaborative planning to gain value enhancement throughout the networked community. This occurs with a shift of business model towards the e-enterprise.

Table 3. Stages of Dynamic Planning Model

	Stage 1	Stage 2	Stage 3
Strategic focus	Self-service	Empowerment	Relationship building
Planning focus	Top-down Training Internal	Bottom-up Self-learning External	Collaborative Value enhancement Community
Outcomes and Performance Gains	Improved operating efficiency (ROI)	Effective resourcing (QWL)	Virtual and economic value added (EVA)

Key: Return on investment (ROI), Quality of working life (QWL), Economic value added
Source: Ash and Burn (2003).

By taking a more holistic approach, executives can turn these stages of a company's transformation into the drivers of e-business excellence. So the central task for senior managers lies in understanding what drives operational excellence in the eERP realm, and then committing the necessary resources (structures, training, planning responsibilities) to the development of the drivers. To this end managers should assess the company's operations by looking at both the traditional and e-business measures. For example Dell and Siemens used the same internal performance measures in both e-business and traditional business operations. Table 3 identifies the measures for outcomes and performance gains and the relationships between them, within the federated planning model. They canvass the measures at the level of employee performance. The use of three research models was specifically intended to give breadth to the study and allow the incorporation of a variety of strategic views which informed the planning process.

5.2 *E-marketplace strategies*

Little theoretical work has been performed that truly helps e-marketplace managers to understand and craft strategy. Brunn *et al.*[50] developed the "Temple framework" to help fill this gap. This theoretical framework represents an holistic understanding of how e-marketplaces, in order to achieve success, must create a powerful setup (for a sound strategic position) to meet the challenges of building liquidity and capturing value for buyers and sellers. Within the setup phase of the framework there is the implication that each buyer's e-procurement strategy must be integrated into the overall procurement strategy.

5.2.1 *Strategic e-procurement model*

The implementations of desktop procurement systems (DPS) designed for the non-professional procurement staff (Segev *et al.* 2001) shows B2B e-Procurement has resulted shorter lead times and lower costs. The focus is an indirect procurement function that includes Maintenance, Repair, and Operating (MRO) items (Figure 7). It brings into play the

All Market Segments Strategy

	NON-CRITICAL	CRITICAL
HIGH (VALUE)	*Services:* • *Engineering* • *Civil* • *Contract mining* • *Maintenance* • *Site management*	*Essential Items:* • *Energy* • *Explosives* • *Chemicals* • *Trucks* • *Loaders*
LOW	*Consumables:* • *Safety* • *Office* • *Travel* • *Industrial* • *Electrical*	*MRO Items: (Most cases)* • *Valves* • *Bearings* • *Electric Motors* • *Belting* • *Pumps*

Figure 7. E-Procurement Strategy for the Global E-Marketplace

Source: Ash and Poezyn (2005).

issue of employee self service that includes retraining for this change in roles, and freeing resources in the compnany's purchasing department for strategic tasks. The final conceptual framework is distilled from the findings of a study by Ash and Poezyn[51] of a Global e-Marketplace (GeM). It is developed as a model of e-Marketplace implementation for sustained innovation and growth. The approach is a strategic collaborative process between alliances where there is a continual review of alignment of the e-business adoption against business objectives. This is quite distinct from the 'one size fits all' approach of centralized planning and allows strategy to evolve with changing market conditions. This approach provides the means to explicitly define and manage relationships between supply network partners and to monitor trends and trigger a revisiting of strategic decisions across the network (Oliver *et al.*, 2003).

GeM has set its sights on growing its offerings within the mining and metals community, "while at the same time broadening the 'footprint' to cover industries such as oil and gas, utilities, steel, and others, where the supply chains characteristics and supplier profiles are very similar"[52]. We can report that recently three large global companies chose to join the e-Marketplace; Nestles, Renault, and Shell[53]. The new benefits scorecard represented in Figure 7 is a strategic approach where process between alliances where there is a continual review of alignment of the e-Procurement adoption against all procurement objectives. The assumption is that an organisation's e-Procurement strategy is a part of its total procurement strategy.

The e-Procurement strategy of the nine cases studied thus far tend to be isolated to the MRO items (shaded), those "critical" items with "low" value. GeM now considers growing into all market segments across its global "footprint" of other industries at all locations. The key business drivers and performance measure of GeM's newest strategic procurement plan is aimed at 'Sustained Innovation and Growth (SIG)'[13].

5.3 *E-supply chain strategies*

Can there be any more profound challenges than those confronting today's supply chains? Are these challenges are here to stay or are more than just the manifestations of a tough economic cycle? Some leaders are acting on this assumption and are thoughtfully considering the implications of the forces creating these challenges. The implications of five key forces, in particular, demand close attention from supply chain professionals[54]:

- the trend toward outsourcing,
- stock market driven cash engineering,
- competitive forces changing the playing field,
- unplanned economic, social, and political events, and
- shorter, less predictable product life cycles.

Two strategic shifts are spearheading the migration to an integrated operating system. The first shift involves the broad recognition that supply chain velocity is fundamental to performance, efficiency, and competitive differentiation. The second strategic shift is the application of systems thinking to the transformation of supply chain models. What's needed is a dramatic new approach that directly responds to the challenges and, at the same time, opens the door to new growth and profit opportunities. A handful of industry leaders are beginning to adopt one such approach through a supply chain model called an integrated operating system. Unlike older models, this new model (Figure 8a) is capable of helping companies outperform weaker competitors by simultaneously reducing working-capital requirements, improving revenue and margin contributions, and improving order-to-delivery predictability and response time.

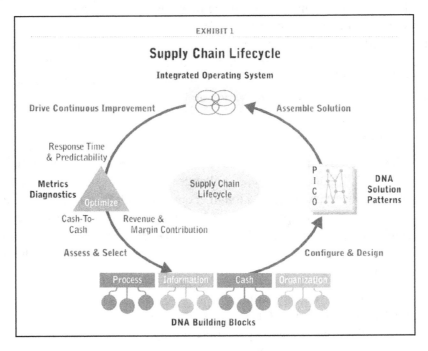

Figure 8a. Supply Chain Product Lifecycles Model

Source: Demers and Sathyanarayanan (2003).

Traditional approaches generally have focused more on moving the product and cash, and less on the information systems and organization-which are at the heart of many of the key challenges. And while traditional models have been successful at optimizing individual functional areas, they have lacked the ability to optimize the entire supply chain. Demers and Sathyanarayanan[54] develop an integrated operating system that can simultaneously improve working capital, enhance revenue and margin, and improve order-to-delivery predictability.

The author's innovative approach is to select and configure a unique blend of capabilities and strategies, or "supply chain DNA," across the dimensions of process, information, cash, and organization. The author has developed a roadmap to executing that approach, and in the process, achieving all three benefits at once.

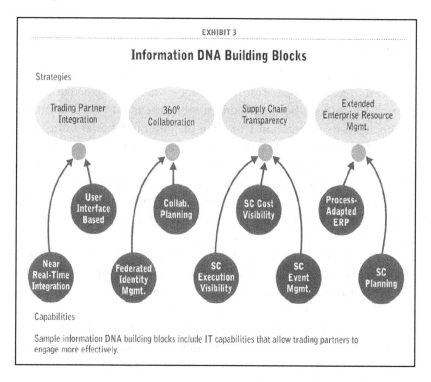

Figure 8b. Supply Chain Product Lifecycles Model

Source: Demers and Sathyanarayanan (2003).

The new model is particularly well suited for companies that are experiencing product commoditization pressures and that understand the need to shift from product innovation to supply chain innovation.

6 Future and Changing Strategies

6.1 *Brave new models in outsourcing*

Outsourcing has come such a long way in recent years that early critics would see little resemblance between today's models and the original concept. No longer a single-process, single-location arrangement, business process outsourcing usually means handing off multiple functions. The expectation is that work will be performed in a variety of locations around the world or "co-sourced" at hybrid-model shared-service centres[55].

6.2 *IT sourcing*

Information technology (IT) has transformed business practices in the last several decades: operations, product strategies, distribution, and customer service have become increasingly dependent on IT. Moreover, IT has changed its orientation from that of pure operational utility in the 1960s and 1970s to that of a competitive weapon in the 1990s and today. These phenomena have affected the way modern organizations are managed, as well as the way IT affects the strategic activities of an organization's value-chain. In particular, aligning an organization's business and IT strategies in order to deliver higher business performance presupposes a strategic business opportunity to which information systems technology is integral[36]. Strategic alignment between business and IT can have a positive business impact only if we see an organization's IT components as parts of a well-integrated organizational system. If business strategy is viewed separately from IT strategy or IT strategy is viewed only as a "support" tool, then there is little likelihood that the above positive impact of strategic alignment can take place.

Table 4. Summary of Conceptual Frameworks for Strategic Sourcing with an Emphasis on Outsourcing Developments

Strategies:	Conceptual Framework	Author(s)	Year	Industry	Case studies	Objectives
1. Sourcing	Strategic Sourcing Model	Welch & Nayak	1992	Manufacture	Multiple	Make or Buy optimization
	Strategy and Structure Model	Chow, et. al.	1995	Logistics	Multiple	Efficiency control cost
	Capability Sourcing Model	Gottfredson, et. al.	2005	Retailing	7-Eleven	Cust. service & market position
2. Outsourcing	Strategic Outsourcing Model	Quinn & Hilmer	1994	Fortune 500s	Multiple	Analysis of benefits versus risks
	Outsourcing Manufacturing Model	Momme	2002	Aalborg	DK & US	Strategic & operational implic'n
	Value from Strategic Outsourcing	Dodd & Renterghem	1997	HR Admin	-	Continued improvement from OS
	The Outsourcing Decision	Stefancic	2004	Admin	-	Benefits realization – Strat. plan
	Outsourcing Relationships	Vining & Globerman	1999	UK, Europe	Literature	Theory built on empirical data
	On partnering	Dent	2002	Banking	1 - USA	Leverage external competencies
	Outsourcing - Different Industries	Blumberg	2002	General	-	Contract services identification
	Globalisation & Offshore Outsourcing	Billi, et. al.	2004	Medical serv.	1 - USA	Outsourcing for collaboration
	"	Robinson & Kalakota	2000	Multiple	Multiple	Bus. Process & IT offshore
	"	Kidane	2004	Multiple	Amex & Dell	Experience and complexity for comprehensive strategy.
3. IT Outsourcing	Strategic IT Outsourcing	Venkatraman & Loh	1994	Fortune 500s	Multiple	Technology to Relationships
	IT sourcing decisions	Willcocks, et. al	1995	Multiple	30	Factors for strategic decisions
	Co-alignment	Pollalis	2003	Multiple	Multiple	Performance from integration
4. e-Sourcing	Team Strategies	Teo and Chan	2004	Finance	4	Contract's partnership
(a) e-Business	Virtual Organising Model	Venkatraman & Henderson	1998	e-Commerce	Multiple	Virtual sourcing strategy and tactics for sustained growth
(b) e-Business	Dynamic Planning Model	Ash and Burn	2003	e-Business	11	3 stages of strategic planning
e-Marketplace	Strategic e-Procurement Model	Ash and Poelzu	2005	Mining	10	e-Procurement integrated with Procurement strategy
e-Supply Chain	Supply Chain Product Lifecycle + 2 Supplementary models	Demers & Sathyanarayanan	2003	IT & Communications	Multiple	Shift in product innovation to supply chain innovation

6.3 *Dynamic sourcing*

In keeping the competitive edge Moore and Wiefels[56] argue there are two fundamental types of business organizations from which companies can choose. The customer-centric organization is optimized for handling low-volume, high-complexity systems, and is linked to the project, evolutions and outsourcing models. The operations-centric organization is best suited to high-volume, low-complexity systems, and is linked to the product, consumables and transaction-services models. There is the implication to change more than the model, "change the strategy."

6.4 *Capability sourcing*

Companies like UPS and FedEx are making their value chains more flexible. Driven by the decline of vertical integrated business model, sourcing is evolving into a strategic process for organizing and fine-tuning the value chain. "The question is no longer whether to outsource a capability or activity but how to source every single activity in the value chain"[12] (p. 132). This is referred to as the new discipline of "capability sourcing."

6.5 *Strategy as ecology (coopetition)*

There is a challenge for organizations in balancing competition with cooperation or collaboration in sustaining the competitive edge. Called "coopetition" this phenomena takes the form of increased cooperation between partners in collaborating to assist the service of customers of partner organizations. Moore[57] argues that such coalitions are like organisms within ecosystems that require nurturing.

References

1. Beinhocker, Eric D. Strategy at the edge of chaos. *The McKinsey Quarterly*, 1, 1997, pp. 24-40; Porter, M.E. *Competing Strategy Techniques for Analysing Industries and Competitors*. Free Press, New York, 1980.
2. Lansiti, M. and Levien, R. Strategy as Ecology. *Harvard Business Review*, 82(3), 2004, pp. 68-78.

3. Kauffman, S.A. Escaping the Red Queen Effect. *The McKinsey Quarterly*, 1, 1995, pp. 118-129.

4. Ticoll, D., Lowry, A. and Kalakota, R. Joined at the Bit, in *Blueprint to the Digital Economy creating wealth in the era of e-business* Don Tapscott, Alex Lowy and David Ticoll, McGraw-Hill, 1998.

5. El Sawy, Omar A., Malhotra, Arvind, Gosain, Sanjay and Young, Kerry M. IT-intensive value innovation in the electronic economy: Insights from Marshall industries. *MIS Quarterly*, 23(3), 1999, pp. 305-335.

6. Wigand, R.T. and Benjamin, R.I. Electronic Commerce: Effects on electronic markets. *Journal of Computer-Mediated Communication*, 1(3), 1995.

7. Rayport, J.F. and Sviokola, J. Exploiting the Virtual Value Chain. *Harvard Business Review*, 73(6), 1995, pp. 75-86.

8. Burn, J.M. and Barnett, M.L. Emerging Virtual Models for Global e-commerce - world wide retailing in the e-grocery business. *Special issue on Global E-Commerce, Special Millennium Issue of Journal of Global Information Technology Management*, 3(1), 2000, pp. 18-32.

9. Quinn, J.B. and Hilmer, F.G. Strategic Outsourcing. *Sloan Management Review*, 35(4), 1994, pp. 43-55.

10. Welch, J.A. and Ranganath, N.P. Strategic Sourcing: A Progressive Approach to the Make-or-Buy Decision. *The Executive*, 6(1), 1992, pp. 23-31.

11. Chow, G., Heaver, T.D. and Henriksson, L.E. Strategy, structure and performance: A framework for logistics research. *Logistics and Transportation Review*, 31(4), 1995, pp. 285-308.

12. Gottfredson, M., Puryear, R. and Phillips, S. Strategic Sourcing: From Periphery to the Core. *Harvard Business Review*, February, 2005, pp. 132-139.

13. Venkatraman, N. and Henderson, J.C. Real Strategies for Virtual Organizing. *Sloan Management Review*, Fall, 1998, pp. 33-48.

14. Ash, C.G. and Burn, J.M. Strategic Framework for the Management of E-ERP Change. *European Journal of Operations Research*, 146(2), 2003, pp. 374-387.

15. Quinn, James Brian and Hilmer, Frederick G. Strategic Outsourcing. *Sloan Management Review*, 35(4), 1994, pp. 43-56.

16. Krause, D.R., Handfield, R.B. and Scannell, T.V. An empirical investigation of supplier development: Reactive and strategic processes. *Journal of Operations Management*, 17(1), 1998, p. 39.

17. Momme, J. Framework for outsourcing manufacturing: Strategic and operational implications. *Computers in Industry*, 49(1), 2002, p. 59.

18. Alexander, M. and Young, D. Outsourcing: Where's the value? *Long Range Planning*, 29(5), 1996, pp. 728-730.

19. Dodd, R.M. and Renterghem, B.M. Measuring for success: Increasing benefit plan value through outsourcing. *Benefits Quarterly*, 13(1), 1997, p. 14.

20. Stefancic, A. The Business Case for Outsourcing. *Employee Benefit Plan Review*, 58(8), 2004, pp. 11-14.

21. Vining, A. and Globerman, S. A conceptual framework for understanding the outsourcing decision. *European Management Journal*, 17(6), 1999, p. 645.

22. Dent, S.M. In uncertain economic times, "smart partnering" pays off. *WorldatWork Journal*, 11(1), 2002, p. 51.

23. Blumberg, L. How to engage in a strategic outsourcing relationship. *Pharmaceutical Technology North America*, 26(7), 2002, p. 74.

24. Billi, J.E., Pai, Chih-Wen and Spahlinger, D.A. Strategic Outsourcing of Clinical Services: A Model for Volume-Stressed Academic Medical Centers. *Health Care Management Review*, 29(4), 2004, p. 291.

25. Karklins, T.J. Global outsourcing of CRM: Techniques and trends. *Customer Inter@ction Solutions*, 21(12), 2003, pp. 48-50.

26. Robinson, M. and Kalakota, R. *Offshore Outsourcing: Business model, ROI, and best practice*, Mavar Press, Alpharetta, GA, 2004.

27. Kidane, A. Offshore outsourcing: business model, ROI, and best practices. *Competitiveness Review*, 14(1/2), 2004, pp. 108-109.

28. Venkatraman, N. Beyond Outsourcing: Managing IT Resources as a Value Center. *Sloan Management Review*, 38(3), 1997, pp. 51-65.

29. Lacity, M.C. and Hirschheim, R. *Information Systems Outsourcing Myths Metaphors and Realities*, John Wiley and Sons, Chichester, 1993.

30. Lacity, M.C. and Hirschheim, R. *Beyond the Information Systems Outsourcing Bandwagon the Insourcing Response*, Wiley and Sons, Chichester, 1995.

31. Lacity, M.C., Willcocks, L.P. and Feeny, D.F. IT Outsourcing: Maximize Flexibility and Control. *Harvard Business Review*, May/June, 1995, pp. 84-93.

32. Currie, Wendy. Using multiple suppliers to mitigate the risk of IT outsourcing at ICI and Wessex Water. *Journal of Information Technology*, 13(3), 1998, p. 169.

33. Venkatraman, N. and Loh, L. The shifting logic of the IS organization: From technical portfolio to relationship portfolio. *Information Strategy*, 10(2), 1994, p. 5.

34. Willcocks, L., Fitzgerald, G. and Feeny, D. Outsourcing IT: The strategic implications. *Long Range Planning*, 28(5), 1995, pp. 59-70.

35. Kishore, R., Rao, H.R., Nam, K., Rajagopalan, S. and Chaudhury, A. A Relationship Perspective on IT Outsourcing. *Communications of the ACM*, 46(12), 2003, p. 86.

36. Pollalis, Y.A. Patterns of co-alignment in information-intensive organizations: business performance through integration strategies. *International Journal of Information Management*, 23(6), 2003, p. 469.

37. Breu, Karin and Peppard, Joe. Useful knowledge for information systems practice: the contribution of the participatory paradigm. *Journal of Information Technology*, 18(3), 2003, pp. 177-193.

38. Teo, T.L. and Chan, C. IT Outsourcing Issues in Singapore: The Vendor's Perspective. 15th Australasian Conference on Information Systems ACIS'2004, Dec. Hobart, Australia, 2004.

39. Viehland, D.W. Critical success factors for developing an e-business strategy. In *Proceedings of 6th Americas Conference on Information Systems* (pp. 911-915). USC, Long Beach, CA, 2000.

40. O'Brien, J.A. *Management information systems: Managing information technology in the Internet worked enterprise*, Irwin, McGraw-Hill, Boston, 1999.

41. Kalakota, R. and Robinson, M. *e-Business2: Roadmap for success*, Addison-Wesley Longman, Reading, MA, 2001.

42. Kalakota, R. and Robinson, M. *e-Business: Roadmap for success* (ch. 2, 7, 8, 9, 12). Addison-Wesley Longman, Reading, MA, 1999.

43. Robey, D., Ross, J.W. and Boudreau, M. Learning to Implement Enterprise Systems: An Exploratory Study of the Dialectics of Change. *Journal of Management Information Systems*, 19(1), 2002, pp. 17-46.

44. Wheeler, B.C. NEBIC: A Dynamic Capabilities Theory for Assessing Net-Enablement. *Information Systems Research*, 13(2), 2002, pp. 125-146.

45. Zahra, S.A. and Gerard, G. The Net-enabled business innovation Cycle and the Evolution of Dynamic Capabilities. *Information Systems Research*, 13(2), 2002, pp. 147-151.

46. Damanpour, Faramarz. E-business e-commerce evolution: Perspective and strategy. *Managerial Finance*, 27(7), 2001, pp. 16-34.

47. Kallio, J., Saarinen, T. and Tinnila, M. Efficient Change Strategies. *Business Process Management Journal*, 8(1), 2002, pp. 80-93.

48. Baldwin, C. and Clarke, K. Managing in an age of modularity. *Harvard Business School Review*, Sep-Oct, 1997, pp. 84-93.

49. Patel, N. Emergent Forms of IT Governance to Support Global e-Business Models. *Journal of Information Technology Theory and Application*, 4(2), 2002, pp. 33-49.

50. Brunn, P., Jensen, M. and Skovgaard, J. e-Marketplaces: Crafting a Winning Strategy. *European Management Journal*, 20(3), 2002, pp. 286-298.

51. Ash, C.G. and Poezyn, A. Use of eMarketplace for Procurement: A Case Study of The Global eMarketPlace, 18th Bled eCommerce Conference, Bled, Slovenia, 2005.

52. *MiningMagazine*. Beyond the bubble. November, 2003, p. 15.

53. Schwartz, E. E-marketplaces make a comeback. *InfoWorld* April, 2004.

54. Demers, D. and Sathyanarayanan, P. Charting the Supply Chain DNA. *Supply Chain Management Review*, 7(6), 2003, pp. 48-54.

55. Brannen, Laurie. Brave new models in outsourcing. *Business Finance*, 9(6), 2003, p. 6.

56. Moore, G. and Wiefels, P. Keeping the competitive edge. *Optimize*, November, 2002, pp. 28-33.

57. Moore, J.F. *The Death of Competition: Leadership and Strategy in the Age of Business Ecosystems*, Harper Business, New York, 1997.

CHAPTER 13

IT-Enabled Innovation in the Multinational Company

Alex Kofinas

Manchester Metropolitan University Business School
Aytoun Street, Manchester M1 3GH
United Kingdom
Email: a.kofinas@mmu.ac.uk

1 Introduction: Heralding a New Economy

From the 1970s onwards the developed world seems to have entered a new paradigm of development, an era of change. Alvin Toffler[1] claimed this change to be the third wave, a wave that would substitute the earlier agricultural and industrial waves. Drucker called it the knowledge society[2]. This phenomenon of change was probably verbalised best by Kondratieff[3] who claimed that there were long economic waves and "during the recession of the long waves, an especially large number of important discoveries and inventions in the technique of production and communication are made, which, however, are usually applied on a large scale only at the beginning of the next long upswing." According to Alan Greenspan, the venerable chairman of the US federal reserve system, we have entered such a period of change in the last twenty years and its main drivers are two inter-related, emergent phenomena: i) a new socio-political paradigm and ii) a new technological paradigm.

Globalization as the new socio-political paradigm provides the context and the impetus for the change in the technological dimension[4,5]. In McLuhan's "global village"[6] actors and institutions become increasingly interconnected leading to an increase in competition as firms move from regional, to national to global competition. In such a knowledge economy organizations can not be "islands of planned co-ordination in a sea of market relations" but they have to be part of a larger network of firms, institutions and social structures[7].

If new technology can bring "factors of production together .... to reduce the cost of organizing spatially ... which improve(s) managerial technique"[18] then, for Coase, such a technology would empower the organization to grow in size and influence. In information technology (IT) management theorists have identified such a technology and the main drive of the new technological paradigm[8]. Its evangelists have promised of new ways of organising, new ways of performing organisational processes and operations, new ways of innovating, and new ways of managerial control[5]. It is often linked to business process re-engineering, restructuring, strategic alliance formation, and organisational diversification - all processes of organizational change. Indeed, during the 1990's most of the promises of IT seem to hold true. Information systems (IS), such as enterprise resource planning (ERP) were created that allowed managerial control of functions within very large corporations[9], intranets and other collaborative software (such as Lotus Notes) were designed for facilitating organizational communications[10], while internet sites were a new venue for commerce leading to the creation of electronic markets[11]. Most important in this argument, much of the knowledge management (KM) trend is, in no small part, related to IT[12], which has led knowledge-intensive industries such as consulting, pharmaceuticals, telecommunications to invest, embrace, and actively promote IT for achieving a competitive advantage[8,13].

The new paradigm has created anxiety in the world of business[14]. Innovation is increasingly seen as crucial for weathering the storms of globalization[15,16] and for sustaining a competitive edge in this uncertain world[17]. IT would be an enabler of this innovation as it could bring about radical technological change and the rapid obsolescence of old technologies and business models[16,19] via diffusion of innovations[20,21]. This drive for an IT-enabled innovation culture has posited a number of challenges to any organization, amplified further by the geographically distributed organizations that characterise such a global economy, such as the large multi-national companies (MNCs).

This new paradigm would result to a different understanding of competition and cooperation. On the one hand globalization has reinforced ideas of co-operative, social networks[8,22], communities of practice or strategic alliances wherein IT may be seen as the glue that keeps such corporate structures together[20,23]. On the other hand it has provided an impetus for an increase in global competition and re-organising of MNCs. This chapter aims to clarify the challenges that IT-enabled innovation has had on MNCs in their quest for global sustainable competitiveness in the global electronic markets.

IT-enabled innovation will be examined from two ontological lenses; first from a New Economy world and second from an a-modern world perspective. The resulting dialectic will be used to address a number of issues present in the relevant literature and, via the formation of a matrix, will enable MNC managers to understand further the complexities of IT-enabled innovation in global electronic markets.

2 The Ontology of IT-Enabled Innovation

2.1 *An exemplar MNC in the New Economy?*

The favourite company of the 1990s, it was voted for six consecutive times the *Fortune* most innovative company and twice the best company to work for[24]. Its humble birth in an unglamorous industry was soon forsaken as its novel business model and its innovative use of technology established it as the industry leader and enabled it to diversify in other related and, increasingly, unrelated industries. It was heralded as an "incubator of grand ideas and large projects"[25] and became an MNC with ambitious projects in the world, stretching from US to India to Japan[26]. In addition, between 1997 and 2001 it utilised IT to come up with innovative ideas and net-ventures that would utilise the emerging global electronic markets to make huge profits[27]. Such ideas were seen as highly innovative, technology-driven and in vogue with the contemporary zeitgeist of globalization and IT[24,28].

Innovation and global should go hand-in-hand with a sustainable competitive advantage and profits in the business arena; for Enron this was not the case. By 2002 it was apparent that together with some real conceptual and technological innovations there had been a number of important financially-inclined innovations, based firmly on old economy precepts and involving shifting massive debt within the company[29]. The investments and expansions in new industries and business revealed a mentality of high risk and gambling[24,30]. The global expansions had unfortunate ending and most were unprofitable[24], while the new business models and the innovative entrepreneurial culture are increasingly seen now as a lot of "pipe dreams" and rhetorical devices. Nevertheless, barring a few sane voices, almost unanimously the business world had been entranced for years by the New Economy vision that Enron conjured.

I use Enron's bankruptcy to highlight, somewhat dramatically, the real dangers MNCs may face if they do not consider alternative ontological views of the world when they examine the importance of IT-enabled innovations in the global electronic markets. It is quite tempting to believe the rhetoric, the managerial talks of a New Economy, the paradigm changes and radical innovation, but the electronic markets have had a disproportionate share of interesting, radical business models, which failed. The two ontological perspectives I am going to present here are extreme; one claims that IT-enabled innovation is radically different from anything we have witnessed before; the second claims that IT-enabled innovation is business-as-usual. The truth for any manager probably lies in-between.

One way to explicate Enron's case is to accept Kondratieff's long-waves theory. Thus Enron was indicative of the uncertainty inherent in a period of radical change and that in spite of its demise some of its innovations were real[31]. Thus what we are currently witnessing a shift that is accompanied with an "especially large number of important discoveries and inventions in the technique of production and communication" which however become commercially available in the upswing of the new wave. Kondratieff subsequently warns the reader that "(i)t is during the period of the rise of the long waves i.e. during the period of high tension in the expansion of economic forces, that, as a rule, the most disastrous and extensive wars and revolutions occur"[3]. Ernon could be part of the disasters Kondratieff predicted. Further musings and the events of the last five years make Kondratieff's warning especially relevant; we witnessed the dot.com bloom and bust, the rise of new technologies such as the mobile wireless telecommunications, biotechnology and the internet while major socio-political events such as the 9/11 terrorist attack, the subsequent upheaval caused by the war against terror, the war in Iraq and the proliferation of weapons of mass destruction have definitely alarmed the global society. It is tempting to read on all these events the coming of a new Kondratieff long wave. In such a world MNCs have to re-invent themselves. They have to utilize the new technologies; change their business models; take advantage of the e-commerce paradigm; adopt new ways of branding and marketing through the internet and mobile telecommunications technology; manage a diverse, disparate, innovative, but often anarchic workforce while allowing enough flexibility and freedom so that the knowledge workers will foster creative, innovative solutions; be global in reach but sensitive to local differences, and be able to handle different alliance configurations and outsourcing arrangements. And then maybe they will be able to ride these waves of change.

Nevertheless this radical innovation drive would not last long. Kondratieff and Greenspan warn us[3,5] that we are approaching a peak in this innovation drive. Soon the new technologies will stabilize and become the standards. Thus the MNCs would heed well to hear Alan Greenspan's cautionary voice: "there are limits to how far globalization and the speed of innovation can proceed, the current apparent rapid pace of structural shift cannot continue indefinitely"[5]. If that is the case then in a short period of time IT-enabled innovations will become standard resources and IT will not matter.

2.2 *The a-modern perspective*

A second response to Enron's failure would be to reject Kondratieff's theory and claim instead that "(w)e have never been modern"[32]. Enron was no different than any of thousands of bankruptcies. An interesting fact to illustrate that; 70-odd years ago an energy company, Insull, was heralded an innovative pioneer, a stalwart of the new era[29]. It brought energy to millions of US households and new innovative business models to the business community, based on novel, exciting technology. But like Enron, its "modern" counterpart, its innovations were not as transformational or real, *but they were presented as such*. By 1932, Insull declared a bankruptcy causing much consternation among business leaders and providing the perfect opportunity for president F. D. Roosevelt to push forward his New Deal[29]. 70 years later a long-lived observer would feel a certain *déjà vu* when Enron, after dismantling the new deal safeguards established under Roosevelt, was to create one of the most spectacular bankruptcies in the American history. Enron like its earlier counterpart failed in old economy fundamentals. If an organization's business should be *"Suaviter in modo, fortiter in re"* – agreeable in manner and strong in substance[33], both Enron and its predecessor, Insull, seem to have focused more on appearance than on substance. Thus we could argue that the New Economy identified by the management literature does not really exist. It is a rhetorical device deployed to suggest that "old economy rules" do not apply to new economy firms. Such a conceptualisation has led to the e-commerce boom and madness where profit did not matter and there was much talk about new models and concepts and the necessary bust as the "new economy" business models crashed like waves onto the old economy. Thus we have been never been modern; we have always been a-modern.

3   The Challenges of IT-Enabled Innovation

This section of the chapter focuses on two themes reiterated in the literature and relevant to IT-enabled innovation. The first is internal to MNCs and has to do with organizational knowledge management and the generation of internal resources to compete in the global context. The second theme is organizationally external to MNCs and focuses on the external threats and opportunities that face MNCs in their drive for expansion in global, electronic markets. A small list of issues relevant to each theme is generated from the literature review and then discussed from both perspectives. The companies that illustrate the thesis of this chapter are instantly recognizable and deeply rooted in the global electronic markets. They serve as mini in-depth case studies to illustrate the issues and challenges that MNCs may face in their pursuit for IT-enabled innovation. Below I have juxtaposed each of the two themes against the two components of the New Economy paradigm; globalization and IT.

Table 1. Challenges for the MNCs in a New Economy

Theme	Information Technology (Technology Paradigm)	Globalisation (Socio-economic Paradigm)
i) Knowledge generation, resources and capabilities	Content-enabled KM (enhancer/competitor)	Relational KM (enhancer/collaborator)
ii) Innovation in the global competitive context	Bound by business model and medium of communication (e.g. Google; Amazon; E-bay) Sub-contracting non-essential functions to state-of-art companies Outsourcing in countries with high technological capability Use of IT systems to integrate and control an expanding alliances network	Bound by geography and socio-politics (e.g. Nokia; ABB) Outsourcing in countries with low wages National Innovation Systems & Culture (e.g. Mobile IT vs IT (NTT DoCoMo and Vodafone), Biotechnology vs Pharmaceutical industry) The Born-global Corporation

3.1 *IT-enabled innovation and organizational knowledge*

In a New Economy ontology the corporate world becomes increasingly global; subsequently for MNCs knowledge that results to commercial innovation would be the main keys for achieving competitiveness. Drucker predicted that the rise of the knowledge economy would thus empower the organizational worker[34]. The workers would have the ability to barter their stock of knowledge as the companies would aim to create new knowledge and bring about innovation[35]. In the knowledge management (KM) literature two main approaches have been suggested to explain the relation of IT to the creation and management of knowledge:

- IT systems such as knowledge management systems[36] that would substitute or facilitate the workers' knowledge-related activities.
- IT systems that would augment and supplement the creative activities of social networks and communities of practice (CoPs) and harness knowledge that would promote innovation. Then the social systems would use IT as one of the mediums to disseminate innovation across organizational and cultural boundaries[37,38].

The former may deal with forms of knowledge such as explicit knowledge[39] or content knowledge[40] while the latter may deal with tacit[39], relational[40] or embedded[41] knowledge. Both the content and the relational approaches to knowledge management accept the importance of human capital and social interaction in creating knowledge. However the content approach has often been criticised for de-emphasizing human capital and de-contextualising knowledge[42,43]. Thus in content approaches, there is much emphasis on the empowerment that IT bestows on the organization over the knowledge worker, and it is offered as a tool to counteract the bartering ability of the knowledge worker[42]. In contrast, the relational approach puts the emphasis on the human element[40]. Knowledge is "mediated, situated, provisional, pragmatic and contested"[41] and is located in communities of practice (CoPs) and is defined by continuous social interactions. Innovation is the result of knowledge-related interactions and collaborations among actors and IT is viewed as innovation's organizational carrier, an important enabling medium for sustaining such global networks and enabling the diffusion of innovation[20]. Both approaches assume that we can manage knowledge and innovation[44] and IT figures as an important element of knowledge management efforts within the organization[45].

These two perspectives on IT-enabled innovation and the knowledge worker present distinctive challenges to the MNC. In the content perspective IT plays a primary role. The MNC has to focus on getting the right alignment of technology to the needs of the organization[46]. Much emphasis is placed on making sure that the implementation of the technology is done with prudence and the approach is often strategic and top-down[47]. A successful enterprise resource planning system, for example, is an IT-enabled medium for the alignment of resources to strategic intent and thus facilitating information transfer across segments of the corporation[46]. IT-based knowledge-sharing systems are considered vital for capturing knowledge and then transferring it across organizational boundaries thus enhancing the innovative capabilities of the organization[42].

The CoPs perspective takes the reverse approach; focusing more on the human interactions as the key determinant of the innovation network they place IT in a secondary role as an enhancer of existing communication patterns and behaviours[40]. The CoPs perspective pays more attention to socially-bound issues such as power[40,48], culture[49] and politics[50]. IT then becomes a medium of control[51] and IT integration an issue of social dimensions[51,52]. Thus according to the relational perspective the focus is on the social relations and CoPs that facilitate knowledge production and relegate information technology as a way of achieving such social interactions. IT is used in a pragmatic fashion and confers a competitive advantage if it assists in strengthening existing relations.

In the a-modern perspective the relation between the worker, knowledge, innovation and IT would differ from both the relational and the content conceptualizations. This third way, though not as clearly articulated it would emphasize that innovation and knowledge creation stem and emerge from innate human creativity[16,44]. Creativity is based on the ability to deal with uncertainty and risk in new ways[53,54]. We have always been creative and innovation is part of human nature. In this emergent perspective of innovation, IT is rendered as just one of the tools or mediators of innovative creativity. Content-based IT systems would be perceived by the emergent knowledge perspective as part of the "corporate immunity system"[55] of the organization, the tendency of the organizational bureaucracy to stifle activities incompatible with its existing line of business[55]. Likewise the relational perspective of knowledge may be perceived as a mechanism of reducing cognitive dissonance within the organization and thus providing the cohesiveness necessary for it to remain functional[56]. Both content and relational perspectives may exert control over organizational norms and social routines that could run counter to the intrinsic independence and loneliness often observed in creative, innovative individuals[16,54]. The silencing of distinct voices within the organization runs counter to the creation of an innovative firm and can lead to an inability for firms to spot radical innovations in the environment, especially when such innovations come from unexpected and seemingly irrelevant directions.

The MNC in the emergent perspective of innovation should use IT judiciously as it cannot confer a sustainable competitive advantage. In this perspective IT can even be seen as a potential disruptor of such radical innovations and can be counter-beneficial. Organizational focus should be on giving innovative, creative people space. The main role of the management would be to allow the physical and organizational space for such creative people within the company and once innovative ideas appear, to provide the support and the resources to promote those that may bring an innovative advantage to the organization[16,44,54]. As the example of the "insanely great"[57] Macintosh computer within Apple, Inc. indicates it is difficult for a company — even for Apple, the pinnacle of innovation in the computing industry — to accept such an approach to radical innovation. The features that contributed to the project's successes led to an estrangement of the project's culture from the rest of the company resulting to a limited diffusion of the technical innovation and the learning generated[57].

The emergent view on knowledge creation and innovation is challenging and even disturbing for MNCs. Creative people may often be found in the periphery of the organization i.e. the parts of the organization that are most cognitively disparate from the organizational core and allow for experimentation[19,54]. The disruptive potential of radical innovation can often be a source of fear rather than excitement within large MNCs as it necessitates the loss of hard-earned capabilities and propagates change and uncertainty[53]. Radical innovators often operate against the conventional wisdom of the organization[54,55]. As agents of incremental or radical innovation they often meet resistance from the advocates of the existing technologies, cue the case of IBM and Apple and their role in the personal computers radical innovation during the 1970s and 1980s[58].

3.2 IT-enabled innovations and competition in the international context

Globalisation has led to a spate of changes in the MNCs' context of competition in the global electronic markets. For example there has been a renewed emphasis and continuous expansion of strategic alliances and business networks to provide access to diverse sources of innovation. This propensity has been noted in a variety of IT-dependant industries; pharmaceuticals[59], computing industry[20] and e-commerce[60]. This thread of thought is linked to the national and regional systems of innovation literature. According to Nooteboom such inter-firm strategic alliances are often defensive in nature[56]. One of the aims of inter-firm alliances is to decrease uncertainty for MNCs by increasing their links with the global environment, a kind of scouting mechanism[56]. Manufacturing and business process outsourcing are driven by cost[61] but innovation and R&D-related outsourcing are often driven by the need to tap global innovation[20]. IT would integrate such global networks; for example ERP and customer-relationship-management software are tools that can help to manage such strategic alliances. For the two main competitors in mobile IT, NTT DoCoMo and the British Vodafone, strategic alliances have become an important part of an aggressive global strategy of expansion. Their partners are diverse; from global technology companies, other alliances involve smaller operators. NTT DoCoMo capitalizes on its lead in mobile technology and its dominance in the secure and highly profitable domestic market to create the global technology networks necessary for promoting its innovative products with much emphasis on Europe and South East Asia[64]. Similarly Vodafone has expanded its operations into South East Asia and with its purchase of J-Phone, the third largest Japanese operator in October 2001, creating a strategically important beachhead in the advanced mobile technology market of Japan[68]. Both competitors aim to provide an integrative, single platform for banking, commerce, games and other entertainment-related activities, thus poising as competitors to a bewildering variety of technology-bound companies such as Sony (and its new portable play-station) and palmOne (the personal digital assistant company), or e-commerce companies such as Amazon and e-Bay[68,69] and in a variety of electronic markets (from product sales to information provision and news brokerage).

An extensive literature on national systems of innovation has examined the importance of government policies in developing the innovative capabilities and networks necessary for MNCs[62,63]. The emphasis has been on the economic, cultural and political geography of innovation. An interesting example of the cultural elements of a national innovation system may be the innovative companies in the mobile-commerce (m-commerce) sector. Arguably issues of culture and local technology have been the main determinant that e-commerce is not as prominent in South East Asia and m-commerce has flourished. Mobile technology has fitted well with the South-east Asian region and played on the capabilities of the region in micro-technology and a culture based on speed, convenience and mobility. The mainstream management literature may glamour on the e-commerce achievements of Amazon and E-bay but mobile operator companies from South-east Asia such as NTT DoCoMo, a spin-off from the Japanese phone company NTT and dominant mobile operator in Japan[64], and LG Telecom that may drive the next radical innovations in IT. South Korean mobile operators have already expanded the usage of mobile technology in mobile banking. People with smart-card handsets can do most simple transactions via mobile-to-ATM connection[65] leading to the transformation of the banking and telecommunications sectors of South Korea with the formation of hybrid operator/bank kiosks within banks. The interest of NTT DoCoMo may lead to a quick spread of these IT-driven innovations well beyond the national boundaries of South Korea[65]. NTT DoCoMo, has shown remarkable growth, most of it attributed to the innovative features of its i-mode offerings, including internet services, games and music[66]. The technological innovations accompanied by a new innovative model of micro-payment have created new electronic markets and facilitated a more flexible approach in Japanese mobile internet than the computer-based model of US and Europe[66]. More important, NTT DoCoMo and other South East Asian operators have been experimenting with technology that would allow the possibility of the mobile handset to function as an electronic wallet[67].

These challenges of innovating in the global context — (a) new organizational configurations and strategic alliances, (b) the importance of culture, and (c) the role of national innovation systems — can be understood from an a-modern perspective as well. Strategic alliances have always existed. First of all if one were to examine the concept of strategic alliances they would unearth a host of diverse activities such as R&D outsourcing in pharmaceutical companies[70], joint ventures among high-tech companies[71], or collaborative buyer-supplier relationships[72]. Despite the rhetoric the New Economy is very fragile if non-existent while politics, geography and other socio-political issues still play a major role in the global markets as one could observe with the phenomenon of outsourcing. With the advent of the rhetoric of globalisation and the resulting perception of heightened uncertainty and urgency firms were to focus on their "core competencies"[73], to take advantage of their "resources" and "capabilities"[74] and to give less focus on all those functions of the company that are not critical for the conferment of sustainable competitive advantage. This rhetoric has promoted a surge of outsourcing in the last fifteen years[61,75] as companies outsourced non-core activities. The surge in outsourcing may be unprecedented in terms of volume but outsourcing itself as a concept is a scarcely new one. IT outsourcing has proved to be particularly challenging[76] and it has proved to be sensitive to a-modern elements of human society such as socio-political frictions. For example the terse relationships between Japan and China have already prompted the Japanese firms to focus their IT outsourcing activities from mainland China to other developing countries[77] with main beneficiaries Malaysia, Thailand and Singapore. The latter has also benefited by the internationalization drive of the Japanese pharmaceutical firms and has been a preferred destination for bio-research outsourcing[61]. In contrast US has repeatedly barred any foreign mobile IT firm to buy into American telecommunications firm citing security reasons[64,69]. As a consequence it has stalled the advent of m-commerce while enhancing indirectly the US-based e-commerce companies that do not yet face the real substitute technology to their computer-based ones. The Japanese government has also been notorious in promoting innovation among the Japanese companies while protecting them from excessive foreign competition[78] and a similar pattern of protective policies is observed in the Chinese government's efforts to facilitate innovation in its domestic industry[79]. Such sensitivity voids the idea of a global, uniform market economy and affects, often directly, the structure of the global electronic markets (see for example how Yahoo! and Google satisfied the internet security demands of the Chinese government in order to secure access in the Chinese market).

3.3 *The born-global corporation and the global electronic markets*

MNCs in the old economy were often stratified according to the internationalization strategies they pursued. One classification views

MNCs as international, global, and transnational[46,51]. In the innovation literature each of these strategies would imply a different IT-infrastructure and different IT commitment from the MNC[46]. Archibugi and Iammarino[80] focused on the nature of organizational innovation and suggest that a firm could pursue innovation that would befit its strategy. They offered a classification of levels of innovation that starts with a relatively local focus of innovation and to end up with IT-enabled global innovations that stem from global technological collaborations[80]. There are many examples of such kind of global collaboration networks, especially from R&D networks in the pharmaceutical industry[20,70]. Very often it is implied that there is a linear progression of internationalization, a progressive globalization process[81] and that governments would need to support this globalization process to facilitate the innovative competitiveness of the firms[80].

However from a New Economy perspective the last ten years seem to have witnessed the rise of a new MNC. Probably the best description of these MNCs is that of the born-global corporations which according to Knight *et al.*[82] are companies that from the beginning of their creation are focused on the global markets. Such corporations may present a challenge to structured, hierarchical approaches to internationalization and innovation since they start expanding internationally from their conception and they actively seek opportunities to expand operations globally. Such companies will enter in competition with MNCs much earlier than common sense would have it and because of their size, they will often be imperceptible by large, established MNCs[82]. Examples abound in the literature and many of the large MNCs of the today come from such born-global companies. Amazon.com, Yahoo! and E-bay are examples of born-global corporations. Due to the nature of e-commerce and the global reach of the internet, almost by default these companies were born-global. They have adopted innovative business models and have used extensively IT for promoting their e-commerce business[60]. Now they have reached a point where they are larger than their competitors in their chosen fields of competition[83]. The phenomenon of the born-global organization puts forward a challenge to the MNCs in two ways:

- Born-global firms increasingly become the main competition for the more traditional MNCs within a global economy, and may quickly emerge as leaders as they redefine industries and competition boundaries.

- The born-globals of today are often portrayed as young (rarely older than a decade), uncluttered from the legacies of the past, IT-savvy and with new business models[60,83,84] and capable of creating new electronic markets.

The current literature often suggests that MNCs should pursue an innovation strategy similar to the born-global firms and use their resources to adjust to globalization, to expand by using IT-enabled business models and innovative networks in order to compete effectively in this New Economy[20,85].

The a-modern perspective would give an alternative view on these born-global corporations. Amazon evolved a business model that directly or indirectly had transformed a number of retailing sectors such as books, CDs and even cars. But is that transformation one of substance or form? Amazon's business model also needed the material infrastructure, the warehouses, the well-organised freighting arm, supplier-based alliances, pricing strategies and investments that we are to find in other brick-and-mortar firms[83]. The much-taunted global strategy of Amazon involved the formation of national subsidiaries in all the major countries and the creation of a rather large infrastructural support. A counter-argument from the New Economy perspective has been that the model has relied on the formation of novel virtual communities and a drive for web-site customization. But the underlying principles such as customer service and customer focus are very old and venerable. The medium has changed but the concepts and ideas are still the same. Amazon does it faster and cheaper but Amazon does qualitatively the *same* thing faster and cheaper. Amazon has been profitable only recently and it had been through some vulnerable, turbulent times, especially when the dot.com bubble burst[60]. Its survival was based on business fundamentals; a sound business model, brand equity and technology patents[60,84]. To focus on Amazon as an exemplar of the New Economy simply because it is a success story is to dismiss the thousands of other e-commerce firms which proved by not surviving the dot.com bust that IT-enabled innovation alone does not bring the new era. The customer perceives a global and innovative company which in reality may resemble the old-style corporations in all ways but one; the medium of interaction and communication. Could it be that "(t)he medium is the message" as McLuhan[86] once had dramatically suggested? Or do we confuse the appearance with substance in order to make the logical fallacy that the two are the same?

4 Conclusions

In this chapter I have solicited the case study of Enron to present two conflicting views on IT-enabled innovation that would be relevant to MNCs. The first view, informed by the New Economy perspective, assumes that IT-enabled innovation is crucial for bringing about innovation and thus creating competitive advantage. The second and opposing view treats this radical New Economy as a rhetoric device and supports the notion that we live in an a-modern society. The MNCs should focus on business fundamentals such as sound business models and a customer-focus. Under this perspective the MNCs' adjustment to the environment should be pragmatic and their use of IT should be judicious. I have exemplified the a-modern economy perspective throughout the chapter by using the same examples I have used to exemplify the New Economy perspective, in essence creating a critical dialectic of IT-enabled innovation. A summary of this dialectic is presented in Table 2.

The theoretical and empirical literature review on the field of IT-enabled innovation so far has not suggested this dialectic between a New Economy perspective and the a-modern economy perspective on innovation. The social reality of IT-enabled innovation would probably lie somewhere in-between these two perspectives. IT has enhanced and enabled innovation in certain companies and industries though whether we have a new Kuhnian shift in paradigms is still uncertain and the rhetoric is probably exaggerated. Decision makers within MNCs can use such a conceptualization map to address the complexity in their macro-environment and to understand where their company is positioned across each of the dimensions. It would enable managers to approach the extant literature in a reflexive dialectic manner: on the one hand with prudence and critical faculty of the a-modern perspective and on the other with the desire and excitement to experiment and try out IT-enabled innovations that may fit the strategy and business model of the given MNC. As Enron warns us adopting a reflexive approach when making decisions on IT-enabled innovation and paying close attention to the socio-political environment and the organizational knowledge-related processes may prove far more useful in handling innovation and uncertainty than faith in little-tested rhetoric of radical innovations and "pipe dreams"[24].

Table 2. The New Economy vs. the a-Modern Economy — Impact Assessment on MNCs

Theme	The New Economy Perspective	The a-Modern Perspective
i) Organizational knowledge creation	Content-enabled vs. Relational KM Manageable innovation IT as an enhancer/collaborator/substitute of the knowledge worker	Emergent knowledge Unmanageable innovation A pragmatic approach to IT as a tool or a medium of communication
ii) Innovation in global competitive context	Business model is affected by IT and thus IT is a powerful medium Global economy exists and IT systems can integrate and control global operations Strategic Alliances/outsourcing/contracting crucial for the competitiveness of the firm National Innovation Systems & Culture are of limited importance as the global electronic markets develop. The aim of IT should be to transcend such constraints and promote electronic markets	Sound business model and strategy are important. IT does not matter The global economy is a rhetoric device Strategic Alliances/outsourcing/contracting have to be thought in pragmatic terms Even in electronic markets there are hidden costs such as geo-political considerations. National and regional systems of innovation, and distribution systems are important

References

1. Toffler, A., *The third wave*. Collins, 1980.
2. Drucker, P., *Managing in a Time of Great Change*. Butterworth-Heinemann Ltd., 1995.
3. Kondratieff, N.D., The Long Waves in Economic Life. *The Review of Economic Statistics*, **17**(6), 1935, pp. 105-115.
4. Archibugi, D., J. Howells, and J. Michie, Innovation systems in a global economy. *Technology Analysis & Strategic Management*, **11**(4), 1999, p. 527.
5. Greenspan, A., Globalization and Innovation. *Vital Speeches of the Day*, **70**(15), 2004, p. 450.
6. McLuhan, M., *Counter-Blast*. Rapp & Whiting, 1970.
7. Richardson, G.B., The Organisation of Industry. *The Economic Journal*, **82**(327), 1972, pp. 883-896.
8. Cooke, P., Regional innovation systems, clusters, and the knowledge economy. *Industrial and Corporate Change*, **10**(4), 2001, p. 945.
9. Ndede-Amadi, A.A., What strategic alignment, process redesign, enteprise resource planning, and e-commerce have in common: enterprise-wide computing. *Business Process Management Journal*, **10**(2), 2004, p. 184.
10. Butler, T., An institutional perspective on developing and implementing intranet- and internet- based information systems. *Information Systems*, **13**, 2003, pp. 209-231.
11. Simons, L.P.A., C. Steinfield, and H. Bouwman, Strategic Positioning of the web in a multi-channel market approach. *Internet Research: Electronic Networking Applications and Policy*, **12**(4), 2002, pp. 339-347.
12. Cabrera, A. and E.F. Cabrera, Knowledge-Sharing Dilemmas. *Organization Studies*, **23**(5), 2002, pp. 687-710.
13. Alvesson, M., Knowledge work: Ambiguity, Image and Identity. *Human Relations*, **54**(7), 2001, pp. 863-886.
14. Anonymous, Leaders: How to make mergers work. *The Economist*, **350**(8101), 1999, p. 15.
15. Liu, V.C. and B.H. Kleiner, Global trends in managing innovation and quality. *Management Research News*, **24**(3/4), 2001, p. 13.
16. Oetinger, B.v., Nurturing the new: patterns for innovation. *The Journal of Business Strategy*, **26**(2), 2005, p. 29.
17. Michie, J., Introduction. The internationalisation of the innovation process. *International Journal of the Economics of Business*, **5**(3), 1998, p. 261.
18. Coase, R.H., The Nature of the Firm. *Economica N.S.*, **4**, 1937, pp. 386-405.
19. Denning, S., Why the best and brightest approaches don't solve the innovation dilemma. *Strategy & Leadership*, **33**(1), 2005, p. 4.
20. Fowles, S. and W. Clark, Innovation networks: good ideas from everywhere in the world. *Strategy & Leadership*, **33**(4), 2005, p. 46.

21. Howells, J., Mind the gap: Information and communication technologies, knowledge activities and innovation in the pharmaceutical industry. *Technology Analysis & Strategic Management*, **14**(3), 2002, p. 355.

22. Brown, J.S. and P. Duguid, Local knowledge: Innovation in the networked age. *Management Learning*, **33**(4), 2002, p. 427.

23. Howells, J.R., Going global: The use of ICT networks in research and development. *Research Policy*, **24**(2), 1995, p. 169.

24. Dahl, C., Pipe Dreams: Greed, Ego, and the Death of Enron/Anatomy of Greed: Unshredded Truth from an Enron Insider/Enron the Rise and Fall/What Went Wrong at Enron: Everyone's Guide to the Largest Bankruptcy in U.S. History/The Smartest Guys in the Room: The Amazing Rise and Scandalous Fall of Enron/Power Failure: The Inside Story of the Collapse of Enron/24 Days. *The Energy Journal*, **25**(4), 2004, p. 115.

25. Laxmi, J., Enron: Restructuring an energy company. *Global Finance*, **14**(5), 2000, p. 80.

26. Carson, M.M., Enron and the new economy. *Competitiveness Review*, **11**(2), 2001, p. 1.

27. Zellner, W., Enron Electrified. *Business Week*, 3691, 2000, p. EB54.

28. Senia, A., Enron enters bandwidth business. *Utility Business*, **3**(3), 2000, p. 28.

29. Cudahy, R.D. and W.D. Henderson, From Insull To Enron: Corporate (Re)Regulation After The Rise And Fall Of Two Energy Icons. *Energy Law Journal*, **26**(1), 2005, p. 35.

30. Sims, R.R. and J. Brinkmann, Enron ethics (or: Culture matters more than codes). *Journal of Business Ethics*, **45**(3), 2003, p. 243.

31. Bruner, B.S.B.a.R., Manager's Journal: What Enron Did Right. *Wall Street Journal*, November 19, 2001, p. A.20.

32. Latour, B., *We Have Never Been Modern*. Harvester Wheatsheaf, 1993.

33. Hopfl, H., 'Suaviter in modo, fortiter in re': Appearance, Reality and the Early Jesuits, in *The Aesthetics of Organization*, S. Linstead and H. Hopfl, Editors. London: Sage Publications Ltd., pp. 197-211, 2000.

34. Drucker, P., *The Age of Discontinuity*. New York: Harper and Row, 1968.

35. Davenport, T.H. and L. Prusak, *Working Knowledge: How Organizations Manage What They Know*. Boston: Harvard Business School, 1998.

36. Walsham, G., Knowledge Management: The Benefits and Limitations of Computer Systems. *European Management Journal*, **19**(6), 2001, pp. 599-608.

37. Brown, J.S. and P. Duguid, Knowledge and Organization: A Social-practice Perspective. *Organization Science*, **12**(2), 2001, p. 198.

38. Sørensen, C. and U. Snis, Innovation through knowledge codification. *Journal of Information Technology*, **16**(2), 2001, pp. 83-97.

39. Nonaka, I. and H. Takeuchi, *The Knowledge-Creating Company: How Japanese companies create the dynamics of innovation*. New York: Oxford University Press, 1995.

40. Hayes, N. and G. Walsham, Knowledge Sharing and ICTs: A Relational Perspective, in *The Blackwell handbook of organizational learning and knowledge management*, M. Easterby-Smith and M. Lyles, Editors. Blackwell, 2003.

41. Blackler, F., Knowledge, Knowledge Work and Organizations: An Overview and Interpretation. *Organization Studies*, **16**(6), 1995, pp. 1021-1046.

42. Alvesson, M. and D. Karreman, Odd Couple: Making Sense of the curious concept of Knowledge Management. *Journal of Management Studies*, **38**(7), 2001, pp. 995-1018.

43. Tsoukas, H., The Firm as a Distributed Knowledge System: A Constructionist Approach. *Strategic Management Journal*, **17**(Winter Special Issue), 1996, pp. 11-25.

44. Snowden, D., Innovation as an objective of knowledge management. Part I: The landscape of management. *Knowledge Management Research & Practice*, **1**(2), 2003, p. 113.

45. Gray, P.H., The impact of Knowledge Repositories on power and control in the workplace. *Information, Technology & People*, **14**, 2001, pp. 368-384.

46. Madapusi, A. and D. D'Souza, Aligning Erp Systems With International Strategies. *Information Systems Management*, **22**(1), 2005, p. 7.

47. Bajwa, D.S., A. Rai, and I. Brennan, Key antecedents of Executive Information System success: A path analytic approach. *Decision Support Systems*, **22**(1), 1998, p. 31.

48. Schultze, U. and R.J. Boland, Knowledge Management Technology and the Reproduction of Knowledge Work Practices. *Journal of Strategic Information Systems*, **9**, 2000, pp. 193-212.

49. Shane, S., Championing innovation in the global corporation. *Research Technology Management*, **37**(4), 1994, p. 29.

50. Marshall, N. and T. Brady, Knowledge management and the politics of knowledge: illustrations from complex products and systems. *European Journal of Information Systems*, **10**, 2001, pp. 99-112.

51. Hanseth, O., C.U. Ciborra, and K. Braa, The control devolution: ERP and the side effects of globalization. *Database for Advances in Information Systems*, **32**(4), 2001, p. 34.

52. Newell, S., C. Tansley, and J. Huang, Social Capital and Knowledge Integration in an ERP Project Team: The Importance of Bridging AND Bonding. *British Journal of Management*, **15**, 2004, pp. S43-S57.

53. Oetinger, B.v., A plea for Uncertainty: Everybody complains about Uncertainty, but it might be a Good Thing to have. *The Journal of Business Strategy*, **25**(1), 2004, p. 57.

54. Stonecipher, H.C., Innovation and creativity: From the light bulb to the jet engine and beyond. *Vital Speeches of the Day*, **64**(12), 1998, p. 370.

55. Pinchot III, G., *Intrapreneuring: Why You Don't Have to Leave the Corporation to Become an Entrepreneur*, 1st Edition. New York: Harper & Row, 1985.

56. Nooteboom, B., A Cognitive Theory of the Firm, in International Workshop on "The Theories of the Firm", Paris, 2002.
57. Nonaka, I. and M. Kenney, Towards a New Theory of Innovation Management: A Case Study Comparing Canon, Inc. and Apple Computer, Inc. *Journal of Engineering and Technology Management*, **8**(1), 1991, p. 67.
58. Oetinger, B.v., From idea to innovation: making creativity real. *The Journal of Business Strategy*, **25**(5), 2004, p. 35.
59. Lacetera, N., Corporate Governance and the Governance of Innovation: The Case of Pharmaceutical Industry. *Journal of Management & Governance*, **5**(1), 2001, p. 29.
60. Filson, D., The Impact of E-Commerce Strategies on Firm Value: Lessons from Amazon.com and Its Early Competitors. *The Journal of Business*, **77**(2), 2004, p. S135.
61. Sen, R. and M.S. Islam, *Southeast Asia In The Global Wave Of Outsourcing: Trends, Opportunities, And Challenges*. Regional Outlook, p. 75, 2005.
62. Cooke, P., New economy innovation systems: Biotechnology in Europe and the USA. *Industry and Innovation*, **8**(3), 2001, p. 267.
63. Archibugi, D. and J. Michie, Technological globalisation or national systems of innovation? *Futures*, **29**(2), 1997, p. 121.
64. Anwar, S.T., NTT DoCoMo and m-commerce: A study in market expansion and global strategy. *Thunderbird International Business Review*, **44**(1), 2002, p. 139.
65. Song, S.-H. and R. Simpson, Mobile Banking Takes Off in South Korea, in *Gartner Research*. Gartner, Inc., p. 11, 2004.
66. McClelland, S., Japan: lessons in growth. *Telecommunications International*, **38**(9), 2004, p. S3.
67. Desai, K., N. Mitsuyama, and C. Bourlias, Japanese Consumers Want Mobile Phones with Enhanced Features, in *Gartner Research*. Gartner, Inc., p. 11, 2004.
68. Anwar, S.T., Vodafone and the wireless industry: A case in market expansion and global strategy. *The Journal of Business & Industrial Marketing*, **18**(2/3), 2003, p. 270.
69. Dodourova, M., Industry dynamics and strategic positioning in the wireless telecommunications industry: The case of Vodafone Group plc. *Management Decision*, **41**(9), 2003, p. 859.
70. Galambos, L. and J.L. Sturchio, Pharmaceutical firms and the transition to biotechnology: A study in strategic innovation. *Business History Review*, **72**(2), 1998, p. 250.
71. Michael, D.H., *et al.*, Case Study: Defining the Social Network of a Strategic Alliance. *Sloan Management Review*, **41**(2), 2000, p. 51.
72. Zagnoli, P. and C. Cardini, Patterns of international R&D cooperation for new product development: The Olivetti multimedia product. *R & D Management*, **24**(1), 1994, p. 3.
73. Prahalad, C.K. and G. Hamel, The Core Competence of the Corporation. *Harvard Business Review*, **68**(3), 1990, pp. 79-91.

74. Barney, J., Firm Resources and Sustained Competitive Advantage. *Journal of Management*, **17**(1), 1991, pp. 99-120.

75. Howells, J., Research and Technology Outsourcing. *Technology Analysis & Strategic Management*, **11**(1), 1999, p. 17.

76. Sadowski, B.M., K. Dittrich, and G.M. Duysters, Collaborative strategies in the event of technological discontinuities: The case of Nokia in the mobile telecommunication industry. *Small Business Economics*, **21**(2), 2003, p. 173.

77. Wiggins, D., B.M. Hayward, and M.R. Burles, Scenarios Show Impact of China/Japan Relationship on the Global IT Industry, in *Gartner Research Report*. Gartner, Inc., p. 18, 2005.

78. Goto, A., Japan's national innovation system: Current status and problems. *Oxford Review of Economic Policy*, **16**(2), 2000, p. 103.

79. Guo, B., J. Chen, and Q. Xu, Perspective of technological innovation and technology management in China. *IEEE Transactions on Engineering Management*, **45**(4), 1998, p. 381.

80. Archibugi, D. and S. Iammarino, The policy implications of the globalisation of innovation. *Research Policy*, **28**(2,3), 1999, p. 317.

81. Zander, I., The formation of international innovation networks in the multinational corporation: An evolutionary perspective. *Industrial and Corporate Change*, **11**(2), 2002, p. 327.

82. Knight, G.A. and S.T. Cavusgil, Innovation, organizational capabilities, and the born-global firm. *Journal of International Business Studies*, **35**(2), 2004, p. 124.

83. Anonymous, eBay and Google march on. *Strategic Direction*, **20**(2), 2004, p. 16.

84. Lumpkin, G.T. and G.G. Dess, E-Business Strategies and Internet Business Models: How the Internet Adds Value. *Organizational Dynamics*, **33**(2), 2004, p. 161.

85. Koudal, P. and G.C. Coleman, Coordinating operations to enhance innovation in the global corporation. *Strategy & Leadership*, **33**(4), 2005, p. 20.

86. McLuhan, M., *Understanding Media: The Extensions of Man*. First Sphere Books, 1968.

CHAPTER 14

The Impact of Internet on Market Structure

Bruno Cassiman and Sandra Sieber
IESE Business School
Avenida Pearson 21, 08034 Barcelona, Spain
Email: bcassiman@iese.edu; sieber@iese.edu

1 Introduction

The Internet affects conventional competitive strategies in at least three different ways: (1) the greater efficiency generated by lower transaction costs and new organizational forms reduce the firm's cost structure, (2) the reduction of consumer's search costs and new opportunities for product differentiation and redefinition affect the consumer's willingness to pay, and, (3) electronic markets affect pricing and allow new pricing mechanisms.

The Internet is an enabling technology[1] that has allowed companies to affect both their demand and costs at the same time creating what Kim and Mauborgne[2] call "value innovations". New entrants or incumbents have been able to radically reposition themselves within an industry, critically affecting the existing industry structure. This has triggered a competitive response, which will lead to a new equilibrium in transformed industries. Therefore, as the Internet simultaneously affects demand and cost, simple comparative statics exercises are unlikely to provide much insight into the effect of the Internet as in many cases the market structure is radically changed. In this sense, in the financial services industry, brokerage has been completely reshaped. In 1997 the market was divided in two main segments, full-service brokerage, with commissions averaging $117 and discount brokerage, operating at $66,[3] with estimated 12 to 14 million discount brokerage accounts, and 40 to 45 million full service brokerage accounts. By that time, online trading was increasing, reaching 3 million online accounts, and with around 60 firms offering online brokerage services at prices as low as $7.95. In the online segment a price war was taking place, as shown in Table 1.

Table 1. Commissions in the Brokerage Industry

	200 Shares at $20	3.000 Shares at $10
Full Service		
Average Commission	$116.90	$672.59
Discount Brokerage		
Average Commission	$66.09	$145.05
Online Brokerage*		
DLJDIRECT	$20.00	$60.00
E*TRADE	$14.95**	$74.95**
FIDELITY BROKERAGE	$14.95	$14.95
DATEK SECURITIES	$9.99	$9.99
AMERITRADE	$8.00	$8.00
SURETRADE	$7.95	$7.95

*Internet Trades
**Active Traders

Sources: Credit Suisse First Boston Corp., Companies, *Business Week*, December 8, 1997.

In 1998, Charles Schwab introduced an expanded Internet offering at a price of $29.95, which included more services than any other online broker, and which significantly hurt the traditional full service segment. As a result, they became the most valued trader in the industry, exceeding Merrill Lynch's market capitalization on one of the last trading sessions of 1998. In response, Merrill Lynch fought back, and included online trading in their offering in October 1999, also at $29.95. The web-based product was packed with research, ease of use, and provided accurate and constantly updated information on accounts, hence including more full-service brokerage than Charles Schwab could offer. As a result, of this and other initiatives Merrill's share price has recovered, and since 2001 Merrill Lynch has consistently outperformed Charles Schwab. But, more importantly, the industry has been completely transformed, offering a different product at significantly lower prices to the customer.

Similar transformations are going on in a whole range of industries, especially in those industries in which information plays a key role, be it as content (such as the media industry), as communication of information (such as the telecommunication industry) or as the infrastructure for information (such as the computer and electronics industry). All these industries have suffered fundamental changes, and are nowadays immersed in a process of industry convergence, and new industries with new competitive dynamics have emerged. In this way, the merger of America Online and Time Warner, completed in January or 2001, aimed at becoming "the world's first Internet-powered media and communications company-which will connect, inform and entertain people everywhere in innovative ways",[4] shows that the transformation of the traditional movie, media and telecommunication companies has just begun, and that industry convergence will be ongoing. AOL Time Warner has opted for an integrated strategy, as it wants to be present in both the content, content aggregation and telecommunication steps of what Valor[5] has called the "online value chain", shown in Figure 1. AOL Time Warner provides content through a variety of companies of the publishing (Time Inc and Time Warner Trade Publishing), filmed entertainment (Warner Bros and New Line Cinema), music (Warner Music Group), and interactive video (AOL Time Warner Interactive Video) industries. These contents are aggregated through their interactive services and properties (America Online), and brought to the customer using their own Internet access provider (America Online), as well as their own networks (Turner Broadcasting, Home Box Office) and cable systems (Time Warner Cable).

Still, it is necessary to better understand the underlying factors that affect industry transformation, as shown in the cases of the financial services and the media and telecommunication industries. In this article we provide a framework that allows us to better understand the impact of Internet on today's competitive landscapes. First, we introduce the concept of value creation, showing that the Internet affects the value creation potential of both the demand and the supply side. Next, we discuss how the increased value creation potential of the Internet has triggered fundamental transformations of industries, thus affecting the potential of firms to appropriate value of this additional value created.

We analyse the main dimensions that affect value appropriation possibilities and conclude in showing that the pricing power of a firm is the result of the combination of value creation and value appropriation opportunities, which may have led to a complete industry transformation that requires not only an adjustment of pricing, but a new competitive approach.

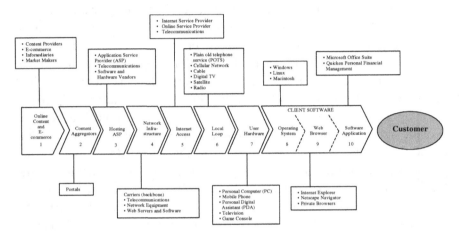

Figure 1. The Online Value Chain

2 Value Creation

Value is created whenever the willingness to pay for an item or service exceeds the (opportunity) cost of providing that item or service. The *potential value created* in an industry is represented by the area between the demand curve, i.e. the maximum willingness to pay of an individual, and, the cost of providing this good to this individual (see Figure 2). For the sake of exposition we will assume a constant average cost, which is equal to marginal cost. The same argumentation can be applied at the individual firm level. Dell for example buys supplies from component manufacturers, hires workers and accesses capital through the stock market. These inputs are transformed into a PC, which is sold to a Dell customer. In the process value is created whenever the willingness to pay of the PC user exceeds the opportunity cost of the resources used to provide this offering. Furthermore, Dell will have a higher profit potential than its competitors whenever Dell is able to create more value than its competitors. We refer to this more-value as *added value*.[6] Whether Dell, in the end, is more profitable than its competitors will depend on Dell's ability to appropriate more of the value created than its competitors. We will discuss the issue of value appropriation in more detail in Section 3.

The effect of the Internet on the potential for value creation therefore depends on how costs of provision of this offering and demand are affected. Figure 3 indicates the effect of changes in demand and costs on the potential value created. In the following sections we discuss the specific effect of the Internet on the cost structure of the firm and demand conditions of the firm and industry.

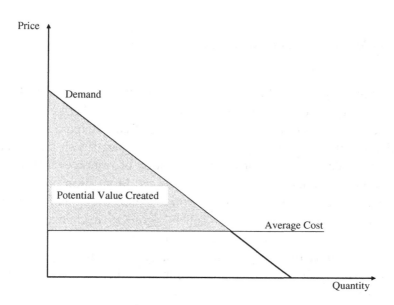

Figure 2. Potential Value Created in Industry

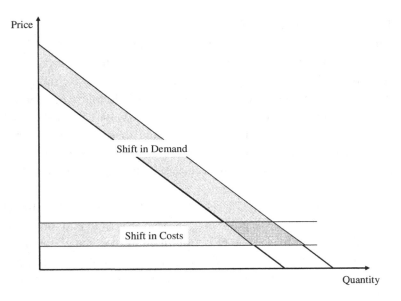

Figure 3. Effect of Internet on Potential Value Created

2.1 *Value creation and the cost side*

2.1.1 *Transaction costs*

The main effect of the Internet on the supply channel has been through the lowering of transaction costs.[7] Milgrom and Roberts[8] distinguish between two types of transaction costs: costs of coordinating and costs of motivating the value system. Those costs associated with coordination include the determination of prices, allocation of resources and location of buyers and sellers to conduct transactions. Motivation costs include the costs generated by information asymmetries and imperfect commitment. When buyers and sellers agree to exchange goods or services, buyers have private information about their willingness to pay and sellers about their opportunity costs, i.e. about the potential value created. This leads to information asymmetries that increase the cost of transacting. Furthermore, the fact that partners in a deal can only imperfectly commit to provide the necessary investments into a project, results in opportunities for hold-up, affecting the initial investments into the project.

Both types of transaction costs exist in the supply channel, but the Internet is unlikely to affect both to the same extent. A priori, one might expect that while the Internet can substantially reduce coordination costs, motivation costs might actually increase. As the Internet allows trades to occur across larger distances and more anonymously, asymmetry of information increases, making trade more difficult. Garicano and Kaplan[9] explicitly study the changes in transaction costs from the introduction of electronic markets for the auctioning of used cars. The authors calculate the potential cost reductions on transaction and production costs for an online auction company.[10] The results estimate a reduction of approximately 52% percent when moving from physical auctions to an online process. While coordination costs seem to be the main drivers of this reduction in transaction costs, the authors do not find evidence for an offsetting increase in asymmetric information for trades on the Internet.

2.1.2 *Organizational forms: Markets versus hierarchies*

The arrival of the Internet has affected coordination costs, hence making alternative organizational forms potentially more appropriate. Markets play a central role in the economy, working as mechanisms of exchange where buyers and sellers match and prices form. Under a hierarchical interaction, value chain activities are governed by managerial control procuring production inputs though established suppliers. Through this organization the cost of searching for other suppliers, writing contracts, etc. is reduced. However, if value system activities are guided through open market relationships the firm will obtain better deals and more competitive prices.

The information technology revolution in general, and particularly the Internet, has reduced the costs of coordinating and information gathering, increasing information transparency for all involved players. As a consequence, under certain conditions it becomes more efficient to conduct transactions through markets instead of using hierarchical organizations. In particular, in the "electronic marketplace", understood as "an interorganizational information system that allows the participating buyers and sellers to exchange information related to prices and product characteristics",[11] transaction costs have been reduced and hierarchical relationships are becoming less efficient compared to market relationships. The role of electronic markets or digital value chain integration in this process has been at the basis of the introduction of new efficiencies and market transparency in the value system of an industry across all value added activities, allowing a deeper integration of the value chains of different organizations that form part of the value system.

These efficiencies come mainly from the reduction in transactional costs making both markets and hierarchies more efficient and shifting the economic organization from hierarchies to markets.[12] According to a recent estimate by the Economist, over 750 networked marketplaces have been developed worldwide.[13] Some of these new marketplaces cover a wide variety of products and an extensive group of buyers and sellers.

The job search market is experiencing some fundamental innovations due to the appearance of an online counterpart. The online recruitment market is clearly growing. Goldman Sachs predicts that online recruitment advertising and related services in Europe will be worth €6.131 million by 2006. According to a study by iLogos Research (April 2001), global use of the Internet for recruiting purposes has increased from 29% of global 500 companies in 1998 to 88% in 2001. In the US the online recruitment market has been steadily growing since its creation, and still in 2004 and 2005 high growth rates have been reported (see Figure 4).

However most of this expansion is through the companies' own corporate websites. Looking at candidate behavior, Forrester Research (June 2001) found that in Europe while newspapers were still the most important source of job advertisements for candidates (62% of candidates used newspapers in their job search, compared to 15% who used job recruitment sites), job recruitment sites attracted twice the number of job seekers than corporate sites.

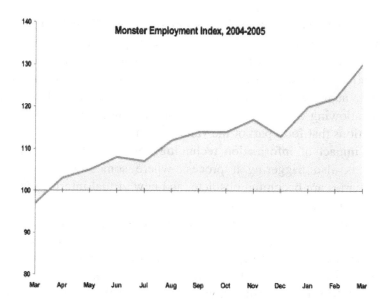

Figure 4. US Online Employment Growth 2004-2005
Source: Monster Online Employment Index
(http://www.monsterworldwide.com/Public_Relations/index_US.html).

Online job search portals, such as the leader of the Spanish market Infojobs.net, are characterized as offering every type of tool to facilitate the recruitment process. They have two types of customer – the companies who want to advertise jobs, and the candidates who are looking for a job – and are able to coordinate their demands in a more efficient way than offline recruiters. They save costs on (a) the publishing of the job offering and CV, (b) the information gathering process for both recruiters and job seekers, and (c) overall time to "match" demand and supply. Hence, although offline recruiting still offers some advantages through the personal nature of the service, the emergence of generic job search marketplaces that could not be efficient before due to the huge coordination costs of matching of job seekers and offers, are significantly changing both the industry and customer behavior, and some of the traditional players are already adopting click and mortar strategies.

Similarly, firms such as Dell Computer and Cisco Systems have shown an impressive growth in value since they found in the Internet a key element of their business architecture. They have automated the coordination of most of their activities, both internal and with external suppliers, achieving greater efficiency and transparency of the value system, allowing a deeper integration of the value chains of different organizations that form part of the value system.

The impact of information technology on the value system of an industry is also triggering a process where some of the traditional intermediaries are becoming obsolete, and new virtual-intermediaries are being incorporated. The repercussion for firms and consumers of this changing environment will depend on the industry and the characteristics of the value system. In most industrialized countries, intermediation margins are close to 33 percent of the final price of goods;[14] this means that an important sector of the economy may be affected. Benjamin and Wigand (1995), for example, have found that in the high-quality shirts market it may be possible to reduce the retail price by almost 62 percent if wholesalers and retailers were eliminated from the value system. The manufacturer now has the possibility of selling its products directly to clients or through integrated retailers that are more efficient, reducing the final sale price and increasing the profit margin.

Sony started selling directly to consumers through the Internet in 2000. Even though the company has only sold 20 percent of its products online until 2005, the impact of this decision on the electronics retail industry has been significant.[15] Similarly, twenty seven airlines, including the big five (American, Continental, United, Northwest and Delta) have banded together to create a unique travel site where these companies will be able to offer fares, ticketing and other services. One of the most important aims of this new initiative is to cut the $5 to $10 dollar commission fees paid to online brokers, in a business that according to Forester will create US$64 billion in online ticketing.[16]

In conclusion, simple "before" and "after" comparisons of outcomes are complicated, as the arrival of the IT revolution has profoundly impacted organizational forms, enhancing the creation of market places, and causing new opportunities for disintermediation and re-intermediation both of internal processes of the firm and the entire value system of an industry.

2.2 *Value creation and demand*

Affecting the willingness to pay of consumers implies shifting the demand curve of consumers. As in the case of cost drivers, demand drivers are affected in different ways by the surge of the Internet. The most important impact has been on the consumer's search costs, which have considerably decreased, as information is instantaneous and buyers can compare the offerings of sellers worldwide. Other drivers, such as brand image and value added services have not been directly impacted by the evolution of the Internet. However, the investment in these types of demand drivers are more important today to achieve a differentiation advantage.[17] Furthermore, the Internet has allowed the firms to become more knowledgeable about their customers. Analyzing click-streams for example provides information that can be used to adjust the offer being made and as such increase the customers' willingness to pay.

In this sense, the emergence of eToys as an online toy e-tailer has significantly impacted the toy industry. Toy buyers (usually parents) arrive at the market with a fixed demand (the child is a product prescriptor), and their total gross willingness to pay is composed by (a) the value of the toy, (b) search cost of the lowest price, and (c) time consumed in the buying process. In the traditional retail world, search costs are high, as different toy stores have to be visited, and the buying process is extremely time consuming (especially during Christmas, in which streets and shopping malls are overcrowded). eToys' selling proposition, with low prices, easy comparison of prices, and little time consumption, was clearly revolutionary in the toy industry. The entry of eToys transformed the toy industry in a fundamental way, and eToys was able to capture sales for a total amount of $107 million during the 1999 Christmas season.

2.2.1 *Search costs*

The Internet has been claimed to reduce search cost. This would increase the net willingness to pay of an individual consumer, shifting out the demand curve for the product on offer. At the same time, the reduction of search costs would imply that substitutes are more easily available. This would reduce the demand for an individual firm, increasing rivalry, leading to lower prices and less price dispersion.[18] In this sense, Brynjolfsson and Smith[19] have found that book prices are 9 to 13 percent lower on the Internet than in brick-and-mortar stores, while music CD prices are 9 to 16 percent lower. In addition, price dispersion has also been reduced. Therefore, and taking into account that, as Stigler says "price dispersion is a manifestation – and indeed it is the measure – of ignorance in the market", reduced search costs seem to be increasing overall market efficiency. Different types of search technologies such as search engines and shopbots, which help consumers to find the lowest prices and bargains, support the transparency provided by online shopping.[20]

Nevertheless, although search costs are lower, the overall effect on prices remains unclear. A survey conducted by McKinsey & Company has found that most online shoppers indeed do not search for lower prices with the intensity it was thought. More than 80% of online shoppers for books, toys and CDs buy from the first site they visit. For durable goods such as electronics, the percentage of shoppers buying on the first site is 76 percent.[21] Furthermore, Janssen and Moraga[22] show that the intuition for the effect of reduced search costs on prices and price dispersion is conditioned by the maturity of the market and the size of the purchase.

2.2.2 *Customization*

Customization of the product involves adding features to the product that the customers value. Therefore, increased customization, i.e. the provision of complementary goods/options, shifts the demand for the product outward. Customers may be willing to pay a premium price for quality service, brand name and trust. For example, Amazon.com, offers a whole range of complementary (and personalized) information on each book they sell, providing an extensive summary, comments from the editor, author, and other readers, as well as information on possible complementary books that a buyer may find interesting to read ("readers that bought this book also bought...”). The company, although charging higher prices than other competitors,[23] retains more that 80 percent of the market share in the online book retail industry. This evidences that not only low prices matter for customers when buying online.

Dell, while having a predefined range of recommended buying options, started offering the complete customization of any of its computers and notebooks through its webpage, opened in 1996. In addition, they have set up a number of forums to ensure the free flow of information with the customer on a constant basis.[24] All of these initiatives have allowed Dell to differentiate from its competitors, charging sensibly higher prices. Although nowadays a number of competitors, such as Apple, have tried to follow this approach, i.e. increasing customization and customer care, Dell continues being the only major computer company able to meet its predictions of profitability, with a market share about 27% of the total personal computer market.

Hence, the combined effect of lower search costs and improved possibilities for customization not only affect demand, but simultaneously change the existing market structure, thus affecting the outcome observed before and after the introduction of Internet.

3 Value Appropriation and Pricing

Achieving cost or differentiation advantages are the most important determinants of strategic positioning. The Internet has created new opportunities to articulate and develop such advantages on the supply side and demand side.[25] As discussed before, the dynamics of competitive advantage in this context can be examined using cost and benefit drivers. These drivers reflect the most important activities that will affect the cost and differentiation advantages with respect to other industry competitors. Lower search costs and customization opportunities have the effect of increasing the buyer's perceived value and lower transaction costs reduce the cost structure of firms, i.e. more value is created. However, these changes have at the same time affected the overall market structure. Therefore, it is not clear how firms can appropriate this added value. Especially on the consumer side there are important challenges in appropriating the added value created by the Internet.

In this sense, eToys had a clear new value proposition, which increased the willingness to pay by offering convenience to the customers. Despite the brilliant start-up, significant challenges for value appropriation appeared during the next months. First, they failed to deliver because they lacked shipping capabilities and were unable to supply the quantities demanded of the hot products. The suppliers were unwilling to cut out their regular customers in moments of product scarcity. Second, incumbents had to react, as the new, superior value proposition was threatening their own sustainability. As a result, the leading US retailer, Toys "R" Us, tried to buy the new entrant eToys in Spring of 2000. As eToys rejected the deal, Toys "R" Us decided to establish an alliance with Amazon.com (hence combining the toy store's merchandising expertise with Amazon's knowledge on web operations, inventory management and fulfillment), thus adopting a click and mortar approach. This in turn affected the value proposition for the customer, as Toys "R" Us now offers additional service as returns are allowed to the brick and mortar stores, increasing the willingness to pay of customers even further. As a result, eToys started running into trouble, selling much less than expected during the Christmas season 2000, and closing their business in Spring 2001. Other pure e-tailers, such as toysmart.com, toytime.com, of redrocket.com already had to shut down operations some months before. Still, the toy retailing business has been reshaped, as online sales have been included in the value proposition of the retailers, price pressure has increased, and more service has to be offered, hence resulting in less value appropriation opportunities.

Nevertheless, not all online businesses have appropriation problems. Firms such as eBay have reported profits since their first year of operations, and their profits are still growing. The company reported a net income of $18.3 million in 1999, increasing it to $568.6 million in 2000, showing an extremely robust business model that will allow them to make an annual profit of around $1 billion in 2005. eBay has profited from being the first mover in the online auction market. It has been able to differentiate itself from the competition by creating and taking advantage of network externalities, and the subsequent creation of lock-in of both buyers and sellers. This has allowed them to reach very high volumes, and, as economies of scale and scope are important, their average costs went down, which in turn gives them a significant advantage regarding their competitors.[26]

The solution to the appropriation challenge crucially depends on the competitive environment: rivalry, entry barriers and the new equilibrium between the firm, its customers and its suppliers. These forces determine the pricing power of the firms in the industry.

3.1 *Rivalry and entry of new competitors*

A senior vice president of Lehman Brothers, New York when talking about the effect of electronic marketplaces on the Chemical Industry noted: "It's pretty clear that with e-business you have more to lose on sales price compared to how much you save on raw materials, simply because you are selling more specialty products and buying more commodity products — where markets are very efficient already — to manufacture them."[27] This reflects the pressure of competition and market transparency on profitability for some industries.

Depending on the market power of firms, the possible value appropriated is completely different. For example, if there is only one firm in the market with all the market power (monopoly) the firm is able to appropriate more of the added value created by the introduction of Internet from consumers and suppliers compared to firms that have no market power.[10] If firms have no market power (competitive scenario) the result is completely different. Prices will be closer to the opportunity cost and there are fewer opportunities for appropriating any value from the consumer side. This implies that buyers will increase their consumer surplus appropriating most of the value created through the introduction of the Internet. Firms only appropriate the added value created from cost reductions in case they are able to reduce prices paid to their suppliers, while prices charged to the consumers do not drop at the same rate. If market rivalry is high and the barriers to entry low, the existing firms will need to decrease prices, giving up a substantial part of the additional value created through the Internet.

The arrival of the Internet has increased rivalry, especially within the online retail channel. Industries with lower entry barriers face greater competitive pressure in the short run reducing aggregate profitability and market prices. Nevertheless, the investment in IT infrastructure and other marketing and branding costs seem to increase entry barriers. In the online book industry, Latcovich and Smith[28] find that Amazon spends 32% of sales on advertising while Barnes and Noble.com spends more than 50%. Offline, Barnes and Noble and Borders spend only between 14% and 20% of sales on advertising. Therefore, the competitive interactions that might be expected in the offline book market should be quite distinct from the online market given this endogenous nature of markets structure. Lucking-Reiley and Spulber,[29] however, argue that entry costs appear to be lower for some dot.coms since new companies can outsource IT infrastructure and software, reducing their initial investment, through the variabilization of a cost that is a sunk costs to incumbents with existing IT infrastructures. Furthermore, easy access to the capital market reduces financial entry barriers. Therefore, increased rivalry will presumably lead to increased price competition.

In the book industry, Bailey[30] examined the impact of the entry of the large brick and mortar book store, Barnes and Noble into the Internet market and the reaction of the incumbent leader Amazon.com. The main result is that the incumbent firm, Amazon, reduced its prices to match the prices of the same basket of books offered by Barnes and Noble (see Figure 5). Interestingly, in this process B&N reduced prices only on the Internet channel, leaving the prices at physical retailers unaffected.

Friberg, Ganslandt and Sandström[31] analyze the problem of price differences across traditional and electronic channels setting up a model comparing in a duopolistic market structure a conventional retail firm and an independent electronic retailer, versus a monopolistic firm who sells in both channels, electronic and conventional. Using a sample from the Swedish books and CDs market they find evidence of lower prices in the online channel for those firms selling exclusively through the Internet. The intuition for this outcome is that monopolistic firms in on-line markets charge a higher price to avoid cannibalizing sales from its conventional retail stores. The independent electronic retailers compete with the conventional firms by charging a lower price. The empirical results also demonstrate significant price dispersion for both traditional and online retail stores. Mazón and Pereira[32] develop a model that generates very similar predictions, but endogenizes the prevailing market structure.

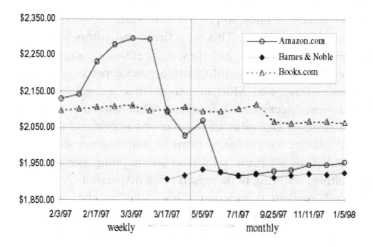

Figure 5. Market Basket Price at Amazon, Barnes & Noble and Books.com

Source: Bailey (1998b).

3.2 *Increased market transparency*

The arrival of the Internet together with powerful search engines potentially creates a perfect information environment where firms selling at the lowest price are posted. The impact on price competition may result in all firms reducing prices to opportunity cost. However, this is not exactly how it works. Following Ellison and Fisher[33] search engines that only post the lowest price retailers will have a short life in the market. Price search engines appropriate some of the value created through the transaction, typically charging a percentage of a transaction that gets completed through their webpage. For example, all e-tailers that are accessed through plaza.terra.es, have to pay a negotiated part of the value of the transaction to Terra, if the user finally buys any item during that connection.[34] If only those firms selling at price equal to opportunity cost are posted, the search engine will be unable to appropriate any value in the long run, as there is no margin left to appropriate. Kephart and Greenwald[35], following Salop and Stiglitz,[36] provide one of the earliest theoretical treatments on how search engines may affect the competition in electronic markets. In their model, firms randomize prices between two types of buyers in order to price discriminate between active bargain searches and non-searchers. This way firms can compete for the active searchers with lower prices, but they compensate by charging a higher price to the others. When an information gatekeeper regulates access to the customers, Baye and Morgan[37] show that the gatekeeper will not provide all firms access to consumers. This way the gatekeeper can appropriate some of the value of transactions performed on its site. Iyer and Pazgal[38] model the choice of firms to join Internet shopping agents. It turns out that not all firms want internet shopping agents to recognize their sites either, resulting in increased price dispersion.

Increased market transparency has lead to the hypothesis that competition in electronic markets will take the form of Bertrand competition, where firms compete purely on prices resulting in lower prices and lower price dispersion and reduced industry profitability. However, the most recent empirical evidence does not support this hypothesis. There exist several empirical studies of prices on electronic markets, most of them focused on books, CDs and software.[39]

The earliest analyses show that prices on the Internet are higher than in the traditional channels. The study reported by Lee[40] compares prices of used cars in conventional and electronic markets from 1986 to 1995. He found that prices where higher on the Internet with respect to conventional channels. A possible explanation for this outcome is that the study was based on prices formed through auctions, where the consumer with the highest willingness to pay is the one who obtains the unique good. This implies that prices for auction markets will usually be higher than traditional markets allowing firms through creative pricing mechanisms to appropriate some of the value created by the Internet. Bailey[41] using a sample of books, CDs and software for US retailers from 1996 to 1997 also found higher prices on the Internet channel. However, the most recent empirical evidence presents a different picture. All the studies on price level, report lower prices on the Internet channel compared to those prices in traditional stores. We have already mentioned Brynjolfsson and Smith's[42] results on book on CD sales on the Internet. Similarly, Clay, Krishnan and Wolff[43] find lower prices on the Internet channel, although they reported significant price dispersion. They reported lowest average prices for New York Times bestsellers (69%) of the publisher's recommended price), higher for computer bestsellers (78%) and the highest for random books (86%). Regarding price dispersion, they found the highest dispersion for NYT bestsellers (28%) followed by computer bestsellers (16%) and the lowest for random books (13%). Given the results about price dispersion reported by Sorensen[44] for the traditional prescription drugs market one would have expected that price levels and dispersion would be lower for more frequently purchased items.

Other studies include used cars, travel agents, life insurance and real state markets.[45] Scott-Morton, Silva and Zettelmeyer[46] found that the average customer pays approximately 2% less for cars bought using online services compared to traditional channels. According to the authors, consumers will benefit from buying online even though dealers will not offer different prices to online and offline customers. However, because of reduced search costs, the internet helps to locate the cheapest dealer in the area, reducing average prices. They found that dealers' gross margins from sales through the internet channel are significantly lower than gross margins earned selling vehicles in the traditional way. However, because online customers are cheaper to serve, the net effect makes dealers better off working through the Internet channel. This indicates that the online branch is able to retain part of the value created on the supply side through reduced transaction costs.

The empirical evidence surveyed suggests the existence of lower prices and lower menu costs on the Internet channel, but an important degree of price dispersion. Deviations from the Bertrand assumptions of product homogeneity, zero search costs and symmetric information lead to price dispersion. Several models have been developed to study the effect of these different assumptions on the Bertrand outcome.[47]

3.3 *New products and pricing mechanisms*

While increased rivalry and market transparency seem to lower value appropriation opportunities for firms, empirical evidence has shown that some firms have been able to create new value appropriation opportunities through the redefinition of their products and the implementation of new pricing mechanisms.

We have already emphasized the importance of customization for value creation, as it increases the customer's willingness to pay. On the other hand, it may also allow firms to appropriate this value, as increased differentiation with regard to their competitors may be achieved. For example, Amazon not only offers books, but also a whole set of complementary information, some of which is based on the analysis of the customer's profile (information of actual and past online behavior stored in Amazon's databases), and therefore the offering is not imitable by any of its competitors. Similarly, Yahoo! bases much of its competitive advantage on the fact that its users have personalized homepages, access their email accounts through their site, and actively participate in the Yahoo! communities, thus creating stickiness that is not easily replicable by any other portal, and that allows Yahoo! to appropriate value through advertising income. In addition, Yahoo! is able to charge different advertising prices depending on the amount of information it has about each user.

Internet also offers new price discrimination opportunities. One very popular new price mechanism is the auction, as it allows companies to almost perfectly discriminate on price, extracting the complete willingness to pay from each customer. In addition, other subtler price discrimination mechanisms include new pricing possibilities in, for example, supermarkets. Peapod, the largest American online grocer, offers coupons and discounts to customers based on each customer's profile, extracting information from repeating customers to capture new potential sales. Hence, for example, a "historical" a cereal consumer that has never purchased a "Tropicana" juice, may well find a "Tropicana" coupon (in form of a banner) during an online shopping session. In addition, Peapod also follows each customer's particular buying process, and may offer a discount on dips while you are buying some chips. All of these initiatives, which are valuable to the customer, as the overall price paid is reduced, result in an increased value appropriation for the producer.

From the preceding analysis it is clear that the Internet has had an important impact on market structure. On the one hand, rivalry and market transparency have increased, difficulting the appropriation of any of the value created through the Internet. On the other hand, endogenous entry barriers and new products and pricing mechanisms have opened new opportunities for firms to appropriate the value created by the Internet.

4 Conclusions

New possibilities on value creation and value appropriation do not only lead to a redefinition of the price equilibrium due to lower transaction costs, search costs, and customization opportunities, increased transparency and its impact on industry rivalry. More and more, the Internet is fundamentally affecting the market structure, as the offering of a firm may fundamentally change, thus affecting competitive dynamics. Entering e-channels with the appropriate strategy can create an enormous competitive advantage for traditional and dot.com companies, although the net effect for a particular firm depends on how its competitive positioning is impacted as Internet comes to the stage. Hence, while sometimes the Internet has allowed firms to simultaneously increase the willingness to pay of customers, and, because of the significant jump in volume, reduce the cost of providing these products and services, value appropriation might be impossible, as rivalry and transparentization of markets may make it impossible to establish a pricing scheme that allows companies to capture the created value. In this sense, we have highlighted the importance of taking into account that on the value creation side, both supply and demand are affected, be it through the reduction of transaction costs, in form of motivation or coordination costs, or the triggering of new organizational forms and work processes on the supply side, or through the reduction of search costs and new customization opportunities. On the other hand, value appropriation and pricing strategies depend on rivalry and new entry possibilities, increases in market transparency, and new products and price mechanisms. The changes that the Internet provokes on the value creation and value appropriation sides will define how overall competitive dynamics are going to change the industry structure.

References

1. Porter, Michael. "Strategy and the Internet" *Harvard Business Review*, March, 2001, pp. 63-78.
2. Kim, Chan and Renée Mauborgne. "Value Innovation: The Strategic Logic of High Growth" *Harvard Business Review*, January-February, 1997, pp. 103-112.
3. Costs for a 200 share trade of a $20 stock.
4. AOL Time Warner Press Release, 11 January 2001.
5. Valor, Josep. "Estrategias y Sostenibilidad de Portales, Proveedores de Acceso a Internet y Empresas de Contenidos: Un Análisis mediante la Cadena de Valor" IESE Occasional Paper 02-4, July, 2002.
6. Brandenburger, Adam and Harborne Stuart. "Value-Based Business Strategy" *Journal of Economics and Management Strategy*, 5(1), 1996, pp. 5-24.
7. Williamson, Oliver. *Markets and Hierarchies: Analysis and Antitrust Implications.* New York: Free Press. 1975.
8. Milgrom, Paul and John Roberts. *Economics Organizations and Management.* New Jersey: Prentice Hall. 1992.
9. Garicano, Luis and Steven Kaplan. "The Effects of Business-to-Business E-Commerce on Transaction Costs" *Journal of Industrial Economics*, 49(4), 2001, pp. 1-23.
10. The company analyzed is Autodaq and operates in the wholesale used car auction market.
11. Bakos, J. Yannis. "A Strategic Analysis of Electronic Marketplaces" *MIS Quarterly*, September, 1991, pp. 295-310.
12. Malone, Thomas W., JoAnne Yates, and Robert I. Benjamin. "Electronic Markets and Electronic Hierarchies" *Communications of the ACM*, 30(6), 1987, pp. 484-497.
13. *The Economist* "Seller Beware," 4 March 2000, pp. 61-62.
14. OECD Report on electronic Commerce (www.oecd.org).
15. Spiegel, Rob. "Sony Shocks Japanese Dealers with Direct Sales Web Site" *The E-Commerce Times*, 2 January 2000.
16. Hillebrand, Mary. "Airlines Band Together to Launch Travel Site" *E-Commerce Times*, 13 January 2000.
17. Latcovich, Simon and Howard Smith. "Pricing, Sunk Costs, and Market Structure Online: Evidence from Book retailing" *Oxford Review of Economic Policy*, 17(2), 2001, pp. 217-234.

18. Janssen, Maartin and Jose Luis Moraga. "Pricing, Consumer Search and Maturity of Internet Markets" Mimeo. 2001.
19. Brynjolfsson, E., and M. Smith. "Frictionless Commerce? A Comparison of Internet and Conventional Retailers" *Management Science*, 46(4), 2000, pp. 563-585.
20. Examples of these type of price search sites are mySimon, Dealtime, Pricewatch and Pricescan.
21. Baker, Walter, Eric Lin, Michael Marn and Craig Zawada. "Getting Prices Right on the Web" *The McKinsey Quarterly*, 2(2), 2001, pp. 54-63; Baker, Walter, Mike Marn and Craig Zawada. "Price Smarter on the Net" *Harvard Business Review*, 79, 2001, pp. 122-127.
22. Janssen, Maartin and Jose Luis Moraga. "Pricing, Consumer Search and Maturity of Internet Markets" Mimeo. 2001.
23. Clay, Karen, Ramayya Krishnan and Eric Wolff. "Prices and Price Dispersion on the Web: Evidence from the Online Book Industry" NBER Working papers. 2001.
24. Magretta, Joan. "The Power of Virtual Integration: An Interview with Dell Computer's Michael Dell" *Harvard Business Review*, 76(2), 1998, pp. 72-85.
25. Porter, Michael. "Strategy and the Internet" *Harvard Business Review*, March, 2001, pp. 63-78.
26. Sieber, Sandra, Rafael Andreu and Joan E. Ricart. "Some Things are New in the New Economy, but it is not Strategy" Working Paper, e-Business Center PWC & IESE. 2002.
27. Stevens, Tim. "E-Rosion?" *The Industry Week*, 13 August 2001.
28. Latcovich, Simon and Howard Smith. "Pricing, Sunk Costs, and Market Structure Online: Evidence from Book retailing" *Oxford Review of Economic Policy*, 17(2), 2001, pp. 217-234.
29. Lucking-Reiley, David and Daniel Spulber. "Business-to-Business Electronic Commerce" *Journal of Economic Perspectives*, 15, 2001, pp. 55-68.
30. Bailey, J.P. "Internet Price Discrimination: Self-Regulation, Public Policy and Global Electronic Commerce" Mimeo. 1998b.
31. Friberg, Richard, Ganslandt Mattias and Mikael Sandström. "Pricing Strategies in E-Commerce: Bricks vs. Clicks" The Research Institute of Industrial Economics. Working Paper No. 559. 2001.
32. Mazón, Cristina and Pedro Pereira. "Who Benefits from Electronic Commerce?" Mimeo. 2001.
33. Ellison, Glen and Sara Fisher. "Search, Obfuscation and Price Elasticities on the Internet" Mimeo. MIT. 2001.
34. If during a session the user only looks around, and buys at any other moment accessing directly the e-commerce site, Terra is not able to charge anything.
35. Kephart, J.O. and A.R. Greenwald. "Shopbot economics" Technical report, IBM Institute for Advanced Commerce. 1998.

36. Salop, S. and J. Stiglitz. "A Theory of Sales: A Simple Model of Price Dispersion with Identical Agents" *American Economic Review*, 72, 1982, pp. 1121-1130.
37. Baye, Michael R. and John Morgan. "Information Gatekeepers on the Internet and the Competitiveness of Homogeneous Product Markets" *American Economic Review*, 91(3), 2001, pp. 454-474.
38. Iyer, Ganesh and Amit Pazgal. "Internet Shopping Agents: Virtual Co-Location and Competition" Mimeo. 2001.
39. See Smith *et al.* for a very complete survey on empirical studies about prices on electronic markets.
40. Lee, Ho Geun. "Do Electronic Marketplaces Lower the Price of Goods?" *Communications of the ACM*, 41(1), 1998, pp. 73-80.
41. Bailey, J.P. "Intermediation and Electronic Markets: Aggregation and Pricing in Internet Commerce" Ph.D. Thesis, Technology, Management and Policy, Massachusetts Institute of Technology, May, 1998a; Bailey, J.P. "Electronic Commerce: Prices and Consumer Issues for Three Products: Books, Compact Discs, and Software," Organisation for Economic Co-Operation and Development, OCDE/GD(98)4. 1998c.
42. Brynjolfsson, E. and M. Smith. "Frictionless Commerce? A Comparison of Internet and Conventional Retailers" *Management Science*, 46(4), 2000, pp. 563-585.
43. Clay, Krishnan and Wolff (2001).
44. Sorensen, A.T. "Equilibrium Price Dispersion in Retail Markets for Prescription Drugs" *Journal of Political Economy*, 108(4), 2000, pp. 833-850.
45. For examples on these industries see Clemons, Hann and Hitt (1998) on travel agencies, Brown and Goolsbee (2000) on life insurance and Crowston and Wigand (2000) on real estate. See Clemons, Eric K., Il-Horn Hann and Lorin M. Hitt. "The Nature of Competition among Online Travel Agents: An Empirical Investigation" Wharton School of Business, Working Paper, 1998; Brown, J.R. and Austan Goolsbee. "Does the Internet Make Markets More Competitive? Evidence from the Life Insurance Industry" *Journal of Political Economy*, 110(3), 2002, pp. 481-507; Crowston, Kevin and Rolf Wigand. "Real Estate War in Cyberspace: An Emerging Electronic Market?" Mimeo. Syracuse University. 2000.
46. Scott-Morton, Fiona, Jorge Silva and Florian Zettelmeyer. "Internet Car Retailing" NBER Working Papers. 2000.
47. See Diamond, Peter A. "Consumer Differences and Prices in a Search Model" *Quarterly Journal of Economics*, 102, 1987, pp. 429-436; Varian, Hal. "A Model of Sales" *American Economic Review*, 70, 1980, pp. 651-659; Shilony, Yuval. "Mixed Pricing in Oligopoly" *Journal of Economic Theory*, 14(2), 1977, pp. 373-388; Stalh, Dale. "Oligopolistic Pricing with Sequential Consumer Search" *American Economic Review*, 79(4), 1989, pp. 700-712; Stalh, Dale. "Oligopolistic Pricing with Heterogeneous Consumer Search" *International Journal of Industrial Organization*, 14, 1996, pp. 243-268; Janssen, Maartin and Jose Luis Moraga. "Pricing, Consumer Search and Maturity of Internet Markets" Mimeo. 2001.

CHAPTER 15

Strategic Transformations in Selected Productive Sectors

Joseph P. McGill

College of Business - Kean University
Union, NJ 07083, USA
Email: jmcgill@kean.edu

1 Introduction

By most accounts, a substantial amount of change in the competitive landscape over the past two decades can be traced to the development and global diffusion of information technologies. New business forms have emerged while others have faded, and entire industries have been transformed. Information technologies (IT) continue to generate waves of change across industries in the same way as earlier technologies such as the telegraph, the electric motor, and the steam engine[1]. As a general purpose technology, IT co-evolve with the architecture of productive activities as well as with the coordination of these activities, and creates value when activities are simultaneously decentralized, specialized, and coordinated[2]. As firms use IT to decentralize and specialize, there are new opportunities to develop our understanding of the dynamics of IT-enabled coordination between firms. This chapter focuses on how IT have transformed relationships among firms in manufacturing, electronic commerce, and research intensive industry sectors, emphasizing a number of contextual factors that may either create or limit these transformations. The contribution of this chapter is to link the IT and strategic management literatures and to provide a starting point for future research that focuses on the intersection of IT and strategy. The chapter unfolds as follows. The next section examines theories of economics and management and their connection with IT-enabled transformation, followed by a selective review of industry sectors focused on manufacturing, electronic commerce, and research and development. The chapter concludes with a synthesis and discussion of IT-enabled transformation.

2 Strategy, Organization and IT

To discuss strategic transformation we must first define what is being transformed. A central focus in the strategic management literature concerns the organizational boundaries of the firm, i.e., why are certain activities integrated within the firm while other activities are performed externally either through collaboration with other firms or through marketplace transactions. To the extent that IT alter boundaries and their coordination in patterned ways, it can be said that IT enable strategic transformation. The following section draws on theories from transaction cost economics[3], the strategic management literature[4,5], and institutional theory[6] to describe the relationship between organizational boundaries and the use of IT for coordination and collaboration.

In the transaction cost economics (TCE) view[3] the choice of internal or external governance for a transaction depends upon the relative cost of administering and performing the activity internally and the cost of exposure to opportunistic behavior by an external supplier of the activity. The type of transaction that creates value usually involves committing specialized resources that are not easily redeployed to other uses. These types of transactions foster opportunism when one firm optimizes its gain at the expense of another firm, for example by "holding up" or renegotiating transaction terms. A firm's know-how, or tacit knowledge, is especially vulnerable to unintended "leakage" when exchange partners are combining knowledge-based resources in co-specialized ways, e.g., collaboration in product or process innovations and in research and learning-oriented activities[6a]. The costs of specifying, monitoring, and enforcing contracts to control opportunism may be quite high thus leading firms to establish "mutual hostages" through joint ventures or bilateral contracts. As the costs of controlling opportunism rise, firms may shift to vertical integration as a cost-minimizing solution to the problem of coordinating co-specialized exchanges[7].

2.1 *Modularity*

Related to the transaction costs view of exchange is the concept of organizational modularity[8]. Modularity describes how the firm's product technology is mirrored in its organization structure and how exchanges of information among organization units (or functions) in the firm incorporate greater or lesser degrees of standardization, for example in product design (R&D) and manufacturing. When the form and flow of information or physical product between units is standardized, each organizational unit has more flexibility to operate autonomously and to handle external disturbances without requiring change to the entire system. Standardized connections among units result in a "loosely coupled" system more capable of recombining units in unique ways to create new systems of interaction. In contrast, highly interdependent units require close coordination and reciprocal adjustments, with changes in one functional area (e.g., in operations, activities, scope, etc.) affecting the performance of other function(s). Organizations with less modular architectures require more mutual adjustment among functional units. While this mutual adjustment increases each unit's knowledge of the overall system and speeds knowledge transfer throughout the entire organization, it also reduces the ability to adjust to exogenous disturbances[9]. To the extent that IT-enabled coordination fosters standardized methods of exchange, for example EDI or inter-firm ERP, firms have more flexibility in choosing whether functions can or should be performed internally or externally. Further, as the number of prospective partners available for exchange through standardized methods increases, the relative cost of internal coordination rises, leading firms to specialize in certain functional activities and externalize other activities that can be more efficiently performed by others.

2.2 *Coordination*

For many firms, the ability to coordinate or bundle their activities with those of their partnering firms provides a basis for competitive advantage[10,11]. In the resource based view (RBV) it is the combination of coordination routines and resources that confer competitive advantage, especially when these combinations of routines and resources are simultaneously valuable, rare, and difficult-to-imitate. Organizational routines differ between firms, and when capabilities provide superior coordination of behavior and resources they become valuable[12,13]. Consider for example Dell Computer's use of private B2B exchanges and proprietary, "in-sourced" information systems that are used to coordinate across multiple firms. The importance of efficiently coordinating multiple echelons of supply in Dell's supply chain is critical to sustaining Dell's position as a low-cost OEM and has led Dell to rely on internal design and development of the IT systems used to control the supply chain, while outsourcing component supply and logistics. The ability of IT to enable coordination of product or service activities independent of the activities themselves is a necessary but not sufficient condition for firms to shift boundaries and coordinate activities in co-specialized ways. IT may enable a firm to achieve market power through, for example, scale economies, differentiation, or positive network effects. Such a firm may dominate its industry value chain and use its market power to specify the "collaborative rules" for other firms wishing to participate in the value chain.

In addition to the resource-based and market-based rationales for IT enabled transformation, non-economic sources of influence include those that are legal and regulatory in nature (e.g., property rights), and those arising from the need to appear organizationally "legitimate". Property rights and patents for example may either limit or encourage firms to adopt a particular business method, or to make research available to other firms participating in research networks. The need to appear legitimate may also encourage firms to adopt IT-enabled organizational structures simply because of uncertainty in their environments, or because they want to appear legitimate to other organizations on whom they are potentially dependent for resources[14]. These institutional pressures can be reflected in bandwagon effects, and in non-economic rationales for the use of supply chain technologies[15].

Figure 1 depicts a typology of IT-enabled transformation based on the dimensions of modularity and inter-firm coordination. Each of the model's four quadrants is described in terms of the rationale and focus of the transformation, and the mechanism of coordination. After reviewing the use of IT in a number of industry settings, we will explore how this framework may help us synthesize what we know about the dynamics of IT-enabled transformation.

Modularity	Coordination	
	Explicit ⇔ **Market**	
Low ⇕ **High**	**I. Craft** Create "converged know-how" and interdisciplinary breakthroughs using IT-enabled tools and artifacts. Examples: Bioinformatics, nanotech simulators. Key factor: Community of practice.	**II. Consolidate** Aggregate and broker distributed transactions to generate positive network externalities. Examples: eBay; C2C & B2B exchanges. Key factor: Trust (transaction visibility).
	III. Chain Disaggregate supply chains to gain from specialization/scale economies; gains captured by lead firms through power/dependence relations. Examples: Dell and component suppliers; "Big 6" automotive OEMs and parts suppliers; Electronic design firms and electronic manufacturing services. Key factor: Bargaining Power.	**IV. Channel** Disintermediate channels vertically while aggregating horizontally, e.g., through bundling. Examples: Amazon, Orbitz, McGraw Hill (Primis). Key factor: Trust (product visibility).

Figure 1. Typology of IT-Enabled Transformations

3 Manufacturing Sector

Over the last two decades, manufacturing firms have faced significant changes in their competitive landscapes as global competition intensified, increasing the need for specialized production and the uncertainty of demand. Facing increased risks to internal investment in production and supply, manufacturing functions that were previously contained within the firm have been externalized, for example through contract manufacturing and supplier markets. Decentralization of production and an increase in the number of firms exchanging information in the production chain have been supported by the parallel development and availability of new information and communication technologies[16]. In the same way the steam engine freed industrial production from dependence on natural water sources for power, information technologies have enabled manufacturing, transportation and communications to be coordinated globally.

IT enable information to be shared between interdependent firms in the supply chain, reducing uncertainty about product/component demand and lowering the cost of misalignment among capacity, inventory, material flows and customer responsiveness. A significant number of IT-enabled supply chain models have demonstrated increasing returns to information sharing for both upstream and downstream firms[17]. This is not surprising given that the internal process activities of firms are tightly coupled with their external information flows, especially for firms in industries such as automobile manufacturing, where firms face high levels of rivalry, high fixed costs and volatility in demand[18]. In spite of the potential value and availability of supply chain technologies, the actual level of implementation appears to be relatively low[19]. In this regard empirical studies show that implementation of supply chain technologies follows a pattern of adoption based on downstream customer requirements, and this pattern appears to be independent of the firm's specific industry or production method[20]. Relative improvement in firm performance is also higher for those firms investing in technology directed toward downstream, rather than toward upstream supply chain activities[21]. Similarly, supplier quality improves when supply chain competencies and capabilities are transferred upstream not only between OEMs and their first tier suppliers, but also between first and second tier suppliers[22]. By managing activities across echelons in vertically complex supply chains, participants become less susceptible to the "bullwhip effect", where disturbances at lower tiers of the supply chain are amplified as they move up through higher tiers[23].

3.1 *Power/dependency relationships*

A number of highly visible firms have been cited as examples of the benefits from IT investment in upstream collaborative activities, such as Cisco's global manufacturing network or Ford's EDI-enabled supply chain. However IT adoption decisions in supply chains appears to depend upon the relative power of downstream and upstream participants. In the automotive industry for example, greater adoption rates by suppliers are associated with greater overall levels of dependency on downstream customers[24]. Larger, more powerful firms are apparently more able than their smaller upstream partners to capture returns to IT investment through scale economies, and thus require upstream partners to make complementary IT investments. However relative power does not guarantee returns on IT investment - the adoption of IT-enabled supply chains in the automotive industry has enabled OEMs and suppliers to benefit from investment in IT only when parallel relational investments have been made[11]. Because of historical and institutional factors that have engendered trust, such as mutual ownership and geographic proximity, Japanese OEMs and their suppliers in particular have benefited from bilateral commitments to exchange know-how and to modify their internal processes. In contrast, the "Big Three" OEMs (GM, Ford, and Daimler-Chrysler) have managed their supplier relationships with a transaction-oriented approach, alternating suppliers based upon bid pricing and the willingness of suppliers to assume technical responsibilities from the OEM[25].

Some researchers have noted that vertical dissaggregation by OEMs and the rise of supplier networks have co-evolved over the last decade and given rise to new forms of intra-industry (meso level) coordination[26]. In the electronics industry for example, supply chain technologies are pervasive across a relatively small number of large contract manufacturers. Since the early 1990's, leading OEM firms such as Ericsson, HP, Lucent Technologies and others have externalized much of their production-related activity, contracting with electronics manufacturing services (EMS) firms to manufacture to the specifications of the lead firm. The top five EMS firms (Solectron, Flextronics International, Sanmina/SCI, Celestica, and Jabil Circuit) have grown annually at around 10% since the early 1990s, and industry sales in 2007 are expected to reach $150 billion USD, demonstrating the magnitude of these shifts[27]. By pooling demand through integrated supply chain activities across multiple lead firms, EMS firms reduce the uncertainty of fluctuating demand while lead firms gain access to scale economies (often by sharing EMS capacity with a competitor) while retaining the knowledge-based resources behind product designs and supply chain configurations[28].

3.2 *Specialization and coordination in supply chains*

The adoption pattern of IT in manufacturing industries may vary
significantly based on the underlying product technologies. Because
an organization's structure often captures its underlying product
technology[8], organizations in industries with componentized products
and standards are more capable of shifting to IT-enabled, network-based
structures[9]. Firms with modular structures are also more structurally
capable of exploration and experimentation because functions such as
product design, sourcing, manufacturing, and logistics are less tightly
coupled, providing an individual functional area with the flexibility to
innovate without requiring adjustments from other functional areas. For
example, in their analysis of 330 U.S. industries, Schilling & Steensma
found the catalysts for organizational modularity in manufacturing to be
complexity (number of unique customer segments served), standardization
of the underlying product technology, and the competitive intensity of
the industry[29]. Standardization of the interfaces between product
components and subassemblies reduces the need for firm-specific
integrating mechanisms. If no competitive advantage is obtained by
combining product-related activities within the firm, then firms can
obtain efficiencies by introducing standardized forms of exchange among
organizational units, thereby increasing the number of potential external
suppliers of the modularized activities[3]. Standardization codifies
knowledge of how components should be linked and enables firms to use
supply chain IT to coordinate information flows rather than vertically
integrating activities. For example, Hitt's study of 548 of the Fortune
1000 firms found that although the use of IT was negatively associated
with vertical integration at the industry level, the negative effect of IT on
vertical dissagregation was even stronger at the firm level[30]. For many
"craft" oriented firms however, low levels of product and organizational
modularity limit the use and the usefulness of supply chain IT to provide
competitive advantage.

   Supply chain technologies in manufacturing also include business-to-
business (B2B) exchanges, which unlike business-to-consumer (B2C)
electronic markets, do not involve disintermediation. B2B exchanges are
typically reverse auctions in which a buyer solicits and evaluates bids

from multiple suppliers, and trading exchanges, where a supplier locates markets for its excess inventories[31]. Other B2B arrangements have evolved more narrowly, i.e., to support exchange between adjacent tiers in a supply chain or to house supply chain information in third-party "hubs". Because B2B exchanges can involve significant investments in the search for and selection of trading partners, particularly in industries with complex manufacturing requirements, many B2B exchanges rely on invitation-only, private exchanges and a limited number of bidders[32]. Notable among B2B exchanges in manufacturing is Covisint, created in 2000 by a consortium (Daimler-Chrysler, GM, and Ford) to provide IT-enabled trading capabilities to the automobile industry. Covisint was initially structured as an IT enabled public exchange to increase the visibility of supply chain opportunities, however Covisint was gradually transformed into a private reverse auction model. This shift was perceived by suppliers as an attempt by the Big 3 OEMs to lower their costs by increasing competitive bidding, and by antitrust regulators as a potential cartel, eventually resulting in the dismantling and sale of Covisint[33].

Despite arguments for the economic benefits of aligning product, organization, and information technology structures, IT adoption decisions are also dependent upon a firm's embeddedness in networks of relations with other organizational actors[34]. In the neo-institutional literature, firms facing uncertainty may adopt new organizational forms even in the absence of a demonstrable economic benefit, because the organizational legitimacy associated with the act of adoption itself enables a firm to obtain resources through its network of relationships[6]. Haunschild and Miner's study of investment bankers showed that firms often imitate the decisions of other firms based on the frequency of adoption among peer firms, as well as on the degree to which peers have positive traits or have experienced positive outcomes from adoption[35]. Normative pressure toward imitation exists across a number of organizational decisions including those dealing with the adoption of IT-enabled inter-firm collaboration[36]. Dependency-based IT adoption patterns in supply chains illustrate how the use and outcomes of IT-enabled collaboration depend not only on economic logic, but also on the consequences for shifts in power relations and legitimacy within the industry.

4 Electronic Commerce

The role of electronic markets in the retail sector has mushroomed, with sustained annual growth rates of 20% and transactions expected to reach USD$100B by 2005 in the U.S. alone[37]. As a result, attention continues to be drawn to e-commerce models as mechanisms of industry transformation and value generation[38]. The following section identifies key findings in the evolution of ecommerce models and examines the role of these models in industry transformation. Miller analyzed a number of today's largest ecommerce firms (e.g., Amazon.com) and noted that these firms began as undercapitalized and poorly positioned start ups[39]. However this asymmetry in resources between established and new firms (such as Amazon.com) may confer flexibility advantages in co-evolving IT and organizational design. Unlike incumbent firms, new firms do not need to coordinate between newly developed routines and established routines and resources that may lack strategic complementarity. Consider for example the need to manage channel conflicts between e-commerce (direct) and reseller (indirect) distribution channels, as is the case with HP-Compaq. Economic models of channel conflict demonstrate optimal profitability when e-commerce (direct) sellers compensate resellers for sales generated through reseller efforts, however monitoring of resellers would incur significant costs not present in direct-only models, such as Dell's[40]. As a consequence, hybrid (direct and reseller) retail models may be at a structural disadvantage relative to IT-enabled, direct-only retail models. Although imitation of new e-commerce models is possible, it is difficult for industry rivals to gain the same advantages in scale economies, learning, and preemptive market positions as those firms who were early adopters of the new models[41]. For industries with the potential for positive network externalities, such as online auctions, early mover advantages may be decisive.

Virtual channels selling retail products high in information content and low in contracting risk have transformed the retail especially for those intermediaries who have only a limited capability to add value through aggregation or other end customer services[42]. Travel agencies, booksellers, and music retailers are but a few examples of businesses that have been disintermediated as online sales channels have increased consumer surplus through pricing and bundling. Orbitz for example was created by airline consortia to provide market transparency and bundled travel services in a way that travel agents and individual airlines could not. The consumer value of an e-commerce model also depends upon how effectively information can be gathered or created, reassembled, and customized to a particular transaction.   Amit & Zott note that consumer value is created when an e-commerce model reduces search costs by increasing the selection range of products and services and by uniquely bundling products and services based on the profile of a specific consumer[40]. Unlike previous marketing investments where natural tradeoffs existed between reach and richness, IT-enabled marketing can be customized to individual consumers, increasing reach and richness simultaneously. In online auction sites for example (e.g., eBay), new markets are formed as reach and richness are increased, creating positive network externalities and positive marginal returns[31].

Although e-commerce models create value, realizing that value depends upon institutional mechanisms that may be external to the transaction. For example, transaction costs rise as individuals devote more time in electronic exchange markets searching for trustworthy transaction partners. While prior experience with a partner can reduce transaction costs, e-commerce transactions are often unique and not part of an ongoing stream of transactions between two parties. Without trust built through prior experience or recourse to a third party for dispute resolution, transaction costs would rise to a level that could make e-commerce transactions unattractive[43]. Institutional mechanisms such as IT-enabled community feedback on the reliability and performance of a seller, third party escrow arrangements, and credit card guarantees are mechanisms that provide a basis for trust. Evidence for the economic value of trust built through IT-enabled feedback is seen in the price premiums that consumers are willing to pay for purchases from highly-rated sellers[44].

5 Research and Development

Many developing industries rely heavily on collaborative research and development activities to overcome significant technological uncertainties. For example, biotechnology and pharmaceutical firms are critically dependent upon inter-organizational research and development activities to create and introduce new diagnostic or therapeutic techniques, yet the uncertainty they face is significant - candidate drugs in pre-clinical development have less than a 1% chance of eventual commercialization[45]. Biotechnology collaborations often involve novel technology combinations, for example, therapeutic discoveries depend upon understanding the link between protein structure and function, which is rooted in the development and convergence of bioinformatics, proteomics, and nano-scale device technologies[46]. IT-enabled inter-organizational activities in knowledge-creation industries such as biotechnology focus on the creation and dissemination of know-how rather than on the systematic coordination of market-based organizational routines, as is the case in industries with more stable product technologies[47]. Inter-organizational collaboration in biotechnology can be IT-enabled in many ways. Knowledge management systems and intermediaries can be networked to capture, distill, and synthesize information from participants and external sources. Salazar, Hackney, & Howells illustrate how the emergence of network "mediators" can improve the availability and relevance of research information[48].

Knowledge is housed and developed within localized communities of practice in which technological or professional specialties are socially embedded processes involving legitimacy and mutual recognition[49]. In industries where knowledge from multiple technological disciplines is converging, the ability to transfer and integrate know-how between communities of practice is critical to the creation of new knowledge. Because knowledge is socially embedded and reconstituted in practice, relational aspects of knowledge transfer are critical to success[50,51,52]. IT-enabled tools or artifacts are important mechanisms for integrating and transferring knowledge between individuals. These bridges include IT-enabled communities that house unique combinations of technological knowledge, provide a cross-disciplinary lexicon, and foster social interaction[53]. IT-enabled tools and artifacts can support exchange across as well as within communities of practice sharing a common disciplinary frontier, for example, the intersection of computational biology and proteomics in the development of protein folding models[54].

In some cases however, the social processes that can be encouraged by IT-enabled virtual communities may lead to unfavorable outcomes. Too much social interaction in teams may cause spillovers of proprietary information between members of a research or project team[55]. Particularly in the case of tacit knowledge that is not yet codified and therefore not yet protected through patenting, knowledge may "leak" across formal organizations through communities of practice[52]. Group dynamics studies have shown that group members sharing common identification develop mutual psychological commitment and increase their exchange of information[56]. When for example firms are engaged in research-oriented strategic alliances, team members may share information that potentially undermines the intellectual property rights interests of the member's organization. The potential for IT-enabled virtual communities to foster the transfer and creation of knowledge also faces institutional limitations from patent protection and property rights laws. For example, the right of academics to use patented knowledge in biotechnology research has recently been narrowed as biotechnology firms seek institutional support for patent protection[57].

6 Discussion

As organization structures and IT have co-evolved, coordinating mechanisms such as hierarchy, stable product technologies, and predictable demand are quickly disappearing. Contract manufacturing, knowledge-based collaborations, supply chains, disintermediation, and remediation have co-evolved with IT, narrowing organization boundaries and shifting attention to the principles governing inter-firm activities.

One way to consider how IT-enabled activities between organizations are coordinated is through models from the literature on strategic alliances. For example, the structures needed to coordinate activities across supply chains in research intensive industries and in markets are similar in many respects to those needed for strategic alliances. These structures include power and dependence relationships, contracts, communities of practice, reputation, and trust. Power and dependence relationships describe the degree to which one firm is dependent upon another for resources and transactions[58]. For example, to the extent that one firm in a supply chain leads or dominates the flow of transactions through that chain to upstream (or downstream) partners, that firm will have bargaining power relative to other firms. In this way one firm can establish direction and coordination for supply chain activities without the need for vertical integration or complex contracts.

When bargaining power is not available, contracts can be designed to create mutual dependence relationships, so that each party involved in a set of transactions will of necessity coordinate with mutually dependent parties. Minority equity positions and joint venture arrangements facilitate the coordination and integration of resources, especially when those resources are complex and knowledge-based[59]. When independent firms must coordinate activities and respond to changing circumstances without renegotiating or creating new contracts, mutual dependence arrangements often provide the incentives and organizing principles needed to maintain coordination of each party's independent activities[3]. Similarly, co-specialized resources are often managed under joint ventures to avoid conflicts over resource commitments or the distribution of profits from joint activities. In research intensive industries such as biotechnology, joint ventures can encourage and accelerate the transfer and creation of knowledge while reducing the risk of unilateral and uncompensated knowledge transfers between organizations.

At the social level, activities and resources can be coordinated through communities of practice[49]. This form of coordination does not necessarily align with the interests of commercial firms, because it is possible for individuals in research collaborations to transfer valuable knowledge to other, possibly competing firms, without recompense or reciprocal transfers of knowledge to the individuals' own firms. IT-enabled hubs for the development and transfer of knowledge exist both for commercial collaborations and for communities of practice, but institutional conflicts over property rights and the control of know-how, although outside the scope of this chapter, are likely to influence future IT-enabled developments in the area of knowledge-based collaboration.

The reputation or social capital of one firm may enable it to coordinate activities with other firms[60], because a firm's reputation can confer advantages in securing resources from other firms and can provide value to other firms. For example, evidence exists that vendors to lead firms with superior reputations are able to capture higher levels of profitability than vendors in chains with less prestigious lead firms[61]. Trust is also a method of organizing IT-enabled activities. For example, the trust built from prior experience with a firm reduces uncertainty about the willingness and capability of that firm to fulfill its obligations in future transactions. In electronic markets such as eBay's, the collective feedback provided by members creates information about trustworthiness that is available to prospective buyers and sellers. Accumulation of transaction information reduces uncertainty and builds social capital that makes sites "sticky" to its members and increases positive network externalities.

Figure 1 offers a typology of IT-enabled organization forms, and synthesizes the key concepts from this chapter. The first axis, *Coordination*, describes the primary mechanism that organizes the transaction. *Explicit* coordination occurs when dependency is created through control over resources or knowledge. *Market* coordination refers to the use of markets as the main method of coordinating activities. The second axis, *Modularity*, refers to the effects of the underlying product technology to require more integrated functioning, e.g., as an integrated hub or nexus of information (*Low Modularity*), or alternatively to differentiate into more modular forms engaged in specialized activities (*High Modularity*).

Quadrant I describes structures involving *Craft* configurations that are usually knowledge-based and focused on co-specialized and dedicated resources. As discussed earlier, collaboration is enabled through knowledge-based, IT enabled tools or artifacts such as visual bioinformatics programs. Explicit organization of the activities may occur through the inter-firm alliances and through shared know-how and socialization in communities of practice. Quadrant II describes transformations that *Consolidate* transactions and activities. The primary organizing principle is trust, usually created through pooling of information and price transparency. Structures in this quadrant often provide positive network externalities because of the self-reinforcing nature of the information collected and shared, as in the case of eBay. Activities are coordinated through market-based decisions rather than dyadic commitments. Quadrant III refers to *Chain* as the basic organizing structure. Structures of this type rely on a lead firm to coordinate activities, usually because the lead firm has obtained a competitive advantage that can provide the firm with bargaining power vis a vis other members of the chain. Lead firms using electronic manufacturing services firms are examples of this type of structure. Quadrant IV is labeled *Channel* to indicate these structures transform the industry by establishing a channel that connects the end consumer of the good with the provider of the good. Through disintermediation and price reductions, the organizing structure reflects commoditization of the product or service. The primary suppliers of the product or service usually have been established prior to disintermediation, making brand awareness and the reputation of the product manufacturers important factors in assuring IT-enabled transactions and activities. As examples, major publishers have legitimized Amazon's disintermediation of book resellers, and major airlines have bypassed travel agencies as intermediaries in the ticketing process, offering direct online transactions with end customers through portals such as Orbitz.

7 Conclusion

This chapter has scanned the strategic management and information systems literatures and provided examples from a number of industries to illustrate how organizations and information technology have co-evolved. In considering how future IT-enabled activities may be transformed and organized, it may be useful to note that IT is at an early stage of development, and as with most general purpose technologies, the maturation process is likely to be long[2]. The ability for IT to continue to restructure relationships and activities in the economic network is tremendous. Because information can be abstracted from virtually all objects and activities, there remains a substantial potential to digitize, integrate, and recombine information in unique ways.

How will new combinations of information and organization originate? In the PC industry for example, technical hobbyists and engineers experimented with alternative designs culminating in the development of Apple and Microsoft[62]. The U.S. radio broadcasting industry had similar hobbyist-based origins, but developed through a number of institutional phases that allocated property rights and defined the industry's structure[63]. Many of the dominant IT-enabled firms of today began as startups with few resources, however they were able to identify the design space and assemble novel combinations of information and activities to create value[41]. It is likely that future IT-enabled transformations will be similarly influenced by technological, economic, and institutional factors.

References

1. Carlsson, B. The digital economy: what is new and what is not? *Structural Change and Economic Dynamics*, 15, 2004, pp. 245-264.
2. Brynjolfsson, E. & Hitt, L. Beyond computation: Information technology, organizational transformation, and business performance. *Journal of Economic Perspectives*, 14, 2000, pp. 23-48.
3. Williamson, O. *The Economic Institutions of Capitalism*, NY: Free Press, 1985.
4. Barney, J. Firm resources and sustained competitive advantage. *Journal of Management*, 17, 1991, pp. 99-120.
5. Porter, M. Market Structure, Strategy Formulation and Firm Profitability: The Theory of Strategic Groups and Mobility Barriers. In John Cady (ed.), *Marketing and the Public Interest*, Marketing Science Institute, 1978, pp. 101-126.
6. Meyer, J. & Rowan, B. Institutional organizations: formal structure as myth and ceremony. *American Journal of Sociology*, 83, 1977, pp. 340-363.
7. Oxley, J. Appropriability hazards and governance in strategic alliances: a transaction cost approach. *Journal of Law, Economics, and Organization*, 13, 1997, pp. 387-409.
8. Henderson, R. & Clark, K. Architectural innovation: The reconfiguration of existing product technologies and the failure of established firms. *Administrative Science Quarterly*, 35, 1990, pp. 9-30.
9. Sanchez, R. & Mahoney, J. Modularity, flexibility, and knowledge management in product organization design. In R. Garud, A. Kumaraswamy & R. N. Langlois (eds.), *Managing the modular age: Architectures, networks and organization design*, New York: Blackwell, 2003, pp. 362-380.
10. Dyer, J. & Singh, H. The relational view: cooperative strategy and sources of interorganizational competitive advantage. *Academy of Management Review*, 23, 1998, pp. 660-679.
11. Santoro, M. & McGill, J. The effect of uncertainty and asset co-specialization on governance in biotechnology alliances. *Strategic Management Journal*, 26(13), 2005, pp. 1261-1269.

12. Nelson, R. & Winter, S. *An evolutionary theory of economic change*, Cambridge, MA: Bellknap Press, 1982.
13. March, J. & Simon, H. *Organizations*, New York: J.Wiley, 1958.
14. Friedland, R. & Alford, R. Bringing society back in: symbols, practices, and institutional contradictions. In W. W. Powell and P. DiMaggio (eds.), *The New Institutionalism in Organizational Analysis*, Chicago: Univ. Chicago Press, 1991, pp. 223-262.
15. Tsikriktsis, N., Gianvito, L. & Frohlich, M. Adoption of e-Processes by Service Firms: An Empirical Study of Antecedents. *Production and Operations Management*, 13, 2004, pp. 216-229.
16. Whitford, J. & Zeitlin, J. Governing decentralized production: institutions, public policy, and the prospects for inter-firm collaboration in U.S. manufacturing. *Industry and Innovation*, 11, 2004, pp. 11-44.
17. Swaminathan, J. & Tayur, S. Models for Supply Chains in E-Business. *Management Science*, 49, 2003, pp. 1387-1406.
18. Childerhouse, P., Hermiz, R., Mason-Jones, R., Popp, A. & Towill, D. Information flow in automotive supply chains — present industrial practice. *Industrial Management + Data Systems*, 103, 2003, pp. 137-149.
19. Patterson, K., Grimm, C. & Corsi, T. Adopting new technologies for supply chain management. *Transportation Research*, 39, 2003, pp. 95-121.
20. Craighead, C. & LaForge, R. Taxonomy of information technology adoption patterns in manufacturing firms. *International Journal of Product Research*, 41, 2003, pp. 2431-2449.
21. Barua, A., Fang, Y. & Konana, P. An empirical investigation of net-enabled business value. *MIS Quarterly*, 28, 2004, pp. 585-620.
22. Park, S. & Hartley, L. Exploring the effect of supplier management on performance in the Korean automotive supply chain. *Journal of Supply Chain Management*, 38, 2002, pp. 46-53.
23. Lee, H., Padmanabhan, V. & Whang, S. The Bullwhip Effect in Supply Chains. *Sloan Management Review*, 38, 1997, pp. 93-102.
24. Sanchez, A. & Perez, M. The use of EDI for interorganisational co-operation and co-ordination in the supply chain. *Integrated Manufacturing Systems*, 14, 2003, pp. 642-651.
25. Dyer, J. & Hatch, N. Using supplier networks to learn faster. *Sloan Management Review*, 45, 2004, pp. 56-63.
26. Sturgeon, T. Modular production networks: A new American model of industrial organization. *Industrial and Corporate Change*, 11, 2004, pp. 451-496.
27. *Businessweek Online*, Two Gems Amid Tech's Dross, 11 October 2002. http://www.businessweek.com/investor/content/oct2002/pi20021011_4447.htm
28. Luthje, B. Electronics contract manufacturing: global production and the international division of labor in the age of the internet. *Industry and Innovation*, 9, 2002, pp. 227-247.

29. Schilling, M. & Steensma, H. The use of modular organizational forms: an industry-level analysis. *Academy of Management Journal*, 44, 2001, pp. 1149-1168.

30. Hitt, L. Information Technology and Firm Boundaries: Evidence from Panel Data. *Information Systems Research*, 10, 1999, pp. 134-149.

31. Pinker, E., Seidmann, A. & Vakrat, Y. Managing online auctions: Current business and research issues. *Management Science*, 49, 2003, pp. 1457-1484.

32. Zeng, A. & Pathak, B. Achieving information integration in supply chain management through B2B e-hubs: concepts and analyses. *Industrial Management + Data Systems*, 103, 2003, pp. 657-665.

33. Koch, C. Covisint's Last Chance; Can an old car guy come out of retirement and save one of the icons of the new economy? *CIO*, 1 December 2002.

34. Granovetter, M. Economic Action and Social Structure: The Problem of Embeddedness. *American Journal of Sociology*, 91, 1985, pp. 481-510.

35. Haunschild, P. & Miner, A. Modes of interorganizational imitation: The effects of outcome salience and uncertainty. *Administrative Science Quarterly*, 42, 1997, pp. 472-500.

36. Teo, H., Wei, K. & Benbasat, I. Predicting intention to adopt interorganizational linkages: An institutional perspective. *MIS Quarterly*, 27, 2003, pp. 19-40.

37. Morgan Stanley. *The global technology data book*, 2004.

38. Amit, R. & Zott, C. Value Creation in e-Business. *Strategic Management Journal*, 22, 2001, pp. 493-520.

39. Miller, D. An asymmetry-based view of advantage: toward an attainable sustainability. *Strategic Management Journal*, 24, 2003, pp. 961-976.

40. Tsay, A. & Agrawal, N. Channel conflict and coordination in the e-commerce age. *Production and Operations Management*, 13, 2004, pp. 93-110.

41. Lieberman, M. & Montgomery, D. First-mover (dis)advantages: retrospective and link with the resource-based view. *Strategic Management Journal*, 19, 1998, pp. 1111-1125.

42. Andal-Ancion, A., Cartwright, P. & Yip, G. The digital transformation of traditional business. *MIT Sloan Management Review*, 44, 2003, pp. 34-41.

43. Pavou, P. & Gefen, D. Building effective online marketplaces with institution-based trust. *Information Systems Research*, 15, 2004, pp. 37-60.

44. Ba, S. & Pavlou, P. Evidence of the effect of trust building technology in electronic markets: price premiums and buyer behavior. *MIS Quarterly*, 26, 2002, pp. 243-268.

45. Rothaermel, F. & Deeds, D. Exploration and exploitation alliances in biotechnology: a system of new product development. *Strategic Management Journal*, 25, 2004, pp. 201-221.

46. National Academies of Science. *Beyond the molecular frontier: Challenges for chemistry and chemical engineering*, Washington, DC: National Academies Press, 2004.

47. Howells, J. Mind the gap: information and communication technologies, knowledge activities and innovation in the pharmaceutical industry. *Technology Analysis and Strategic Management*, 14, 2002, pp. 355-370.
48. Salazar, A., Hackney, R. & Howells, J. The Strategic Impact of Internet Technology in Biotechnology and Pharmaceutical firms: insights from a knowledge management perspective. *Information Technology and Management*, 4, 2003, pp. 289-301.
49. Brown, J. & Duguid, P. Organizational learning and communities-of-practice: Toward a unified view of working, learning and innovation. *Organization Science*, 2, 1991, pp. 40-57.
50. Giddens, A. *Central Problems in Social Theory*, Berkeley, CA: University of California Press, 1979.
51. Santoro, M. & Gopalakrishnan, S. The institutionalization of knowledge transfer activities within industry-university collaborative ventures. *Journal of Engineering and Technology Management*, 17, 2000, pp. 299-319.
52. Kogut, B. & Zander, U. Knowledge of the firm, combinative capabilities, and the replication of technology. *Organization Science*, 3, 1992, pp. 383-397.
53. Brannback, M. R&D collaboration: role of Ba in knowledge creating networks. *Knowledge Management Research & Practice*, 1, 2002, pp. 28-38.
54. Minkel, J. How Informatics Unites Teams. *Drug Discovery & Development*, 8, 2005, pp. 26-31.
55. Hamel, G., Doz, Y. & Prahalad, C. Collaborate with your competitors - and win. *Harvard Business Review*, 67, 1989, pp. 133-139.
56. Janis, I. & Mann, L. *Decision making: A psychological analysis of conflict, choice, and commitment*, New York: The Free Press, 1997.
57. Lee, P. Patents, Paradigm Shifts, and Progress in Biomedical Science. *The Yale Law Journal*, 114, 2004, pp. 659-695.
58. Pfeffer, J. R. *The external control of organizations: a resource dependency perspective*, New York: Harper and Row, 1978.
59. Gulati, R. Does familiarity breed trust? The implication of repeated ties for contractual choice in alliances. *Academy of Management Journal*, 38, 1995, pp. 85-112.
60. Alvarez, S., Barney, J. & Bosse, D. Trust and its alternatives. *Human Resource Management*, 42, 2003, pp. 393-404.
61. Subramani, M. How do suppliers benefit from information technology use in supply chain relationships? *MIS Quarterly*, 28, 2004, pp. 45-74.
62. Jackson, M., Mandeville, T. & Potts, J. The Evolution of the Digital Computation Industry. *Prometheus*, 20, 2002, pp. 323-336.
63. Leblebici, H., Salancik, G., Copay, A. & King, T. Institutional Change and the Transformation of Interorganizational Fields: An organizational history of the U.S. broadcasting industry. *Administrative Science Quarterly*, 36, 1991, pp. 333-363.

CHAPTER 16

The Evolution of
New Social Relations and Structures

John Cawood
Department of Information and Communications
Manchester Metropolitan University
Rosamond Street West
Manchester M15 6LL
United Kingdom
Email: j.cawood@mmu.ac.uk

1 Introduction

The role that technologies play in social transformation has become an increasingly important focus of research as information and communications technologies reach ever more deeply into all aspects of our public and private activities. Where once the effects of technology were felt mainly in the way we work, today, ICTs support our leisure activities and inhabit our homes. In recent years, the technical capacities once found only in large organisations are now deployed in household devices and services. As work, leisure and the family evolve, many observers identify new technologies as the main engine of social change.

The first "information society" theorists associated innovation in information processing technology with the transformation of work, the decline of the nation state and the creation of new social and political arrangements. More recently, claims have been made that the growth of the Internet and the advent of the Web have led to the construction of virtual communities in cyberspace where electronic landscapes replace the times and places in which human relations were previously created. In these new on-line communities we can reconstruct our identities or develop multiple selves by choosing alternative genders and personal characteristics.

Some observers celebrate these ideas and claim that digital technologies are transforming our society for the better. Others agree that microelectronic networks are changing our social arrangements but are wary of the results. Fragmentation of community, isolation of the individual and the privatisation of culture have all been laid at the door of technological innovation. Critics of these opposing but essentially similar positions argue that whilst ICTs have certainly affected social and economic forms, deeper structures remain unchanged. This debate is not a new one. The nature of the relationship between technological innovation and social structures is a long-standing focus of discussion in the social sciences. However, as the pace of technical innovation accelerates, an understanding of how organisational forms, family structures, community activities and personal identity are related to new technologies of production, communication, administration and leisure has become ever more important.

In the early 1960s, the association of digital computing and information processing with the major structural changes taking place in industrial nations prompted the development of a series of related theories which identified a fundamental shift in the nature of society. This chapter begins with a review of some key examples of those theories which seek to account for the role of ICTs and information in creating new forms of social structure. Here, the underlying issue of technological determinism will be addressed and a guide given to the differing perspectives and methodologies which have arisen from approaches such as post-modernism and post-industrialism.

The emergence of the Internet and the convergence of computing technology with communications systems saw the emergence of new socio-technical models. Theories of the "information society" gave way to discussion of the "virtual" and the "network" society. The proliferation of e-mail, bulletin boards and then Web-based communications strengthened the expanding interest in the part played by ICTs in community activity, on-line culture and the construction of individual identity. The second part of the chapter will examine theoretical models of social structures in the age of the Web and the growth of research into network culture, community and identity.

As ICTs became more and more a part of our home life, the consumption of technologies and their shifting meanings stimulated other avenues of investigation. Today, cellular radio and wireless technologies have added a new dimension to discussions of social relationships as school children, political organisations and family members have devised uses for ICTs which their designers had never envisaged. In the last part of the chapter, the consumption of ICTs in households will be discussed in relation to changes in family structure and emergent patterns of home life. Throughout the discussion, key concepts will be highlighted and specific methods of undertaking research into the forms of socio-technical relations will be indicated.

2 Post-Industrialism and the Information Society: ICTs in Socio-Economic Change

Current discussions of the digital, the virtual, the information and the network society have their origins in the academic and popular studies which sought to explain the deep-seated social, economic and cultural shifts which began to affect industrial societies in the 1960s and early 70s. Most of these accounts saw computing and communications technologies, explicitly or implicitly as the fundamental determinant of change.

From the 1960s, industrial and commercial structures centred on the nation state began to fragment in the face of increased globalisation of markets, production and finance. Collectivist notions of welfare and community gave way to privatised, market orientated approaches. The influence of organised labour declined as the location of manufacturing industry moved to lower wage economies and firms increased productivity through technical innovation. Jobs migrated to the service sector. Besides the growing importance of information technologies and information itself in these changes, several observers picked out the key role played by the globalisation of communications. This involved technical innovation – telecommunications networks, satellite systems, etc – but also the construction of what Webster[1] has called a common "symbolic environment". Not only did communications technologies support the international operation of manufacturing, financial and marketing activity but consumers in ever wider parts of the world were provided with "common images," mainly by trans-national media corporations. Thus the changes which were taking place had a cultural as well as a social and economic dimension. If workers in New York, London and Tokyo were increasingly working with information technologies, they were also watching the same films, reading the same books and tuning in to the same television programmes.

The concept of a post-industrial society (PIS) was an early attempt to characterise the changes which were under way. PIS theorists discerned the end of industrial capitalism and the advent of a service and leisure economy. They drew attention to science and technology as key social components, the emergence of new social groupings defined by non-economic criteria, the distinctive importance of information in technology and the decline of traditional social conflicts. In France, Alain Touraine[2] foresaw new social divisions emerging as high-technology production developed requiring new groups of workers with specialist knowledge and high skill levels. In the USA, Matchlup[3] and later Porat[4] drew up categories of "information industries" and used quantitive studies of their growth to argue for the emergence of an information economy. Daniel Bell[5] argued that in information society knowledge and information would replace labour and capital as central economic factors. This economic transformation was accompanied by a shift in social structure and these changes were qualitative as well as quantitative. In contrast to many information society theorists and to their critics on the Left, Bell believed that the social, political and cultural realms had separate existences and that society could not be analysed as a single system.

Bell's work was the most comprehensive and influential representative of several theses which developed the post-industrial analysis into a theory of the information society. Alvin Toffler's concept of a *Third Wave*[6] in which industrial society is transformed into information society is the most well know of a series of futurologies which included Naisbitt's *Megatrends*[7] and Masuda's *The Information Society as Post Industrial Society*[8]. Popularisation of the more serious analyses were often expressions of cheerful technological determinism (see below) in which the inevitability of (beneficial) information and communications technologies was allied to warnings of the dire social and economic consequences which would surely follow failure to embrace them.

As Christopher May[9] has observed these early analyses of the post-industrial, information society prompted further accounts of the "new age" which themselves contributed to the construction of a socio-economic "reality". Concepts developed by information society theorists were used in the formulation of policies designed to create just such a society. The information society zeitgeist soon permeated the more practical world of commercial policy and economic strategy. As early as 1982, the Science Council of Canada used the idea of the information economy to underpin its national strategy for microelectronics[10]. By 1986, British Telecom was using Toffler's term, The Third Wave, as a title for its pamphlet on the "telecommunications revolution" and Masuda's ideas have been adopted by Japanese planners. A decade later, the idea of the transformation from an industrial to an information society was taken as given by the proponents of local informatics initiatives and strategic planners in the European Commission. Quoting Toffler, the Secretary General of the EU Regional Information Society Initiative framed his 1998 report in the context of a move from an "Industrial Age in which capital has been the main factor of production" to "the dawn of the Information Age"[11]. A brief glance at the current Website of the European Union's Information Society Project[12] shows that the concept of the information society is still used both as a description of a changing social structure and also as a rationale for promoting such change.

3 Technological Determinism

All theories which seek to explicate the relationship between social structures and technological innovation must confront, explicitly or implicitly, the question of cause and effect. According to Mackenzie and Wajcman, technological determinism is "the single most influential theory of the relationship between technology and society"[13]. Many of popular accounts of the "impact of ICTs", quite a number of academic analyses and almost all commercial and public policy statements are marked by technological determinism. In the determinist perspective, technology has an autonomous existence and has "effects" or "impacts" on society. The arrow of causation points from technology to society. A common version sees technologists as applying scientific knowledge which has been "discovered" in fundamental research. This applied science (technology) then causes social changes of various kinds. Forecasts of how ICTs will relate to future social change are particularly prone to "TD". For example, throughout the 1980s, it was forecast that new technology would lead to the "paperless office". Hindsight shows us that in many ways the exact opposite has occurred.

In any assessment of theories which seek to explain of the role of ICTs in evolution of social structures, the key failures of technological determinism need to be borne in mind. Firstly, experience has shown us that the same technologies deployed in different contexts are associated with widely divergent social changes. Thus, at the level of the organisation, the introduction of technologies which improve the efficiency of manufacture or information handling can lead to job losses in times of economic recession but to job creation in periods of economic growth. Similarly, at the national level, cable TV has flourished in the USA but lags behind satellite broadcasting in the UK. Secondly, technologies do not suddenly appear fully formed but are shaped by the social structures which produce them. There is no immutable trajectory prescribed by a technology's essential technical characteristics. For instance, cultural, social and political factors have meant that both public telephone networks and broadcasting systems have had quite separate and distinct developments in the USA, France and Great Britain. Some critics of technological determinism have argued that technologies are socially constructed. For instance, Bijker, Pinch, Hughes and others[14] suggest that the final forms of technologies as far apart as bicycles and electricity supply systems result from the interaction of social interests which hold differing interpretations of their nature and purpose. This is not to argue that technologies do not have effects but that the relationship between the technical and the social is far more complex than the one-dimensional and one-directional concept of technical determinism.

Despite these telling criticisms, technological determinism is still very much alive in commercial and political discourse and in popular accounts of technical change. To many technical, managerial and commercial professionals, to many policy makers and to many everyday observers, the determining effects of ICTs are "obvious". Critics from the social sciences are seen as either naïve or proponents of the opposite pole of the determinist continuum – social determinism. However, the perspective of social construction and other approaches such as actor-network theory[15] show that there are ways out of the determinist continuum which give us more fruitful analyses of the relationship between technology and social change.

4 Post-Modern Perspectives on ICTs

Theorists of the information society such as Bell, Porat and Touraine used mainly orthodox social science concepts to make sense of a changing social and economic landscape. For Lyotard[16], Baudrillard[17] and other post-modern theorists the world has changed in so many fundamental ways that these concepts are no longer adequate to describe what is happening.

Post-modern accounts acknowledge the role of information and communications technologies but see a world beyond progress. Where Bell and others saw science and technology as a motor of socio-economic change, for post-modern writers, science is no more than another form of discourse, a component of culture. In such a perspective, there can be no meta-theory of the information society which explains the working of information and communications technologies in social transformation.

Postmodernism is important to any discussion of ICTs and changing social relations since it has helped shift the focus of debate. In the 1970s and 80s, post-industrial and information society theories sought to give global analyses of changing socio-economic structures and were typically concerned with changing patterns of work and production. In the 1980s and 90s, post-modern theorists concerned themselves with culture, the consumer and the presentation of identity. Post-modernism rose to prominence during the period of rapid expansion of the Internet and strongly influenced the study of the cultures and communities which developed in "cyberspace". This research will be examined later. However, the issues raised by post-industrial analyses did not go away. David Lyon[18] has suggested that two themes stand out in both approaches. One is the so-called digital divide – the growing social and economic inequality associated with the development of microelectronic technologies. The other is the greater potential for social control which they make possible.

5 From Information to Network Society: Social Structure in the Age of the Web

Information society and post-modern accounts, in their different ways seek to explain the role of information and communication technologies both in the change of social and economic structures and in the transformation of our individual actions and sense of identity. In his three volume analysis of the information age, Manuel Castells[19] has brought these two strands together and argues that networks are the defining feature of social, economic and cultural practices.

Castells uses a diverse and extensive range of quantitative and qualitative resources to argue that the accelerating and revolutionary development of information and communications technologies, the restructuring of capitalism and the demise of the Soviet Union and other forms of "statism", and the rise of social movements such as environmentalism and feminism are creating a new type of society. These three dynamics engender a new social structure (a network society), a new economy (the global informational economy) and a new "virtual" culture. For Castells, network flows (capital, information, images, symbols, etc.) become more important than the social interests which they represent. In this way, a technological determination (the deployment of ICTs) underpins a new social determination (the power of network flows). In such a social structure it becomes crucial to be present in a network. More powerful and dynamic networks dominate weaker networks.

Castells argues that states, business, media and religious organisations are no longer the locus of power. Instead, wealth, power, information and images are spread through global networks and circulate in a system which constantly reconfigures itself and whose location is independent of traditional geography. Movements such as feminism, environmentalism, and nationalism are engendered by a tension between the new network logic and identities rooted in traditional social forms.

Since new electronic media transcend time and space social groups exist in different times and spaces. Some live in the instantaneous time of electronic systems, other in the traditional time of everyday life, marked out by the clock. Similarly, whilst one social class lives in the virtual space of the Web, another is bound by the traditional locations of city and countryside.

The transcendence of the space of places (traditional geography) by the space of flows (see above) produces "timeless time" as the Web technology of the hyperlink and the menu of the graphical user interface break the linearity of clock time and allow temporal compression, instantaneous communication and asynchronicity (the time shift of computer mediated communication and the VCR). These features of network logic result in a culture of "real virtuality" where the real world is captured and reproduced in a virtual setting. Experience is not just represented on the screen as image but appearances on screen become the experience.

6 Critics of Information and Network Society Theories

Van Dijk[20] argues that Castells takes network logic too far in claiming that networks have become the basic units of society. Rather, present society combines "organic communities and virtual communities". The former are composed of "the remaining direct relationships between individuals, shrinking households and other associations of living and working using mainly face-to-face communications in conditions of co-presence. The latter are called virtual because here associations between people are not tied to the same particular time, place and other physical conditions."

Van Dijk's comments represents the views of many who endorse the view that the present era marks a turning point in social development but are not altogether happy with notions of "information" or "network societies". However, there are other scholars who acknowledge the significance of ICTs and information but insist that the central feature of the present is its continuity with the past. Perhaps the clearest expression of this position and the strongest criticism of the whole information society concept from Bell to Castells has come from the American political economist Herbert Schiller. Similar analyses have been put forward in the UK by Garnham[21] and more recently by May[22].

In *Information Inequality*[23] and many previous works, Schiller argued that the increasing significance of information and ICTs in contemporary society is not an indication of a fundamental transformation of its social structure but derives from the needs of advanced capitalism. If we look behind the hyperbole of cyberspace and the spin on virtual reality, claimed Schiller, we will find market pressures to make profit, information inequality shaped by social class and the dominance of corporate institutions. In this perspective, it is media corporations such as Time Warner and software companies such as Microsoft which shape the content of television news and determine the types of computer programme which are written.

7 Culture, Community and Identity

Whilst Castells' concept of the network society is perhaps the most extensive analysis of social change in the age of the web, it drew on a growing body of research which focused on the culture of Internet use, the new forms of community which were appearing online and the use of the Web as a medium for identity presentation. Information and communications technologies shape the way we view events. They convey images of other people and places and affect the ability of those who own and control the media to influence our sense of self and the world we belong to. Many researchers argue that all new media technologies from talking drums to mobile phones bring about a reconstruction of identity and community by offering new modes of reflection, perception and experience to those who control or use them.

Drawing on postmodernist ideas, Turkle[24], Stone[25] and others have analysed culture, identity and community in cyberspace by studying virtual environments, such as chatrooms and MUDs (Multi-User Domains). This school of thought introduced the notion of the 'virtual self'. Sherry Turkle explores virtual environments, using the method of participant observation. She claims that in on-line communities we (re-)invent our identities and have the possibility to develop a truer self or multiple selves by choosing our gender and personal characteristics.

Internet researchers have extended the ethnographic method developed by participant observers to create virtual ethnography. Christine Hine[26] discusses this technique and argues that the Internet is both a site for cultural formations and a cultural artefact which is shaped by users' understandings and expectations. However, Hine rejects postmodern notions of the Net as a site for the end of authenticity and the idea that it transcends space and time. Instead, she suggests that the Internet produces multiple orderings of space and time which cross the boundary between off-line and on-line.

Celebrating the Internet as a space to express one's identity freely or as a democratic sphere which devolves power, Rheingold claims that:

> Virtual communities are social aggregations that emerge from the Net when enough people carry on [computer-mediated] public discussions long enough, with sufficient human feeling, to form webs of personal relationships in cyberspace ... these new media attract colonies of enthusiasts because CMC enables people to do things with each other in new ways, and to do altogether new kinds of things - just as telegraphs, telephones, and televisions did.[27]

This perspective is both an analysis of the changes affecting traditional communities and the proposal of an alternative. According to Rheingold, as more and more informal public spaces disappear from our real lives so technology offers the utopia of interactivity, which can bridge the gaps caused by social separation and difference. To Rheingold, the net is the ultimate flowering of community, where individuals choose the community to which they belong: there is no longer any need to create a new place, merely to choose from the menu of those available. Steven Jones argues that this is a community like those in the arts, a community of common interest rather than common location[28]. It is suggested that in the Net we have a tool which will "revitalise the public sphere", the domain where we come together to deal with matters of general interest. In this way, local and national politics might be recast in an "e-democracy" which breaks down hierarchies and overcomes the domination of the traditional media. Critics such as Robins[29] have argued that whatever the attractions of virtual communities, we are all still part of a real world. Others see virtual communities as extensions of existing communities and point to an earlier electronic technology, the telephone, whose use has reinforced existing social networks and personal interactions rather than establishing new ones.

Recent empirical and ethnographic research on the construction of personal Web pages by teenagers and the design of commercial sites aimed at young people gives support to the view that existing social structures and relationships shape new net-based activities. Bober (2002)[30] has found that the personal web sites of 14-18 year olds show a marked differentiation by gender. Commercial websites show the same kind of gender differentiation in their content that is found in teenage magazines. Boy's personal homepages are populated by sports images and commercial sites for girls have fashion, beauty and celebrity sections. Young people's net-based leisure activities again show how existing practices are mediated by new technologies. Leisure activities on the Internet are similar to those off-line but their distribution is altered by the opportunities and constraints of the technology. For instance, in Bober's sample shopping as a leisure activity for girls fell from the choice of just under 82% off-line to just fewer than 24% on-line[31]. Reasons for this include the ineligibility of under-18s for credit cards and the fact that on-line shopping does not have the social dimensions of its off-line counterpart. Such findings run counter to the theories of cyborgs and multiple identities. They suggest that the changes which digital technologies effect do alter our behaviour but they do so within the framework of existing social relationships. Society may be experiencing long term secular change but technology is not precipitating dramatic shifts in deeper social structures.

The cultural approach is not restricted to individual and communal activities in the virtual time and space of computer networks. According to Raymond Williams[32], culture is one of the key concepts in modern social knowledge. To understand social structures, we must study cultural meanings and values. Willams puts forward a social definition of culture in which meaning plays a crucial role. In such a perspective "culture is a description of a particular way of life which expresses certain meanings and values not only in art and learning but also in institutions and ordinary behaviour". Recent elaborations of cultural approach to social relations add technology to these categories. Thus the study of the social relations of ICTs demands an analysis of technology as a cultural product. In a cultural analysis of ICTs, we seek to clarify the meanings of digital technologies and the implict and explicit values which they represent in a particular way of life. The notion of a technology as a cultural artefact which has a common cultural meaning is similar to the idea of "collective representations" which sociologists suggest provide the shared understandings which bind individuals together in society.

Stuart Hall, Hugh Mackay, Paul du Gay and others[33] have developed the concept of the cultural circuit to investigate the ways in which technological artefacts are brought into our everyday lives and in so doing affect social transformations. According to this model, the effects of technologies are not determined primarily by the circumstances of their production: their social import is symbolic as well as economic. Traditionally, social science has seen the mode of production as the key determinant of the meaning of a technology. To oversimplify, it was assumed that a product's manufacture decides its form, purpose and use. In contrast, cultural theorists argue that the processes of consumption, identity construction, representation and social regulation of technologies are of equal moment to production. It is the articulation of some or all of these "moments" which shapes the variable and contingent outcome of a technology. These processes are said to constitute the cultural circuit. To become a cultural artefact an ICT such as a mobile phone, personal computer or disc-player must move through the various moments of the cultural circuit and in so doing acquire cultural meaning. The technology does not have an intrinsic meaning in itself.

For instance, a device such as the I-Pod is the product of a particular organisational culture (in this case the Macintosh Corporation). The characteristics of that culture affected the way in which the I-Pod was developed and, ultimately, whether it was to be commercially successful. Macintosh designers had to have an image of the potential consumers and a notion of their interests and desires before any physical artefact or software could be produced. In their marketing activities, advertisers had to construct representations that allowed consumers to identify with the product. Connotations of "high tech", "mobility", "style", "youth" and so on were used to give the new product meaning. Thus symbolic as well as physical work is required to bring a technology into our culture.

However the work does not stop there. Consumers may "read" the new technology according to the intended "text" of the designers or they may not. Technologies may be "read" in ways which have never occurred to their designers. Recent information and communications technology provides a multitude of examples. Personal computers were sold to parents as technologies which would benefit the educational development of their offspring. But children sat in their bedrooms and played computer games. Mobile phones were initially designed for business and professional use. Today we use them to chat and keep in touch with our children, even their basic function of speech communication is subverted as teenagers opt to text their friends. Such "negotiated" and "oppositional" readings show the active nature of consumption and provide feed-back to producers who modify technologies to take account of changing meanings.

Finally, the formal and informal rules on how and when we use technologies change as their meanings are extended, altered or replaced. Technologies such as the television, mobile phone and personal cassette or disc player blur the boundaries between the private and public sphere. We conduct private conversations on mobile phones in public spaces such as trains and shops. Thanks to devices such as the Walkman, we can listen to rock music, classical concerts or learn French irregular verbs as we cycle, skateboard or commute to work. Initially, unfamiliar behaviour of this kind goes against established classifications of public and private space by being both public and private simultaneously. However, whilst efforts have been made to regulate the use of mobile phones and personal stereo players, as we adjust to the new technologies and as producers modify products to take account of public concern so our notions of what constitutes normal behaviour change and we adjust our classification.

The cultural turn in the study of the role of technology in social change reflects the increased importance of cultural practices and institutions in our society. The growth of the mass media, the globalisation of film, television and fashion as well as finance and manufacture have affected the way in which we live our lives and the ways in which we relate to one another and see ourselves. In addition, social scientists have come to see culture as equal to economic and political processes in the constitution of the social world. If we are to understand the role of microelectronic technologies in social change then we must add cultural to social and political epistemologies. Moreover, culture is not simply the domain of the arts and humanities but includes technologies. Computer networks, mobile phones, DVD players and the electronic point of sale terminal at the local supermarket are all cultural artefacts in the same was as works of literature or watercolours.

8   ICTs and Changing Social Relations in the Household

The notion of technology as a powerful symbolic as well as a material resource has been brought to bear on the transformations that are taking place in the household as well as in the wider community. Once again, this is not an entirely new debate. The role of the telephone and the radio in our domestic lives has been under scrutiny for at least 70 years. Claims that television has led to illiteracy, delinquency and other social ills have been investigated by social scientists since the 1950s. Nevertheless, the degree of penetration which new microelectronic products have achieved is such that some researchers see a study of ICTs in the home as especially significant for an understanding of social change. In particular, attention has been drawn to the way in which shifts in household relationships are interacting with new technologies to break down the traditional boundaries of the home and are contributing to changes in family relationships.

When new technologies arrive in a household both space and time have to be found for them. The place, purpose and context of a home computer or DVD might seem unproblematic but researchers such as Silverstone, Hirsch and Morley[34] show that technologies have to be "domesticated" and that in doing so the dynamic of the household is affected. Household members interact with one another and with the technology. They may have different objectives and there can be conflict as well as consensus. Gender and age are two obvious differentiating factors. The uses and non-uses made of telephones, computers and digital games by teenage boys and overworked housewives or by fathers and daughters are the stuff of situation comedies but there are serious points to be made here. Access to ICTs by household members is regulated by social relationships in the household. Decisions on what is interesting, useful, educational and so on reflect domestic power relations.

Moores[35] has argued that boundary marking is of crucial importance in the experience of home. Boundaries can be marked between the household and the world outside or internal divisions within the home. Limits may be set on use of the internet in the periods before school examinations and some families use software to control children's access to websites. At the same time, household technologies can be boundary breakers. Young people can use them to take more power for themselves. Marshall[36] identifies the home computer as a site of contest between adult and adolescent and the teenage bedroom as a new source of anxiety for parents as technologies facilitate the fragmentation of family experience.

Television and the Internet also break geographical and cultural boundaries by connecting us to experiences beyond our immediate localities. We inhabit electronic as well as physical landscapes. The election of an American president, political protest in the Ukraine and the devastation caused by the Indonesian tsunami are brought into households around the world, as the events themselves unfold. Television, the Web and more recently DVD bring the culture, values and life styles of North America to traditional communities in the most remote areas of the world. The Internet enables a multitude of alternative perspectives to reach into homes where once information and entertainment came only through channels regulated by government or controlled by large corporations. However, recent computer-mediated technologies seem to play a different social role in the household to that attributed to traditional broadcast technologies.

When families gathered around the radio and later the television, shared experiences were a focus of domestic life[37]. Home computers and games consoles, on the other hand, shut out the domestic, psychologically connecting the user or player to other physically distant or virtual individuals. At the same time, a psychological barrier is erected which "screens out" those who are physically present. In a similar manner, ICTs make public spaces available in the privacy of our homes even as they allow us to undertake private activities in public. The same technologies which electronically connect us to a wider community contribute to our isolation by removing the necessity to leave our homes to seek information, participate in leisure activities or make social contact. Technological innovation interacts with changes in household relationships and with socio-technical changes taking place outside the home. For instance, James Stewart[38] has found a crossover between home, work and other activities which appears to be increasing as individual ownership of devices replaces the shared domestic technologies of earlier years.

The increased diffusion and changing role of domestic technologies can be seen as indications of a wider transformation of social arrangements in the home. Jacques Donzelot[39] suggests that a "withdrawal to interior space" is taking place. Jonathan Gershuny[40] and others contend that households have shifted from units of production to units of consumption. Mackay[41] argues that the increased domestic consumption of ICT-based devices and services is part of a broader retreat to the home and garden. These views accord with the idea that ICTs and other household technologies are part of the process of *privatisation*. Privatisation, the retreat from public or collective activity, is, according to Raymond Williams[42] is one of two long term social trends. The other is *mobilisation*, the break up of communities and the movement to towns and cities which was initiated by industrialisation.

Recent quantitive research tends to support views on privatisation. The amount of leisure time spent at home in the wealthier economies has risen to about 80%[43]. ICTs are increasingly consumed in the home to provide experiences, services and leisure activities which, a generation ago, might have been sought outside it. According to a recent UK Government survey[44], the most popular of household leisure activity for a four week period in 2002 was watching television (99% of those surveyed), followed by listening to the radio (88%). These participation rates have been constant since 1996. However, the proportion of adults listening to recorded music has grown steadily over the last 25 years from 62% in 1977 to 83% in 2002. More dramatically, by the third quarter of 2004, 52 per cent of households in the UK (12.9 million) could access the Internet from home, compared with just 9 per cent (2.3 million) in the same quarter of 1998. About half of adult Internet users had bought or ordered goods, tickets or services.

The shifting pattern of the use of ICTS in the home needs to be seen in the context of the changing nature of the household[45]. In the ten years between 1971 and 1991, there was a significant decline in the average size of household in Great Britain from nearly 3 to just under 2.5 persons. In 2002 the average number of persons per household was 2.31. Since 1971 there have also been changes in the composition of households. Most striking is the increase in the proportion of one-person households, and of households headed by a lone parent. Between 1971 and 1998, the overall proportion of one-person households almost doubled to 31%. The proportion of households with dependent children headed by a lone parent rose from 4% of all households in 1979 to 7% in 1993. It has remained relatively constant since then. Many observers identify a link between such changes in household structure and the diffusion of ICTs.

9 Conclusion

In this brief survey of analyses of socio-technical transformation, we have seen that notions of the nature of social change and of the role played in it by information and communications technology vary considerably. Theories of post-industrialism and the information society have given way to concepts of the network society in which social structures and relationships are mediated by the net. Rejecting the possibility of a meta-theory of society, post-modernists have argued that technology should be considered as a form of discourse. Cultural theorists have maintained that the social import of technology is symbolic as well as economic. This notion of technology has been deployed in studies of virtual communities and of the use of ICTs in households. Economists of information have used quantitative methods to demonstrate that the way we work has been transformed and that information has replaced labour and capital in a restructuring of the economy. Ethnographers have developed qualitative techniques which facilitate the construction of identity on the Web and have revealed social transformations in the household.

All of these analyses show that, at least on some level, social structures and social relationships are affected by innovation in information and communications technologies. The key questions are at what level and in what way? Are digital technologies associated with radical social transformation on the scale of the Industrial Revolution or do they serve to perpetuate existing social arrangements? Are the changes which we have noted at the level of the communities and the household evidence of a wider societal change? It is clear that many of the claims made about ICTs are informed by a heavy dose of technological determinism and attention has been drawn to its several failings. The history of earlier technologies suggests that we ought to treat present developments with caution. Many of the claims made about the impact of the Internet resurrect debates about domestic electrification, the telephone and other old technologies which once were new.

Robin Mansell in her study of the patterns of social and technical interaction notes that new forms of social structure and relationships do not simply replace existing ones[46]. Rather, present arrangements inform emergent structures and socio-technical change may produce improved or worsened social outcomes. Moreover there is no generic model of an information or network society which meets the interests of all social actors. In the long term, new modes of social and technical interaction may result but the studies referred to in this chapter show that present social structures and relationships and the technologies which mediate them are all in a state of change. As Mansell reminds us, these are the very factors which shape future structures.

References

1. Webster, F. *Theories of the Information Society*, London: Routledge, 1995, p. 144.
2. Touraine, A. *The Post Industrial Society*, New York: Wildwood House, 1974.
3. Matchlup, F. *The Production and Distribution of Knowledge in the United States*, Princeton, NJ: Princeton University Press, 1962.
4. Porat, M.U. *The Information Economy: Sources and Methods for Measuring the Primary Information Sector*, Washington, D.C.: U.S. Department of Commerce,

Office of Telecommunications, 1977; Porat, M.U. *The Information Economy: Definition and Measurement*, Washington, D.C.: U.S. Department of Commerce, Office of Telecommunications, 1977.

5. Bell, D. *The Coming of Post Industrial Society: A Venture in Social Forecasting*, Harmondsworth: Penguin, 1974.

6. Toffler, A. *The Third Wave*, New York: Collins, 1980.

7. Naisbitt, J. *Megatrends: Ten New Directions Transforming Our Lives*, London: Sidgewick & Jackson, 1982.

8. Masuda, Y. *The Information Society as Post Industrial Society*, Bethesda: Maryland, 1983.

9. May, C. *The Global Information Society: A sceptical view*, Cambridge: Polity Press, 2002, p. 8.

10. See Cordell, A. *The Uneasy Eighties: The Transition to an Information Society*, Ottawa: Science Council of Canada, 1985.

11. Hughes, G. (ed.) *Shaping the Information Society in the Regions: The Experience of the IRISI Initiative*, Brussels: European Commission, 1998.

12. See the thematic portal of the European Information Society Project Office at http://europa.eu.int/information_society/index_en.htm

13. Mackenzie, D. & Wajcman, J. *The Social Shaping of Technology*, 1st ed. Buckingham: Open University, 1985, p. 4.

14. Bijker, W.E., Hughes, T.P. & Pinch, T. (eds.) *The Social Construction of Technological Systems*, Cambridge MA: MIT Press, 1987.

15. See, for example, Law, J. & Hassard, J. (eds.) *Actor Network Theory and After*, Oxford: Blackwell and Sociological Review, 1999.

16. Lyotard, J.-F. *The Postmodern Condition: A Report on Knowledge*, Manchester: University of Manchester Press, 1984.

17. Baudrillard, J. *America (1986)*, London: Verso, 1988.

18. Lyon, D. *Postmodernity*, 2nd ed. Buckingham: Open University, 1999, p. 66.

19. Castells, M. *The Information Age: Economy, Society and Culture,* I *The Rise of the Network Society*, Oxford: Blackwell, 1996; Castells, M. *The Information Age: Economy, Society and Culture,* II *The Power of Identity*, Oxford: Blackwell, 1997; Castells, M. *The Information Age: Economy, Society and Culture,* III *End of Millennium*, Oxford: Blackwell, 1998.

20. Van Dijk, J. *The Network Society: Social Aspects of the New Media*, London: Sage, 1999, p. 24.

21. Garnham, N. *Capitalism and Communication: Global Culture and the Politics of the Information Age*, London: Sage, 1990.

22. May, C. *The Information Society: a Sceptical View*, Malden: Polity Press, 2002.

23. Schiller, H. *Information Inequality: The deepening social crisis in America*, New York/London: Routledge, 1996.

24. Turkle, S. *Life on the Screen: Identity in the Age of the Internet*, London: Wiedemfeld & Nicolson, 1995.

25. Stone, A.R. *The War of Desire and Technology at the Close of the Mechanical Age*, Cambridge, MA: MIT Press, 1995.

26. Hine, C. *Virtual Ethnography*, London: Sage, 2000.

27. Rheingold, H. *The Virtual Community: Homesteading on the Electronic Frontier*, London: Secker and Warburg, 1994, pp. 3, 5-6.

28. Jones, S.G. Community in the Information Age, in Jones, S.G. (ed.) *Cyberspace: computer mediated communication and community*, London: Sage, 1995.

29. Robins, K. Cyberspace and the world we live in, in Robins, K. (ed.) *Into the Image: culture and politics in the field of vision*, London: Routledge, 1996.

30. Bober, M. *Boys and Girls on the Net: the role of gender in the on-line practices and representations of young people*, paper presented at Crossroads in Cultural Studies, Fourth International Conference of the Association for Cultural Studies, Tampere, Finland, 2002.

31. Bober, M. *Can the Internet Replace the Mall? How e-commerce affects the shopping experiences of young people*, paper presented at Consumption and the Post-Industrial City: first conference in the series, The European City in Transition, Weimar, Germany, 2001.

32. Williams, R. *Keywords: a vocabulary of culture and society*, London: Fontana, 1976.

33. See Mackay, H. (ed.) *Consumption and Everyday Life*, London: Sage, 1997.

34. See Silverstone, R., Hirsch, E. and Morley, David. The Moral Economy of the Household, in Silverstone, R. & Hirsch, E. *Consuming Technologies: media and information in domestic spaces*, London: Routledge, 1992.

35. Moores, S. *Satellite Television and Everyday Life: articulating technology*, Acamedia Research Monograph 10, Luton: University of Luton Press, 1996.

36. Marshall, P.D. Technophobia: video games, computer hacks and cybernetics, *Media International Australia*, 85, 1997, pp. 70-78.

37. See Morley, D. *Family Television: cultural power and domestic leisure*, London: Routledge, 1986; Holmes, D. Virtual identity: communities of broadcast, communities of interactivity, in Holmes, D. (ed.) *Virtual Politics: identity and community in cyberspace*, London: Sage, 1997, pp. 26-45.

38. Stewart, J. Investigating ICTs in Everyday Life: Insights from research on the adoption and consumption of new ICTs in the domestic environment, *Cognition, Technology & Work*, 5(1), 2003, pp. 4-14.

39. Donzelot, J. *The Policing of Families*, London: Hutchinson, 1980.

40. Gershuny, J. *Social Innovation and the Division of Labour*, Oxford: OUP, 1983.

41. Mackay (ref. 33, p. 264).

42. Williams, R. Culture and Technology, in *Towards 2000*, London: Chatto and Windus, 1983.

43. Tomlinson, A. Home fixtures: doing it yourself in a privatised world, in Tomlinson, A. (ed.) *Consumption, Identity and Style: marketing, meanings and the packaging of leisure*, London: Routledge, 1990.

44. See summary of *Living in Britain, Supplementary Report, Sport and Leisure*, UK National Statistics Online at http://www.statistics.gov.uk

45. All statistics in this paragraph are from the *Living in Britain - the 2002 General Household Survey*, UK National Statistics Web site (ref. 44).

46. Mansell, R. (ed.) *Inside the Communications Revolution: evolving patterns of social and technical interaction*, Oxford: OUP, 2002, p. 256.

CHAPTER 17

Knowledge Management, Technology and Organization

J.-C. Spender
Leeds University Business School
Leeds LS2 9JT, United Kingdom
Email: jcspender@yahoo.com

1 Introduction: Thinking about Technologies and Organizations

Technology is often seen as an exogenous resource to be integrated into the production function, providing an ROI. So technologies seem to differ in terms of their contributions. They also differ in terms of the products and services they make possible, and thus the markets that might be entered. Such strategic views might be balanced by concern whether a new technology fits others already integrated into the firm, whether it leads to incremental or radical changes in firm's processes. Are new skills or understandings required to make use of the new technology? These puzzles reflect our not being quite sure what we mean by 'a technology' or, indeed, 'an organization'. Ihde[1] points out technology is not science – for science is in the realm of ideas while technology is 'in the world'.

The concept of 'being in the world' usefully narrows what we might understand by a technology. Ihde offers a number of contrasts to the conventional view that technology is neutral and simply refers to the tools we use in whatever way we decide. But a tool is only understood as such when we can distinguish it from a mere object, and this is a consequence of our knowing how to use it. It gathers whatever meaning it has from the practices it enables. A catheter, a condenser, or a cruise missile gathers meaning from the way it is used, not from the engineering knowledge employed in its production, or the money spent on its construction. Technology as neutral object or technique is that which has no use-based meaning. Ihde follows up by pointing out that to use a technology is to take part in a life-world; technology and culture

365

become entwined. Thus an atom bomb is a metaphor for the society that produces it; just as developing the means of its production changes the society that produces it. There is a crucial indeterminacy here for the technologies we use interact with and on us, shape our sense of expertise and thus of ourselves, and in doing so they change our sense of them.

A similar indeterminacy or slipperiness can be found in the literature on organizations. Morgan[2] offers several ways of framing an organization, ranging from machine to community to psychic prison. Classical organization theory sought abstract rules of, say, structure and span of control, which could apply to all organizations and be held in the realm of thought as design principles. Likewise the analysis of markets and the pursuit of optimum solutions would be rational abstractions, and the techniques for creating and managing organizations – best managerial practices perhaps – would be rational yet neutral. But organizations are 'in the world' and exist beyond the mind, becoming part of the context in which they come into being and persist. Consequently our notions of organization are as culturally contextualized as our notions of technology. Knowing how to manage them is less a matter of applying universal principles than of knowing what works in a particular context and, as such, the organization itself begins to converge on the notion of a technology.

Our organizing also reflects the technological context of our organizations. Adam Smith[3] recorded a way of making pins, a technology, that implied a particular division of labor and way of organizing. Designing an automobile and the division of labor appropriate for its manufacture become one and the same. It seems probable that 19th Century mill factories took their form reflecting at least two 'technologies'[4]. Prior to the industrial use of electricity, power was moved by belt and shaft. This technique entails high transmission losses, minimized when the factory is completely spherical. The mills' cubic form was a workable approximation. Management too was exposed to information losses and made most effective by walking around, personal supervision within the factory as a spherical 'panopticon'. But with the spread of electrical power and with the development of information technologies such as the telegraph, alternative factory layouts became viable. Mass-production assembly-lines which control the pace and process of assembly re-cast these ideas and opened up different ways of integrating management with materials processing; notions that Woodward[5] explored. Although the questions she asked may have lost their edge today, her intuitions were powerful. We argue bringing technologies and organizations within the same framework will tell us more about their integration. We suggest both are forms of organizational knowledge.

Whatever we might mean by a technology or an organization remains extremely ambiguous until we take their context and 'being-in-the-world-ness' into account. Only then can we see their interplay. Contingency theory is one approach[6-8]. But contingency theory presumes a universal system for classifying context. This moves it out of the world and into abstraction. How can we construct a managerially relevant approach to technology and organization in which both are in-the-world rather than mere abstractions?

2 A Knowledge-Based Approach

Knowledge management is a discourse with the capacity to reach beyond rational abstractions and engage practice as in-the-world as well as being conceptualized as the implementation of rational decision-making. It depends on how we theorize practice. The notion of technology as distinct from design implies instantiation and a 'knowing how' that engages the world rather than stands apart from it as a 'knowing about' – distinctions popular in the knowledge management (KM) literature and referencing the work of Ryle[9] or James[10]. Likewise we can redefine organizations as systems of practice, rather than systems of authority relations, rules, or routines. Practice is in-the-world and must deal with the reality of the Second Law of Thermodynamics, with frictions and transaction costs where entropy rises[11]. Paying attention to organizational practice, we see the gap between design and implementation and develop notions of expertise, practical skill, and tacit knowledge that help us understand how organizations in-the-world actually operate[12-14].

Integrating technology into an organization is seldom straightforward. The process is one of *bricolage*, muddling through and taking advantage of whatever lies to hand[15,16]. Both technology and organization are implementations in the world, whether the knowledge is 'embedded' as organizational routines, heuristics, or habits, 'embodied' as the expertise of employees, 'embrained' in management's mental maps, 'encoded' in the organization's policies and signs, or 'encultured' in their communications[17], or explicit and tacit, to employ Nonaka and Takeuchi's[18] typology. Technology implies knowledge, just as organization does. But we need to develop the idea further before we can think about their integration. One familiar metaphor is of the organization as a machine-like structure, and here technology as machine-like fits right in. But this misses our interest in the problematic relationship between technology and organization. Where are its people, and what must they know?

Our paper begins with an analysis of the KM literature to see how knowledge is defined and theorized. We see various epistemologies being adopted to frame the term 'knowledge'. In particular we see profound differences in the ways the KM literature defines data, meaning, and practice (Figure 1). Knowledge-as-data and knowledge-as-meaning are relatively familiar. Knowledge-as-practice is less so and much more difficult to pin down. Here we find the terms 'skill' and 'tacit knowledge' used widely, generally with references to Polanyi[18,19]. Given the difficulty of defining 'tacit' and so making it part of a theory[20] we understand it generally as a rhetorical device to point readers towards knowledge-as-practice. The distinctions underlying Figure 1 are grounded in contrasting epistemologies, so our three types appear incommensurate, implying that data, meaning, and practice cannot be compared; they are 'apples and oranges'. Nor is it easy to understand how they come to be integrated by managers.

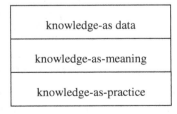

Figure 1. Three Types of Knowledge

Our first thoughts are generally shaped by our background in rational decision-making. We see that data is drawn into a decision-making model to be computed within a system of meaning that stands apart, epistemologically, from the data being computed. Once computed, the conclusion is enacted, and this is normally what we mean by practice. As the chapter proceeds we shall move away from this and surface the way the practice's context actually provides the underlying basis for making the connections between data, meaning, and practice. To anticipate our final conclusions, we shall find the incommensurability between the three knowledge types remains secure only so long as we presume the context is universal, abstract, and unbounded. Then there can be no connections. The data has only one meaning. It is objective, corresponds with reality and there are no sustainable alternatives. Likewise practice is the enactment of goal-oriented rational decisions. But where the context is bounded, our knowledge becomes bounded, the distinctions between data, meaning and practice begin to dissolve and connections appear. Data becomes more subjective and dependent on meanings which could be otherwise, and meanings are no longer pure abstractions but reflect particular contexts and interests, and so could also be otherwise. Under such circumstances effective practice calls for an intimate knowledge of the context of action that goes far beyond mere recognition of the goals sought by the various actors. The resulting knowledge-based theory is grounded on forms of practice shaped by the context and its limits rather than on any axioms like abstract rationality. In this sense the paper's origin lies in Simon's[21-23] analysis of bounded rationality and managerial action under conditions of uncertainty. He argued famously that under conditions of complete knowledge (certainty) there would be no call for a theory of administration for everyone would then know exactly what to do. But the world of practice is never completely known. Rules can never be entirely sufficient to their implementation and much of our surprise about reality is that we find ourselves beyond our rules. It is the resulting uncertainty of our being-in-the-world that creates the managerial task. Likewise a technology often appears as a set of instructions, but their meaning and use, appearing at the interface with its users, is always ambiguous.

3 Data versus Information

We know a hard drive carries data. But however hard we look at the data it cannot tell us what it means. Meaning is grounded in us and what we do, it is what our minds add to the data – we connect the dots in a system of meaning, a frame for cognizing within which we are comfortable placing the data, and turning it into information. The data can be a number – fine and precise, but as information we need to know whether the number refers to a temperature, a bank balance, or this week's casualties, etc. This seems simple enough but is so often glossed that we tend to miss that communicating data – which IT systems do well – is utterly different from communicating the meaning of the data, which generally has to be known before the recipient can understand the data.

Communicating 'information' gets these two ideas tangled up. Where does meaning come from? Are we born with a basic understanding of what is going on around us, a sort of geneto-cognitive 'boot program'? Absorptive capacity is a popular term in our literature and it refers to our ability to acquire further knowledge[24]. But it is always about leveraging old meaning into new and does nothing to tell us about how the processes of acquiring first meanings begin. As soon as we 'problematize' meaning by suggesting the relationship between data and meaning is neither self-evident nor necessary, in the sense of reflecting reality, we realize meaning is what we create in our heads as a product of our imagination. Meaning cannot be extracted from data through rigorous analysis or grounded theorizing[25]. But are there constraints on our imagination, will things mean whatever we want them to mean?

Once we separate data and meaning, melded together in the term 'information', we see differences in our notions of learning and management's roles. When knowledge is defined as data, learning implies more data. We might call this the 'accretion' model. We learn as we sit at a desk and are given more facts, or as we read more books. Learning theorists know this is an impoverished theory in the sense it is so simplistic and tautological it tells us nothing of importance. When knowledge is meaning, we see learning as the acquisition of a framework of meaning or an improvement to one we already have in place. This contrast is evident in Kuhn's[26] thesis of scientific advancement. Normal science is the elaboration or accrual of 'facts' within a seemingly stable framework. Revolutionary or radical progress occurs when there is a 'paradigm shift', a move to a new system of meaning. These ideas are familiar from the analysis of different types of innovation[27]. Meaning is constructed subjectively as an act of imagination, so management's role in the creation of new meaning is to invent it and convey it and, perhaps, to clarify the constraints on others' imagination by setting limits.

We cannot describe a meaning system without referring to the data it holds; it is a net that captures only what we have imagined as possible. So we cannot know meaning until it is attached to something. It is an abstraction that must be instantiated just as we illustrate the mathematical concept of differentiation by differentiating a particular function. Anthropologists tell us cultures differ, and can be indicated by differences such as might arise between Inuit and English notions of marital fidelity – or of snow. Though data and meaning differ they are equally aspects of information. When we mark what we have as 'data', we stress specific observations and push the observer's frame into the background, taking it for granted. When we call it 'meaning' we foreground and problematize the observer's frame. We ask 'why do you attach that meaning to that data?'

Knowledge managers and regular managers too need to be conscious of the difference between data and meaning. As communications theory recognizes, it is easy to transfer data so long as the recipient has an appropriate meaning system with which to absorb what is being communicated. But communicating new meaning is quite different for that would lead the recipient see the data being received in new ways. While it is easy to talk about meaning as an 'act of imagination', it is less easy to be clear about the circumstances under which this is either possible or necessary. It requires a model of man unfamiliar to rationality-committed academics. On the one hand we have Man the Decision-Maker, driven by data, even when riven with biases[28]. On the other Man the Meaning-Creator, confronting a universe of stimuli (pre-data) and data that is uncomprehended[29]. In short, one dimension of KM is always about collecting and analyzing information, while another is about managing our responses to uncertainty, recognizing the absence of information (Figure 2).

4 From Imagination to Practice

Our conceptual method is to seek defining differences, in this case epistemological, that must then be overcome by managerial creativity. The early KM literature was influenced by work in decision-making and systems theory, in particular that of Ackoff. In a 1989 paper, he proposed the now widely used DIKW model (data, information, knowledge, wisdom) model[30]. It suggests a Jacob's Ladder of increasing knowledge power. His proposal is actually a 5-step one, embracing data, information, knowledge, understanding, and wisdom. He argued data is without meaning – it just <u>is</u>, like the 'pre-data' stimuli mentioned above. Information is data with meaning. Knowledge exists when we have useful aggregations of information. Understanding is interpolative, enabling one to generate new knowledge from old, and it differs from knowledge as learning differs from memorizing. Finally, he defined wisdom as bringing understanding into the context of the human condition. This typology may be more popular than useful since its underlying differences remain submerged beneath poorly defined every-day terms.

But we can say three things. First, we can see knowledge is a problematic concept – after several millennia philosophers are still unable to agree on what it is – and we should not raise our hopes of better insights too hastily. Indeed there is paradox around what it means to theorize about knowledge. Would such understanding be a form of meta-knowledge, or just more knowledge, and how would we tell the difference anyway? Second, we have two dominant epistemologies or frameworks within which academic knowledge is presently hung: realism and idealism[31]. Realism, which embraces various forms of positivism, starts out from the assumption there is a knowable reality 'out there'. Science seeks to understand this as its subject with probing experiments which expose our hypotheses to falsification. The alternative epistemology is idealism or interpretivism. It is more about the cognitive 'in here' and assumes we can never have certain or immediate knowledge of what lies beyond our minds. Following Descartes, we can only be certain of the 'in here'.

While the realist position seems obvious and commonsensical to most of us, for several hundred years we have had to grapple with having no certain knowledge of this assumed reality. We learned from the Ancient Skeptics that we have no 'frame-free' data. In a variation on the skeptical theme Vico suggested centuries ago that whatever we know we must first imagine[32]. If we are limited to the realist and idealist positions, as are most discussions about knowledge and its management, an interesting assumption about practice tends to follow. It is always preceded by thought, of which it is therefore the enactment[33]. We are stuck with this single way of explaining practice, and other kinds are beyond explanation and get dismissed as irrational, inexplicable, or otherwise deviant. We arrive at one of the most fundamental assumptions of organizational and managerial theorizing – that managers can, or should, control organizations by shaping the decision-making thoughts of the business's customers, employees, associates, competitors, etc. This leads to our third point – that if practice is only explicable by referring to the ideas that shape it, we have no need of a theory of knowledge-as-practice.

We can argue that KM is only interesting because it points to another notion of knowledge-as-practice, which is why the term tacit seems so fundamental to our discipline. We need some additional conceptual devices to justify a theory of practice, and so make our case for knowledge-as-practice. The clue is to distinguish between situation (a) in which we assume rationality, and can focus on the data and meaning required to make decisions and articulate them into practice, and (b) in which we appeal to our natural creativity to overcome the knowledge absences (Figure 2). At a deeper level we must problematize consciousness itself and thus the rationality or reasoning that stands upon it. This questioning is explicit in the debate between Vygotsky[34] and Piaget[35], theorists of the development of human consciousness[36]. Both had a huge impact on development education and learning theory[37]. At the risk of gross over-simplification we can say both recognized consciousness as problematic, something to be constructed which could be otherwise, neither 'natural' nor the given facility presumed in *homo economicus*.

K	Managing what we have	Responding to what we lack
Data	Rational decision-making	Data collection and systematic discovery
Meaning	Communicating meaning	Constructing meaning and heuristics
Practice	Executing decisions	Explorative practice

Figure 2. Extended Scope of a K-Based Theory of Organization

Consciousnesses are not alike. Piaget argued what we call consciousness unfolds during the child's first four or so years – at which point reasoning, memory, observation – especially the observation of self – have fallen into place. The process is genetically-given. Vygotsky, starting with the same problematic, argued that consciousness is socially shaped through interactions between child and parent or other 'care-givers'. For Vygotskians these interactions are not purposive in the conventional goal-directed sense, rather they precede and shape consciousness. It is no great leap from here to appreciating that what we do does, in fact, have a significant impact on how we think about ourselves and our world. Our work shapes our identity, as Marx suggested. This is especially true of 'professionals', those whose work stands on a rigorous body of knowledge, typically controlled by others[38]. Medical doctors, within their own special body of knowledge, surely see the world quite differently than do priests, or pilots, or engineers. This leads to a richer theory of practice that distinguishes sharply between (a) purposive practices oriented towards organizational goals and (b) practices that are simply about us, in the sense of the ongoing task of shaping, maintaining and protecting our consciousness – what we might call our identity.

Practicing managers learn to be sensitive to the relationship between peoples' work and their attitudes. There is much sociology about how workers protect their identities as they resist the power structures in which they are embedded. Decorating one's cubicle, Dilbert's columns aside, is one way in which we personalize our workplace and so try and possess it psychologically. Roy's[39] observation of 'gold bricking', working ahead of the piece-rate so one has the flexibility to go for a smoke or chat to someone elsewhere in the plant, is a classic. In managerial terms, given a broader theory of organizational practice, we can distinguish three kinds of practice: goal-oriented, identity-oriented, and an unexplained residue. We see three practices rather than the two – purposive and irrational – suggested by rationalists like Argyris. Our framework also recalls Bales's[40] classic work on group activity, and his distinction between task orientation and group maintenance activities. Here we propose identity-constructing practice as *ex definitio* prior to and outside consciousness and thus the possibility of being explained as purposive. Consciousness is re-defined to make conceptual space for both reasoning and imagination, recalling Adam Smith's comment that what demarcates the human race is our senses, our ability to reason and, most significant for our analysis, our imagination[41]. This three dimensional model of Man was shared by the other Enlightenment philosophers such as Locke and Hume.

At this point the reader may be wondering where the technology-organization discussion fits. But recall we began by suggesting technology and organization may be similar phenomena from a knowledge point of view. We must overcome our inclination to think of them as different simply because technology is so often physical hardware while organizations are 'soft' social or authority systems. Each shares our three types of knowledge. Likewise each suggests a theory of learning, for more data is not the same as establishing or changing meanings – and neither is the same as creating and sharing new practices. Managing each is different. Data is not problematic for those in the realist position; reality is presumed to exist so observations of it seem straightforward. Managers can initiate the discovery of data, and its collection, transportation, and delivery. But the focus of the idealist or interpretive position is meaning. Managers create meaning through acts of imagination and may then need to communicate it (Figure 2). Many theorists, following Durkheim and including Kuhn, suggest meaning-making is a collective project[42,43].

Practice belongs to a third epistemology, one in which there are external and internal constraints over the imagination. The imagination is not in the world. As it comes into the world it confronts constraints that can be associated with the psychological world, as in the discussion above of the growth of consciousness, or with the physical world, such as the Second Law of Thermodynamics, or with the social world, such as the Law, custom, and belief. Practice is always particular, in-the-world, unique, created afresh, constrained also by the unique time/space situation in which it takes place. Managers shape practice by communicating their thoughts and by their decision-making, but also by manipulating the constraints to the imaginings of the others' over which they have power.

5   From the Knowledge We Have to the Knowledge We Haven't

The central theme in the KM literature is of managing knowledge assets (Figure 1). In the section above we introduced the complementary conception of KM as responding creatively to knowledge absences (Figure 2). The first is focused on how to allocate the organization's knowledge to best effect – to collect and deliver data, to manage meaning, or to discover and transfer best practice. The second plunges us into practice, and is more about identifying the acts and practices of imagination that managers perform when confronting uncertainty, circumstances under which they have inadequate data or need to create meaning. Or rather this is a way of defining an essential managerial activity which many, not only those wearing the title of manager, perform within organizations. This is the realm of heuristics rather than rationality. Simon[22,44-47] bade us pay close attention to heuristics, rules which cannot be justified theoretically but deal practically with uncertainty and knowledge absences and justified pragmatically. We pick up the challenge Simon[23] presented us with his concept of 'bounded rationality' absent which there is little need for managers and none for an administrative science. Overall KM may be more to do with the bounds to rationality than with revisions to decision-making under certainty, and this leads us towards a broader notion of KM (see Figure 3).

We are familiar with the reason-dominated left side of Figure 3. But our proposals about KM open up a right-hand creative side as well. This can take us far beyond the causality and control aspects of reason-dominated KM to cover the management of acts of imagination. Clearly these cannot be made subject to predictive causal laws so the analysis must focus on its constraints, bounds, and limits.

Type of Knowledge	Consciousness		
	Reason-dominated		Imagination-dominated
	Static	Dynamic	Dynamic
Data	Rational Decision-making	Hypothesis testing and communication	Awareness
Meaning	Paradigms communicated through language, narrative, or observation		Creating new meanings, paradigm shifts
Practice	Enacting established logical rules	Goal-oriented learning, evolving new rules	Explorative practice and the production of consciousness

Figure 3. A Broader Range for a New KM

Paradoxically our empirical tradition focuses on practice, on doing experiments, ultimately prioritizing practice as the final source of meaning, and this is central to the radical constructivist epistemology we touch on next. We also discover practice as inherently creative, for even when it seems to be the enactment of a decision, this is an abstraction in the realm of thought and the circumstances of its enactment in the world are always unique. Practice's creativity inevitably places it beyond the bounds of a completely rational analysis, for that necessarily abstracts something general from the particular and creates the unbridgeable gap between anticipation and experience[48]. Practice takes place in a real world constrained by all its experienced constraints and complexity. Thus the idea of controlling practice by controlling the actor's decision-making can never be entirely effective because as we think we select only a sub-set of the world we have experienced and managers have no means of foreclosing the tacit processes of selection[20].

The gap between thought and experience connects us to this question about the tacit that permeates the KM literature. Some see tacit knowledge as under-articulated knowledge of the same basic type as well-articulated explicit knowledge, i.e. it is equally in the mind but difficult to put into language and so communicate to others[49]. Others see it as in a different domain altogether and point to embodied knowledge or practical skills[15,17,50]. However, following Gourlay[20], we suggest that what is tacit about all our knowledge, and remains inexplicable because it is the result of our creativity, is not so much its poor codification and articulation of what is essentially explicable, but rather its embodiment in the processes of selection which, as we have seen above, must precede all explicit knowledge. In its essence what is tacit is our sense of ourselves and our identity.

The strength of Polanyi's example of bicycle-riding is that both novice and expert experience the same context of activity and receive the same sense-stimuli. But the two riders differ radically in what they attend to; the novice does not yet know how to pay attention correctly to balance and hand motion, so mis-selecting from the various stimuli being received. In contrast, the expert has learned, through imaginative experiment or instruction, how to attend selectively and so construct a workable model of the situation which thereby seems coherent. Likewise expert radiographers see the same X-ray films as their novice colleagues, but know better what to pay attention to. In short, tacit knowledge is evidence of human imaginative activity, whether physical or mental. It becomes the coherence we put into the world as we make it sensible, and is necessarily prior to and forever distinct from any subsequent knowledge of the world. Without the tacit knowledge that we alone create we can have no explicit knowledge for we cannot be conscious of the world. It is our attitude towards the world, as Polanyi[19, 51] argues, how we pay attention.

At this point we turn our whole analytic schema upside down and instead of starting our theorizing with rational thought at the top left corner of Figure 3 we start at the bottom right with raw practice. Instead of saying, along with Ackoff, that data just exists, we say practice, because it is in-the-world simply exists. In philosophical terms we replace rational man, *homo economicus* or *homo sapiens* with *homo ludens*[52], or *homo faber*[53], or Man the *bricoleur*[15,54] – Man who explores the world as a matter of natural creative practice, and drawing on the resulting experience, rather than intellectually through hypothesized causal models of the world. Thus we prioritize practice over thought and reasoning, and become exposed to being surprised by experiencing the world in its variety and richness, as opposed to protecting ourselves and restricting our experience to what we can learn by testing hypotheses[55].

6 On Radical Constructivism

Even with a scheme of KM that covers rational analysis and imaginative practice and, at the same time, three types of knowledge, it is still not quite clear how we are to pull the cells of Figure 3 together. A rich notion of practice helps us do this. As indicated already, we can approach practice in at least two ways, by (a) treating it as the enactment of a goal-oriented cognition, or (b) understanding the constraints to explorative imaginative practice. The first prioritizes thought over action, the second reverses them. There are echoes of exploitation and exploration here[56], for explorative practice is essentially unplanned, with activity preceding analysis, problemistic in the sense of being driven by the need to address some problem[57]. Explorative practice is ultimately about paradigm shifts in the domain of practice, instead of just in meanings, about imaginative extensions that may lead to radically different patterns of practice. They change the discipline just as Reg Harris and Lance Armstrong transformed competitive cycling. How they did this is incomprehensible (or seems tacit) to ordinary cyclists. When we do not understand it we tend to assume they are simply doing what we know to do, but better. In fact this is not the case for their practices are quite different.

To grasp these breakthroughs one must have experienced the limits and constraints oneself. Musicians provide examples. Haydn changed classical music forever by inventing the string quartet, just as Hendrix changed guitar playing. Most of us are outsiders to these domains of skillful practice, uncomprehendingly observing the new practice. We sense something is different but do not know the boundaries that have been transcended. Nor are these breakthroughs mere happenstance. On the contrary, they arise from considerable imaginations confronting the constraints of the medium, and will only occur after prodigious disciplined effort. Newton and Einstein remarked the insights they created came about only because they were able to focus their imaginations and, in particular, carry the constraints in question in their 'mind's eye' for months at a time.

The central puzzle behind an epistemology of practice is the relationship between practice and thought. Absent any links we are unable to say anything about practice; we are condemned to observing it without comment. If the links are too close and determining, we need not observe practice – it can be collapsed into the analysis of the thinking behind it. The key to understanding KM as a discipline, therefore, is not merely to see the discontinuity between the realist and idealist positions – between data and meaning. This is already well understood and does not lead to anything new. The conceptual barrier from which Simon retreated but which practicing managers must cross is to unhook practice from decision-making as framed within either realism or subjectivism. In this sense, and at its most powerful, KM is a fundamental critique of rational decision-making, and begins a follow-through to the challenge presented by Simon's of bounded rationality.

But what can we say about the relationship between thought and practice? Isn't talking about practice just more thinking? Radical constructivism gives us some clues. Like most philosophical positions there is variety here, and many disagreements too. But a summary of key points might go like this. Rorty[58] introduced 'anti-representationalism'. The argument is that both realists and idealists focus on creating representations to use in meaningful truth-capturing statements, the former referring to the 'real' as a warrant for their representations, the latter to their subjective conceptualizing. Anti-representationalists consider such efforts misdirected and argue instead that language should only try to capture our experience of practice. As such it provides a guide to further practice rather than saying anything about the reality that provides the practice's context. We are limited to knowing the practice not the reality in which it takes place. Our reality is neither 'out there' nor 'in here'; the only reality we can know is our own experience of their interaction. This is the only knowledge that is 'in the world'. Our experience, and its interaction with the ideas retained in our memory, is all we have to go on.

The core of radical constructivism is that we waste our time trying to 'represent' the 'out there' reality for it is forever unknown to us. But at the same time it does not seem useful to deny its impact on us; death arrives, entropy happens, gravity rules. But we cannot grasp our experience of this or reality's constraints over our practice, with representations alone. Rather we must focus on modeling our experience and using those habits and artifacts to direct our practice since it takes place within, and is bounded by, an unknowable context. What does this mean in practice, so to speak? Pickering's[59] analysis of the ways in which scientific explanations are developed in the laboratory is helpful for non-philosophers. He shows the fundamental assumption of radical constructivism is that when we use our imaginings to guide our actions, we run up against the world and may find things do not turn out as expected. We may be surprised. We experience the world falsifying our practice, somewhat parallel to Popper's[60] understanding of experimental evidence as falsifying our ideas. But in Popper's work it is representations of reality (hypotheses) that are being falsified. In radical constructivism, it is our ordering of our experience that is being falsified. To confuse the two is to slip back into realism.

Radical constructivism survives the skeptical critique of the realist and idealist positions while also allowing our interacting with the world to constrain our imagination. Social constructionists and some neo-institutionalists presume the final constraint on the imagination is the given-ness of the social process and structure itself[61]. In addition to its awareness of the social and psychological constraints, radical constructivism allows the physical (non-cognitive) limits over our actions to impress themselves onto our experience without, at the same time, insisting we build representations of them. Again, in a radical constructivist epistemology there are forms of explorative practice that precede thought, so complementing the Vygotskian arguments presented earlier. This drives the necessary wedge between thought and practice.

These days no discussion of radical constructivism is complete without some reference to its contemporary cousin epistemology, critical realism[62]. The contrasts between the two are considerable, though the details need not detain us beyond pointing to what each takes as the cornerstone of its position. It is important to appreciate all epistemologies deal with similar questions, all framed within a set of presumption about the nature of reality, of the human being, of thought, of experience, of the interactions between these, and so forth. Realism, in all its varieties prioritizes the real as a coherent and undeniable aspect of our existence. Radical constructivism prioritizes human agency and thus differs sharply. The critical aspect of critical realism deals with the gulf between the presumed 'intransitive' or unchangeable reality, and our 'transitive' or changeable appreciation of it as the 'actual', so critical realists charge that to confuse the two is to commit the 'epistemic fallacy'. The realist aspect of critical realism is that the actual is a field of determining causal relations that stand apart from our subjective constructions of them. In this sense critical realists discount human agency and creativity. As a consequence critical realists argue the methods by which the actual may be researched are compatible with those used in the natural sciences, and that sociological notions such as 'society' can be presumed to exist in the same way as physical objects comprise the Natural universe[63].

Given our focus on relating organization and technology, we need only to get a sense of what difference it might make to shift from a radical constructivist perspective to a critical realist one. The key is that in this chapter we presume technology and organization are alike, both human artifacts, equally evidence of our agency and creativity. Thus organization is a technology and vice versa. The two can, and need to be, researched in the same way, in this case as the changeable results of our imagination rather than as stable systems of causality. But critical realism allows the actual is changeable, transient evidence of the intransient causal relations that lie behind it. Thus the critical realists and radical constructivists converge as the former see the intransient relations as bounds to the actual, and the latter look to the experienced constraints on their imagination as the limits of what can be considered viable. Consequently our entire discussion can be re-framed within a critical realist discourse. But part would be missed, the part, for instance, crucial to Willmott's[63] discussion of Laclau's work, i.e. the importation of human creativity as we attend to our bounded rationality and the 'constructed' uncertainty which, from a constructivist point of view, separates the bounded universe of human experience from the universality of the intransient relations presumed by realists. Thus radical constructivists are disinclined to attach much significance to the causal relations comprising reality while critical realists seem to dismiss human agency as they prioritize the ordered world beyond us.

7 Pulling KM Together

Thus by embracing creativity, our KM opens up a richer understanding of organizations as bodies or locations of data, meaning and practice, and of the management of such knowledge. It confronts rather than suppresses the distinctions between data, meaning, and practice and between rational decision-making and imaginative acts (Figures 2 and 3). These distinctions drive the theory; without them there is nothing new. The underlying agenda is radical, a critique of the rational decision-making model on which so much of our analysis is grounded – even though it suppresses any discussion of uncertainty, creativity, constraints, power, and emotion. Yet we know these are central to the crucial problems of the disciplines that converge on managerial theorizing[57,64,65].

As we progress from the top left corner of Figure 3 to its bottom right corner we move from abstractions about organizational knowledge towards the on-going immediacy and pervasive sense of present in practice. We contrast knowledge assets, static, against the on-going processes of knowing and learning. We reject the normal assumption that sufficient information is available to think through to an optimal decision. We leave the Eden-like comfort zone at the matrix's top left corner where we are not challenged to make sense of the data. But when it becomes inconsistent with our experience we have a meaning problem and cast about for alternatives. Not finding any we look, perhaps, to 'expert practitioners', to those able to deal with our problem in practice even while being unable to explain what they are doing. All this is about shrinking from embracing and theorizing our imagination and creativity as we move from the first side of KM. The second side is about our imaginative and creative practices as we respond to uncertainties and a lack of knowledge rather than handing our responsibilities as managers over to others. Creativity is always in play in organizational life and the suggestion that everyone is being rational and following rules is patently ridiculous. Rationality is useful only when people's creativity brings that rationality into the world. The basic poverty of much managerial and organizational theorizing lies in its reluctance to think 'out of the box', leave the rationality-bound comfort zone at the top left of Figure 3, and embrace the creative aspects of the other side of the matrix.

When Simon[23] proposed bounded rationality he was ambiguous about its causes, but was writing primarily as a cognitive psychologist. On the one hand he pointed out our limited computational abilities, on the other our limited information gathering capabilities. Here we supplement rather than ignore the idea of the psychological constraints on the imagination. The popularization of the Vygotskian work of Lave and Scribner as 'communities of practice' shows the widespread acceptance of social constructionism[66-71]. The imagination is clearly constrained in the context of shared practice, indeed the essence of a 'community of practice' is agreement on context, not on shared concepts or purpose[72,73]. But such theorizing cannot escape the realist's criticisms of idealism or deny their modernist zeal for finding causal mechanisms for all phenomena. The importance of radical constructivism is that it accepts all constraints, from both the realist and idealist sides of the philosophical house.

Others are working along lines similar to those suggested here, though without explicitly adopting the same epistemologies. But they certainly provide additional insights. Carlile[74,75], for example, sets up a three-way discussion based on realist, idealist, and pragmatist positions. Thiétart[76] does something similar, exploring organizational science's methodologies and differentiating its positivist, interpretive, and constructionist paradigms. Patriotta[77] makes subtle use of breakdowns of practice (irruptions) to surface the underlying cognitive models. But none of this work depends upon a theory of knowledge-as-practice like that proposed here. Nor does any of it position KM as a radical critique of the rational decision-making approach.

At this point we seem to have ignored completely one part of the KM literature, that about the ownership of organizational knowledge[78,79]. One of the penalties for using the term knowledge is it is so expansive – indeed it can embrace everything known or sought after. The ownership discussion is not really about the epistemologically defined problematics of knowledge management; it is simply an exploration of the limits of the institutional practices prevalent in capitalist society, about how to capture knowledge – whatever it is – as a tradable asset. Confusion arises when we think achieving ownership of knowledge resolves its problems with uncertainty. This is a mistake for ownership and creativity are unrelated. Owning an uncertain situation cannot be a way of dealing with it, in spite of Williamson's[80] suggestions to the contrary. Inasmuch as there is a connection it is because ownership can be used to sharpen the constraints to the actors' imaginings. Other aspects of knowledge ownership yet to find their way into the KM literature are (a) computer and information security, ownership in the cyber – rather than legal sense, and (b) our rights to privacy and the legal and institutional apparatus of others' knowledge about us. New technologies are pressing such new problems onto the agenda and bear greatly on their integration into the organization.

Recalling Figure 2, the left hand column stresses rational approaches. The right-hand column stresses creative practice as a visceral and natural response to uncertainty and the constructivist-assumed source of all human knowledge. The left presumes our rationality, the right our imagination. After evolving practice we may codify it into heuristics, attach meaning to our experience, and develop language to enable us to collect and analyze what we call data. When we start with data and rational decision-making in mind, we start at the top left of the matrix. When that fails because of insufficient data, we collect additional data, or create it through systematic scientific practice. On other occasions we lack the ability to make sense of the data and look for new patterns of meaning. Under the press of experiencing surprise and uncertainty, we are moved away from the top left and down towards the bottom right. Eventually we have neither data nor meaning and have to confront our being-in-the-world directly, as a matter of explorative practice alone. To be human is to respond to such uncertainty with practice – often first codified and so learned through play[52].

8 Conclusion: The Relationship between Organizations and Technology

The point of exploring the KM literature is to re-define both organization and technology and so theorize their interaction. A KM approach lets us move to a view of the organization as a complex of systems of data, systems of meaning, and systems of practice, where by practice we mean both goal-oriented and identity-creating[11]. The term system does not imply they are well-formed, displaying closure and logical coherence. They are not autopoietic and bounded[81]. All human systems are open and time dependent. As a result each must have its own learning processes, just as each carries its own implications about what managers must contribute to the system. These illuminate how the organization interacts with its context, both shaping and being shaped by it, as structuration theory suggests[82]. Organizational meanings are the creative consequences of interacting, in the radical constructivist sense, with an experienced context.

How then should we consider technology? A technology, like every organization, has its data, meaning, and practice dimensions. We tend to begin with the practice dimension, the fact that things work in a particular way and not otherwise. A technology is first and foremost a system of constraints over practice, only secondly a set of production possibilities. But at the same time a technology has meaning, it is inevitably constrained by the attitudes and interests from which it sprang; though there is no deterministic relationship between practices and meanings. They can be un-hooked. Practices can always be co-opted to other meanings; they are not morally neutral. The data's dimensions depend on meanings adopted and implemented, but these too will be un-hooked and re-interpreted when a paradigm shifts. We might analyze the interaction of technology and organization along three dimensions (Figure 4). The conventional machine-model analysis focuses on the fit between $D(o)$ and $D(t)$; any uncertainty $D(u)$ is suppressed. This model has little explanatory power. It provides little insight into what happens when organizations embark on technological change. We need to surface other dimensions, the meanings and practices embedded in the technology. Only then can we make comparisons with the patterns of meaning and practice already in place in the organization and integral aspects of its identity. Only then can we anticipate how their interactions will lead to 'external learning'.

Figure 4 implies a technology as a complex of systems of data, meaning, and practice, like every organization. But they also differ. An organization is a dynamic arrangement, a buzzing network of evolving people and relations within and without. Human systems are robust and have built-in uncertainty resolution capabilities arising from our natural creativity; although not so great as to approach autopoiesis[83,84]. An autopoietic system is one able to generate its own resources and become informationally independent of its context. But a technology has none of this. What we mean by a technology is more or less an organization without people and, as such, emasculated, without the human systems' dynamic uncertainty-resolving capabilities. Creativity is the consequence of bringing people into the system; thus an actor-network is an organization rather than a technology[85]. A technology cannot tolerate uncertainty, for that arrests its functioning. Recall the idea of fault-tolerant computing, that system's robustness arose because it was redundant, i.e. there was more than the minimal system involved. Redundancy is not an indication of creativity; it is the result of deploying such excess resources that when failures occur, the system degrades gracefully as opposed to precipitately[86]. Because of our creativity individuals and social systems are inherently robust and resilient rather than redundant[18].

Putting the organization's uncertainty resolution processes in the column next to technology in Figure 4 is merely re-stating Thompson's[87] approach to bounded rationality, for it is here that we find the 'boundary-spanning' process. We move towards Luhmann's[88] notion of technology and organization as semi-autonomous social systems that interact only through the immediacy and in-the-worldness of practice and the 'irritations' that that produces[89]. To say that technology evolves endogenously, as Romer[90] suggests is fundamental to economic growth, is to mistake a social system for a mechanical one. Human creativity is the litmus test of the difference between these types of system.

So what are we to conclude? Our hope is to provide some novel tools for considering the interaction of technology and organization. Inasmuch as we can tease out the implications of Figure 4, it is that two knowledge-specific struggles are always under way in organizations. On the one hand there is the data-driven design of the organization and the evaluation of how a technology might fit within it. This analysis lies within the realm of complete rationality and presumes both the technology and the organization can be adequately described. In addition, though the reasoning is contingent on the organization's objectives, we argue for a neutrality, saying the facts are thus and so, that this technology is more efficient than that. In contrast, we propose that changing technology is really a term for changing organizational practice. We are changing production functions, not just hardware. This necessarily disrupts the existing socio-technical system and the identities of all involved. New interactions and new learning occurs and lead to a stable social system only when viable new identities co-evolve with the new practices. Analyzing these requires an understanding of organizational power and the various actors' emotions, as well as the constraints resulting from the technology's physicality and logic.

K	Organization		Technology
	Certainty	**Uncertainty**	
Data	D(o)	D(u)	D(t)
Meaning	M(o)	M(u)	M(t)
Practice	P(o)	P(u)	P(t)

Figure 4. The Interaction of Technology and Organization

These analyses complement and compete with each other for priority. We cannot adopt a realist position that simply presumes the meaning or impact of a technology, independent of its use and users. Doing this involves standing apart from the consequences – and senior managers sometimes ignore their responsibilities this way. They may know little of the organization's creativity and presume those within the organization are completely malleable, without identities grounded in their own systems of meaning and practice. We often say people are resistant to change because we know change upsets current patterns. But we can sometimes be surprised how readily people change when they believe changes will enhance their power and identity. Their expectations are the consequence of making new meanings from the data they have gotten. The key to managing this, we suggest, is creative boundary management, recognizing that both technology and organization are actually created and re-created on the fly by the actors involved as they experience new constraints. Sometimes we know these feel like opportunities, at other times they are threats. But, presented with new situations, people deploy their imagination and practical creativity to push forward and resolve inconsistencies and conflicts, and open up new knowing at all three levels of knowledge.

References

1. Ihde, D., *Philosophy of Technology: An Introduction*. New York: Paragon House, 1993.
2. Morgan, G., *Images of Organization*. Newbury Park CA: Sage Publications, 1986.
3. Smith, A., *The Wealth of Nations, Books I - III*. London: Penguin Books, 1986.
4. Pacey, A., *The Maze of Ingenuity: Ideas and Idealism in the Development of Technology*. 2nd ed. Cambridge MA: The MIT Press, 1992.
5. Woodward, J., *Industrial Organization: Behaviour and Control*. London: Oxford University Press, 1970.
6. Donaldson, L., *The Contingency Theory of Organizations*. Thousand Oaks CA: Sage Publications, 2001.
7. Burns, T. and G.M. Stalker, *The Management of Innovation*. London: Tavistock Publications, 1961.
8. Lawrence, P.R. and J.W. Lorsch, *Organization and Environment: Managing Differentiation and Integration*. Boston MA: Harvard University Press, 1967.
9. Ryle, G., *The Concept of Mind*. London: Hutchinson, 1949.
10. James, W., *The Principles of Psychology*. Vol. I & II. New York: Dover Publications, 1950.
11. Spender, J.-C., Organizations are Activity Systems, Not Merely Systems of Thought. *Advances in Strategic Management*, 12B, 1995, pp. 153-174.
12. Scarbrough, H., ed. *The Management of Expertise*. Basingstoke: Macmillan Press, 1996.
13. Chi, M., R. Glaser, and M.J. Farr, eds. *The Nature of Expertise*. Hillsdale, NJ: Lawrence Erlbaum Associates, 1988.
14. Sternberg, R.J. *et al.*, *Practical Intelligence in Everyday Life*. Cambridge: Cambridge University Press, 2000.
15. Harper, D.A., *Working Knowledge: Skill and Community in a Small Shop*. Chicago IL: University of Chicago Press, 1987.

16. Brown, J.S. and P. Duguid, Organizational Learning and Communities-of-Practice: Towards a Unified View of Working, Learning, and Innovation. *Organization Science*, 2, 1991, pp. 40-57.

17. Blackler, F., Knowledge, Knowledge Work and Organizations: An Overview and Interpretations. *Organization Studies*, 16(6), 1995, pp. 1021-1046.

18. Nonaka, I. and H. Takeuchi, *The Knowledge-Creating Company: How Japanese Companies Create the Dynamics of Innovation*. New York: Oxford University Press, 1995.

19. Polanyi, M., *Personal Knowledge: Towards a Post-Critical Philosophy*. Corrected ed. Chicago IL: University of Chicago Press, 1962.

20. Gourlay, S., Knowing as Semiosis: Steps Towards a Reconceptualization of 'Tacit Knowledge', in *Organizations as Knowledge Systems*, H. Tsoukas and N. Mylonopoulos, Editors. Basingstoke: Palgrave Macmillan, 2004, pp. 86-105.

21. Simon, H.A., *Administrative Behavior: A Study of Decision-Making Processes in Administrative Organization*. 1st ed. New York: Macmillan, 1947.

22. Simon, H.A., *The New Science of Management Decision*. New York: Harper & Row, 1960.

23. Simon, H.A., *Administrative Behavior: A Study of Decision-Making Processes in Administrative Organization*. 2nd ed. New York: Macmillan, 1958.

24. Cohen, W.M. and D.A. Levinthal, Absorptive Capacity: A New Perspective on Learning and Innovation. *Administrative Science Quarterly*, 35, 1990, pp. 128-152.

25. Dougherty, D., Grounded Theory Research Methods, in *The Blackwell Companion to Organizations*, J.A.C. Baum, Editor. Oxford: Blackwell, 2002, pp. 849-866.

26. Kuhn, T.S., *The Structure of Scientific Revolutions*. 2nd ed. Chicago IL: University of Chicago Press, 1970.

27. Henderson, R.M. and K.B. Clark, Architectural Innovation: The Reconfiguration of Existing Product Technologies. *Administrative Science Quarterly*, 35(1), 1990, p. 9.

28. Kahneman, D. and A. Tversky, Prospect Theory: An Analysis of Decisions Under Risk. *Econometrica*, 47, 1979, pp. 262-291.

29. Weick, K.E., *Social Psychology of Organizing*. 2nd ed. Reading MA: Addison-Wesley, 1979.

30. Ackoff, R.L., From Data to Wisdom. *Journal of Applied Systems Analysis*, 16, 1989, pp. 3-9.

31. Delanty, G., *Social Science: Beyond Constructivism and Realism*. Minneapolis MN: University of Minnesota Press, 1997.

32. von Glasersfeld, E., *Radical Constructivism*. London: Routledge/Falmer, 2002.

33. Argyris, C., *Reasoning, Learning and Action: Individual and Organizational*. San Francisco CA: Jossey-Bass Publishers, 1982.

34. Vygotsky, L.S., *Mind in Society: The Development of Higher Psychological Processes*. Cambridge MA: Harvard University Press, 1978.

35. Piaget, J., *Psychology and Epistemology: Towards a Theory of Knowledge*. London: Allen Lane, 1972.

36. Webb, E., *Philosophers of Consciousness*. Seattle WA: University of Washington Press, 1988.
37. Tharp, R.G. and R. Gallimore, *Rousing Minds to Life: Teaching, Learning, and Schooling in Social Context*. Cambridge: Cambridge University Press, 1988.
38. Abbott, A., *The System of Professions: An Essay on the Division of Expert Labor*. Chicago IL: University of Chicago Press, 1988.
39. Roy, D., Quota Restriction and Gold-Bricking in a Machine Shop. *American Journal of Sociology*, 67, 1952, pp. 427-442.
40. Bales, R.F., *Interaction Process Analysis*. Cambridge MA: Addison-Wesley, 1950.
41. Skinner, A., Adam Smith, the Philosopher and the Porter, in *Knowledge, Social Institutions and the Division of Labor*, P.L. Porta, R. Scazzieri, and A. Skinner, Editors. Cheltenham: Edward Elgar, 2001, pp. 35-51.
42. Jones, R.A., *Emile Durkheim: An Introduction to Four Major Works*. Newbury Park CA: Sage, 1986.
43. Sandelands, L.E. and R.E. Stablein, The Concept of Organization Mind, in *Research in the Sociology of Organizations*, S. Bacharach and N. DiTomaso, Editors. Greenwich CT: JAI Press Inc., 1987, pp. 135-161.
44. Simon, H.A., Bounded Rationality and Organizational Learning. *Organization Science*, 2(1), 1991, pp. 125-134.
45. Simon, H.A., The Many Shapes of Knowledge. *Revue d'Economie Industrielle*, 88(2e), 1999, pp. 23-39.
46. Simon, H.A., Making Management Decisions: The Role of Intuition and Emotion. *Academy of Management Executive*, 1, 1987, pp. 57-64.
47. Simon, H.A., *The Sciences of the Artificial*. 2nd ed. Cambridge MA: MIT Press, 1981.
48. Tsoukas, H. and N. Mylonopoulos, Introduction: What Does it Mean to View Organizations as Knowledge Systems, in *Organizations as Knowledge Systems*, H. Tsoukas and N. Mylonopoulos, Editors. Basingstoke: Palgrave Macmillan, 2004, pp. 1-26.
49. Boisot, M., *Knowledge Assets: Securing Competitive Advantage in the Information Economy*. Oxford: Oxford University Press, 1998.
50. Kusterer, K.C., *Know-How on the Job: The Important Working Knowledge of the "Unskilled" Workers*. Boulder CO: Westview Press, 1978.
51. Polanyi, M., *The Study of Man*. Chicago IL: The University of Chicago Press, 1959.
52. Huizinga, J., *Homo Ludens: A Study of the Play-Element in Culture*. Boston MA: Beacon Press, 1955.
53. Bergson, H., *Creative Evolution*. New York: Rowman & Littlefield, 1983.
54. Brown, J.S. and P. Duguid, Organizing Knowledge. *California Management Review*, 40(3), 1998, pp. 90-111.
55. Dewey, J., *Experience and Education*. New York: Macmillan, 1938.
56. March, J.G., Exploration and Exploitation in Organizational Learning. *Organization Science*, 2, 1991, pp. 71-87.

57. March, J.G. and H.A. Simon, *Organizations*. New York: John Wiley, 1958.

58. Rorty, R., *Objectivity, Relativism, and Truth: Philosophical Papers Vol 1*. Cambridge: Cambridge University Press, 1991.

59. Pickering, A., *The Mangle of Practice: Time, Agency, and Science*. Chicago IL: University of Chicago Press, 1995.

60. Popper, K.R., *The Logic of Scientific Discovery*. London: Hutchinson, 1968.

61. Gergen, K.J., *Toward Transformation in Social Knowledge*. 2nd ed. New York: Sage Publications, 1994.

62. Fleetwood, S. and S. Ackroyd, eds. *Critical Realist Applications in Organisation and Management Studies*. London: Routledge, 2004.

63. Willmott, H., Theorizing Contemporary Control: Some Post-Structuralist Responses to Some Critical Realist Questions. *Organization*, 12(5), 2005, pp. 747-780.

64. Nelson, R.R. and S.G. Winter, *An Evolutionary Theory of Economic Change*. Cambridge MA: Belknap Press, 1982.

65. Cyert, R.M. and J.G. March, *A Behavioral Theory of the Firm*. Englewood Cliffs NJ: Prentice-Hall, 1963.

66. Rogoff, B. and J. Lave, eds. *Everyday Cognition: Its Development in Social Context*. Cambridge MA: Harvard University Press, 1984.

67. Tobach, E. *et al.*, eds. *Mind and Social Practice: Selected Writings of Sylvia Scribner*. Cambridge: Cambridge University Press, 1997.

68. Scribner, S., Studying Working Intelligence, in *Everyday Cognition: Its Development in Social Context*, B. Rogoff and J. Lave, Editors. Cambridge MA: Harvard University Press, 1984, pp. 9-40.

69. Cole, M. and S. Scribner, *Culture and Thought: A Psychological Introduction*. New York: John Wiley & Sons, 1974.

70. Hacking, I., *The Social Construction of What?* Cambridge MA: Harvard University Press, 1999.

71. Kukla, A., *Social Constructivism and the Philosophy of Science*. London: Routledge, 2000.

72. Knorr-Cetina, K., *Epistemic Cultures: How the Sciences Make Knowledge*. Cambridge MA: Harvard University Press, 1999.

73. Amin, A. and P. Cohendet, *Architectures of Knowledge: Firms, Capabilities, and Communities*. Oxford: Oxford University Press, 2004.

74. Carlile, P.R., Transferring, Translating, and Transforming: An Integrative Framework for Managing Knowledge Across Boundaries. *Organization Science*, 15(5), 2004, pp. 555-568.

75. Carlile, P.R., A Pragmatic View of Knowledge and Boundaries: Boundary Objects in New Product Development. *Organization Science*, 13(4), 2003, pp. 442-455.

76. Thiétart, R.-A., ed. *Doing Management Research: A Comprehensive Guide*. London: Sage Publications, 2001.

77. Patriotta, G., *Organizational Knowledge in the Making: How Firms Create, Use, and Institutionalize Knowledge*. Oxford: Oxford University Press, 2003.

78. Nonaka, I. and D.J. Teece, eds. *Managing Industrial Knowledge: Creation, Transfer and Utilization.* London: Sage, 2001.

79. Teece, D.J., *Managing Intellectual Capital: Organizational, Strategic, and Policy Dimensions.* Oxford: Oxford University Press, 2000.

80. Williamson, O.E., *Markets and Hierarchies: Analysis and Antitrust Implications.* New York: Free Press, 1975.

81. Maturana, H.R. and F.J. Varela, *Autopoiesis and Cognition: The Realization of the Living.* Dordrecht, Holland: D. Reidel, 1980.

82. Bryant, C.G. and D. Jary, *Giddens' Theory of Structuration: A Critical Appreciation.* London: Routledge, 1991.

83. von Krogh, G. and J. Roos, *Managing Knowledge: Perspectives on Cooperation and Competition.* London: Sage, 1996.

84. Bakken, T. and T. Hernes, eds. *Autopoietic Organization Theory: Drawing on Niklas Luhmann's Social Systems Perspective.* Copenhagen: Copenhagen Business School Press, 2003.

85. Law, J. and J. Hassard, eds. *Actor Network Theory and After.* Oxford: Blackwell, 1999.

86. Perrow, C.B., *Normal Accidents: Living with High-risk Technologies.* New York: Basic Books, 1984.

87. Thompson, J.D., *Organizations in Action: Social Science Bases of Administrative Theory.* New York: McGraw-Hill, 1967.

88. Luhmann, N., *Social Systems.* Stanford CA: Stanford University Press, 1995.

89. Hernes, T. and T. Bakken, Implications of Self-Reference: Niklas Luhmann's Autopoiesis and Organization Theory. *Organization Studies*, 24(9), 2003, pp. 1511-1535.

90. Romer, P.M., Endogenous Technological Change. *Journal of Political Economy*, 98(Supplement), 1990, pp. S71-S102.

CHAPTER 18

Knowledge and Labor Theories of Value: Can they be Reconciled?

Stephen Jaros
Department of Management, Marketing and E-Business
Southern University
Baton Rouge, Louisiana 70813, USA
Email: sjaros3@cox.net

1 Introduction

Traditionally, researchers operating from Critical perspectives on work have adopted the Classical-economic (e.g., Locke, Ricardo, Smith, Marx) view that labor, typically conceptualized as manual labor, is the source of value in business firms, and that labor processes are the locations where value is created[1]. However, prompted by the emerging importance of information and communication technology in today's global political economy, Jacques[1], echoing earlier claims of the development of a "post-industrial society"[2] and of a "network" society[3] proposed replacing the Classical/Marxian focus on labor as the loci of value with the notion that "knowledge", or more specifically, "learning processes" which leverage ICT, would serve as a better root metaphor for understanding the nature of value creation in contemporary capitalism. This proposal suggests that knowledge and learning systems, often embedded in non-human assets such as communication networks, workflow configurations, robots, and computer information systems, have usurped the role of production labor as the source of value in modern corporations. Jacques proposes that a "knowledge theory of value" (KTV) would better capture the "spirit" of global capitalism than does the Classical "labor theory of value" (LTV). His focus was on

---

[1] "Labor process" is a Marxian-derived term that is closely related to what most mainstream business analysts would refer to as a "production process". As Marx notes, "The elementary factors of the labor-process are 1, the personal activity of man, *i.e.*, work itself, 2, the subject of that work, and 3, its instruments." (Marx, 1876, p. 167).

developing a KTV as a "constructive metaphor", one that could help us better-understand modern workplaces and the broader political economy.

This chapter has three purposes. The first is to determine if a KTV and a LTV are mutually exclusive. This involves re-evaluating evidence of the "correctness" of Jacques's view that knowledge/ICT has largely replaced labor as the source of value in global capitalist production processes. If it has, then there is no need to "reconcile" a KTV with an LTV. I conclude that it has not, and therefore (purpose 2) describe how they can be reconciled. The third purpose is to assess the political utility of this reconciliation. In other words, what is the value of a theory of value that recognizes both knowledge and labor inputs? Speaking from a critical-political perspective: irrespective of the empirical correctness of the LTV or KTV or any theory of value, what is the value of using the KTV as a "metaphor" to describe global capitalism and advance the economic welfare of all employees, technical or manual? Thus, this chapter is aimed at addressing political issues that have arisen from a critical-Marxian intellectual tradition.

2 Has Knowledge Replaced Labor as the Loci of Value?

Jaros[4] analyzed Jacques's proposal to determine if existing evidence supports the key empirical assumption underlying his work – that information and learning processes really have changed the "nature of work", such that their management and implementation has replaced "labor" as the primary source of value. Essentially, Jacques's proposal answers in the affirmative a question posed by Cawood in this handbook: "are digital technologies associated with radical social transformation on the order of the industrial revolution, or do they serve to perpetuate existing social arrangements?" (p.10). Jaros concluded that the evidence is mixed. There is evidence that firms are "leveraging knowledge" and ICT systems to create value more than they ever have, which supports the view that a KTV that replaces the LTV is justified. In contrast, other evidence supports the point of view that labor is still a dominant loci of value-creation.

2.1 *Evidence for the ascendance of knowledge and ICT processes as a source of value*

Some researchers argue for the growth of and importance of information, marketing, and communication systems in value creation. For example, Willmott[5] commenting on the "dot-com bubble" of the late 1990s, argues that the ability to manage and manipulate information has become the critical business activity. Willmott notes that the success of dot-com start-ups in attracting investment capital was largely a function of the entrepreneur's ability to manipulate information – to put on a "show" for investors that convinces equity markets that the start-up could leverage the internet to produce enormous rates of return, as well as the ability of finance experts to develop business plans that could convince equity markets of the future profitability of companies that existed solely on paper at the time. Willmott notes that for dot-com entrepreneurs seeking investment capital, the equity market *was* their product/service market. Investors were the "customers" that these entrepreneurs were trying to appeal to, and their ability to manipulate information and convince investors of their mastery of ICT as a source of value was critical to their success/failure in attracting capital.

Willmott's analysis is representative of a much larger analytical stream that touts the rise of "symbolic analysts" or "knowledge workers"[6] and their role in value-creation. Finance experts, software engineers, strategic planners, public relations consultants, lawyers, research scientists, etc. – they utilize ICT to generate, manipulate, and disseminate knowledge that creates value for shareholders[7]. And this view is not confined to academia: according to the CEO of Siemens, one of the world's largest corporations, between 60% and 80% of the company's value-added is generated by knowledge management[8].

This burst of exuberance over the perceived growing impact of knowledge and ICT processes on value creation has spawned a cottage industry of consultants (e.g., the "Knowledge Management Resource Center"; "Knowledge Management" magazine), academicians (e.g., the "Research Program in Social and Organizational Learning" at George Washington University; the "Organizational Learning and Instructional Technologies Program" at the University of Mexico; the "Electronic

Journal of Knowledge Management"), and combinations of both (e.g.,
Peter Senge's "Society for Organizational Learning"; the "Knowledge
Management Research and Practice" journal) that investigate and
disseminate "best practices" in information management, leveraging
knowledge and learning processes, implementing ICT, etc. to create
value-added in organizations. Thus, there is evidence that management
practitioners and academicians recognize the importance of knowledge
as the locus of value creation in today's global economy.

2.2 *Evidence against the notion that knowledge/learning processes have become the loci of value creation*

However, some evidence points in an opposite direction. Other
researchers argue that globalization is characterized by parallel processes
of firm-level skills upgrading on the one hand and "firm de-
knowledging" on the other. For example, Littler and Innes[9] present
evidence from a study of 4000+ Australian firms that suggest that while
some firms have upskilled in response to ICT implementation, others
have, as a result of downsizing and de-layering processes, been de-
skilled. While Littler and Innes focus on the concept of "skill", not
labor, their work has implications for this research, because their findings
challenge the notion that info-globalization processes have been
characterized by the "replacement of manual skill by knowledge" and by
a general up-skilling trend, because their findings indicate cross-currents
of both up-skilling and de-skilling. Littler and Innes propose that the de-
skilling trend is actually the predominant one, though not as highly
visible (in the media and academia) as the upskilling trend.

While Littler and Innes analyzed firm-level, not job-level, skill
changes, they claim their data support an "insecurity thesis", which
proposes that while some high-profile information technology sectors
have experienced up-skilling, this has been dwarfed by a less-publicized
but underlying trend towards jobs growth in low pay, de-skilled, service
and manual labor. Thus, manual labor, not information-processing
systems, may still serve as an important and substantial source of value.
This argument echoes Ritzer[10] whose "McDonaldization" hypothesis
suggests that even though ICT innovations in the realm of the internet,

cyberspace, virtual reality, etc. have captured the fascination of the mass and business media, exploitation of low-wage service and manual labor remains a bedrock feature of global capitalism, and this bedrock feature reveals itself in downsizing and de-layering strategies, often characterized by a shift in production from high-wage 1st world countries to low-wage 3rd world countries.

Likewise, champions of "Business Process Re-engineering" approaches to improving efficiency and productivity, in part by using ICT, such as Hammer[11] initially argued in favor of 'radical' organizational change that disregarded the 'human factor' in work processes, treating employees as essentially interchangeable, and dictating change to them in a top-down manner. But, after many BPR efforts failed, and this failure was determined to be at least in-part caused by a loss of "organizational knowledge" due to employee attrition and alienation, many BPR advocates modified their approach to include an incorporation of "human" or "socio-technical" factors into the process[12].

Similarly, evidence from consulting research suggests – at least in the USA – some disenchantment with "knowledge management" and ICT initiatives that were touted as revolutionary sources of new value creation. Many firms now have "knowledge management officers" or "Chief Information Officers" to run ICT programs, but returns on investment in organizational learning and knowledge management have been difficult to quantify: "labeling a project a KM initiative is asking for trouble. It invites philosophical discussions about the nature of knowledge and political debates over who owns it. There's also a good chance people won't understand what you're talking about. "KM is like CRM. It means a hundred different things to a hundred different people," says Novell CIO Debra Anderson, who avoids the term altogether."[13]. Similarly, Voelpel, Dous, and Davenport[14] argue that during the "knowledge management hype" of recent years, many firms launched knowledge management and ICT initiatives, but "most of these initiatives did not provide the benefits they had promised" (p. 9). This gap between the "promise" or "hype" of KM and the realities of implementation echo the 1980s "expert systems" phenomenon, which attempted to codify human capital into physical and "knowledge" capital via user interface $\leftrightarrow$ inference engine $\leftrightarrow$ knowledge base interaction. Billions of dollars of private and public money were invested in expert and AI systems, and expectations were sky-high about the commercial potential, but the results were disappointing[15].

   These findings suggest a middle tack between Jacques's notion of knowledge as the dominant source of value in the modern capitalist firm, and the work of critical theorists that have rejected his proposal in favor of the LTV, or any theory of value including the LTV. Available evidence suggests that the "exploitation" of manual labor is still a source of wealth in many organizations, and yet the management of knowledge work, learning processes, and the efforts of "symbolic analysts" who leverage ICT to generate/manipulate information is becoming a dominant feature of managerial work as well, suggesting that both labor and information contribute to value creation.

2.3 *Knowledge and labor in the "labor" (production) process*

However, this "middle tack" notion raises a theoretical conundrum: How can they be reconciled? Recently, in reply to Jaros[16], Jacques[17] questioned the epistemological consistency of a middle tack approach. He suggests that while knowledge could be readily added to the Labour Theory of Value, perhaps as a factor of production, ".... The coherence of that, and the limitation of thinking in new terms, would be that the system could still rest upon the epistemological basis that labor IS value and knowledge influences how this value is utilized by societies. (Conversely) in a knowledge theory, labor could be a factor influencing how knowledge is utilized, but a knowledge theory would make the epistemological statement that knowledge or ICT IS value. To try and build one system in which labor and knowledge are value would be analogous, to me, with trying to build a Copernican-Ptolemaic system of astronomy. It is possible to incorporate either into the other, but not accept the base assumptions of both simultaneously. It is not that either is more true in any objective sense. Rather, each requires us to accept as root beliefs something that we are required in the other system to believe is false". Thus, Jacques argues that "knowledge" and "labour" are incommensurable metaphors for understanding value production dynamics.

At root, this notion seemingly presumes two characteristics of the LTV and KTV: (1) that there can be but a single basis of value, i.e., that either labor or knowledge doesn't just create value but "is" value, and (2) that "value" has no tangible existence or foundation, or at least if it does, it isn't measurable . When one says that "labour" or "knowledge" is *the* source of value in capitalist production, one is invoking a particular "lens" or paradigm through which to view the world. And a lens that is not inherently any more or less "correct" than any other lens. The parallels with post-modernist perspectives on political economy (which argue that there are no "real" bases to any social-economic constructs) should be clear.

In contrast, this chapter proposes that knowledge and labor can serve as bases of value creation within contemporary global firms and that this can be assessed in different kinds of *labor processes*. "Labor processes" are heterogeneous, and one characteristic that distinguishes one kind of labor process from another is how knowledge and labor are leveraged to create value. One implication of this perspective is that neither the LTV nor the KTV can be considered "correct" at the firm level. Every firm consists of multiple labor processes, which leverage knowledge and labor to create value. Both knowledge and labor, therefore, contribute to the totality of value created by the firm. Additionally, contra post-modernist perspectives, "value" does have an empirically verifiable basis, and identifying that basis is crucial to understand wealth creation and distribution processes in modern work organizations. I argue that Jacques unjustifiably views value-creation processes as "black boxes" that cannot be explicated with any kind of reasonable precision.

3 Reconciling Knowledge and Labor Theories of Value

As noted above, the basis of the proposed reconciliation is a shift in level of analysis from the firm to the labor process. "Labour process" is a Marxian-derived term that is closely related to what most mainstream business analysts would refer to as a "production process". As Marx notes, "The elementary factors of the labour-process are 1, the personal activity of man, *i.e.*, work itself, 2, the subject of that work, and 3, its instruments."[18]. This definition highlights the notion that a labor process is a *productive* activity; it produces goods and services that have value to someone. It consists of a goal (the subject of work – the creation of value), personal activity that is purposeful (oriented to achieving the goal) and which utilizes tools and instruments to that end. Labor processes can be individual or social in nature. A man or woman who makes a product or grows food by themselves constitutes a labor process, but more typically of course, labor processes consist of multiple individuals working in a coordinated manner in organizations.

A couple additional points on the term "labor process": A reader unfamiliar with Marxian/Critical organizational research might wonder why I am using the term "labor process" if what we are really talking about is typically known as a "production process", i.e., a process that involves combining multiple production inputs – equipment, technology, labor, knowledge, etc. – to make a product or deliver a service. The reason is that this chapter is designed to address issues that are of particular import to Marxian-flavored organization theory, which utilizes Marxian terminology like the "labor process", which in turn reflects Marx's view – a view echoed by many critically-oriented organizational scholars – that labor is the unique source of value-added in production processes.

Another point about the concept of a "labor process" is that it is a theoretical abstraction, not necessarily an ontologically "real" phenomenon[19]. The "labor process" represents an artificial "bracketing-off" of some kinds of organizational activity for detailed analysis. Typically, what is bracketed off is a production or service delivery process in a particular organization – a factory floor, a retail store shopping area, a customer service center, a software design facility, a data processing center, a call center, etc. These physical settings and the technologies utilized are of course real, but the bracketing-off is an abstraction, because "value chains" extend far beyond what goes on in a particular organizational production process. For example, the supplies and raw materials that are utilized in the first workstation of a firm's production process (one boundary of a "labor process") are of course themselves the product of "labor processes" in other organizations, and the finished product that rolls off the end of the assembly line (the other boundary of a labor process) is then an input to other labor processes involving marketing activities, transport & distribution activities, etc.

So ultimately the boundaries of any labor process are arbitrary in the sense that they are an artificial construction of the researcher – but that is true of arguably all constructs in organizational behavior. As with all theoretical abstractions, what matters is the practical need to focus analytical attention on something manageable by the researcher (we cannot study everything about value creation all at once), and whether the abstraction facilitates the production of new knowledge about something that is "real" in the world. In the case of drawing general conclusions about the process of value creation, I believe that any given labor process is likely to be representative of what happens in the "bracketed off" portions of the value-chain, though of course the specifics may vary depending on the degree of empirical difference between the labor process that is isolated for analysis and what is bracketed off.

3.1 *Linkages between labor and knowledge in value-creation processes in labor processes*

Just about all human productive processes leverage knowledge and labor, often via ICT, thus these production factors are almost always linked: At a basic biological level, as living beings, humans are the *result* of the transmission of knowledge contained in the genetic code from organism to organism. Likewise, this transmission of knowledge via the genetic code typically requires the "personal activity of man", i.e., the labor of having sex. So which comes first, or which can best be described as being *the* locus of value (human) creation? It is a chicken-or-egg conundrum, since both activities are equally critical to the "value-creation" process. It is also a comparatively simple labor process. Primitive labor (the sex act) is combined with primitive knowledge (knowing that sex acts lead to pregnancy, transmission of a genetic code) to create "value" (a baby).

But what about a labor process like in-vitro fertilization, in which ICT and chemical processes are used to extract semen and ovum, cryofreeze embryos and then "knowledge workers" (doctors) implant the embryo? Jacques might argue that the relative contribution of labor and knowledge to value creation change when advanced technology is introduced. Here, the labor process is much more complex than the comparatively simple act of having sex and letting nature take its course. Advanced bio-technology that did not exist for much of human history is leveraged to create human life that otherwise could not be created by natural biological processes. Isn't it reasonable to say that the leveraging of knowledge – the knowledge needed to "artificially" create a human embryo by chemically combining a sperm and egg in a laboratory, is the critical value-added event? Perhaps, but then consider the labor – the personal activity of people – involved in the process as well: the labor performed by the bio-chemist to combine the sperm and egg in the petrel dish, and by the doctor to implant it in the wall of the uterus, is surely just as "advanced" as the knowledge that underlies this activity. The labor process is complex with respect to knowledge leveraged, but it is also complex with respect to the labor activity performed. Thus, we have the chicken-egg conundrum yet again – both activities are seemingly equally critical to value-creation.

And when we shift to the level of producing goods and services in a market economy these linkages are inescapable. For example, it is clear that *purposeful* labor of the kind Smith, Ricardo, and Marx identified as a component of a labor process is impossible without knowledge – knowledge of what one is trying to accomplish, and how to use the tools and materials at hand. An auto worker cannot build a car until an engineer has designed it, and the "value" added by the auto worker will not be realized unless marketers are successful at designing effective marketing strategies. ICT links all of these internal work processes, and work processes in other firms that are part of the focal firm's supply chain. Thus, any labor process necessarily combines knowledge with labor to create and realize value, and is embedded within a broader system of value-chains within and across firms.

However, does this mean that we can't say anything more than that knowledge and labor contribute *equally* to value-creation in all labor processes? Above, we described labor processes in which the level of knowledge and the level of labor – simple or advanced – were equal. By "simple labor" I mean labor that is low-skill, meaning that large numbers of people are capable of performing it. By "simple knowledge", I mean that the knowledge leveraged requires little education and is readily-easily grasped by large numbers of people. In contrast, the in-vitro labor process is characterized by comparatively *advanced* labor and advanced knowledge. The knowledge leveraged about how machines and chemical processes can be used to artificially implant an embryo requires years of education and is not readily known to most people. Likewise, the labor performed to extract a sperm and egg, to combine them chemically to create an embryo and to implant the embryo is high skill – comparatively few people have the skill to perform it because the physical actions are complex and require significant training.

But what about labor processes that combine advanced knowledge with simple labor, or advanced labor with simple knowledge? Software design might be thought of an example of the former. The knowledge needed by the software engineer to develop the computer programs that constitute the software package is advanced, but the labor used to code the software – to type the computer language that creates the code – is simple. The work of athletes such as NBA basketball players or professional figure skaters would exemplify the latter. The knowledge needed to execute a basketball play or an ice skating routine is simple and readily graspable without much education, but the physical labor performed – shooting a basketball or executing a triple-jump at a professional standard of performance – is advanced.

If advanced factors provide more value-added than simple factors, then it might be true labor processes that combine advanced knowledge and simple labor leverage knowledge *more* than labor to create value, and that labor processes that combine advanced labor and simple knowledge leverage labor more than knowledge to create value. But is this true? This raises the issue of how we assess "value".

3.2 *Value = "socially necessary" inputs to production, assessed by cost*

Put simply, I agree that Jacques is fundamentally correct in that, existentially speaking, "value" is ultimately un-knowable. No product, service, or input to production is *inherently* valuable, i.e. has a value independent of the people who utilize it, attempt to measure it, etc.

"Value" is not an objective physical or material characteristic. However, contra Jacques and postmodernist perspectives, *economic* value, the value of inputs and outputs of economic processes, can be indirectly assessed – by price. The price of an input reflects – admittedly imperfectly, like all reflections – the underlying collective subjective valuations held by economic actors. Or in Critical-Marxian terms, economic value reflects what is "socially necessary" about an input, whether that be labor or knowledge, or some other productive input.

Given this formulation, I propose that advanced production factors are more valuable than simple ones, because the "social necessity" of advanced factors is greater. They are *scarcer*, and therefore effective demand for them is likely to be greater (or in other words, only those who are willing to up their valuation to a point where demand = supply will be able to acquire them), which will be reflected in a higher price-valuation. What matters in determining value is not the type input (e.g., labor or ICT), nor the specific or necessary role it plays production – but its advanced or simple nature. Air, for example, is absolutely necessary for any production process involving humans, because without it everyone would die. But air is typically not scarce, so it usually has no economic value.

So I propose that labor processes that combine advanced labor with simple knowledge leverage labor more than ICT to create value, since the price of labor should make up a greater part of the price of the product than the price of knowledge-information systems will. In these cases, we can propose that labor can properly be described as the primary loci of value. The converse should be true of labor processes that leverage advanced knowledge and simple labor to create value. In labor processes that leverage simple knowledge and simple labor, or advanced knowledge and simple knowledge, neither one can be fairly described as the loci of value creation.

Our conclusion is that both the KTV and LTV are incorrect in their pure form, but can be reconciled – in the sense that we can identify when knowledge or labor is the foci of value creation – by testing their propositions at the level of the labor process.

4 Empirical Verification of Relative Contributions of Knowledge and Labor to Value

Testing the propositions that the value-added of labor and knowledge will hinge on whether the factor is advanced or simple would seem to be a straightforward task – adding up the cost of labor and the cost of knowledge/information management for a given labor (production process) and comparing them. But this raises some accounting issues – cost allocation issues – that must be clarified.

4.1 *Knowledge and labor costs*

How much money does an organization spend to manage knowledge? Some costs would clearly seem to fit in this category:

- ICTs that process knowledge within a labor process and between labor processes;
- computer hardware and software systems that store and permit the analysis of information within a labor process;
- salaries/wages of managers and technicians who design, implement, and supervise knowledge systems (IT technicians, software engineers, knowledge managers, etc.) within a labor process;
- costs of controlling knowledge in a labor process (i.e., security measures to prevent unauthorized access and to prevent industrial espionage).

Also, since many knowledge-management systems are organization-wide, intended to facilitate knowledge transfer across labor processes, we have to allocate these system-wide costs to the labor process (think of this as "knowledge-management overhead"):

- rent and maintenance of machines and facilities dedicated to the generation/acquisition, storage, retrieval, and dissemination of knowledge in the organization as a whole;
- the cost of managing intellectual assets such as copyrights, trademarks, patents;
- costs of managing organization-wide programs specifically dedicated to knowledge generation and transfer (e.g., Siemens's "ShareNet" program[20]).

Labor costs would include:

- wages, salaries, benefits paid to production workers, service workers, and maintenance workers within a labor process who maintain the tools and equipment they use to make products or deliver services;
- costs of controlling labor (human supervision costs, electronic surveillance costs, etc.).

4.2 *Costing difficulties of informal knowledge management and learning processes*

Perhaps the most vexing costing difficulty lies in putting a price on the management of informal aspects of knowledge management and learning processes. Some knowledge management scholars argue that knowledge processes that create value in organizations have both a formal and an informal component. According to Brown & Duguid[21] A "knowledge production process" involves "organizational learning", which encompasses processes of knowledge recognition (identifying information as potentially useful to the organization), knowledge acquisition (selecting knowledgeable employees, environmental scanning/ benchmarking, tapping experiential knowledge), knowledge dissemination (communication – codified via information technology, tacit via organizational culture/stories)[22] and knowledge institutionalization in formal rules/practices[23].

The cost allocation categories described above capture the price the organization pays for most of the formal aspects of "knowledge production" within a labor process, but what about the informal aspects – the production of "tacit" knowledge that is generated and transmitted by organizational cultures? Chartrand[24] argues that tacit knowledge is "knowledge that cannot be explicated or codified, and cannot be transmitted by prescription. It can only be passed on by practice and demonstration. This restricts diffusion to personal contact." Accounting for tacit knowledge is difficult, because it is not explicitly paid for by the organization.

Because tacit knowledge is generated by experience, and can only be transmitted by the possessor's ability to demonstrate the knowledge and for the receiver to emulate what has been demonstrated, tacit knowledge is produced by *learning* processes. Individuals or teams learn how to create and recognize tacit knowledge as they do their jobs, and organizations learn to emulate what the team or individual has learned, meaning that the knowledge is disseminated via cultural processes throughout the organization[25]. Of course, researchers who study organizational learning have developed fine-grained distinctions between different kinds of learning (e.g., Argyris & Schon's single-, double-, and triple-loop learning) for both tacit and explicit/formal knowledge, but for our purpose what matters is how the tacit processes can be accounted for in terms of the value they provide to an organization.

To this end, Nanoka & Takeuchi's[26] our-component framework of knowledge conversion between tacit and explicit (socialization, externalization, internalization, and combination) is useful. Fundamentally these conversion processes are individual in nature – they take place in the mind of a particular employee – and are not characteristics of an organization, per se, though the organization can take steps to provide an environment that facilitates conversion. As Acosta[27] notes, individuals and organizations are incapable of simply "taking in" data. Rather, the questions we ask as we search for information, what we find, how we make sense of it, and what we do with it are "all guided and constrained by our mental models (in the case of individuals), and paradigms and cultural lenses (in the case of organizations embedded in social systems)." (p. 17). Jacques[28] makes a similar point with his argument that the central problem of managing knowledge is one of "learning capitalization". Jacques notes that "..learning is the property of the worker or the workgroup until it is applied. Once applied, it becomes knowledge and can be capitalized... but it is the learning, not the knowledge that is the source of value" (p. 208).

The implication being that, whatever the *process* by which learning occurs and whatever the specific form that learning takes (i.e., single-loop, double-loop, tacit to explicit, explicit to tacit, etc.), and whatever ICT is leveraged in the process, what matters to the organization in a value-creation sense is how the knowledge generated by the employee is utilized on a wide scale, is "made apparent" to the organization. Therefore, management of explicit knowledge, and the price the organization pays for it, which is captured by the cost factors cited above, can stand as a proxy (albeit an imperfect one) for the value-added of tacit knowledge, since explicit knowledge represents tacit knowledge that has been "made apparent", disseminated throughout the organization. Tacit knowledge which has not been made apparent, which is confined to a single employee or a small number of employees, or even small inter-firm "communities of practice"[2] that span organizational boundaries, is not likely to add much value-added to the organization[29]. The organization is not leveraging the knowledge; the isolated employees are, sometimes even to hold down productivity (i.e., the employee uses the tacit knowledge he gains to trade-off "leisure" for work). Thus, these guidelines for costing out the price that an organization pays for labor and knowledge inputs could provide the data needed to categorize a labor process as knowledge or labor intensive.

5 Political Implications

If the "reconciliation" of the Labour and Knowledge Theories of Value proposed here has empirical validity, what are the political implications for researchers who study organizational behavior from critical-Marxian perspectives with an eye toward improving the economic position of workers and other lower-level employees?

5.1 *Implications for Marxian notions of "exploitation"*

Traditionally, critical scholars have objected to what they call the "exploitation" of workers under capitalist production processes. According to Marx, under capitalism, workers are exploited in the sense that they (collectively speaking, at the firm-level) receive less in pay and benefits than the value of the output they produce[30]. Capitalists are able to appropriate this "surplus" output because they own the means of production (tantamount to the "means of survival", at least in the short run) and workers do not, so capitalists have workers over a barrel, so to

---

[2]A broader 'community of practice', one that spans organizational boundaries or encompasses many employees, might be an exception, because the tacit knowledge may be so widely-shared within the organization that the firm realizes non-trivial, and positive, value-added.

speak, when bargaining for wages. Thus, in Roemer's[31] terms, exploitation is a product of unequal asset distribution between workers and capitalists. Also, Capitalists are aided in this exploitation by the "invisible" nature of exploitation under capitalism, which (unlike in feudalism or slave-production) is not obvious. The worker appears (to himself) to be free to choose for whom to work for, and therefore does not perceive the exploitative nature of the working *relationship* among all employers and employees.

Exploitation is regarded as a universal characteristic of capitalist production, one that flows from the logic of the Classically-derived LTV. As such, critical organizational theory has oriented itself towards trying to develop a short-run political programme aimed at ameliorating the effects of exploitation (e.g., social-welfare programs that transfer, via government taxes, capitalist-appropriated wealth back to workers), and a long-run program of ending that exploitation entirely, via the replacement of capitalism with socialism[32]. However, the implication of the analysis presented in this chapter is that the replacement of capitalism by socialism is, at the systemic level, unjustified, because at the level of the labor process, "labor" is not always the primary source of value-added. Sometimes, perhaps most of the time, "knowledge" is, meaning that worker exploitation is not an inherent, universal feature of capitalist production. Replacing capitalism with socialism could constitute throwing the proverbial baby out with the bath-water, since the political-economic "good" done by ending exploitation in those labor processes where it exists could come at the expense of the (greater) benefits achieved by leveraging knowledge in others, since in both cases it is the profit imperative which drives the business owner to produce value-added.

Another point worth making is that critical theorists often confuse levels of analysis. They often point to the low wages received by *individual* workers as evidence of *systemic* exploitation[33]. However, if we look at the return to labor at the systemic (firm) level, we often see that workers collectively receive more in pay/benefits than owners do. The per-person return is far less, but the overall return is often far greater. This may still mean that workers are being exploited – the value of the work they do may exceed what they are paid – but rhetorically/politically, it puts the issue in a different perspective.

Thus, this analysis posits that the critical researcher should consider abandoning efforts aimed at replacing capitalism with socialism, and instead focus on the ameliorative programs that can lessen the hardship of laborers who find themselves unable to earn a living wage (short-run welfare relief, establishment and enforcement of the right to form unions, training programs that make workers more valuable, etc.).

5.2 *Implications for the politics of Jacques's KTV*

In proposing the development of a Knowledge Theory of Value, Jacques argues that the LTV was an appropriate way to conceptualize work during Marx's era, when the "oppression of workers" was the central political, ethical, and economic problem to be addressed. But according to Jacques, this state of affairs no longer holds. Value is now created by ICT, utilized by knowledge workers such as finance experts, software engineers, marketing consultants, public relations personnel, design experts, and lawyers, all of whom tend to be highly paid and for whom an "exploitation" argument is unlikely to be persuasive to the public at-large. Even production workers are now expected to be quasi-knowledge workers; with many firms implementing TQM programs, employee involvement programs, Just-in-Time inventory programs and the like, which attempt to leverage the manual laborer's creativity and judgment by "up-skilling" his/her ability to utilize ICT to leverage knowledge.

However, this chapter argues that labor exploitation still does exist, if we look beyond the experiences of workers in the advanced western economies and observe what is happening on a global level. Many firms that are lauded as exemplars of the new "knowledge economy", such as Nike and Wal-Mart may in fact derive a significant proportion of their profits via the low wages of their international work-forces. A focus on highly-paid US and European workers may miss what is happening overseas in third world countries. Examples would include U.S. car companies paying Mexican workers $9 an hour in pay/benefits compared to $55 an hour for U.S. workers, or Nike sub-contractors paying teenage girls 50 cents an hour in Bangladesh or Vietnam to make shoes that sell for $150 to US teenagers. These workers can hardly be called "knowledge workers" and it is likely that labor, not knowledge, is what is being leveraged to produce value-added in these production processes. And as Littler and Innes found, there is empirical evidence that many firms in the developed world are sacrificing allegedly valuable knowledge workers at a rate higher than they are shedding manual laborers. In other words, there is little reason to think that worker "oppression" is no longer a serious moral/political problem, or that low-knowledge, low-skill production labor is no longer a foci of value creation in many firms, even if we jettison the core principles of the Labor Theory of Value.

References

1. Jacques, R. Theorizing knowledge as work: the need for a knowledge theory of value. In C. Prichard *et al.* (Eds.), *Managing Knowledge.* London: Macmillan. 2000.
2. Bell, D. *The coming of post-industrial society: a venture in social forecasting.* Harmondsworth: Penguin. 1974.
3. Castells, M. *The information age. Economy, Society, and Culture I.* Oxford: Blackwell. 1996.
4. Jaros, S. *The "knowledge theory of value" part II: its implications for Labour Process Theory and firm-deknowledging.* Paper presented at the 2004 AOM Meetings, New Orleans, Louisiana, USA, 2004a; Jaros, S. Jacques's (2000) call for a "knowledge theory of value": implications for Labour Process Theory. *Electronic Journal of Radical Organization Theory*, 8(1), 2004b.
5. Willmott, H. From knowledge to learning. In C. Prichard *et al.* (Eds.), *Managing Knowledge.* London: Macmillan. 2000.
6. Reich, R. *The Work of Nations.* New York: Vintage. 1991.
7. Castells, M. *The Internet Galaxy: Reflections on the Internet, Business, and Society.* London: Oxford University Press. 2002.
8. Fink, G. & Holden, N. The global transfer of management knowledge. *Academy of Management Executive*, 19, 2005, pp. 5-9.
9. Littler, C. & Innes, P. Downsizing and de-knowledging the firm. *Work, Employment, and Society*, 17, 2003, pp. 73-100.
10. Ritzer, G. *The McDonaldization of Society.* London: Sage. 2000.
11. Hammer, M. Reengineering Work: Don't Automate, Obliterate. *Harvard Business Review*, July-August, 1990, pp. 104-112.
12. Galliers, R. & Baker, B. An approach to business process reengineering: The contribution of socio-technical and soft OR concepts. *INFORS*, November, 1995.

13. Dragoon, A. Knowledge Management by any other name.... *CIO magazine*, 15 October 2004.
14. Voelpel, S., Dous, M. & Davenport, T. Five steps to creating a global knowledge-sharing system. *Academy of Management Executive*, 19, 2005, pp. 9-23.
15. Vasallos, V. & Venkatasubramanian, S. Technology transfer in the software industry: the case of AI. Stanford Computer Industry Project. 1995.
16. Jaros, S. 2004b.
17. Jacques, R. Personal correspondence. 15 September 2004.
18. Marx, K. *Capital*, volume 1. New York: Vintage. 1867. p. 167.
19. Knights, D. & Willmott, H. *Labour Process Theory*. London: Macmillan. 1990.
20. See Voelpel, *et al.*, 2005.
21. Brown, J.S. & Duguid, P. Organizational learning and communities-of-practice: Toward a unified view of working, learning and innovation. *Organization Science*, 2(1), 1991, pp. 40-57.
22. See Brown & Duguid, 1991; Heavens, S. and Child, J. *Mediating individual and organizational learning: The role of teams and trust.* Paper presented at the Organizational Learning Conference, Lancaster University, 6-8 June 1999.
23. Huber, G.P. Organizational learning: The contributing processes and the literature. *Organization Science*, 2, 1991, pp. 88-115.
24. Chartrand, H. *The Competitiveness of Nations in a Global Knowledge-Based Economy.* Unpublished Ph.D. dissertation. 2003. http://members.shaw.ca/competitivenessofnations/
25. Argyris, C. & Schon, D. *Organizational learning II: Theory, method, and practice.* Reading, MA.: Addison-Wesley. 1996.
26. Nonaka, I. & Takeuchi, H. *The Knowledge Creation Company: How Japanese Companies Create the Dynamics of Innovation.* Oxford: University Press. 1995.
27. Acosta, A. *A Diversity Perspective on Organizational Learning and a Learning Perspective on Organizational Diversity.* Paper presented at the AOM meetings, New Orleans. 2004.
28. Jacques, R. 2000.
29. Wenger, E. Communities of Practice: Learning as a Social System. *Systems Thinker*, June, 1998.
30. Sowell, T. *Marxism: Philosophy and Economics*. NY: Quill. 1985.
31. Roemer, J. Second thoughts on property relations and exploitation. *Canadian Journal of Philosophy*, 15(Supplementary volume), 1989, pp. 257-266.
32. See Thompson, P. Disconnected Capitalism: Or why employers can't keep their side of the bargain. *Work, Employment, & Society*, 17, 2003, pp. 359-378.
33. See Jaros, S. 2004a.

CHAPTER 19

Information Technology-Enabled Innovation: A Critical Overview and Research Agenda

Angel Salazar[*] and Steve Sawyer[†]

[*]Manchester Metropolitan University Business School
Aytoun Street, Manchester M1 3GH, United Kingdom
Email: a.salazar@mmu.ac.uk

[†]Pennsylvania State University
301F IST Building, University Park, PA 16802, USA
Email: sawyer@ist.psu.edu

1 Introduction

Contemporary studies have broadened our insights about the roles which information technology (IT) plays in supporting innovation in organizations and markets. These studies have also showcased an ever-expanding range of theoretical perspectives. The diversity of issues, levels and perspectives illustrated in the contributing chapters of this handbook raises relevant questions about the degree of theoretical development and integration, and the extent to which a clear cumulative body of knowledge is emerging.

While the diversity of approaches is impressive, there is little integration among them, making coherent innovation models and organisational strategies enabled by IT elusive. This is particularly apparent in the context of new industry dynamics, as the evolving use of the Internet demonstrates. Increasingly, scholars stress the need to cross-fertilize ideas by considering diverse theoretical levels of analysis which take into account the *processes* and *outcomes* of IT-enabled innovation within organisations and markets[10-15]. The articulation of processes and outcomes requires the acknowledgement of the inter-level dynamics, transformational attributes and symbiotic effect of information technology in organizations and markets[19].

Here we engage in a critical overview of selected representative studies focusing on IT-enabled innovation at the level of the organisation and markets. The purpose of this review is to update our understanding and help scholars develop more robust and integrated theories of IT-enabled innovation. We make the case that scholars of IT in organizations are best served by adopting theoretical perspectives and research designs that systematically combine the study of research questions related to both *process* and *outcomes* of IT-enabled innovation at various levels of analysis. In doing this, we draw from Markus and Robey's[34] and Klein *et al.*'s[35] work and extend it by explicitly discussing how the level of analysis affects the establishment of valid and meaningful causal relationships. Second, we highlight the usefulness and also possible limitations of strategic management and economic theories. Here we will discuss the pros and cons of variance and process research approaches. Third, we point to recent theoretical developments such as relational and dynamic capabilities, knowledge management and organizational learning, social networks, neo-institutionalism, and adaptive structuring. Finally, we discuss some of the remaining problematic theoretical areas and suggest possible extensions and integration of current strategic management and organization theories.

2   Defining IT-Enabled Innovation

Here we start by broadly defining IT-enabled innovation as *"the patterns of actions, relationships, processes and outcomes embedded in the virtualisation of social relations, knowledge exchange and learning, and value-adding activities spanning the organisational boundaries of the firm"*. More specifically, IT-enabled innovation is characterised by the emergence of virtual organisational forms and collective cognitions based on complex, interdependent relational network of actors and value-augmenting activities, where innovation and learning originates from enabling dialogue and knowledge exchange. In addition, distinguishable patterns of social relations, knowledge exchanges and value-adding activities are *inter-dependant of their technological, economic, social and political ecosystems.*

The implementation and exploitation of IT is enabling innovation in the context of much wider organisational and market transformations. Firms are outsourcing aspects of their value chain and relying more on strategic alliances and collaborations with specialist and intermediary companies in the hope of becoming more flexible in their production and faster to market. To do this, these firms are entering into strategic alliances and engaging networks of firms through electronic means. This includes the emergence of firms whose business strategies and marketing, production and innovation activities are essentially wholly enabled by IT infrastructures, applications and services. These are key drivers for providing completely new products and services. The use of IT makes possible contractual and collaborative relationships which are characterized by multi-channel transactional and relational processes, and which may span different activities of the value chain. These uses of IT help to alter the structure and basis of competition and collaboration within markets[21-24].

For example, Nambisan[5] highlights the relationship of new IT and new organisational forms and innovation, leading to virtual customer-supplier product innovation communities. From a practical stance, a group of firms can use Internet technologies in such a way that it can interconnect information systems across multiple research, development and production sites and let information flow across organisational boundaries[70]. For instance, the biotechnology industry has offered appropriate contexts for this type of empirical issues. Before the advent of Internet technology, drug development had traditionally been based on long and costly activities, which was normally performed in-house by large pharmaceutical companies, such as AstraZeneca, Pfizer, and GlaxoSmithKline. These pharmaceutical companies are adopting IT both at the intra-firm and inter-firm level. Large companies and their specialist biotech supply firms engage in virtual inter-organisational networks with their partners acting essentially as knowledge brokers in many of the value-creating activities of drug discovery, development and commercialization. For other relevant examples in the media industries see Cassiman and Sieber, Chapter 14 of this volume.

3 Establishing Causal Relationships

Traditional variance approaches are concerned with "establishing necessary and sufficient causation between dependent and independent variables. Such an approach to knowledge creation is valuable in contexts that are stable and where the boundaries of the phenomenon under consideration are clear"[32] (p. 223). Traditional variance studies in IT tend to focus on a particular level of analysis, be it organisation, individuals or groups inside the organisation, or a network of organisations.

Scholars assume that organizations are somehow homogenous and that causal patterns and relationships of IT-enabled innovation are directly reproduced at all levels. For example, work psychologists and organisational sociologists who study IT implementation tend to study identity and cultural aspects of individuals and groups. Those groups would tend to be treated as homogenous, and the causal relationships assumed to be duplicated across levels.

The level of analysis issue within and across organizations has been addressed previously in widely cited papers in the specialised IT literature by Markus and Robey[34], and the more general organisation science literature by Klein *et al.*[35]. We draw from this work and extend it by explicitly discussing how the level of analysis affects establishing valid and meaningful causal relationships.

The existing corpus of IT studies spans from the micro to the macro aspects. The theoretical foundations range from an institutional emphasis on cognition and normative social structures within and across organisational boundaries, to an economics-inspired focus on the structure and competition within markets[24-26]. Relevant research questions both focus on and span different levels of analysis. For instance, some micro studies have focused on how firms' organisational characteristics influence their ability to adopt and deploy IT. At the macro level, some studies have often focus on how the strategic effects of IT on industry structure are mediated by changes in regulation[27-30].

Traditional variance studies often raise the level of analysis to assess aggregated economic impact of IT on national and regional economies, and global industries. For instance, studies have focused on the economic performance and the scale of industry transformation and innovation, and the adoption and diffusion trajectories of e-Business technologies and services in a given market or region. Variance analyses are useful for identifying factors that affect the variation in levels of adoption observed across markets and across organisations.

The above are indeed relevant research issues and questions, but IT studies tend to focus on a particular level of analysis, the macro or the micro, for theory development. As others have noted, the distinction among levels of analysis is often blurred. And, macro (i.e., markets) researchers can learn more about organisational phenomena by engaging studies at the meso (i.e., networks of collaborating firms) and micro-level (i.e., individuals inside the organisation) than they currently do by focusing primarily on an aggregated level of analysis[25].

Very few studies have attempted to articulate the inter-dependent *competitive and strategic* (i.e., establishing cross-level causal relationships, and measuring performance outcomes and aggregated impact on competitiveness), and *organisational* aspects (i.e., investigating causal relationships, enabling conditions and processes at the micro and meso levels) of IT-enabled innovation. This inter-level dynamics of IT implementation and the constant blurring of boundaries in context to innovation activity have as a consequence the growing significance of articulating both the social phenomena and value-adding activities at multiple levels of analysis in studying organisations and markets[25].

Also, the inter-organisational and temporal nature of virtual business networks also requires the modification of the variance model in which inter-organisational institutional context is explicitly recognized. Traditional variance studies are less useful for examining questions about the dynamics of the mechanisms or processes of change and innovation. Variance studies often cannot account for the order and sequence of events that unfold in institutional and organisational change processes being studied in context to IT-enabled innovation. Variance studies are limited in that they assume that a *fixed* number of predicting variables identified at a particular time *determine* actions or decisions regarding the organisational phenomena under study. Variance explanations also assume that an identifiable set of independent and contingent variables *can* be both identified and used to explain phenomena at a particular level of analysis[25]. Process analyses make clear that some factors treated as external contingent forces in variance models need now be regarded as part of the relevant emergent organisational interactions[33].

Unfortunately, very few scholars have, however, made explicit their analytical framework they use to link the organisational level with the inter-organisational level, and explain how outcomes and relationships at organisational levels are related and/or replicated at the market level. For instance, Gittell and Weiss's[8] framework linked intra- and inter-organisational coordination in context to patient care. Organisation design and network perspectives and a process approach are combined to span multiple levels of analysis, focusing on factors that contribute to effective coordination at one level and can also generate effective coordination at other levels. The authors contend that coordination of patient care, enabled by IT in this case, is an important organisational phenomenon that cannot be examined without crossing levels of analysis. The authors contend that organisation decision shapes networks and that information systems act as linking devices supporting a virtual organisational network spanning internal organizational boundaries. Gittell and Weiss's study, however, explicitly disregards what are the relevant value-adding activities and decisions, and how coordination and collaboration lead to new knowledge exchange configurations that align the organization with the overall requirements of patient care and alert them about new opportunities in the external environment.

While information technology-enabled innovation is increasingly being associated with a wider range of inter-organisational, market and institutional dimensions, the micro organisational level still remains problematic[8,31]. Fundamental unresolved questions remain such as:

- Are patterns of IT-enabled innovation reproduced across levels? More specifically, are patterns of *social relations, knowledge exchange and learning, and value-adding activities* produced at the intra-organizational/micro level reproduced at the inter-organizational/macro level, and vice versa?
- How are patterns of IT-enabled innovation related across levels of a social system? More specifically, how do relational and cognitive characteristics, and structural and market conditions interact at organizational and market levels?

As structures of meaning inhabit every level of analysis, there is an opportunity to understand the relationship between micro and macro levels by encouraging analysis at multiple level of analysis using process research approaches, as well as promoting variance studies that explicitly establish connections across levels and across time.

4 Strategic Management and Economic Theories

Strategic management theories have traditionally been useful to investigate which strategies add value, which mechanisms can reduce costs, and which designs of inter-organizational networks are cost-effective. More recent studies have been associated with theories and concepts from pricing and auction theory, contract theory, network externalities[14], intermediation, disintermediation and reintermediation, aggregation and disaggregation[36], value chain framework and business model concept[37], resource based views of the firm[38], and transaction cost economics[30], which are strongly rooted on the economic view[39,40]. From the transaction cost economics perspective, for example, IT is seen as a means of reducing transaction costs between the buyer and supplier, coordination costs in multiparty bargaining, and communications costs for suppliers (see Table 1a).

Let us illustrate these issues with an example. Berthon *et al.*[39] highlight relevant research issues from a strategic management perspective. The key questions these authors investigated were: *what are the key transaction costs associated with electronic markets, and how is technology affecting these costs; what is the within- and between-company potential for dis/reaggregation and dis/reintermediation; what is the dominant form of economic coordination and mode of interplayer interaction; and which form of Web-enabled organisation is most efficient within a given context?* The authors, not surprisingly, based their framework on transaction cost theory and the notion of social capital. Financial services and electronic procurement markets have offered appropriate contexts for this type of study. In summary, research issues confronted by strategic management scholars include the performance and governance of internet-based firms and electronic markets[42].

Likewise, Cassiman and Sieber, Chapter 14 of this volume, focused on the roles of the Internet and new opportunities for value creation. They highlight the on-going transformation in those industries in which information plays a key role, be it content (such as the media industry), communication of information (such as the telecommunication industry) or infrastructure for information (such as the computer and electronics industry). For instance, the merger of America Online and Time Warner gives evidence of the early stages of transformation of traditional movie, media and telecommunication companies. AOL Time Warner provides content through a variety of companies of the publishing, filmed entertainment, music, and interactive video industries. These contents are aggregated and brought to the customer using their own Internet access provider (America Online), as well as their own networks (Turner Broadcasting, Home Box Office) and cable systems (Time Warner Cable). Cassiman and Sieber also show that new technology simultaneously affects demand and costs structures leading to a radical transformation of existing market structures. Furthermore, as the Internet impacts industries in several ways simultaneously they find that simply analyzing the effect of Internet on pricing behavior and price dispersion misses the point of industries being transformed, which clearly affects the pricing power and possibilities of individual firms.

In this post-Internet era, where value maximization is seen as a key factor, researchers are applying strategic management theories to investigate strategies to add value and mechanisms to reduce transaction costs, and analyze the strategic role of partners and intermediaries within selected markets[14,39,40]. For instance, the five forces model of Porter[52] advocates independence and power over buyers and suppliers, and competition against rival firms becomes the strategic focus. The specialised strategic IT literature is not short in relevant examples illustrating the strategic value and impact of IT on business networks, including aspects of global product innovation, operational and logistics excellence, improved customer relationships, strategic alliances and knowledge acquisition. Exemplar cases include Ford's EDI-enabled supply chain network[67], Marshall's value innovation network[68], Cisco's global supplier integrated network[69], and BioSpace's global R&D and knowledge management network[70]. Other issues include how the adoption of internetworking technology influences organisational form. For instance, Brews and Tucci[91] applied the transaction costs economics perspective to analyse the impact of internetworking technology on organisational form.

One of the problems of applying transaction-cost logic to the study of IT-enabled innovation networks is that economic optimisation becomes the overriding focus of analysis[43]. Moreover, strategic management theories rest on the problematic assumption that adaptive behaviour is a natural feature of most formal organisations and business networks[11,55]. That is, it is relatively unproblematic for organisations to gain competitive advantages through the rapid emulation of successful competitors or the adoption of business models enabled by IT. However, alternative forms, and other additional aspects, of coordination to the price systems involve social relationships and dialogue[44,45]. Strategic management theories based on economics and traditional variance approaches have clear limitations for explaining collaborative behaviour in context to IT-enabled innovation[49-51]. Most firms operate in a mixed competitive environment with relational and competitive characteristics[50].

Relational characteristics of business networks are more complex and less understood than transactional or competitive characteristics. Relational characteristics are reflected in buyers and sellers forming strong, long-term relationships in a very similar way to single organisations. As organisations vertically disintegrate and outsource services, collaboration and coordination with external organisations becomes increasingly important for achieving high performance outcomes. Thus, 'pure' market mechanisms are often insufficient for coordinating the resulting relational interdependencies among organisations, thus requiring explicit attention to the design of mechanism for managing inter-organisational networks[8,45]. Other controversial issues include the limitations of the economic-oriented strategic management theories such as TCE for example, to account for institutional and organisational aspects, including the role of professions and associations, and consumer and partner trust formation[46,47].

Table 1a. Theoretical Developments and Questions for Further Research

	Focus & Authors	Questions for Further Research
1. Strategic Management and Economic Theories (e.g., TCE, Resource Dependence)	- Value adding strategies, cost reducing mechanism, cost-effective inter-organisational designs. - Kambil and Heck 1998, Brynjolfsson and Hitt 2000, Cassiman and Sieber 2001 & 2006, Kraemer and Dedrick 2002, Amit and Zott 2002, Berthon et al 2003, Banker and Kauffman 2004, Brews and Tucci 2004.	What are the key transactions costs associated with electronic markets? How technology is affecting these costs: what is the within- and between-company potential for dis/reaggregation and dis/reintermediation? What is the dominant form of economic coordination and mode of interplayer interaction; and which form of IT-enabled organisation is most efficient within a given context? What aspects of internet business models are most likely to be adopted and diffused at different organisational/market levels? What are the structural and organisational conditions for a given level of adoption to take place?
2. Relational and Dynamic Capabilities Views	- Obtaining and sustaining competitive advantage through the development of a set of distinctive organisational capabilities. - Wheeler 2002, Zahra and George 2002.	What are the key organisational capabilities and knowledge exchange mechanisms required for the successful implementation of IT-enabled innovation, and what are the unique, inimitable attributes of these capabilities? How do these capabilities are mobilised and recombined, and what are the relevant organising and learning processes? What are the necessary contextual conditions for creating distinctive dynamic capabilities that enable sustained IT-enable innovation?
3. Knowledge Management and Organisational Learning	- Emergent hybrid perspective based on positivist (i.e., information sharing) and interpretivist (i.e., social interaction) views. - Schultze and Boland 2000, Newell et al 2001, Nambisan 2002.	What are the boundaries of effective customer involvement in new product development set by new technologies? How should organisations establish and govern a customer community of value creation with permeable boundaries? What is the significance of network relationships and new forms of interacting, leading and organising? What patterns of social structuring of organisational activity have greater impact on the utilisation of information technology?

Table 1b. Theoretical Developments and Questions for Further Research

	Focus & Authors	Questions for Further Research
4. Social Network Theory	- Impact of information systems on network structure, structural effects of internetworking, formation of inter-organisational networks. - Kreiner and Schultz 1993, Ebers 1997, Lee and Pennings 2002, Brews and Tucci 2004, Roijakkers et al 2006.	Which features of organisational network design give rise to effective coordination at more than one level of analysis? What are the specific characteristics of these personal communication networks underlying alliance networks and how do they affect the effectiveness of inter-firm learning? How do characteristics of the overall alliance network interact with specifics of the personal communication network in influencing inter-firm learning? How is IT implementation affecting communication, information processing and decision-making within and across organisational boundaries? How are boundaries likely to be redrawn as a result of an increased in the adoption and diffusion of IT? Which aspects are likely to be subject to individual and organisational agency?
5. Neo-Institutional Theory	- Organisational fields, institutional environments, normative and cognitive elements of institutions, mimetic processes of form replication. - Mitev 1996, West 2000, Helper and MacDuffie 2003, Crowston and Myers 2004, Seror 2006, Pentland 2006.	What effects do institutional structures have on virtual networks? How do business networks' structural and cognitive organisational characteristics influence their ability to adopt and deploy IT? How the effects of IT on industry innovative performance and firm organisational structure are conditioned by the structural and cognitive dynamics of customer-supplier networks?
6. Adaptive Structuring and Practice Perspective	- Symbiotic relationship between IT development and organisational forms. Individual shape structuring processes and relationships. - Newell et al 2001, Schultze and Orlikowski 2004, Barret 2006.	How does IT implementation cause changes in social relations, and in knowledge exchange and learning at the individual, group, organisational and inter-organisational level? What are the intervening contextual conditions affecting those changes?

5 New Theoretical Developments

We have identified at least five areas of growing research activity regarding IT enabled innovation: relational and dynamic capabilities, knowledge management and organizational learning, social networks, neo-institutionalism, and adaptive structuring (see Tables 1a & 1b). We have chosen to review these five areas because they explicitly address the process nature of social relations, and knowledge exchange and learning aspects, which are central to our previous definition of IT-enabled innovation. Each one of these theoretical perspectives has the potential to extend the breadth of intellectual space of strategic management relative to IT IT-enabled innovation.

5.1 *Relational and dynamic capabilities views*

The relational perspective argues that actions of organisational agents are driven by personal motives and emotions, and do not necessarily relate to opportunistic profit-seeking behaviour, and in these cases the rational-actor assumption that underlies the economic-oriented views fails[54,55,56]. From a relational view, organisations and markets are re-conceived as "resource-flows, information flows and webs of significance"[44] (p. 123). Presently, there is little direct empirical comparison of the relational perspective to the more common economic perspectives. In addition, the concept of dynamic capabilities has become a major focus of scholars and practitioners in the strategy field. This view gives special attention to obtaining and sustaining competitive advantage through the development of a set of distinctive organisational capabilities, rather than through conventional strategies based on industry structure and positioning. The more contemporary conception of the dynamic capabilities view has been enriched by other theoretical perspectives such as the resource-based view and the relational view, and more recently the knowledge management and organisational learning perspective. This evolution in the conceptualisation of dynamic capabilities has been accompanied by an increasing number of empirical studies published in strategic management literature, and more recently in the IT management literature. For instance, Wheeler[6] identified and measured the organisational capabilities that comprise the ongoing work net-enablement in electronic markets. He lays out a 'Net-Enabled Business Innovation Cycle' (NEBIC) theory rooted in strategic management's dynamic capabilities perspective and the notion of absorptive capacity. 'Net-enablement' is seen as a dynamic capability with four constructs: choosing emerging and enabling information technologies; matching economic opportunities with enabling IT; executing business innovation; and assessing customer value. Dynamic capabilities are seen as leading to resource configurations that generate value-creating strategies, which can be imitated and developed through multiple learning paths. In this view 'creating customer value' is the dependent variable from an economic variance view, and 'net-enablement' is a process variable from a socio-organisational view. The main research questions that we would like to highlight here are: *what are the key organizational (and relational) capabilities required for the successful implementation of IT-enabled innovation, and what are the unique, inimitable attributes of these capabilities?* Also, *how are these capabilities mobilized and recombined, and what are the relevant organising and learning processes?* And, w*hat are the necessary contextual conditions for creating distinctive dynamic capabilities that enable sustained IT-enabled innovation?*

5.2 *Knowledge management and organizational learning*

The knowledge management and organisational learning view of IT-enabled transformation is a second contemporary thrust in strategic management. In the more specialised IT literature, the role of collaboration, knowledge sharing and learning in competitive strategies and innovation are highlighted. The intensity and pace of innovation in knowledge-intensive and hypercompetitive markets has brought the need for organisations to exploit their collaborative networks to boost their own innovation capacity. Scholars have reviewed the role that IT plays in promoting information and knowledge sharing, collaboration and coordination both inside and across organisational boundaries; transformational attributes include the role that information technologies have on re-shaping inter-organisational collaboration and innovation. In this work, they acknowledge the symbiotic relationship between the approaches for information technology development and the emergence of inter-organisational forms and structures[58,59,60,61].

IT-enabled innovation can be characterised by two broad assumptions about the nature of knowledge: (a) the content, intensity and frequency of the knowledge production and sharing actions; or (b) the social patterns or structure of the connections between heterogeneous actors across multiple levels[62,63,64]. The first assumption advocates that information and knowledge can be made explicit and be transferred easily regardless of the characteristics of the organisational context. The second assumption acknowledges a more reflective "interpretative" view -that information and knowledge sharing are characterised by being highly tacit and inter-dependent on the social setting. Likewise, IT-enabled innovation can be characterised by two broad assumptions about the nature of learning: (a) that learning primarily occurs within individuals, or (b) learning is the result of a wider and richer socialization process. There has been a progressive shift away from thinking about knowledge as a commodity or asset that organisations have or may acquire, towards the study of knowing as something that individuals and teams do and how this can in turn be harnessed by the firm. Mutually supportive relationships must exist among organizational members since knowledge creation is a social process.

Some scholars have attempted to combine these two positivist (e.g., information sharing) and more interpretive (e.g., social interaction, knowing) views about knowledge and learning[64,65]. For instance, Nambisan[5] investigated the knowledge creation issues, customer interaction, and motivations in a computer-mediated and community-oriented environment. The main research questions here are *what are the boundaries of effective customer involvement in new product development set by new technologies; and how should organisations establish and govern a customer community of value creation with permeable boundaries?*

Scholars need to move away from first-order questions such as *how effectively organizations are using information technology to collect and disseminate knowledge which can be harnessed to gain competitive advantage,* towards second-order questions such as *what is the significance of network relationships and new forms of interacting, leading and organising?* and *what patterns of social structuring of organizational activity have greater impact on the utilisation of information technology?*

5.3 *Social network theory*

There is a growing literature that examines when, where, why, and how organisations engage in inter-organisational networking. An important research issue has been the impact of information systems on network structure[71]. Related issues include the structural effects of internetworking and the formation of inter-organisational innovation networks[72-75]. Inter-organisational forms can take the shape of interconnection between firms, such as strategic alliances and federated organisational structures enabled by inter-organisational information systems.

Ebers[73] (p. 13), however, warns us that "we know much less about how inter-organisational networking relationships are built, develop, and dissolve. That is, we know little about the intermediate processes, the steps and activities that translate motives into particular network structures and about the contingencies that facilitate and constrain these relationships and processes". Also, it is assumed by the economic perspective that organisations are free to make choices about potential partners without reference to wider institutional or industry norms[76].

As noted in Section 3, Gittell and Weiss[8] examined the coordination of patient care crossing levels of analysis. Their premise is that organisation design is both shaped by and shapes social networks. Information systems are conceptualized as linking devices, which support organisation design to create a virtual organisation. This leads to questions regarding *which features of organisational network design give rise to effective coordination at more than one level?*

In Chapter 11 of this volume, Roijakkers, Duysters and Sadowski-Rasters studied learning in the context of the personal social communication network underlying alliance networks. Their critical examination of the networking literature showed that a number of important research questions that relate to communication networks and strategic alliances have, until now, remained largely unanswered. They point out that most studies of alliances and networks do not include an evaluation of lower-level communication networks through which tacit technical knowledge has to be transferred and new technologies have to be learned into their analysis of the effectiveness of inter-firm learning. The main unresolved questions they highlight are *what are the specific characteristics of these personal communication networks underlying alliance networks and how do they affect the effectiveness of inter-firm learning? How do characteristics of the overall alliance network interact with specifics of the personal communication network in influencing inter-firm learning?*

In addition, other critical questions we would like to highlight are *how is IT implementation affecting communication, information processing and decision-making within and across organizational boundaries? How are boundaries likely to be redrawn as a result of an increased in the adoption and diffusion of IT? Which aspects are likely to be subject to individual and organizational agency?*

5.4 *Neo-institutional theory*

Neo-institutional theory is articulated primarily at the macro level of analysis, concerning itself with such phenomena as social institutions, organisational fields, institutional environments and societal sectors. The neo-institutional approach is also concerned with cognitive elements of institutions: the frames through which meaning is made and social action constructed. Neo-institutionalism focuses attention to institutional effects, such as the ways organisations and their members are influenced by, and influence, institutionalized rules and institutional environments. Institutional processes create both cognitive and structural constraints, or an 'iron cage' in Max Weber's terms[20]. Institutionalised modes of organizing can provide legitimated ways of proceeding in inter-organisational interaction. These modes may, in turn, hinder free choice and innovation. As established inter-organisational activity becomes widely accepted, organisational actors may be affected by the increased risks of innovating (i.e., modifying and expanding the network), the demand for further reflection, and the potential reduction of legitimacy[77].

The specialised IT literature has given comparatively less explicit attention to the relationship between institutional contexts and inter-organisational networks embedded in those contexts. Relatively few variance studies have primarily focused on the effect of environmental factors or forces, often together with organisational factors, on the adoption of inter-organisational systems and the development of business networks in the context of innovation[78-80].

Neo-institutional analysis can take into account both the isomorphic and the constitutive nature of institutional forms and processes of formation of Internet-enabled business networks. IT scholars have not yet appropriately studied organisational forms at birth and birth and survival rates, or the mimetic processes of form replication and the distinct institutional and socio-organisational forces shaping these processes. West[83] found that the institutional context within which organisations operate exerts an influence on their choice of organisational form, drawing on an information-processing and institutional *contingent* approach to understanding optimal organisation structure. Likewise, Helper and MacDuffie[84] investigated the evolution of electronic business in the auto industry, and their effects on consumer and supplier relationships, focused in part on the industry value chain relative to employee unions. Anand *et al.*[48] examined a mechanism through which organisational fields are constituted in the music industry. They conclude that markets can serve as a magnet, around which groups of actors consolidate, and that cognition of markets occurs through the creation, distribution and interpretation of a web of information about the market.

Neo-institutional researchers have, to date, shown far less concern with the origin of form (as the product of ongoing interaction of individual members). Endogenous organisational dynamics are rare in accounts of institutional change. The dynamics of organisational transformation and innovation is also treated different by institutional researchers. Institutional theorists suggest that organisations become more similar over time because of normative processes that reward similarity (e.g., IT education and accreditation promoting particular codes of conduct and collective cognition).

Most neo-institutional analyses, like many traditional strategic management studies, tend to regard the relationship among contextual economic and regulatory factors *and* the content of innovation and transformation as deterministic. The more embedded an organisation is in its institutional and market environments; the more likely it is that their relationships will be symbiotic. There have been very few authors who have investigated the enabling role of information technology in several markets.

In Chapter 7 of this volume, Seror developed a neo-institutional framework for analyzing the future development of virtual infrastructures in service delivery systems illustrated in the health care context. Market dynamics and control mechanisms define the logic of system structures, processes and ideologies. Ideology, defined as the integrated theories and values that constitute a coherent socio-political system, is expressed in patterns of stakeholders' participation in the financing, administration, and regulation of service delivery, including the roles of government, service providers, and consumers.

In Chapter 10, Pentland, using organizational ecology as a starting point, outlines a framework for studying the ecology of inter-organizational routines in e-commerce. Net-based technologies are distinctive because they require integration with the systems of other organizations, as well as one's own internal systems. From the received literature, Crowston *et al.*[33] investigated the interplay between structure and information technology in the real estate industry, while Mitev[86] investigated the failure of implementation and adoption of a computerised reservation system within the French railways. Crowston and Myers[15] successfully developed a framework and investigated transformation enabled by information technology using three theoretical perspectives in the real estate industry. Their analysis included the economic analysis of IT-induced reduction in cost of locating properties and disintermediation of real estate agents, the institutional analysis of the use of IT mandated by the regulatory environment and the role of rules and agreements between agents in transactions, and the socio-organisational analysis of the role of agents in contextualizing information from databases and use of IT to support social networks of agents, customers and other professionals.

From the neo-institutional perspective, remaining central research questions spanning levels of analysis are *what effects do institutional structures have on virtual networks? How do business networks' structural and cognitive organisational characteristics influence their ability to adopt and deploy IT?* Also, while economic and macro structural issues (i.e., return of investment, size of firms) are widely discussed in variance-based studies of IT, the dynamics of inter-organisational business networks and changing institutional environments have not yet been properly analysed and integrated at the organisation, network and market levels, e.g. *how are the effects of IT on industry innovative performance and firm organisational structure conditioned by the structural and cognitive dynamics of customer-supplier networks?* Other questions that can be addressed by adopting a process view based on an neo-institutional stance include: *what aspects of Internet business models are most likely to be adopted and diffused at different organizational/market levels, and what are the structural and organizational conditions for a given level of adoption to take place?*

5.5 *Adaptive structuring and practice perspectives*

Increasingly, researchers are acknowledging the symbiotic relationship between the approaches for IT development and the emergence of organisational forms in the context of innovation. From the adaptive structuring perspective, which is informed by Giddens'[87] structuration theory, individual social agents try intentionally and reflexively to shape structuring processes and relationships in order to coordinate the activity within an organisation or network. Recent studies have observed that inter-organisational networks can be facilitated by explicit and ongoing adaptation of technology to changing contexts of use.

In Chapter 2 of this volume, Barrett reviewed key dimensions of intraorganizational and interorganizational forms, which can be facilitated by advances in IT, and the potential of the IT to enable changing organizational forms. His review included the technological imperative, structurational approaches, and an extended discussion of the emerging perspective of 'practice lens' approach.

Schultze and Orlikowski[88] analyzed the implications of using IT to mediate electronic brokerage relationships that are enacted through work practices and interactions of actors representing customer and provider firms. The authors view business-to-business settings as typically maintained through inter-personal interactions between customers and their providers. They adopt a 'practice' perspective to examine the structural and interpersonal elements that produce and are produced by everyday activities, arguing that a practice lens requires neither a choice between a macro- and a micro-level of analysis, nor a conflation of the two. Further, this practice lens directs attention to how macro-phenomena are constituted by micro-interactions, and how those micro-interactions, in turn, are shaped by macro influences and effects.

Likewise, Newell, Scarbrough and Swan[65] investigated the adoption of intranet technology as a vehicle for encouraging organisation-wide knowledge sharing within a large, global bank, focusing attention on the enabling and dis-enabling effects of intranet technology on the processes of communication, collaboration and social coordination. They find that intranet adoption helped to reinforce the existing functional and national boundaries with electronic fences. They advocate that the intranet can be conceptualised as an interactive and decentred technology, which therefore has the potential for multiple interpretations and effects.

The main research questions that we would like to highlight here are: *how does IT implementation cause changes in social relations, and in knowledge exchange and learning at the individual, group and organizational level? What are the intervening contextual conditions affecting those changes?*

6   Further Intersections and Research Agenda

In this section we critically discuss how recent theoretical developments can be applied to the remaining problematic empirical areas illustrated in sections four and five. These theoretical developments applied to the IT domain are contributing to partially filling the knowledge gap: Wheeler's[6] "Net-Enabled Business Innovation Cycle" adopting a relational and dynamic capabilities view, Nambisan's[5] 'hybrid' knowledge-based view on virtual new product development communities, Schultze and

Orlikowski[88] and Barrett (Chapter 2 of this volume) using adaptive structuring and practice perspective. These novel studies are moving from contingent causality of variance to a process logical structure of analysis, and from a unitary level to multi-level analyses.

While new insights from recent studies like those reviewed above have broadened our understanding of IT-enabled innovation (e.g., virtual collaboration, value-creation and organizational change), there is still little empirical evidence as to how intra- and inter-organisational innovation and market dynamics can be articulated. Additional empirical evidence and relevant integrative analyses are required to illuminate the formulation of coherent competitive strategies and the promotion of more effective organisational forms and processes.

First, the dynamic capabilities perspective should be further developed using more contemporary notions derived from the knowledge management and organisational learning perspectives. This would enable fresh investigations of the dynamic organisational nature of strategic IT-enabled innovation. This pluralistic combination of perspectives need to emphasize the strategic value of higher order resources allowing the generation of and renewal of core capabilities and competitive advantage, as well as the significance of self-reinforcing tacit knowledge exchanges and learning processes.

Second, future studies should extend strategic management theories with neo-institutional analysis to account for isomorphism and the constitutive nature of institutional forms and processes of formation of Internet-enabled business networks and markets, which has so far been a neglected area. While management studies have already developed robust frameworks combining, for instance, strategic and neo-institutional perspectives[81,82], there are, however, very few IT studies following that route. Some new IT studies are starting implicitly to bring together strategic management and neo-institutional theories. For instance, Jin and Robey[46] extended a market-level analysis based on transaction-cost economic with neo-institutional theory and social network theory in order to explain the emergence of 'cyber-mediaries' in electronic commerce in retailing. Beside the economic benefits of reducing buying time and providing new products and services, Jin and Robey found that 'cybermediaries' persist in electronic form because they are institutionalised structural forms, which conform to regulative, normative and cognitive expectations, and are therefore seen as legitimate. They also found that 'cybermediaries' occupy strategic positions in complex social networks, thereby acquiring social power. The previously noted study by Crowston and Myers[15] successfully developed a framework and investigated transformation enabled by information technology using three theoretical perspectives in the real estate industry[85]. These studies need to be supplemented by new research combining the focus on institutional norms of the institutional perspective with the strategic management perspective explicitly addressing *how and why new cognitive and structural forms of such strategic networks of firms and electronic-enabled ecosystems are created and replicated.*

Third, a focus on adaptive structuring, relational, and knowledge management views can supplement strategic management theories and assist researchers in gaining deeper and richer insights about the relational aspects of inter-organisational interactions and the endogenous dynamics of knowledge-intensive firms. A problematic issue dictated by emergent global and distributed innovation scenarios is: *what are the social processes and intervening conditions by which individuals build and maintain their explicit and tacit knowledge exchanges in the context of these virtual environments?*

Fourth, extending the strategic management perspective *with* neo-institutional theory *and* adaptive structuring perspectives at various levels of analysis has the potential to explain second-order transformation in the context of innovation. As one of the growing area of controversy focuses on *how people within organisations come to share cognitions and norms about appropriate innovative behaviour, and how different organisational forms or designs develop*, the neo-institutional and adaptive structuring perspectives need to be integrated by researchers attempting to fully understand IT-enabled innovation.

The above intersections should contribute to advancing our understanding and build more robust and integrated theories. Researchers need to further develop their theoretical frameworks and research designs using the above intersections in order to systematically combine macro market and institutional forces, and micro organisational forces shaping

IT-enabled innovation, and also integrate variance (e.g., antecedents and consequences) with process approaches. Methodologically, scholars should incorporate market-level data analysis with organisational-level data analysis in order to capture the complex dynamics of inter-organisational networks and markets[81,89]. Analyses spanning multiple levels and approaches will contribute to understanding issues of causation and reproduction of form in complex virtual organisations and markets[90].

References

1. Wiesenfeld, Batia M., Raghuram, S. and Garud, R. Communication Patterns as Determinants of Organisational Identification in a Virtual Organisation, *Organisation Science*, 10(6), 1999, pp. 777-790.
2. Ahuja, M.K. and Carley, K.M. Network Structure in Virtual Organisations, *Organisation Science*, 10(6), 1999, pp. 741-757.
3. Rothaermel, F.T. and Sugiyama, S. Virtual Internet Communities and Commercial Success: Individual and Community-level Theory Grounded in the Atypical Case of TimeZone.com, *Journal of Management*, 27, 1999, pp. 297-312.
4. Chatterjee, Patrali. Interfirm Alliances in Online Retailing, *Journal of Business Research*, 57, 2002, pp. 714-723.
5. Nambisan, Satish. Designing Virtual Customer Environments for New Product Development: Toward a Theory, *Academy of Management Review*, 27(3), 2002, pp. 392-413.
6. Wheeler, Bradley C. NEBIC: A Dynamic Capabilities Theory for Assessing Net-Enablement, *Information Systems Research*, 13(2), 2002, pp. 125-146.
7. Rice, J. and Juniper, J. High Technology Alliances in Uncertain Times: The Case of Bluetooth, *Knowledge, Technology & Policy*, 16(3), 2003, pp. 113-124.
8. Gittell, J.H. and Weiss, L. Coordination Networks Within and Across Organisations: A Multi-level Framework, *Journal of Management Studies*, 41(1), 2004, pp. 127-151.
9. Yip, George S. Global Strategy in the Internet Era, *Business Strategy Review*, 11(4), 2000, pp. 1-14.
10. Coghlan, David. The Interlevel Dynamics of Information Technology, *Journal of Information Technology*, 13, 1998, pp. 139-149.
11. Sarkar, M., Butler, B. and Steinfield, C. Cybermediaries in Electronic Marketspace: Toward Theory Building, *Journal of Business Research*, 41, 1998, pp. 215-221.
12. Straub, D. and Watson, R.T. Research Commentary: Transformational Issues in Researching IS and Net-Enabled Organisations, *Information Systems Research*, 12(4), 2001, pp. 337-345.

13. Holmqvist, Mikael. A Dynamic Model of Intra- and Interorganisational Learning, *Organisation Studies*, 24(1), 2003, pp. 95-123.

14. Banker, R.D. and Kauffman, R.J. The Evolution of Research on Information Systems: A Fiftieth-Year Survey of the Literature in *Management Science, Management Science*, 50(3), 2004, pp. 281-298.

15. Crowston, K. and Myers, M.D. Information Technology and the Transformation of Industries: Three Research Perspectives, *Journal of Strategic Information Systems*, 13, 2004, pp. 5-28.

16. Allen, J. and Kim, J. IT and the Video Game Industry: Tensions and Mutual Shaping, *Journal of Information Technology*, 20(4), 2005, pp. 234-244.

17. Howard, M. Collaboration and the '3 Day Car:' A study of Automotive ICT Adoption, *Journal of Information Technology*, 20(4), 2005, pp. 244-255.

18. Sawyer, S., Wigand, R. and Crowston, K. Redefining Access: Uses and Role of Information and Communication Technologies in the US Residential Real Estate Industry from 1995 to 2005, *Journal of Information Technology*, 20(4), 2005, pp. 213-223.

19. Steinfield, C., Markus, M.L. and Wigand, R. Exploring Interorganizational Systems at the Industry Level of Analysis: Evidence from the US Home Mortgage Industry, *Journal of Information Technology*, 20(4), 2005, pp. 224-233.

20. Baum, J.A.C. and Rowley, T.J. Companion to Organisations: An Introduction. In Joel A.C. Baum (Ed.) *Companion to Organisations*, Blackwell Publishers, Oxford, 2002.

21. McLoughlin, I. and Jackson, P.F. Organisational Learning and the Virtual Organisation. In P. Jackson (Ed.) *Virtual Working: Social and Organisational Dynamics*, Routledge, 1999.

22. Snow, C.C., Lipnack, J. and Stampts, J. The Virtual Organisation: Promises and Payoffs, Large and Small. In Cary L. Cooper and Denise M. Rousseau (Eds.) *The Virtual Organisation*, Trends in Organisational Behavior, Volume 6, Wiley & Sons, 1999.

23. Cohen, S.G. and Manking, D. Collaboration in the Virtual Organisation. In Cary L. Cooper and Denise M. Rousseau (Eds.) *The Virtual Organisation*, Trends in Organisational Behavior, Volume 6, Wiley & Sons, 1999.

24. Child, J. and McGrath, R.G. Organisation Unfettered: Organisational Form in an Information-Intensive Economy, *Academy of Management Journal*, 44(6), 2001, pp. 1135-1148.

25. Salazar, Angel. Understanding Organizations, Networks, Markets and Industries in the Internet Age: A Multi-Theoretical Review and Suggestions for Theory Building, MMUBS Working Paper Series, 2004.

26. Zahra, S. and George, G. The Net-Enabled Business Innovation Cycle and the Evolution of Dynamic Capabilities, *Information Systems Research*, 13(2), 2002, pp. 147-150.

27. Kambil, A. and Heck, E. van. Reengineering the Dutch Flower Auctions: A Framework for Analyzing Exchange Organisations, *Information Systems Research*, 9(1), 1998, pp. 1-19.
28. Brynjolfsson, E. and Hitt, L.M. Beyond Computation: Information Technology, Organisational Transformation and Business Performance, *Journal of Economic Perspectives*, 14(4), 2000, pp. 23-48.
29. Cassiman, B. and Sieber, S. El Impacto de Internet sobre la Estructura de los Mercados, *Economia Industrial*, 339, 2001, pp. 13-24.
30. Amit, R. and Zott, C. Value Drivers of e-Commerce Business Models. In M. Hitt, R. Amit, C.E. Lucier and R.D. Nixon (Eds.) *Creating Value: Winners in the New Business Environment*, Blackwell Publishing, 2002.
31. Damsgaard, J. and Lyytinen, K. Contours of Diffusion of Electronic Data Interchange in Finland: Overcoming technological barriers and collaborating to make it happen, *Journal of Strategic Information Systems*, 7, 1998, pp. 275-297.
32. Garud, R. and Van de Ven, A.H. Strategic Change Processes. In A. Pettigrew, H. Thomas and R. Whittington (Eds.) *Handbook of Strategy and Management*, SAGE Publications, 2002.
33. Crowston, K., Sawyer, S. and Wigand, R. Investigating the Interplay between Structure and Information and Communications Technology in the Real Estate Industry, *Information Technology and People*, 14(2), 2002, pp. 163-183.
34. Markus, M.L. and Robey, D. Information Technology and Organisational Change: Causal Structure in Theory and Research, *Management Science*, 34(5), 1988, pp. 583-598.
35. Klein, K., Dansereau, F. and Hall, R.J. Levels Issues in Theory Development, Data Collection and Analysis, *Academy of Management Review*, 19(2), 1994, pp. 195-229.
36. Kauffman, R.J. and Walden, E.A. Economics and Electronic Commerce: Survey and Research Directions, *International Journal of Electronic Commerce*, 5(4), 2001, pp. 5-116.
37. Wigand, Rolf T. Electronic Commerce: Definition, Theory and Context, *The Information Society*, 13, 1997, pp. 1-16.
38. Park, N.K., Mezias, J.M. and Song, J. A Resource-based View of Strategic Alliances and Firm Value in the Electronic Marketplace, *Journal of Management*, 30(1), 2004, pp. 7-27.
39. Berthon, P., Ewing, M., Pitt, L. and Naude, P. Understanding B2B and the Web: the Acceleration of Coordination and Motivation, *Industrial Marketing Management*, 32, 2003, pp. 553-561.
40. Geoffrion, A.M. and Krishnan, R. E-Business and Management Science: Mutual Impacts (Part 1 and 2), *Management Science*, 49(10), 2003, pp. 1275-1286.
41. Raisch, Warren D. *The eMarketplace: Strategies for Success in B2B eCommerce*, McGraw Hill, New York, 2001.

42. Grover, V. and Saeed, K.A. Strategic Orientation and Performance of Internet-based Businesses, *Information Systems Journal*, 14, 2004, pp. 23-42.
43. Christiaanse, E., Diepen, T.V. and Damsgaard, J. Proprietary versus Internet Technologies and the Adoption and Impact of Electronic Marketplaces, *Journal of Strategic Information Systems*, 13, 2004, pp. 151-165.
44. Kallinikos, Jannis. Cognitive Foundations of Economic Institutions: Markets, Organisations and Networks Revisited, *Scandinavian Journal of Management*, 11(2), 1995, pp. 119-137.
45. DiMaggio, P. and Louch, H. Socially Embedded Consumer Transactions: For What Kinds of Purchases Do People Most Often Use Networks? *American Sociological Review*, 63, 1998, pp. 619-637.
46. Jin, L. and Robey, D. Explaining Cybermediation: An Organisational Analysis of Electronic Retailing, *International Journal of Electronic Commerce*, 3(4), 1999, pp. 47-65.
47. Pavlou, P.A. and Gefen, D. Building Effective Online Marketplaces with Institution-based Trust, *Information Systems Research*, 15(1), 2004, pp. 37-59.
48. Anand, N. and Peterson, R.A. When Market Information Constitutes Fields: Sensemaking of Markets in the Commercial Music Industry, *Organisation Science*, 11(3), 2000, pp. 270-284.
49. Clay, K., Krishnan, R., Wolff, E. and Fernandes, D. Retail Strategies on the Web: Price and non-Price Competition in the Online Book Industry, *Journal of Industrial Economics*, 50, 2002, pp. 351-367.
50. Easton, G. and Araujo, L. Evaluating the Impact of B2B e-commerce: A Contingent Approach, *Industrial Marketing Management*, 32, 2003, pp. 431-439.
51. Kim, E., Nam, D. and Stimpert, J.L. The Applicability of Porter's Generic Strategies in the Digital Age: Assumptions, Conjectures and Suggestions, *Journal of Management*, 30(5), 2004, pp. 569-589.
52. Porter, Michael. Strategy and the Internet, *Harvard Business Review*, March, 2001, pp. 62-78.
53. Powell, J.H. and Wakeley, T.M. Evolutionary Concepts and Business Economics: Towards a Normative Approach, *Journal of Business Research*, 56, 2003, pp. 153-161.
54. Dyer, J.H. and Singh, H. The Relational View: Cooperative Strategy and Sources of Interorganisational Competitive Advantage, *Academy of Management Review*, 23(4), 1998, pp. 660-679.
55. Stabell, C. and Feldstad, O. Configuring Value for Competitive Advantage: on Chains, Shops and Networks, *Strategic Management Journal*, 15(3), 1998, pp. 303-317.
56. Foss, Nicolai J. More Critical Comments on Knowledge-based Theories of the Firm, *Organisation Science*, 7(5), 1996, pp. 519-523.

57. Boer, M., Van den Bosch, F.A.J. and Volberda, H.W. Managing Organisational Knowledge Integration in the Emerging Multimedia Complex, *Journal of Management Studies*, 36(3), 1999, pp. 379-399.

58. Orlikowski, W. and Robey, D. Information Technology and the Structuring of Organisations, *Information Systems Research*, 2(2), 1991, pp. 143-169.

59. Orlikowski, W., Yates, J., Okamura, K. and Fujimoto, M. Shaping Electronic Communication: The Metastructuring of Technology in the Context of Use, *Organisation Science*, 6(4), 1995, pp. 423-444.

60. Orlikowski, Wanda. Improvising Organisational Transformation Over Time: A Situated Change Perspective, *Information Systems Research*, 7(1), 1996, pp. 63-92.

61. Hinds, P. and Kiesler, S. Communication across Boundaries: Work, Structure, and Use of Communication Technologies in a Large Organisation, *Organisation Science*, 6(4), 1995, pp. 373-391.

62. Dierkes, M., Berthoin-Antal, A., Chid, J. and Nonaka, I. *Handbook of Organisational Learning and Knowledge*, Oxford University Press, Oxford, 2001.

63. Argote, L., McEvily, B. and Reagans, R. Managing Knowledge in Organisations: An Integrative Framework and Review of Emerging Themes, *Management Science*, 49(4), 2003, pp. 571-582.

64. Borgatti, S.P. and Foster, P.C. The Network Paradigm in Organisational Research: A Review and Typology, *Journal of Management*, 29(6), 2003, pp. 991-1013.

65. Newell, S., Scarbrough, H. and Swan, J. From Global Knowledge Management to Internal Electronic Fences: Contradictory Outcomes of Intranet Development, *British Journal of Management*, 12, 2001, pp. 97-111.

66. Swan, J., Newell, S., Scarbrough, H. and Hislop, D. Knowledge management and innovation: networks and networking, *Journal of Knowledge Management*, 3(4), 1999, pp. 262-275.

67. Webster, Juliet. Networks of Collaboration or Conflict? Electronic Data Interchange and Power in the Supply Chain, *Journal of Strategic Information Systems*, 4(1), 1995, pp. 31-42.

68. El Sawy, O., Malhorta, A., Gosain, S. and Young, K.M. IT-Intensive Value Innovation in the Electronic Economy: Insights from Marshall Industries, *MIS Quarterly*, 23(3), 1999, pp. 305-333.

69. Kraemer, K.L. and Dedrick, J. Strategic Use of the Internet and e-Commerce: Cisco Systems, *Journal of Strategic Information Systems*, 11, 2002, pp. 5-29.

70. Salazar, A., Hackney, R. and Howells, J. Strategic Impact of Internet Technology in Biotechnology and Pharmaceutical Firms: Insights from a Knowledge Management Perspective, *Journal of Special Topics in Information Technology and Management*, 4(2/3), 2003, pp. 289-301.

71. Holland, C.P. and Lockett, G. Mixed Mode Operation of Electronic Markets and Hierarchies. In Mark Ebers (Ed.) *The Formation of Inter-Organisational Networks*, Oxford University Press, 1997.

72. Kreiner, K. and Schultz, M. Informal Collaboration in R&D: The Formation of Networks Across Organisations, *Organisation Studies*, 14(2), 1993, pp. 189-209.

73. Ebers, Mark. Explaining Inter-Organisational Network Formation. In Mark Ebers (Ed.) *The Formation of Inter-Organisational Networks*, Oxford University Press, 1997.

74. Lee, K. and Pennings, J.M. Mimicry and the Market: Adoption of a New Organisational Form, *Academy of Management Journal*, 45(1), 2002, pp. 144-162.

75. Brews, P. and Tucci, C.L. Exploring the Structural Effects of Internetworking, *Strategic Management Journal*, 25, 2004, pp. 429-451.

76. Marchington, M. and Vincent, S. Analysing the Influence of Institutional, Organisational and Interpersonal Forces in Shaping Inter-Organisational Relations, *Journal of Management Studies*, 41(6), 2004, pp. 1029-1056.

77. Phillips, N., Lawrence, T.B. and Hardy, C. Inter-Organisational Collaboration and the Dynamics of Institutional Fields, *Journal of Management Studies*, 37(1), 2000, pp. 23-40.

78. King, J., Kraemer, K., McFarlan, F., Raman, K.S. and Yap, C.S. Institutional Factors in Information Technology Innovation, *Information Systems Research*, 5(2), 1994, pp. 139-169.

79. Kumar, K. and Dissel, H.G. Sustainable Collaboration: managing Conflict and Cooperation in Interorganisational Systems, *MIS Quarterly*, September, 1996, pp. 279-300.

80. Wang, S. and Cheung, W. E-Business Adoption by Travel Agencies: Prime Candidates for Mobile e-Business, *International Journal of Electronic Commerce*, 8(3), 2004, pp. 43-63.

81. Oliver, Christine. Sustainable Competitive Advantage: Combining Institutional and Resource-based Views, *Strategic Management Journal*, 18(9), 1997, pp. 697-713.

82. Roberts, P.W. and Greenwood, R. Integrating Transaction Cost and Institutional Theories: Toward a Constrained-Efficiency Framework for Understanding Organisational Design Adoption, *Academy of Management Review*, 22(2), 1997, pp. 346-373.

83. West, Jonathan. Institutions, Information Processing and Organisation Structure in Research and Development: Evidence from the Semiconductor Industry, *Research Policy*, 29, 2000, pp. 349-373.

84. Helper, S. and MacDuffie, J.P. B2B and Modes of Exchange: Evolutionary and Transformative Effects. In Bruce Kogut (Ed.) *The Global Internet Economy*, MIT Press, 2002.

85. Palmer, D.A. and Biggart, N.W. Organisational Institutions. In Joel A.C. Baum (Ed.) *Companion to Organisations*, Blackwell Publishers, Oxford, 2002.

86. Mitev, Nathalie N. More than a Failure? The Computer Reservation Systems at French Railways, *Information Technology & People*, 9(4), 1996, pp. 8-19.

87. Giddens, A. *The Constitution of Society: Outline of the Theory of Structuration*, Political Press, Cambridge, 1984.

88. Schultze, U. and Orlikowski, W. A Practice Perspective on Technology-Mediated Network Relations: The Use of Internet-based Self-Serve Technologies, *Information Systems Research*, 15(1), 2004, pp. 87-106.

89. Mahoney, J.T. and Sanchez, R. Building New Management Theory by Integrating Processes and Products of Thought, *Journal of Management Inquiry*, 13(1), 2004, pp. 34-47.

90. Klein, K.J., Tosi, H. and Canella, A.A. Multilevel Theory Building: Benefits, Barriers and New Developments, *Academy of Management Review*, 24(2), 1999, pp. 243-248.

91. Brews, P. and Tucci, C.L. Exploring the Structural Effects of Internetworking, *Strategic Management Journal*, 25, 2004, pp. 429-451.

Index